D1606251

RACE & RHYME

RACE & RHYME

Rereading the New Testament

Love Lazarus Sechrest

WILLIAM B. EERDMANS PUBLISHING COMPANY

GRAND RAPIDS, MICHIGAN

Wm. B. Eerdmans Publishing Co.
4035 Park East Court SE, Grand Rapids, Michigan 49546
www.eerdmans.com

© 2022 Love Lazarus Sechrest
All rights reserved
Published 2022
Printed in the United States of America

28 27 26 25 24 23 22   1 2 3 4 5 6 7

ISBN 978-0-8028-6713-1

Library of Congress Cataloging-in-Publication Data

A catalog record for this book is available from the Library of Congress.

Chapter 2, "Neighbors, Allies, Frenemies, and Foes," is used with the permission of Wipf & Stock Publishers. A version of this chapter originally appeared as "Enemies, Romans, Pigs, and Dogs: Loving the Other in the Gospel of Matthew," *Ex Auditu: An International Journal of Theological Interpretation of Scripture* 31 (2015): 71–105.

"Between Ourselves," copyright 1976 by Audre Lorde, "Outlines," copyright 1986 by Audre Lorde, "School Note," copyright by Audre Lorde. From *The Collected Poems of Audre Lorde* by Audre Lorde. Used by permission of W. W. Norton & Company, Inc.

To Paige and Audrey.
Thanks for all you've taught and for all you've forgiven.
You are a constant source of inspiration and hope.

CONTENTS

vii

CONTENTS

Contents

FIGURES AND TABLES

PREFACE

In this book, I have described and attempted to model a disciplined method by which we identify and analyze situations in contemporary life that "rhyme" with the situations addressed in the Bible. The method is the one that I've engaged over fifteen years of teaching students to cultivate a biblically shaped imagination for use in moral reasoning about race relations in the United States. It has been profoundly moving to watch students adopt a posture that takes the Bible and their racialized social contexts seriously while eschewing easy moralistic answers. I have learned much from their struggles to do the imaginative, imprecise, and messy work of challenging their own associations and finding fresh ways to live out the faith.

While this book was gestated and born during my years teaching on the progressive edge of evangelicalism, I have always had a complicated and often uncomfortable relationship with this movement. Evangelicalism is effectively blind to matters of race and privilege and rampant with prejudice against sexual minorities. Politically the movement foregrounds the interests of the unborn, while my politics are equally one-sided in emphasizing the interests of living Black and minoritized bodies. While teaching among people who shared my love of the Bible and my belief that it ought to make a difference in how we live, I found many in this movement who imprisoned the text in the past. Some of these interpreters were preoccupied with theologies that miss the weightier matters of justice, dignity, freedom, and grace that should mark the lives of every disciple. And it is this concern for justice, dignity, freedom, and grace in real life that first drew me to interactions with interpreters who read the Bible through the lens of their own cultural experience. Although many in this school lacked my presuppositions about the Bible, I soon realized that they frequently saw things in this holy and beloved book that others didn't. When I didn't agree with them, I soon learned that I couldn't dismiss them. Sometimes their readings were troubling; other times they made my heart soar. I was eventually utterly captivated by their ways and now count myself among their number.

Though I began working through the lens of a hermeneutics of trust, there was a dawning recognition that trust did not entail, at least for me, willful blindness. What I offer here is an attempt at balancing two convictions: My love for the God of the Bible on the one hand and my distaste for trying to "save" a text and make excuses for it on the other, as if God needs me to do that. So when some manner of the peace I made with this text or that fails to persuade, so be it. After all these years of wrestling, I was bound to publish or risk not agreeing with the self who began this journey. When I did my doctoral studies in the early 2000s, it was nearly impossible to do African American or womanist biblical interpretation. There was a lack of available mentors, few publishing outlets, and broad marginalization of this work in White-normed interpretive circles where there is scant acknowledgment of the influence of the interpreter's social location on the production of meaning. Though I had wonderful mentors and friends in those days, no one was available to me in my field who could help me navigate the marginalization of womanist and African American voices in biblical studies. My own womanist voice did not begin to emerge until many years after graduation, and I am still in the process of becoming.

Though I have the discipline-spanning curiosity of the medievalist, I also share a modern academic's disdain for the dabbler. While I attempt to read widely in the disciplines engaged in the various chapters, I necessarily fall short of mastery. Still, I hope that specialists in these respective fields may discern my attempts to avoid the most egregious errors. If there is an arrogance here of attempting a monograph that breaches the rituals and expectations of scholarly guilds, it is one I share with my interdisciplinary womanist sisters. I am convinced that reflection on the complex problems of race and gender requires insights from diverse domains of knowledge.

There are many people to thank. I have the deepest gratitude and never-ending love and admiration for my partner and husband, Edward A. Sechrest Jr., a prince among humans. My two daughters, Paige Allyson Sechrest and Audrey Jordan Sechrest, are brilliant, beautiful, and outstanding leaders each. Boundless love, affection, and thanks also go to my mother J. Rachel Lazarus, my sister Rosalind R. Williams, and the memory of my grandmother Corine Cross Lazarus Hand. All of these family members made me who I am, and because of them, I thank God daily for who I'm from. I love you all more than words can say.

I am grateful for colleagues in the African American Biblical Hermeneutics section at SBL, especially Herb Marbury and Randall Bailey, and for longtime friends whose encouragement through the years has meant the world: Willie Jennings, J. R. Daniel Kirk, Mitzi Smith, Joel Marcus, Susan Eastman, Mignon Jacobs, and Reggie Williams. I am no less grateful for new colleagues and friends at Columbia Seminary: for President Leanne Van Dyk, who made it possible for me to get this book over the finish line, every last one of my beloved friends on the faculty, and Karen Wishart-Christian, Ann Clay Adams, and Mike Medford, without whom I would be lost.

Students and colleagues in the "Race and Identity in the New Testament" course I taught at Fuller Theological Seminary from 2007 to 2018 were essential dialogue partners. All of them have gone on to do groundbreaking work in congregations, non-profits, ethics, theology, law, and education. I'm so grateful for Janna Louie, Estella Low Jee Leng, Troy Kinney, Nicole Rivas, Philip Allen, Jeff Liou, Trey Clark, Craig Hendrickson, Nathan Daniels, Jenelle Austin, and Bryson White.

There remains one final note. My first monograph, *A Former Jew: Paul and the Dialectics of Race*, was among the first to make historical claims about the nature of race and ethnic identity in antiquity, arguing that these social constructions are relevant for understanding the New Testament and other texts in the period. While history is still very much engaged in *Race and Rhyme*, in this book I am interested in exploring how the Bible shapes our social lives and imaginations relevant to these topics. The Bible reflects the limitations of culture, but it does not transcend culture. God has deigned to work God's will through imperfect human beings, each trapped within their own cultural and perceptual biases. Does the God revealed in the Bible have anything to say through it to the mammoth problems of race, racism, and White supremacy? I believe so, and this is my attempt to elucidate some of what I see there.

Love Lazarus Sechrest

ABBREVIATIONS

AB	Anchor Bible
AME	African Methodist Episcopal
ANE	Ancient Near East
ANTC	Abingdon New Testament Commentaries
AT	Author's translation
b.	Babylonian Talmud
BDAG	Frederick W. Danker, Walter Bauer, William F. Arndt, and F. Wilbur Gingrich. *Greek-English Lexicon of the New Testament and Other Early Christian Literature.* 3rd ed. Chicago: University of Chicago Press, 2000
BECNT	Baker Exegetical Commentary on the New Testament
BETL	Bibliotheca Ephemeridum Theologicarum Lovaniensium
BibInt	Biblical Interpretation
BNTC	Black's New Testament Commentaries
CBQ	*Catholic Biblical Quarterly*
CEB	Common English Bible
CRT	Critical Race Theory
HB	Hebrew Bible
HT	*Haustafeln* or Household Code
HTR	*Harvard Theological Review*
ICC	International Critical Commentary
JBL	*Journal of Biblical Literature*
JETS	*Journal of the Evangelical Theological Society*
JSJ	*Journal for the Study of Judaism*
JSNT	*Journal for the Study of the New Testament*
JSNTSup	Journal for the Study of the New Testament Supplement Series
JTS	*Journal of Theological Studies*
Liddell-Scott	Henry George Liddell, Robert Scott, and Henry Stuart Jones. *A Greek-English Lexicon.* 9th ed. Oxford: Clarendon, 1996

LNTS	Library of New Testament Studies
lit.	literally
LXX	Septuagint
m.	Mishnah
NASB	New American Standard Bible
NCBC	New Cambridge Bible Commentary
NET	New English Translation
NETS	New English Translation of the Septuagint
NIB	New International Version—1984 UK edition
NICNT	New International Commentary on the New Testament
NIGTC	New International Greek Testament Commentary
NIV	New International Version—1984 US edition
NJB	New Jerusalem Bible
NLT	New Living Translation
NovT	*Novum Testamentum*
NRSV	New Revised Standard Version
NT	New Testament
NTL	New Testament Library
NTS	*New Testament Studies*
OT	Old Testament
par.	parallel
PNTC	Pillar New Testament Commentary
SBL	Society for Biblical Literature
SBLSBS	Society of Biblical Literature Sources for Biblical Study
SNTSMS	Society for New Testament Studies Monograph Series
s.v.	"See under the heading" (from *sub voce*, literally "under the word")
t.	Tosefta
TNTC	Tyndale New Testament Commentaries
WBC	Word Biblical Commentary
WUNT	Wissenschaftliche Untersuchungen zum Neuen Testament
ZKG	*Zeitschrift für Kirchengeschichte*
ZNW	*Zeitschrift für die neutestamentliche Wissenschaft*

RACE AND ASSOCIATIVE REASONING

History doesn't repeat itself—but it does rhyme.

—attributed to Mark Twain[1]

Race and Rhyme

During the third weekend of November 2016, I attended the annual gathering of religious studies scholars at the combined meetings of the American Academy of Religion and the Society for Biblical Literature in San Diego. That weekend many of us were reeling in shock, trying to absorb Donald Trump's election as the forty-fifth President of the United States. We were a diverse group of scholars studying phenomena across a broad range of global religious traditions. Some of us were persons of faith and many of us were not. Judging from hallway conversations in and around the sessions I attended, few were supporters of the new President, likely reflecting national opinion polls for this educational demographic. Everyone seemed shocked by the coincidence of factors that had combined to allow Trump to take the presidency even though he secured nearly three million fewer votes than his competitor. Many were outraged that 46 percent of the electorate had handed the nation's welfare over to a narcissistic, racist, misogynistic, Islamophobic, transphobic, and homophobic bigot.

That weekend Rev. Dr. William Barber addressed the conference, and his remarks articulated a framework for processing these events. Barber, the architect of the Moral Monday movement and co-chair of the Poor People's Campaign, spoke of our present moment as a manifestation of what he called the third American Reconstruction. According to Barber, the election of Donald Trump represented another scene in the story of the United States where

---

1. Though this saying is attributed to Mark Twain, its provenance is difficult to trace. See https://quoteinvestigator.com/2014/01/12/history-rhymes/.

the forces of White[2] supremacy reasserted dominance in resistance to apparent progress in racial justice. The first American Reconstruction was a backlash to the emancipation of enslaved Blacks. The second, masquerading as the War on Drugs, was a reiteration of White racial dominance over Blacks and Latinx people in a "new Jim Crow" regime of physical segregation and social control in an era of mass incarceration.[3] For Barber and others, the election of Donald Trump and the increase of open and unabashed White supremacist rhetoric in the wake of that election was a backlash against the browning of America. It was the dawn of an age in which Whites would no longer be the majority group in the country, only its largest single minority group. Signified by the Obama presidency, this moment was, in fact, different from those other backlash eras. While the first American Reconstruction focused on a Black-White binary around male citizenship rights, the third one is multiethnic and intersectional. This new Reconstruction occurs as Blacks, Indigenous peoples, Asian Americans, Pacific Islanders, Latinx people, and women have (contested) access to the ballot. While the second Reconstruction required mass demonstrations to win the right to vote, this new one requires mass mobilization of nonengaged voters to defeat voter suppression. The analogs to the first Reconstruction era in the antebellum south aren't perfect, but they do rhyme.

This book is a collection of essays united by a common methodology that I call associative hermeneutics, a method based on analogical reasoning. This hermeneutic involves a disciplined attempt to find the "rhyme" between contemporary issues and biblical texts. The essays in this book use this method to explore examples of group conflict found in New Testament narratives and the tensions underlying epistolary discourse. Parts of the Bible are not at all helpful as a foundation for contemporary ethics, like the genocide in the Old Testament Conquest narrative (Josh. 8–11) or the passages that enshrine slavery (Eph. 6:5–9) and the oppression of women (1 Tim. 2:9–15). Still, the ancient church is a fascinating site for the exploration of intergroup tensions. The earliest documents in the New Testament exhibit the strains in the early Christian

---

2. In this book, I capitalize words that refer to subpopulations by race or ethnicity. This practice is ubiquitous in our society when referring to Asian-, Latinx-, Irish-, and Native-Americans, etc. Though contested, we can see it with increasing frequency when using the term "Black" to refer to African Americans. Less common, however, is my practice of capitalizing "White" when referring to that group of Americans: "To not name 'White' as a race is, in fact, an anti-Black act which frames Whiteness as both neutral and the standard." For a more detailed but still accessible comment on this antiracist practice, see the source for this quotation in Nguyễn and Pendleton, "Recognizing Race in Language." On the other hand, I preserve capitalization practices from source material when using direct quotes.

3. Alexander, *New Jim Crow*.

movement as it transitioned from a sectarian group in the larger landscape of first-century nascent Judaisms into a Gentile-inclusive association that would survive on the fringes of the Roman Empire and later sweep the West. While some New Testament scholars rightly focus on how interpreters and biblical narratives are complicit in the rise and advance of Empire,[4] I am interested in how these narratives can bear witness to early struggles about group identity amid more powerful influencers. Thus this book attempts to find places where reflection on intergroup conflict, ethnoracial tension, and power dynamics in the New Testament promotes liberative reflection on race relations in contemporary life. There is no attempt to collapse the ancient narratives in the Bible into the much more complicated problems in modern society. As interesting as the rhymes that show similarities in human dynamics across the ages are, the complicating and syncopating tempos that interrupt the similarities and create new melodies are, to my mind, infinitely more fascinating. They force us into a living relationship with the word of God and compel us to pay attention as God continues to speak in and through contemporary situations.

I hope that the discussion of this hermeneutic stimulates renewed critical engagement with the biblical text with contemporary problems in mind. Yet, it is better to describe it as an approach that illuminates the reading strategies that Black folk and others have been using for as long as they have been preaching. The use of analogy and associative reasoning in ethics, as discussed here, is an interpretive move found in many works.[5] In other words, the observation about how people of color center their experience in reasoning from their own experience to the text and back again is not a new one. Here I offer analogy as a method for doing biblical moral reflection via the womanist aims of liberation for Black women and other marginalized communities and the critique of misogynistic and oppressive ideologies wherever they appear in biblical narratives or occur in biblical reflection. What emerges is *a heuristic device that allows a disciplined exploration of spaces where the similarities between our lives and the lives of those*

4. Throughout this book I capitalize "Empire" when referring to it as a collection of values or ideologies. The word appears in lowercase type when referring to historical political entities like the Babylonian or Roman empires.

5. E.g., Jennifer Kaalund's dialogical reasoning in *Reading Hebrews and 1 Peter*. Richard Hays's work in New Testament ethics (see esp. his book *Moral Vision*) has influenced me in its use of analogy as a method for doing biblical moral reflection, though the organizing principles we use for analogical work with New Testament texts differ. Whereas Hays uses cross, community, and new creation as focal images for New Testament ethics, I center the womanist values of liberation for Black women and other marginalized communities and the critique of misogynistic and oppressive ideologies wherever they appear in biblical narratives or emerge from biblical reflection.

who lived ages ago follow the fundamentals of human experience while simultaneously forcing attention to spaces where slavish attention to these ancient stories leads us into morally compromised postures. Though I bring the practice of analogical reasoning to questions about race and race relations, this method will be fruitful for cultivating biblical ethics on any number of topics or issues in modern life.

I begin by situating associative hermeneutics vis-à-vis the aims and values of womanist biblical interpretation. Next, I illustrate the use of associative hermeneutics via interaction with a narrative text (Acts 6:1–6) and an epistolary text (1 Tim. 2:8–15). I've used both of these texts to introduce this method to students in seminary classrooms. Though I define relevant terminology from the study of racial and ethnic studies in each of the following chapters, the third section of this chapter presents major concepts in the study of race and racism that will be helpful when engaging these chapters. Finally, this introduction ends with an overview of each subsequent chapter, describing their basic structures and identifying the central rhyme or analogy that governs the dialogue between the focal biblical texts and the issues in race relations examined there.

Womanist Hermeneutics

Womanist interpretation shares many of the aims and methods of African American hermeneutics. Mitzi Smith's compelling account in *Insights from African American Interpretation* is an excellent introductory text for these disciplines. Smith maintains that one of the principal aims of African American hermeneutics is to unearth, mine, and reconstruct the history of biblical interpretation among Black peoples. According to Smith, enslavers used racially biased interpretations of the Bible to rationalize their dehumanizing treatment. Through catechesis, they attempted to inscribe in the very souls of Black people the notion that Blacks are inferior and to convince them that their subordinate social position in relation to White people was fitting and natural. Practicing an early and implicit "hermeneutics of suspicion," many enslaved people were suspicious of the Bible or the White man's interpretation of the Bible. Thus, for Smith, another important aim of African American interpretation is to counteract ideologically driven Eurocentric interpretations that consciously or unconsciously support the subordination of Blacks along with overlapping sexism, classism, and bias against the queer community.[6]

6. M. J. Smith, *Insights*, 47: "Peoples, cultures, and ideologies are prioritized, minimized, or obliterated in the process of and as a result of biblical interpretations. It matters who sets the table (determines the agenda) and who sits at the proverbial table (the invitees). It matters what is included or excluded from the menu and guest list; the two are interconnected. It matters who teaches and what texts they select to be taught. It matters what or whose questions, issues,

The relationship between African Americans and the Bible is historically fraught since the Bible was a weapon of psychological, spiritual, and physical abasement. As Smith describes African American experience with the Bible during and after slavery, she maintains that "God's unmediated self-revelation remains a central aspect of African American biblical interpretation," an assertion that grounds and legitimizes Black people's authority to read and interpret the biblical text.[7] The capacity to receive unmediated divine revelation was critical for the appropriation of the Christian faith among Blacks when so many of its central precepts were deployed against their humanity during slavery. Thus, African American interpretation "honors the sacredness and legitimacy of black lived experiences" and includes the production of revelation and knowledge about God, sacred texts, and their contexts.[8] Acknowledging the problematic ideologies in the text, these interpreters do not confuse the biblical text with God. This "hermeneutical intuition" was not a theological stumbling block that threatened the African ancestors' faith in God, Jesus Christ, or the Holy Spirit.[9] African American biblical interpreters aim to produce interpretations that are relevant for Africana communities.

Even as of the publication of her book in 2017, Smith notes that African American interpretation remains a deeply marginalized activity in the scholarly guild. According to Smith:

> While all approaches to biblical interpretation are contextual and ideological, contemporary scholars tend to reserve such designations for minoritized interpretive approaches and not for the dominant, mainstream methods. African American biblical interpretation is an unapologetically, undeniably interested, ideological, culturally determined, contextual approach to reading biblical texts and contexts, as well as readings and readers of biblical texts and contexts. . . . In fact, minority opinions are ignored or dismissed as illegitimate and/or not scholarly and thus marginally engaged, if at all.[10]

Noting that Black scholars use historical-critical methods even as these recede in importance against the priority to produce knowledge that helps liberate

and concerns are raised, avoided, silenced, treated as marginal, or as (ir)relevant. It matters how we approach and understand the biblical texts (its characters and narratives) and the God about which they testify. African American biblical scholars have not understood the biblical text as a flawless and self-interpreting historical artifact, lacking pretext, context, or bias."

7. M. J. Smith, *Insights*, 12.
8. M. J. Smith, *Insights*, 76.
9. M. J. Smith, *Insights*, 65–66.
10. M. J. Smith, *Insights*, 14–15.

the community, she insists that the distinction between exegesis and eisegesis that the academy constructs is a somewhat superficial one. She says that "we are always, all of us, reading *into* the text." For Smith, the sanctions against eisegesis in mainstream Eurocentric scholarship betray an unconscious or conscious insistence that "application," that is, the demonstration of relevance, is substandard.[11] For Black interpreters, "that which lies behind the text does not determine the questions to be asked of the text; a search for the ancient historical context does not drive the hermeneutical task."[12] This commitment to exploring issues in front of the text helped me introduce these methods to evangelical students. Though initially wary of these methods, many of these students would give them a second look when I argued that evangelicals of all people should be interested in these methods, given their deep commitments to the idea that the Bible is relevant for everyday life.

Though it shares many of these aims and methods, an account of womanist interpretation proper must include Alice Walker's oft-cited definition of a womanist in *In Search of Our Mothers' Gardens*:

> *Womanist 1.* From *womanish*. (Opp. of "girlish," i.e., frivolous, irresponsible, not serious) A black feminist or feminist of color. From the black folk expression of mothers to female children, "You acting womanish," i.e., like a woman. Usually referring to outrageous, audacious, courageous or *willful* behavior. Wanting to know more and in greater depth than is considered "good" for one. Interested in grown-up doings. Acting grown up. Being grown up. Interchangeable with another black folk expression: "You trying to be grown." Responsible. In charge. *Serious.*
>
> *2. Also:* A woman who loves other women, sexually and/or nonsexually. Appreciates and prefers women's culture, women's emotional flexibility (values tears as a natural counterbalance of laughter), and women's strength. Sometimes loves individual men, sexually and/or nonsexually. Committed to survival and wholeness of entire people, male and female. Not a separatist, except, periodically, for health. Traditionally universalist, as in: "Mama, why are we brown, pink, and yellow, and our cousins are white, beige, and black?" Ans.: "Well, you know the colored race is just like a flower garden, with every color flower represented." Traditionally capable, as in: "Mama,

---

11. M. J. Smith, *Insights*, 74, emphasis added.
12. M. J. Smith, *Insights*, 17.

I'm walking to Canada and I'm taking you and a bunch of other slaves with me." Reply: "It wouldn't be the first time."[13]

Though Walker is a critically acclaimed and award-winning writer of Black women's fiction, this set of values crystalized womanist thought across various disciplines, including theology, ethics, and biblical interpretation. Now situated more and more in the biblical studies academic guild in recent years, womanist biblical interpretation did not grow out of African American biblical interpretation so much as both are outgrowths of Black theology. Womanist interpretation exists alongside feminist interpretation and integrates Black theology with womanist theology and ethics. While the methods used in African American interpretation and womanist interpretation are similar in that these modes both center the experience, culture, and thought of African Americans, the values of womanist interpretation present in Walker's definition above are dominant among womanist interpreters.

Katie Cannon is credited as the first scholar to articulate an explicitly womanist theology,[14] and the disciplines of womanist theology and ethics have thrived ever since. Some of the leading scholars in the field appear in two major anthologies: Emilie Townes's anthology *A Troubling in My Soul: Womanist Perspectives on Evil and Suffering*[15] and the 2011 collection edited by Katie Cannon, Emilie Townes, and Angela Sims, *Womanist Theological Ethics: A Reader*.[16] Katie Cannon's description of the aims of womanist interpretation is an early expression of the values that would come to dominate womanist interpretation. Her 1995 essay "Womanist Interpretation and Preaching in the Black Church" describes how womanist interpretation and preaching critiques and rethinks ministerial

---

13. Walker, *In Search of Our Mothers' Gardens*, xi; emphasis Walker's. An earlier, shorter definition appeared early in Walker's short story "Coming Apart," which was first published in 1979.

14. For an introduction to Katie Cannon's thought see Cannon, *Katie's Canon*. For a short article-length treatment of the origins and history of womanist biblical interpretation see Gafney, "Black Feminist Approach to Biblical Studies." To see a thorough treatment of the origins of womanist thought and especially its relationship to feminist interpretation in a book-length treatment see Junior, *Womanist Biblical Interpretation*.

15. Townes, *Troubling in My Soul* contains essays by Karen Baker-Fletcher, Katie Geneva Cannon, M. Shawn Copeland, Cheryl Townsend Gilkes, Jacquelyn Grant, Patricia L. Hunter, Cheryl A. Kirk-Duggan, Clarice Martin, Rosita DeAnn Mathews, Jamie T. Phelps, Marcia Y. Riggs, Emilie Townes, Delores S. Williams, Francis Wood.

16. Cannon, Townes, and Sims, *Womanist Theological Ethics* contains essays by Karen Baker-Fletcher, Katie Geneva Cannon, M. Shawn Copeland, Kelly Brown Douglas, Cheryl Townsend Gilkes, Marcia Y. Riggs, Angela D. Sims, Emilie Townes, and Renita Weems.

roles and the distribution of power within the Black church community, resisting the role of the Black preacher as principal interpreter of Scripture. Implicitly
articulating the analogical character of Black preaching, Cannon narrates how
"gospel stories about Jesus are linked back to quite definite events of the Greco-
Roman world and to the life of the present-day community. . . . The narrative
strategies of black religious lore recapitulate the lives and decisive actions of
biblical ancestors who are not thought to belong merely to the past, but are
considered also to be living, in, with, and beyond their faith descendants. . . . In
other words, Bible stories are relived, not merely heard."[17]

Hebrew Bible/Old Testament scholar Renita Weems was the first womanist biblical scholar. In her frequently cited essay on the aims of womanist
interpretation, she insists that Black women need to reflect on sexism, racism,
and classism in ways that classical feminism and Black theological reflection
sometimes elide. Seeing womanist work as a corrective to the narrower interests of White feminisms and Black liberation, Weems maintains that womanist
interpreters understand that "meaning takes place in the charged encounter
between socially and politically conditioned text and socially and politically
conditioned" readers. Womanists privilege no one reading or reading strategy
over another but employ various approaches, offering their readings as one of
many possible interpretations.[18] According to Weems, womanist interpreters
refuse to sanction oppressive stories in the Bible like the rape of Tamar in Genesis 34, the butchering of the Levite's concubine in Judges 19, or the prostitute
anointing Jesus's feet with her tears and hair in Luke 7. Womanists aim to break
the hold that these texts have on the imaginations of Black women and refuse
to excuse them because they allegedly serve some larger purpose. For Weems,
"part of rereading androcentric texts can entail choosing not to read them at
all . . . breaking the cycle of uncritically retelling and passing down from one
generation to the next violent, androcentric, culturally chauvinistic texts and
resisting where necessary the moral vision of such texts."[19] She encourages
readers to raise questions about texts, authors, and the assumptions embedded
in them. Readers should use their imaginations to retell the story in a way that
gets at hidden truths. Most importantly, they should take responsibility for the
impact the stories have on the lives of others, especially those who take the
stories to heart and try to live up to them.[20]

---

17. Cannon, "Womanist Interpretation and Preaching," 34.

18. Weems, "Re-Reading for Liberation," 25–26; Gafney, "Black Feminist Approach to
Biblical Studies."

19. Weems, "Re-Reading for Liberation," 28.

20. Weems, "Re-Reading for Liberation," 30.

Defining womanism as "black women's feminism," Wil Gafney's *Womanist Midrash* exemplifies the deep commitment to the interdisciplinarity of womanist interpretation.[21] This groundbreaking work develops the method named in its title as a combination of womanist interpretation with classical rabbinic Jewish midrash. Explicitly naming how "womanist midrash" mutually fuels and is empowered by her experience in the pulpit, Gafney reiterates her focal concern with the marginalized people in the text and those who read it. She focuses on women's stories and the features in the story that most interest women, emphases often missing in worship settings inside and outside of the Black church. Noting the hundreds of unnamed women in the Hebrew Bible, Gafney's work intentionally centers these women by offering names for some of the unnamed among them while listening for and giving voice to their stories.

Classic rabbinic midrash examines every word and feature of the text for revelatory possibilities. Like womanist interpretation, it questions the text and fills in the gaps and silences in the text with wisdom that makes it possible to live with the text in new moments. In her introduction, Gafney calls on the Black church modality of reading with a "sanctified imagination" to describe how womanist work analogously fills in the gaps by telling the story behind the story:

> The concept of the sanctified imagination is deeply rooted in a biblical piety that respects the Scriptures as the word of God and takes them seriously and authoritatively. This piety can be characterized by a belief in the inerrancy of Scripture and a profound concern never to misrepresent the biblical texts. In this context the preacher would be very careful to signify that what he or she is preaching is not in the text but is also divinely inspired. In this practice a preacher may introduce a part of the sermon with words like "In my sanctified imagination . . . ," in order to disclose that the preacher is going beyond the text in a manner not likely to be challenged, even in the most literal interpretive communities. The sanctified imagination is the fertile creative space where the preacher-interpreter enters the text, particularly the spaces in the text, and fills them out with missing details: names, back stories, detailed descriptions of the scene and characters, and so on.[22]

As someone who has long intuited that the apostle Paul's reading strategy seems at times oddly familiar, my soul danced when I read this description of the hermeneutics of the sanctified imagination. With her ingenious method-

---

21. Gafney, *Womanist Midrash*, 6.
22. Gafney, *Womanist Midrash*, 3–4.

ological synthesis, Gafney has articulated the power and valence of African American and other reader-response strategies for those who have been slow to credit them with legitimacy in the guild by showing how they are analogous to the centuries-old practices of the rabbis.

Intent on writing an accessible introductory text, Nyasha Junior in her *Introduction to Womanist Interpretation* tries to help students understand the complex intersections between feminist interpretation and activism and womanist interpretation and activism.[23] She argues that womanist interpretation does not arise from feminist interpretation but rather is an outgrowth of African American women's longstanding engagement with the Bible from the nineteenth century and beyond. She persuasively sustains this project through the first half of the book, tracing the rise of feminist interpretation alongside the separate increase of African American womanist interpretation. Junior's judgment in the second half of the book that there is a lack of precision in defining womanist approaches is a stance that has been less well received. Despite noting the same values and emphases mentioned above, Junior concludes that there is a lack of precision in womanist biblical approaches, especially when differentiating womanist theology, ethics, and religious studies from womanist biblical interpretation. In this latter judgment, I think she misses an opportunity to call attention to the structural disadvantages caused by the diminished numbers of Blacks in biblical studies that result from White normativity about the contours of biblical studies. The result is that there are fewer Blacks in biblical studies than in any other discipline in theological education or religious studies. It is not unusual to find minoritized theologians and ethicists doing interdisciplinary work in Bible to bring its perspectives to their work for the sake of members of the community who do not have access to anyone with formal training in biblical studies. Michael Brown's summary of an earlier, similar moment where Black theologians lacked the benefits of access to scholarly trained African American interpreters gets at a similar point:

> Unlike . . . other contextual approaches . . . black theology has suffered from two somewhat related problems. The first is the traditional disinterest among American biblical scholars in theologies of liberation. . . . The second problem has been the traditional absence of African Americans in the guild of biblical studies. When black theology emerged, very few African American biblical scholars were practicing in the academy. . . . For

23. Junior, *Womanist Biblical Interpretation*. Though Junior writes a book on the topic, she explicitly denies that she is a womanist interpreter (p. xxi).

the enterprise of black theology this absence was critical. Because of the contextual character of black theology, it would be impossible for anyone other than an African American biblical scholar to interpret Scripture through the symbol of blackness. Thus was born a critical need for black theologians: African American scholars of the Hebrew Bible and the New Testament—scholars who could explicate the scriptural basis for this liberatory theological enterprise.[24]

In 2015, the same year that Junior's book was published, Mitzi Smith published *I Found God in Me: A Womanist Biblical Interpretation Reader*. Smith identifies four generations of womanist scholars who were trained and publishing in biblical studies: two women in the first generation (Drs. Renita Weems and Clarice Martin), eight women in the second generation (Drs. Gay Byron, Cheryl Anderson, Valerie Bridgeman, Madeline McClenney-Sadler, Margaret Aymer, and Raquel St. Clair), four scholars in the third generation (Drs. Stephanie Buckhanon Crowder, Wil Gafney, Love Sechrest, and Mitzi Smith) and six in the fourth generation (Drs. Lynne St. Clair Darden, Shanell Teresa Smith, Kimberly Dawn Russaw, Febbie Dickerson, Yolanda Norton, and Vanessa Lovelace), in effect identifying a total of twenty women. Perhaps reflecting similar concerns about the dearth of biblical scholars who can address the Bible through the prism of Black womanhood, fourth-generation womanist biblical scholar Febbie Dickerson challenges womanist biblical scholars to bring all of their training in historical-critical methods to the task of challenging old stereotypes, debunking cultural constructs, and imagining new realities.[25]

Smith's essay in *I Found God in Me* describes the persona of womanist interpreters as prophetic and iconoclastic activists who are accountable to grassroots African American women who struggle for voice and representation. According to Smith, a womanist biblical scholar prophetically "confronts and names oppressions in texts, contexts, readers, readings, and cultures" through a selective engagement with texts that resonate with Black women.[26] They speak truth to power and risk demonization as prophetesses but avoid overgeneralizations and the logic of "pull-yourself-up-by-your-boot-straps" exceptionalism. For Smith, aspirational goals that emerge from the prosperity gospel do nothing more than further burden oppressed Black women. Concerned for the liberation of the entire community, though not at the expense of Black women's health and whole-

24. M. J. Brown, *Blackening of the Bible*, 18.
25. Dickerson, "Acts 9:36–43," 151.
26. M. J. Smith, "This Little Light of Mine," 113.

ness, womanists iconoclastically resist descriptions of the Black male pastor as the undisputed authority in the Black church. They challenge slave imagery in depictions of God and rebuke oppressive texts that diminish or silence women.[27] Explicitly naming a throughline among womanist scholars in many fields, Smith maintains that womanists reject complicity in the oppression of sexual minorities, noting that "the black church has failed on any significant scale to be an activist for gender inclusivity and sexual orientation."[28]

Theologian Kelly Brown Douglas also names values in womanist biblical interpretation. She suggests that it unleashes a liberative agency that attends to marginalized perspectives because "no theology emerges in a social, historical or cultural vacuum, and neither does any particular interpretation or approach to Scripture. Both theological and biblical discourse is shaped by the complicated historical realities of the persons conducting them."[29] Insisting that biblical materials themselves infer the invalidation of traditions of tyranny and terror, a womanist approach to biblical interpretation "begins with the recognition that our society and many of our churches . . . [are] marred by interlocking and interactive structures of domination."[30] While signifying powerlessness, marginality also comes with the power of a liberative agency.[31] Her essay unpacks her theological understanding of God's preference for the poor and marginalized, noting "God's election of the enslaved Israelites and not the enslaving Egyptians" and the fact that the incarnate God entered "human history through a manger and not Herod's palace."[32] For Douglas, the words that the first shall be last and last first in Mark 10:31 foretell a vision of transformed human relationships in perichoretic imitation of the relationships within the triune God.[33]

Hence for Douglas, womanist biblical scholars have several vital dispositions.[34] First, they name their privilege, which frees them to seek the perspectives of the most marginalized. Second, they engage the biblical stories from the perspective of the most marginalized, for example, entering the Sarah and Hagar narrative by reading through Hagar's perspective, a view that challenges the idea that God acts as a liberator in this story.[35] Third, as Douglas highlights

27. M. J. Smith, "This Little Light of Mine," 119–20.
28. M. J. Smith, "This Little Light of Mine," 122.
29. Douglas, "Marginalized People, Liberating Perspectives," 41.
30. Douglas, "Marginalized People, Liberating Perspectives," 41–43.
31. Douglas, "Marginalized People, Liberating Perspectives," 41–43.
32. Douglas, "Marginalized People, Liberating Perspectives," 45.
33. Douglas, "Marginalized People, Liberating Perspectives," 45–46.
34. Douglas, "Marginalized People, Liberating Perspectives," 41–43.
35. Here Douglas highlights Delores Williams's reading of this narrative in *Sisters in the Wilderness*.

in a different article, they utilize a hermeneutics of suspicion in reading the biblical texts since some stories lend themselves to oppressive interpretations that diminish life and freedom for all kinds of people. These "texts and/or interpretations must be held under 'suspicion,' critically reevaluated and perhaps lose authority."[36] Though it can perhaps be understood as a positive restatement of the third disposition above, Douglas essentially adds a fourth task in the same article by saying that "we are constrained to always find the liberative strand of the Bible in relation to the struggles of others. We are to resist any temptation to do otherwise, if indeed our theologies are accountable to the marginalized voices of our communities."[37]

A Liberative Hermeneutics of Suspicion

Douglas's fourth task is where this present book focuses. In keeping with womanist values, I find liberative strands of New Testament teaching while also suspiciously rooting out how the associations I detect are at odds with contemporary realities regarding the marginalized. I use associative hermeneutics and womanist values to interrogate the limits of analogies between the Bible and modern conditions of racism. *In other words, having found a liberative text or reading, I also attend to the ways that the text may introduce illiberative, oppressive, or otherwise harmful elements at the intersection of the text in question and larger issues surrounding contemporary race relations.*

Deployment of any hermeneutic must start with a clear understanding of the nature of the Bible before engaging theories about how to read it. With such an understanding of the nature of Scripture in hand, I think that a hermeneutic of suspicion and an associative hermeneutic can achieve complementary ends and achieve readings informed by attention to the concerns of the marginalized. Associative hermeneutics begins with the recognition that biblical texts are all historically conditioned. They reflect the human cultures that shaped and influenced the imaginative worlds of all these human authors and editors. They reflect beliefs about the nature of existence, human anthropology, technological limits, and the cosmological horizons of people living in the past. Contemporary readers should not feel bound to live within these parameters for purposes of heralding the holiness of these Scriptures.

As an example of this kind of critique, Renita Weems honors the central place that the Bible has in shaping the Black church, but in so doing recognizes the way that the notion of election and the concomitant behaviors attached to

36. Douglas, "When the Subjugated Come to the Center," 37.
37. Douglas, "When the Subjugated Come to the Center," 42.

it rhymes with the ideologies of privilege that prevail in White dominant culture today.[38] I suggest that at its core, this is associative hermeneutics at work. However, the methodology offered here would call for reflection on where the similarities between election and privilege diverge. As Weems suggests, the notion of manifest destiny embedded in much White American ideology and the biblical ideology of election do indeed have much in common. Both exhibit a sense that God has ordained access to resources and provision, and both foster an entitlement to those resources, despite whatever unjust ways they are allocated in a given historical moment. Yet it is important to add that there is a significant difference: the idea of election in the Bible was bestowed as comfort upon a ragtag, poor, marginalized, and enslaved people, while the concept of American manifest destiny was appropriated by a fledgling empire, fresh off a series of military victories and anxious to stretch its muscle against less well-endowed marginalized peoples. This caveat does not somehow invalidate Weems's original insight. Her insight is thickened by adding the reminder about how dangerous the notion of election can become when an underprivileged group emphasizing election later acquires power and privileges that slide easily and tragically into imperialistic behavior. Indeed, this situation might resonate today with marginalized Palestinians vis-à-vis the ideological proclivities of the modern nation-state of Israel.

An associative womanist hermeneutic insists that we engage the ugly details in some biblical narratives. We must resist illiberative injunctions to sustain spousal abuse (1 Pet. 3:6), injunctions that prohibit or inhibit feminine agency (1 Cor. 14:34; 1 Tim. 2:9–15), commands to commit genocide (Josh. 6–8, 10–12), or those advocating submission to brutal governments (Rom. 13). A reckoning with the nature of Scripture demands that we recognize that Scripture does not speak with one voice, nor does it always say the same thing on the same topic. The stories and testimonies span centuries and a myriad of social conditions. Women lead and govern in Judges, sit silently in 1 Corinthians (when not prophesying!), and have standing as apostles in Romans 16. The Bible itself bears witness to the myriad of possible readings as New Testament authors regularly reappropriate Old Testament texts, often twisting them out of all recognition from their original settings. Such situations thereby fuel our imaginative reappropriations as generations of Bible readers have done in their own prayer closets, praying the psalms and reimagining their own enemies in the place of the ancient enemies named in the original. The Bible itself attests to imaginative

38. Weems, "Womanist Reflections"; M. J. Smith, "Knowing More"; also see M. J. Smith and Lalitha, *Teaching All Nations*.

and playful appropriation of stories and texts in new circumstances far removed from those imagined by their original authors and editors, and these reappropriations are still at work today among people of faith, both learned and lay.

A hermeneutic of suspicion helps us remember that uncritical appropriation of texts can do irreparable harm to the marginalized. What I propose is the use of an additive principle: We can read the Bible from the point of view of its first readers, that is, from the perspective of ancient Israelites and marginalized Jewish and mostly Gentile converts to the early Christian movement, *and* we should also read the Bible from the perspectives of the most marginalized peoples today, those both inside and outside of Christian churches.[39] An associative hermeneutic is a way of fostering an imaginative, fruitful, and useful but *critical* dialogue between these two standpoints, figuring out where they are aligned and where we need additional resources to engage contemporary matters of morality or ethics.

The critical lens of Howard Thurman's grandmother, Nancy Ambrose, is one often cited in introductions to womanist interpretation, here as told by Kelly Brown Douglas:

> Howard Thurman tells of his grandmother. He relates his grandmother saying to him: "During the days of slavery . . . the master's minister would occasionally hold services for the slaves. . . . Always the white minister used as his text something from Paul. At least three times a year he used as his text: 'Slaves, be obedient to them that are your masters . . . as unto Christ.' I promised my Maker that if I ever learned to read and if freedom ever came, I would not read that part of the Bible."[40]

Douglas goes on to hold the critical lens of Thurman's grandmother in tension with the faith of her own grandmother in a way that resonates with the aims of associative hermeneutics:

---

39. Cf. D. S. Williams, *Sisters in the Wilderness*, 146–47: "The point here is that when non-Jewish people . . . read the entire Hebrew testament from the point of view of the non-Hebrew slave, there is no clear indication that God is against perpetual enslavement. . . . Equivocal messages and/or silence about God's liberating power on behalf of non-Hebrew, female slaves of African descent do not make effective weapons for African Americans to use in 'wars' against oppressors."

40. Douglas, "When the Subjugated Come to the Center," 42; citing Thurman, *Jesus and the Disinherited*, 30–31. For possibly the first use of this story by a biblical scholar see Weems, "Reading Her Way," 61–62; and M. J. Smith, who uses this story to introduce African American interpretation broadly in *Insights*, 6.

I realize that for my grandmother the Bible was more than simply a story about an Israelite people and their God. It was even more than a story about Jesus. In the Bible, Mama Dorsey found her own story; and the story that she found was enough to get her through whatever her days would bring because it demonstrated the sure and certain faith that God would bring better days, if not for her then certainly for her four grandchildren.[41]

Our proto-womanist marginalized mothers and grandmothers had the good sense to find the rhyme between the Good Book and their own conditions, and they followed that rhyme to life and liberation in Christ.

Taking the Bible Seriously but Not Literally

Thus womanist hermeneutics attends to African American women as readers and meaning makers, as people who are participating and extending the biblical narrative horizon by emphasizing liberative readings of texts. These practitioners engage texts through the lenses of their own experiences as people shaped by Scripture and living in a world that falls short of biblical ideas about the relationships between humans, creation, and God. I suggest that this hermeneutic participates in the broader trajectory of Black faith and preaching that encourages readers of the biblical text to see themselves as participants in the drama played out on its pages. It is an interpretive poetry that correlates the shape of the biblical text with the material conditions of Black women and men "who live in a world that is not of their choosing."[42]

This hermeneutic can be critiqued from both the left and the right. On the left, one could argue that by reading oneself into the text, one fails to reckon that the text is an ancient artifact and a product of vastly different cultures. Such a hermeneutic runs the risk of taking the text too seriously and literally by leaving its readers in bondage to ancient mores and traditions that have no place in the modern world. On the right, one could argue that associative hermeneutics allows someone to make the text say anything; in other words, it is a method that fails to take the text seriously enough. Both of these criticisms are important. Below I outline the mechanics of associative hermeneutics that contemporary readers interested in the liberation of Blacks and other marginalized peoples can adapt and note elements of the method that account for these criticisms.

41. Douglas, "When the Subjugated Come to the Center," 37.
42. Willie Jennings, personal communication.

So taking up a complaint from the right, inasmuch as Black readers read themselves into the text, does that result in a deformation of the text so that the text becomes something different from what its author intended? This outcome is certainly possible, though the way we talk about the interaction between text and reader is itself the product of interpretive choices. In some ways, the ideas that authors intend to convey through writing are lost at the point of the production of the text. As authors, we want to communicate our ideas for consumption by an audience that we envision. But whether the text ever achieves its intended communicative goals is something that lies outside of any author's control, ancient or modern alike. In that respect, the interplay between the Bible and contemporary African Americans on the one hand and between the Bible and the first readers on the other hand are relationships that differ in degree but not in kind. In other words, contemporary readers, African Americans, and all other modern readers are more likely to miss an ancient author's communicative intent than were the audiences to which that ancient author wrote. Yet, that same possibility of misunderstanding existed for the first readers of the Bible as well, even though it might have happened to a lesser degree. Indeed, *all readers* of texts create new relationships with the texts they read. When texts and readers share a worldview and a set of common experiences, accurate communication becomes more possible, but the risk of miscommunication is always present. Modern readers share a distance from the ancient author's experience, which means that recovering the author's precise intention is always a fragile undertaking.

However, if at a minimum we can say that the Bible is great literature—and it is surely that and more—then it shares with other such great literature the capacity to evoke responses to similarities in the human condition. In my view, it speaks with power precisely because it captures the experience of a people's understanding of God in a way that reminds me of how I encounter analogous phenomena. The struggles the people of God experience in reconciling the woes and dangers of a life lived at the mercy of the whims of powerful elites *rhymes* in some respects with how my people today live lives on the edge of exploitation by the 1 percent. I hear echoes of my own pleas to God in the poems and prayers of the psalter; I thrill at the stories of bondage and liberation and trace the shape of the journey of my own people in the rough outlines of slaves leaving Egypt. I set my face in a contemporary pulpit with the same flint in my eye as when John warned his people that there is no compromise possible with the ravening beast of Empire.

Let us now take up a different critique of associative hermeneutics from the left: Why should someone seek practices of interpretation that take the text "seriously though not literally" if they involve a wholesale embrace of practices and sensibilities that simply have no place in modern life, like slavery or genocide or ethnocentrism or misogyny? Those trained and disciplined by the enterprise of historical-critical biblical interpretation must quickly point out in agreement with these critics that however much I may read myself into the stories of the text, these stories are not, in fact, my own. Thus, a reading strategy that takes the biblical text seriously is one that interprets texts with sensitivity to the peoples, literatures, and historical and cultural contexts of the Bible, one that takes the Bible as an artifact of particular peoples located in lands and traditions that are vastly different from our own. However, it is also necessary to recognize that attending to historical peoples, literatures, and cultural contexts in interpretation is, in my mind, a matter of rendering the same courtesies to the ancient author that I would want extended to my own attempts to communicate about the values and concerns that animate my writing. A reading strategy that takes the text seriously but not literally will attend to the matters celebrated in doctoral seminars and seminary classrooms. Matters of genre and critical exploration of the historical, narrative, social, and political tensions in the text may all be engaged when reading the Bible with interest in centering the concerns of African American readers and interpreters. These matters help illuminate the distance between the ancient artifact and the modern condition in a way that allows readers to improvise on biblical harmonies.

So a reading strategy for African American women that takes the text seriously is also one that takes the circumstances of the contemporary reader and the communities to which she belongs seriously. It must explore the differences between the ancient world and the modern world as seriously as it tries to recover details about the historical circumstances that gave rise to the text. The modern reader must reckon that even if there are points of contact between the events reflected in the text and modern life, there will almost certainly be issues in contemporary life that will complicate a morally responsible, if biblically analogous, response. For example, readers who look to emulate Paul in their moral prescriptions will have to contend with the fact that Paul wrote with an expectation that the coming of the Lord would quickly redeem his audience in his lifetime. Thus, whatever one makes of his attitudes about marriage, his commands do not have long-range planning in mind in the way that moderns will inevitably have when reading his epistles two millennia later. Likewise, when one encounters anti-Jewish rhetoric in the gospels, contemporary readers will have to reckon with a long Christian history of racist crusades and anti-Semitism when attempting to use them as the basis for moral reasoning in the twenty-first century. No matter what the household codes tell us, we know that slavery is a dehumanizing evil and, in the United States, a racist institution as well. We've already seen what happens when people have taken those commands literally, making the Bible complicit in one of the most morally reprehensible human institutions ever devised. Encountering the Bible as human literature that has been divinely superintended and coauthored by people constrained by culture and limited horizons makes us better positioned to read it as morally responsible agents embedded in different cultures but struggling with similar problems that arise from the human condition.

Race and Associative Hermeneutics

Reading with an eye toward questions of race relations and gender arrangements will inevitably involve having our eyes drawn to the situations, stories, and characters in the biblical texts that depict intergroup conflict and those that feature women. For example, the case of the widows and disciples in Acts 6:1–6 seems analogous with, though not identical to, modern discourse about restorative justice. The story is about vulnerable Greek-speaking widows from the Jewish diaspora overlooked by the local Aramaic-speaking Jews in the daily distribution of food. The story also involves ethnic differences mediated via language (Greek vs. Aramaic) and geographical difference (Judeans vs. non-Judeans), characteristics that contributed to the minority status occupied by the impoverished widows and which may also have led to their marginalization in the food distribution. To solve the problem, the apostles appoint seven men to oversee the distribution. Notably, the men promoted to lead the food distribution more equitably had Greek names, thus presumably sharing some of the lived experiences of those overlooked Greek widows. Presumably, they would have identified with the widows' circumstances and been less inclined to neglect their needs. Other interpreters are puzzled that these new, well-qualified leaders are instructed to confine their activity to "serving tables" (Acts 6:2). Mitzi Smith notes the hierarchy that seems to be at work in the text, highlighting how the disciples assign the seven Greeks to the more menial task of serving at tables while they continue the vital task of preaching and teaching.[43] Have the Jews from outside of Judea been assigned to lower status positions? Is there an ethnic hierarchy at work?

Hence, the story rhymes with elements in the discourse about contemporary affirmative action that seeks to elevate persons from resource-constrained minority communities as a way of redressing a presenting inequity while more

43. Smith and Kim, *Toward Decentering the New Testament*, 98.

privileged others continue to reserve for themselves the most desirable work and reward structures. By contrast, Demetrius Williams sees a liberative element here. He observes the appropriateness of the fact that the Greek-speaking Philip and Stephen are the ones who take the first steps in moving the boundaries of the early Christian movement beyond Jerusalem.[44] Hence reading Williams together with Smith would imply that while the apostles hire the Seven to do the most menial of tasks, the assignment nonetheless left them well-placed for advancement into a growth opportunity of evangelism in the diaspora. This reading would reprise the biblical theme that God works through the marginalized, the least of these, the youngest, and the last one chosen.

Though some interpreters see this as a story about the appointment of new leaders in a diaconate (cf. Num. 11), the comment about growth in Acts 6:1 ("Now during those days, when the disciples were increasing in number") suggests that Luke thought that the conflict imperiled growth in the early Jesus community, perhaps by alienating diaspora Jews. The similar and bracketing growth comment in 6:7 ("the number of the disciples increased greatly in Jerusalem, and a great many of the priests became obedient to the faith," AT) suggests that the *solution* empowered additional growth among the priestly class.[45] In other words, it may be that the *harmonious* resolution of the ethnic conflict over resource sharing in the story paid off by increasing the winsomeness of the early Christian movement, attracting a group from the people's leadership class who were the most learned and pious among them. Affirmative action in contemporary life shares some of these dynamics since it too attempts to redress neglect and lack of access to vitally important resources. One might also say that as a very conservative approach to redressing centuries of stolen wages lost in slavery, affirmative action is also a solution that *harmoniously* seeks to reduce ongoing ethnic conflict. Nevertheless, though it has significant differences with this simple story and does not address the complexities of modern racial discrimination, the idea that something like affirmative action has a place in the center of what it means to be a Christian community via Acts 6 is compelling. Acts 6 thus not only prepares for stories about the movement's growth beyond the tight ethnic circle in Jerusalem, but it is also at least partly about creating safety for a minority community amid the hostility—or inhospitableness—of a majority culture.

44. D. K. Williams, "Acts of the Apostles," 225.

45. Since I occasionally use English translations for purposes of illustrating the meaning of Greek terms and phrases, I use the abbreviation AT to indicate the translations that are mine own.

The Poetics of Associative Reasoning

This interpretation of Acts 6:1–6 is based on associative reasoning, a reading strategy using analogical language that attempts to find similarities between events, notwithstanding profound cultural differences between them. Associative thinking is thus at the heart of interdisciplinary scholarly work and is hence relevant for womanist interpretation, which is also interdisciplinary by nature. In business literature, associative reasoning is the capacity to draw insights from one domain and bring them to bear in a different environment. This capacity is viewed as the taproot of the innovative adaptations that power new markets and give birth to technological advances.[46] As metaphors, analogies are also key strategies in theological and philosophical discourse. In a discussion about metaphorical language about God, Sallie McFague explores how metaphor works in the philosophy of science. Metaphor is central in how we engage the unknown as we connect what is unfamiliar with that which is more familiar, sorting out how new phenomena are both like and unlike what we already know. According to McFague, metaphorical statements "always contain the whisper, 'it is and it is not.'"[47] Especially important in language that describes God, metaphorical language about God requires multiple models that correct and challenge each other. Exploring the similarities and dissimilarities in these models helps avoid distortions from over-focus on a single metaphor. Using a single metaphor to describe God simply cannot do justice to the range of biblical testimony and thus lapses into idolatrous error.

Theorists examining metaphor or analogy often quote Aristotle, who wrote that "facility with metaphor cannot be taught and is a mark of genius, demanding as it does a sensitivity to similarity and dissimilarity . . . and the elusive relation between them" (*Rhetorica* 1405a7; cf. *De Poetica* 1458b13–17, 1459a).[48] As a skill, associative reasoning may come easier for some than for others, but anyone can cultivate this capacity. One can expand one's ability to make assessments in a field through maturity, education, and training. Exercises that can develop a repertoire in this area involve finding or imagining common characteristics among a gathering of objects that appear to be unrelated.[49] For example, using the four rows shown below, an associative reasoning game

46. Dyer, Gregersen, and Christensen, *Innovator's DNA*.

47. McFague, *Metaphorical Theology*, 13; also see Burrell, *Analogy and Philosophical Language*, 98.

48. Translated from Burrell, *Analogy and Philosophical Language*, 73; also see Chaitin, "Metonymy/Metaphor."

49. For example, Dyer, Gregersen, and Christensen, *Innovator's DNA*, 255, discusses a

might ask players to find or create a connection, one row at a time, that links the three objects on the row in question.[50]

a. trombones, scientists, playgrounds
b. a gymnastics competition, a track meet, a bank
c. a car, a baseball bat, hot sauce in a handbag
d. a shepherd, the White House, sheet music

Notice that the associative thinking underlying the examples above is embedded in culture, as is true of all intellectual capacities. Non-native English speakers might struggle with making one or more of these sample associations, and people outside of a particular African American demographic might wrestle with at least one of these associations:

a. they all have slides
b. they all have vaults
c. "swag" in Beyoncé's 2016 *Lemonade* video album
d. they all have staffs

Since analogies are extended metaphors, it can be helpful to examine metaphorical language as a precursor to a discussion of analogical reasoning. Martin Luther King Jr. was well known for his poetic genius and used figurative language in ways that involved "a startling juxtaposition of apparently unlike entities that initially provokes puzzlement" as in phrases like "the iron feet of oppression"; the "dark chambers of pessimism"; and the "tranquilizing drug of gradualism."[51] Thus, in literature, associative thinking is figurative language that transfers meaning from one object to another unlike object. The transfer of meaning occurs by

---

game that helps players excel in making these associations by playing "What's the connection?" Given random words, players find and create a connection between them:

Hands, salt, spray paint (Answer: Things you shake)
Trombones, scientists, playgrounds (Answer: They all have slides)
A Gymnastics Competition, A Track Meet, A Bank (Answer: They have vaults)
A Shepherd, The White House, Sheet Music (Answer: They have staffs)
Cow, School, Bar (Answer: Things with bells)
Fire Trucks, High Dive Towers, House Painters (Answer: Things with ladders)
Taste, Ear, Rose (Answer: Things that have buds)
A French Bank, Oscar Mayer, From Here to Eternity/My Way/White Christmas (Answer: Things with Franc[k]s)
50. From a website for the 2016 Tribond™ game on www.tribond.com.
51. These examples are given in Lischer, *Preacher King*, 123–24.

imaginatively twisting the ordinary meaning of a word so that when it is transferred to a different idea, the proper use of the transferred word applies innova-
tively to the other idea. For example, a "workhorse" is a description given to a
member of the equine species that has been bred for endurance and strength to
haul massive loads that are many times heavier than the horse itself.[52] Yet among
people who share similar cultural referents, an employee who is a "workhorse in
the department" is recognizable as someone who is a tireless office laborer who
does more than their fair share of work, rather than a literal reference to a large
animal with hooves and a mane that has been set loose in a skyscraper. Thus a
metaphor, originating from a Greek word meaning "to transfer,"[53] is figurative
language that suggests that one object really is another one, implying a comparison or transfer of meaning between the two. In the metaphorical phrase "You
are the light of the earth," Jesus suggests that his disciples are agents who will
bring knowledge of God's actions in Christ to others who metaphorically inhabit
darkness because of their ignorance of God's ways and God's will.[54]

David B. Burrell examines the role of language in the practice of philosophy
and notes the central role of analogical expressions, maintaining that they are
a privileged set of terms that are the bedrock of language and philosophical
inquiry.[55] For the purposes of this discussion, I repeat here several properties
of analogical expressions identified by Burrell that are helpful. First, analogical expressions are readily employed across different contexts despite the
differences in meaning, as seen in Barber's analogy between the Trump era
and Reconstruction described in the opening of this chapter.[56] Second, Burrell maintains that the use of analogous expressions assumes the capacity to
understand and specify as necessary what the two expressions have in common between them, facilitating a meaningful application of one term to the
analogous term or situation.[57] Third, we can observe that over time common
analogical usages expand potentially even to the point where the metaphorical association itself becomes standardized, possibly even to the point where
the origin of the expression is lost (e.g., "crocodile tears").[58] Finally, it will be
helpful to remember Burrell's argument that formulations of analogies include

---

52. A draft horse bred for hauling massive loads can weigh as much as a ton (2,000
pounds) but can pull as much as twenty tons or more.

53. "To transfer": μεταφέρω.

54. Nørgaard, Busse, and Montoro, *Key Terms in Stylistics*, 107.

55. Burrell, *Analogy and Philosophical Language*.

56. Burrell, *Analogy and Philosophical Language*, 206.

57. Burrell, *Analogy and Philosophical Language*, 75, 206, 220–21, 223.

58. https://www.psychologytoday.com/us/blog/the-red-light-district/201511/do
-crocodiles-really-cry.

the capacity to assess, evaluate, or recognize the degree of common ground and difference embedded in the formulation.[59] This last is in keeping with Aristotle's conviction that a metaphor "must be fitting . . . that is, [it must] fairly correspond to the thing signified" (*Rhetorica* 1405a10).[60] In other words, analogical thinking demands the active presence of judgment.[61]

Consequently, analogies are extended metaphors that also establish a relationship between two things. While metaphors establish relationships between objects that may not appear to be similar at first glance, analogies examine the common characteristics between like objects. In an expression first articulated by Aristotle, analogies often take the form of a mathematical proportion "A is to B just as C is to D," expressed mathematically as

$$A : B :: C : D$$

and this proportion expresses the idea that the relationship between A and B is similar or analogous to the relationship between C and D. Though the symbols are a helpful shorthand for discussions about analogies, we must keep in mind that the use of the mathematical expression could convey the sense of a greater degree of precision than actually exists; similarly, the concise mathematical formula elides the fact that analogies express both similarity *and* dissimilarity.[62] In other words, a precise statement that "X is analogous to Y" virtually demands the addition of some qualifying statement "with respect to Z." That is, we need some way of limiting the applicability of the analogy; otherwise, we are asserting that A is the same as or identical to B rather than a statement of an analogical relation between A and B.[63] For example, in the reading of Acts discussed above, we could say that Acts 6:1–6 is analogous to affirmative action *with reference to* empowering minorities who have been disadvantaged economically, though the two situations are vastly different in terms of why, how, and to whom the reforms are administered.

Hence in biblical interpretation or biblical ethics, we would say that a biblical situation *is analogous to* a modern situation when the two situations share crucial characteristics or social dynamics. If there are enough shared and sa-

59. Burrell, *Analogy and Philosophical Language*, 17, 22, 30, 207.
60. Burrell, *Analogy and Philosophical Language*, 73.
61. Burrell, *Analogy and Philosophical Language*, 208, 230.
62. Burrell, *Analogy and Philosophical Language*, 10 and passim. In other words, we cannot overemphasize the difference between the expression "::" ("analogous to/proportionate to") and the one signified by "=" ("equals").
63. Burrell, *Analogy and Philosophical Language*, 14.

lient properties between them, then the results of the biblical situation, that is, the moral response to the situation described in the text, will be analogous to a biblically informed moral response to the modern dilemma. In the language of math logic, we would see:

$$S_B : S_M :: R_B : R_M$$

So, when the biblical situation S_B is analogous to or rhymes with the modern situation S_M, we can surmise that the relationship will hold when considering some of the other aspects of the two situations, including the moral reasoning in the characters' situational responses. Recognizing that all analogies break down at some point and that no analogy is ever perfect, we strive to discern the measure and extent of the assonances and dissonances of analogical correspondences with biblical literature. It means that we must turn a bare rhyme that correlates two culturally distinct situations into a fully fleshed out poetics that moves toward a biblically shaped and morally responsible response to contemporary dilemmas in African American life. Thus, this method presupposes an in-depth understanding of *both the historical context and the modern dilemma* to draw parallels regarding the social dynamics in the ancient situation.

Though we will examine specific biblical texts below, figure 1.1 (on p. 26, below) imagines a modern dilemma that seeks biblical guidance about choosing leaders. This example uses a simplified version of a biblical moral—when God chooses a king, the people's harvest is bountiful—and aligns it with the modern dilemma about choosing leaders. This biblical story rhymes with questions today about electing presidents and prime ministers but takes place in a more diverse society with people from a range of gender expressions in a vastly more complex economic environment. Construction of an analogy requires iterating where and how the details in the two contexts differ until one is satisfied that there is enough correspondence to warrant aligning the stories from the two different temporal contexts. In this case, we construct a possible modern situation and response that aligns with the simple biblical story: If we choose leaders with godly character (whatever their ethnicity or race; whether male, female, or gender fluid), the people's economic well-being flourishes.

In teaching this method to students, I've found that it achieves the goal of helping my students take the Bible seriously but not literally. By practicing this method, students do creative, nuanced, and imaginative biblical moral reasoning. The appendix shows a sample of student work on an analogical

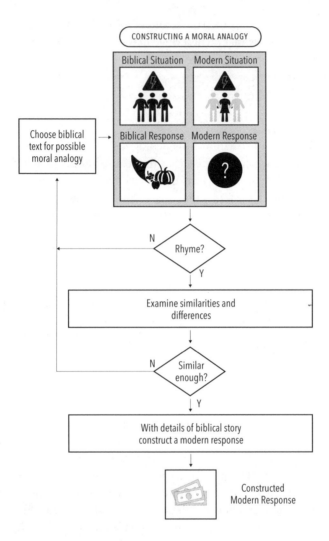

Figure 1.1. Associative Hermeneutics

reasoning assignment.[64] The component sections of the assignment are heuristic devices to aid the cultivation of the judgment required in associative reasoning. In particular, the analogy table required on page two of the project

64. Though I did receive permission to share this particular student's work shown here, I have nonetheless protected the author's identity in this sample.

(see appendix) assists students in fleshing out the poetics of a rhyme between a narrative episode in the New Testament and exploration of a contemporary dilemma in race relations. The table helps them correlate events in a biblical situation with the parameters of a current issue in race relations, helping them find biblical resources for liberative solutions.

Over the years, I've found that students are much more likely to succeed when engaging biblical narratives than while interacting with other biblical genres.[65] Because narratives provide more information about the biblical situation, it is usually easier for them to identify conditions and problems in a modern experience that rhyme with the conflict in the biblical stories. They struggle a bit more with epistles, for instance, which require going behind the text to excavate the underlying social situation that prompted the epistle's writing before making persuasive associations with contemporary issues. For the same reason, the book of Revelation is most difficult of all, requiring the ability to do some level of epistolary mirror reading as well as the ability to negotiate the symbol universe of early Jewish and Christian apocalyptic writing.

The Analytics of Associative Reasoning

We can illustrate a critical analysis of analogical reasoning for moral reflection by considering 1 Timothy 2:8–15. In its context, it is a text that biblical literalists see as a prooftext prohibiting female leadership in the church and in society. This text and others like it have done irreparable harm to the women in Black churches and in other churches that take the Bible seriously and literally. The so-called "male headship" promoted in this text is a prime culprit in sanctioning the sometimes dangerous, exploitative, and oppressive power of the Black pastor in Black churches, mainly peopled by Black women.[66] The use of this text is dangerous in that engagement with it may signal some agreement with its gender-biased message of female subordination when that is farthest from my intention. Nevertheless, I have used it in classes, albeit gingerly, because

---

65. Similarly Hays, *Moral Vision*, 295: "the narrative texts of the New Testament are fundamental resources for normative ethics." Likewise Hays later writes: "whenever we appeal to the authority of the New Testament, we are necessarily engaged in metaphor-making, placing our community's life imaginatively with the world articulated by the texts" (298–99).

66. See Riggs, *Plenty Good Room,* for a nuanced analysis of the sexual-gender oppression in the Black church. Further, her engagement with Scripture in the constructive portion of this work offers intriguing examples of associative reasoning. Also see Nadar, "Paradigm Shifts in Mission," for a womanist reading of this text that similarly resists the oppression of Black South African women in churches.

doing so illustrates the critical role of culture in the interpretive task when juxtaposing ancient values with a contemporary social context. I have found that associative reasoning with this text exposes the function of culture in interpretation, illustrates the importance of critiquing misogynistic assumptions latent in biblical texts, and helps demonstrate the liberative value of a hermeneutics of suspicion.

Literarily, the text is a passage from one of the New Testament documents called the Pastoral Epistles, and close readings of this group of epistles (1 Timothy, 2 Timothy, and Titus) suggest that they share a language and a set of concerns about a believer's reputation in their broader society. Arising from these texts is the idea that disciples must be concerned about public decency. They must recognize that the behavior of individuals in the group will reflect on the early Christian movement at large.[67] As with any New Testament epistle, moral reflection requires reconstruction of the ecclesial situation that prompted the sending of the letter, and in this case interpreters may be frustrated by the pseudonymous authorship of 1 Timothy. But even though the details of the debates animating 1 Timothy are now lost to history, it seems clear that controversies were roiling the churches in Ephesus and exploding into view in public arguments, as attested by themes across the Pastoral Epistles.[68] In 1 Timothy 2:1–4, the author hopes that a peaceful and stable society will provide the optimal context for the church's growth. Concern in this text that the faithful will maintain decorum that will adorn the church's reputation manifests itself in gendered proscriptions about male behavior (2:8–9), and in 2:9–15 the author is especially concerned that women exhibit culturally appropriate demeanor in public.[69] Further, 1 Timothy 2:13–14 ("it was not Adam who was deceived . . .") suggests that, for this author, women are easily deceived, and intellectually and morally incapable of detecting error, ideas that were widespread in the culture (e.g., Philo, *On the Sacrifices of Abel and*

---

67. 1 Tim. 2:2, 9–10, 12, 15; 3:1–13; 5:7, 24–25; cf. 2 Tim. 1:7; Tit. 2:2, 5, 7–8, 10, 12.

68. 1 Tim. 1:7–9, 2:8; 5:13; 6:3–5; 2 Tim. 2:14, 16–18, 23–24; 3:6; 4:3–4; Tit. 1:6–7, 9–11; 3:2, 9–11.

69. Similarly, Plutarch's *Moralia, Advice to Brides and Grooms,* Babbitt 142C–E: "Theano, in putting her cloak about her, exposed her arm. Somebody exclaimed, 'A lovely arm.' 'But not for the public,' said she. Not only the arm of the virtuous woman, but her speech as well, ought to be not for the public, and she ought to be modest and guarded about saying anything in the hearing of outsiders, since it is an exposure of herself; for in her talk can be seen her feelings, character, and disposition. . . . For a woman ought to do her talking either to her husband or through her husband, and she should not feel aggrieved if, like the flute-player, she makes a more impressive sound through a tongue not her own."

Cain 103; Aristotle, *Politics* 1259b).[70] The underlying logic is that in a culture where it was considered indecent for women to speak or act in public, and where women were considered irrational and lacking in intellectual capacities, the pastor forbids women to teach or lead because such would severely undermine the credibility of the church.

Taking the Bible seriously but not literally means reckoning with the fact that it is impossible to strip the culture out of the biblical narratives so that we only concern ourselves with its timeless and transcendent principles, as some might argue.[71] One of the most critical dynamics in biblical ethics and biblical interpretation is that the reader must always read the text with attention to the vast cultural gap between the ancient text and the reader who is embedded in a vastly more complex society as we carry out ethical responsibilities vis-à-vis biblical interpretation to the communities from which we emerge. This text asks disciples to comport themselves in culturally appropriate ways and gives instructions about the proper demeanor for male public discourse and public prayer, and women's dress and public comportment (1 Tim. 2:8–15). In the address to women, the passage issues culturally appropriate examples anchored to prevailing anthropological assumptions about women's capacities, resulting

---

70. Philo, *Special Laws* 1.201, Colson: "So too with the two ingredients which constitute our life-principle, the rational and the irrational; the rational which belongs to mind and reason is of the masculine gender, the irrational, the province of sense, is of the feminine." Similarly, Aristotle, *Politics* 1259b, Rackham: "The male is by nature superior, and the female inferior; and the one rules, and the other is ruled. . . . Of household management we have seen that there are three parts—one is the rule of a master over slaves . . . another of a father, and the third of a husband. A husband and father rules over wife and children, both free, but the rule differs, the rule over his children being a royal, over his wife a constitutional rule. For although there may be exceptions to the order of nature, the male is by nature fitter for command than the female, just as the older and full-grown is superior to the younger and more immature. . . . The relation of the male to the female is of this kind [with different outward forms and names and titles of respect], but there the inequality is permanent. The rule of a father over his children is royal, for he receives both love and the respect due to age, exercising a kind of royal power. . . . The freeman rules over the slave after another manner from that in which the male rules over the female, or the man over the child; although the parts of the soul are present in all of them, they are present in different degrees. For the slave has no deliberative faculty at all; the woman has, but it is without authority, and the child has, but it is immature. So, it must necessarily be with the moral virtues also; all may be supposed to partake of them, but only in such manner and degree as is required by each for the fulfillment of his duty. . . . Clearly, then, moral virtue belongs to all of them; but the temperance of a man and a woman, are not, as Socrates maintained, the same; the courage of a man is shown in commanding, of a woman in obeying."

71. Hays, *Moral Vision*, 299–300.

in prohibitions for feminine public agency. These behavioral sanctions are all in service of establishing a credible Christian witness in society so that the faith will be appealing and winsome to outsiders, so that, as verse 4 puts it, everyone may be saved and come to the knowledge of the truth.

As Hebrew Bible scholar Wilda Gafney puts it, "the reprehensible gender and sexual mores of the Stone and Iron Ages are still in effect for some of the women, men, boys, and girls living in the Digital Age."[72] However, twenty-first-century human anthropology in the West is different from anthropological assumptions in the first century. Today many of us should and do hold that women and men are intellectually equal. If female public action brings shame on the Christian movement in antiquity, the opposite situation prevails today. In other words, an analogous reading of this text today would hold that it would bring shame on Christians to *prohibit* women from public speech and activity because now Black women in the United States can receive the same developmental and educational opportunities as men and, at least theoretically, can serve as CEOs and governors, vice presidents and prime ministers. In a culture that proclaims that *women's rights are human rights*, this text would prompt us to shield the church from disgrace. We would do everything we could to avoid the suggestion that women are not fit for leadership intellectually or morally, stereotypes that are profoundly damaging to Black women who are subject to stereotypes about feminine incompetence as well as ideas about Black intellectual inferiority. Thus, a liberative reading of this text would involve, first, a critique of its ancient gender-biased assumptions about the capacities of women. Second, a liberative interpretation might simultaneously use the text to promote culturally appropriate behavior regarding female agency that is a credit to the church by celebrating feminine accomplishments in all kinds of public, sacred, and secular spheres. In other words, in this new cultural moment of female empowerment, this reading promotes an *inversion* of the literal injunctions in the text to enable the performance of the text in a different cultural context that is analogous to its original moral trajectory. In conversations about race and gender, students were also quick to realize that this reading of 1 Timothy 2 that interrogates similarities and differences in knowledge about human anthropology across time also has implications for a biblically informed posture toward sexual orientation today. This reading suggests that it would discredit Christian practice if Christians insisted on demonizing LGBTQIA+ differences in a culture that recognizes that the range of human sexuality and gender expression is far broader and more complex than what was known in the New Testament period.

72. Gafney, *Womanist Midrash*, 83.

This reading of 1 Timothy 2 demonstrates that an associative hermeneutic can help bridge the chasm between situations today and those rooted in geographically, culturally, and temporally distant cultures. But we must also ensure that an associative hermeneutic will interrogate both the specifics of the text at hand and the specifics of the contemporary moral dilemma. Therefore, since no analogy is ever perfect, we need to add constraining elements to our methodology that help articulate the limitations of the metaphorical associations. The chief function of these refining factors is to identify the extent of the analogy to avoid doing moral violence in an analogy that fails to take the complexities of the modern dilemma seriously. The use of metaphor and analogy as a tool in biblical hermeneutics will only ever be as helpful as the critical review of an attempted correlation of the biblical teaching with complex modern problems. Hence, I suggest two methodological additions to the basic intuitive discernment of an association between a situation narrated or assumed in the Bible and a current dilemma. These two framing questions can help construct morally responsible analogies and examine the spaces where the analogy breaks down.

We can express the first addition to the method as a question that helps establish the limit of the poetic details of a rhyme between the Bible and contemporary life by stimulating thought on the unintended consequences of a wholesale, uncritical application of the biblical text for modern life (see figure 1.2):

Poetic limit question: Given a rhyme between a current situation and the biblical passage/situation, what is the *modern equivalent of an unexamined idea* in the biblical passage?

Suppose we were to ask this question about the analogy that we explored earlier in Acts 6:1–6. In that case, we might decide to look closer at details in the text about selecting the new leaders from the ethnic minority subgroup. We could begin by framing our intuition about a rhyme between Acts 6 and affirmative action in the terms used in the framing question about the limitation of the analogy:

Poetic limit example: Affirmative action that helps minoritized people control needed resources after neglect is analogous to Acts 6:1–6, where minoritized Greek-speaking leaders are put in charge of the food distribution to ensure that minoritized Greek-speaking widows receive better access to food. If this is so, what is the *modern equivalent* of making sure that the Greek leaders were "of good standing, full of the Spirit and of wisdom" (Acts 6:3)?

An implied modern equivalent of Acts 6:3 might involve making sure that affirmative action programs ensure that selected minorities are "qualified" to

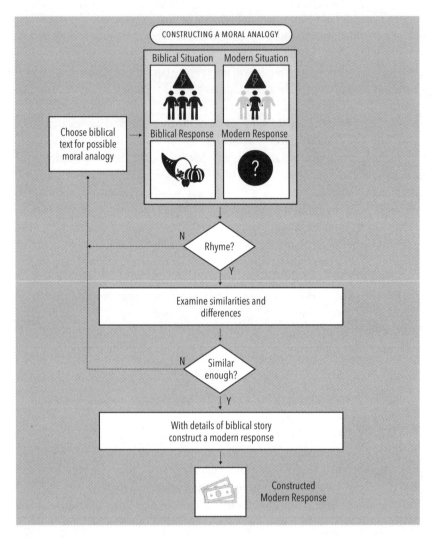

Figure 1.2. The Analytics of Associative Hermeneutics

do the job at hand. Critics might find in this caveat a wedge by which others could bring down the entire modern affirmative action apparatus since there is among opponents of affirmative action an unstated biased assumption that minorities are unqualified for positions, roles, or participation in institutions from which they have been previously excluded. Indeed, the history of welfare programs to relieve poverty in this country has faltered on just this point, as

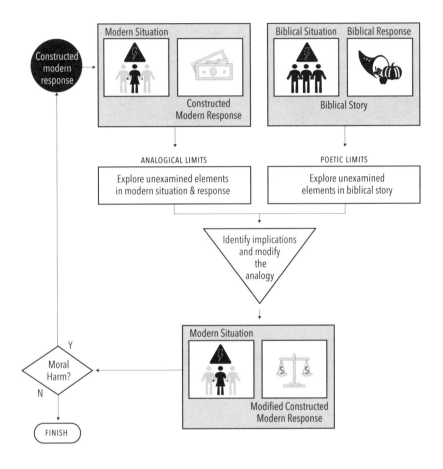

legislators intentionally refrained from putting benefits directly in the hands of minority communities because of a so-called lack of human capital in these communities capable of managing poverty relief resources.[73] These actions short-circuited financial independence and left these communities dependent

73. Quadagno, *Color of Welfare*.

on biased distribution systems. Therefore, the framing of the analogy is helpful in that it attends to the idea that it was *control of resources* by minority leaders that achieved the harmonious result, relieved the suffering of the neglected and overlooked minoritized communities, and increased the appeal of the early Christian movement to others. A consideration of the contemporary history of the racialized defacement of the modern welfare state shows that failure to empower the minoritized community by investing its leaders with real authority will no doubt fail to achieve results analogous to the winsome ethnoracial harmony normalized in Acts 6.

While the question about the poetic limits invites iterative reflection on the details of the biblical account,[74] a second methodological intervention helps stimulate thinking on the complexity of the modern dilemma that participates in the analogy (see again figure 1.2). Specifically, this second framing question identifies issues associated with the contemporary problem that may not be addressed in the passage at hand: the limitations on the analogy for contemporary ethics. This question aims to stimulate fruitful reflection about how other dynamics in modern life might complicate, inform, or augment a more rounded and robust biblically shaped moral response:

> *Analogical limit questions:* If a given current situation is analogous to a biblical passage/situation, is there some element in the contemporary case unaddressed in this biblical passage/situation? Are there other biblical texts that can inform this situation?

Use of this framing question might involve statements of a rhyme and questions as follows for each of our sample texts:

> *Analogical limits example 1:* Acts 6:1–6 selects minoritized Greek-speaking leaders to control food distribution to ensure that neglected Greek-speaking widows receive better access to food, and this is analogous to affirmative action that helps redress neglected African Americans. However, is there something in this text or outside of it that addresses *reparations for accumulated losses* by minoritized communities?

74. In student assignments, I invite students to reflect on multiple elements/verses/characters in a given passage to help flesh out the poetic shape of a broadly discerned rhyme through iterative use of framing question 1. Likewise, framing question 2 can be iteratively engaged to determine the limitations or constraints on a rhyme between a passage and a contemporary problem. See the appendix for the heuristic devices used to aid students in their biblical moral reflection.

Analogical limits example 2: First Timothy 2:1–15 exhorts female believers to display culturally relevant public demeanors that will reflect well on the church (2:9–15) and lead outsiders to align with it (2:1–4), actions that are analogous to activities that affirm women leaders in modern life, which reflect well on the church's public witness. However, how can we address situations when instead of quietly and peacefully obeying authorities to improve the reputation of the faith (cf. 2:1–4) *believers should protest or resist authority figures* to win or preserve a good reputation for the faith?

The second set of questions that probe the limits of biblical analogy move from modern life back to the text, while the earlier set of questions that flesh out the poetic shape of the rhyme between the text and contemporary life start with the biblical text and then move to the reader's context. In the first example, the framing question about the limits of the rhyme or analogy between affirmative action and Acts 6 explores a case where the modern dilemma of African American economic deprivation is longstanding and institutionalized, orders of magnitude more complex than the situation of the Hellenistic widows. The contemporary dilemma poses whether the simple solution in Acts 6 is formulated at a scale necessary for justice claims inherent when the bias at issue lasted for over four hundred and fifty years. The question is whether Acts 6 is even the best biblical analog for the centuries of African American economic deprivation. A womanist might answer that the Exodus from Egypt after hundreds of years of slavery is a better fit:

> I'll make it so that when you leave Egypt, the Egyptians will be kind to you and you won't go away empty-handed. Every woman will ask her neighbor . . . for their silver and their gold jewelry as well as their clothing. (Exod. 3:21–22 CEB)

Similarly, and with an eye on the gender dynamics of the Acts story, we should not fail to interrogate the assumption that minority *male* representatives share enough of the social location of the deprived widows as we attend to the intersectional complexities about how an affirmative action response would need to be crafted today. There is evidence, for instance, that White women benefit from affirmative action in the United States while also being among its fiercest opponents, and these factors should nuance our ethical response to the analogy.[75]

75. Massie, "White Women Benefit Most from Affirmative Action."

Similar questions prevail in the second example from 1 Timothy 2, about whether the biblical analog can address contemporary dilemmas. The analogy in 1 Timothy 2 is predicated on the idea from the text that cultural relevance makes a vital contribution to the creation of behavioral norms. While the particulars of dress and decorum vary widely across the centuries, the idea from the text that the comportment of believers has a bearing on how appealing the faith is to outsiders makes it possible to align the culturally specific details of 1 Timothy 2:8–15 with a modern register. But the question about protest and resistance in the second example probe the analogical limits of this correlation. These questions ask whether the norm about tranquil social relations in 1 Timothy 2:1–4 best positions the church for broad appeal in the public square in all situations. The mass civil protest during the summer of 2020 about the injustice done to Breonna Taylor might offer a clear example here. Taylor, a Black woman in Louisville, Kentucky, was killed in an improperly executed "no-knock" police raid while sleeping in her own bed, in a home that was only tangentially associated with the person of interest in a criminal investigation.[76] I would argue that Christian involvement in the massive protests against routine and unaccountable police violence against Black women, children, and men that summer *does* comport with Christian witness. Several biblical narratives and texts, including the prophetic resistance exhorted in Acts 4 and Revelation 11, could sanction demonstrations of a public and holy unrest about injustice. In other words, we never expect that a given biblical passage alone can address all of the issues in a contemporary moral dilemma, not to mention the fact that we need to appeal to theological, theoretical, and political resources in addition to the Bible. Questions about analogical limits prompt close readings of contemporary moral questions, even as questions about the poetic shape of an ethical response require close readings of a biblical text. The appendix shows heuristic frameworks that invite students to do exposition of the poetic shape of a moral analogy and reflect on limitations and complicating factors in analyzing them.

I've found that the 1 Timothy 2 example is especially useful in getting students to think through the idea that culture is an ever evolving but constant presence in human life. The inherently amorphous nature of culture can't be excised from the biblical story, like stripping the husk from corn and leaving only the good kernels, any more than culture can be expurgated from our contemporary stories. Because every jot and tittle of the New Testament is culturally conditioned, it is impossible to distinguish timeless truth in the New

---

76. For more on the unjust killing of Breonna Taylor and the protests in its aftermath, see Oppel, Taylor, and Bogel-Burroughs, "What to Know about Breonna Taylor's Death."

Testament from culturally conditioned elements.[77] First Timothy 2 insists that cultural norms are an important resource for thinking about Christian witness and should not be ignored as they are in more literalistic approaches. The method calls for an imaginative synthesis of two cultural moments, based on the idea that human drives, motivations, loves, and fears operate in many different cultural landscapes, not because of the similarities in cultures but because of similarities in the human condition. This method allows a biblically shaped imaginative synthesis where such factors in the human condition correspond but allows freedom from wooden and literalistic application that overdetermines the similarities between biblical times and today and ignores their mammoth differences. Further, by iterating between a metaphorical reading of the biblical text and a critical assessment of the contemporary horizon, this reading strategy prevents an uncritical adoption of first-century culture on the one hand or a reductionistic engagement with contemporary culture on the other.

Race Relations and the New Testament

With a new language for analogical reasoning from the previous section in hand, we lack only a brief survey of key concepts in the study of race and racism before engaging the liberative readings of New Testament texts herein. Each chapter in this book introduces terminology and concepts from the study of race and ethnicity germane to the issue(s) engaged there. However, it will be helpful to situate some of the major concepts in this domain before diving into discussions of narrower issues. Before providing an overview of the remaining chapters in this book, in the next section I define the key terms in the study of race relations: *ethnicity*, *race*, *racism*, *privilege*, *prejudice*, and adjacent terms such as *racialization*, *stereotypes*, and the concept of *White supremacy*.

Know the Score: Key Terms in the Study of Race and Racism

Primarily regarded as a social construction of the modern era, race is perhaps better seen as humanity's most dangerous myth and virulent superstition.[78] There is no standard definition of race nor a unifying theory that engages its relationship to similar concepts such as "ethnicity" and "nation," one reason

---

77. Hays, *Moral Vision*, 299; see also pp. 291–313 for additional explication of the use of metaphor and analogy in doing New Testament ethics.
78. Yudell, *Race Unmasked*, 2.

why the study of race is interdisciplinary across the natural sciences, social sciences, and humanities. While some believe that race is wholly different from ethnicity, others maintain that race is a special case of ethnic identification, a natural and primordial characteristic of human society existing from antiquity. Originally the terms *race, nation,* and *ethnic group* were used synonymously, each of them emphasizing common descent or a widely held myth of common descent.[79] It is better to say that *race* and *ethnicity* represent socially constructed, imagined communities that do not represent natural, biological, primordial, or essential human properties but groups assumed to share some physical, cultural, or socioeconomic realities. These communities are constructed through boundaries drawn by the group either in isolation or, more often, in combination with powerful outside actors. It's also important to say that the constructed or imagined nature of race and ethnicity is in tension with the tangible social effects of racial and ethnic identity. In other words, these communities may be imagined, but the results of membership in a disadvantaged ethnic or racial group have real-life consequences on salary, health, mortality, education, housing, and ordinary public interactions, whether while shopping or in encounters with police and other authorities.

One common set of definitions tries to differentiate race and ethnicity by suggesting that race focuses on physical descent and kinship and the physical, mental, or moral characteristics that are assumed to accompany them, while ethnicity focuses on culture. However, this way of defining race becomes problematic to the degree that it associates pejorative or inferior physical, mental, and moral characteristics with a biological category. These associations are better seen as the product of processes of *racialization* when a group is marginalized or dehumanized via social assumptions about the group. If race highlights physical descent, common usage for the term *ethnicity* tends to focus on a people group's culture and geographical location, with attention to the customs, dress, food, religion, language, etc. of a nation, race, group, or cult. Ethnicity is often associated with what is foreign or exotic.

People can change ethnicity via a shift in language, dress, or even surname, but it is difficult or impossible to change race. Thus, some who try to differentiate ethnicity from the closely connected concept of race might insist that race is a special subclassification of ethnicity, characterized by unusually rigid group boundaries based on skin color. Others look at the two concepts through the

---

79. For more information on the transhistorical social construction of concepts such as race, ethnic group, and nation from the NT period until the modern period, see Sechrest, *Former Jew.*

prism of conflict, defining race as involving extraordinarily high levels of conflict. However, this schema falters upon categorizing some conflict as "racial" that might otherwise be classified as "ethnic" (e.g., Tutsis vs. Hutus in Rwanda; Catholics vs. Protestants in Northern Ireland; or Israelis vs. Palestinians in the occupied West Bank territories). Further, it is challenging to distinguish race from an ethnic group or religious group when thinking about groups like Jews or Arabs, which may cut across all these categories depending on context. Because of the definitional and disciplinary ambiguities, I prefer using the hybrid term *ethnoracial* to signal how it is frequently difficult to differentiate the concepts of race and ethnicity.[80] What is far more important in my judgment is the examination of the processes by which Whites and people of color are racialized by the hierarchical ordering of ethnoracial groups in society.[81] In other words, Whites are every bit as much of a racialized group in US society as are African Americans, Asian Americans, Indigenous Americans, or Latinx Americans.

There is much more agreement about defining the term *racism* as a hierarchical system of advantage based on race than the terms encountered above. However, precision is still needed when adjudicating whether a given person or act should be considered racist.[82] In contemporary US society, White culture is regarded as normative and the ideal to which all other groups must aspire for acceptance. In other words, the histories, doctrines, practices, and cultural artifacts of Whites are assumed as the standard for all. Hence, *White supremacy* can be defined as the ideology that centers on whiteness, and we can note how it creates and sustains institutions and practices that promote the social, political, and economic dominance of Whites and the disadvantage of people of color.[83]

When determining whether something should be labeled racist, Omi and Winant helpfully introduce a framework for precision in this area. They define a *racial project* as the combination of the representational elements of race with the attendant institutional and structural aspects of racism.[84] A racial project or narrative is considered *racist* if it creates or perpetuates already existing hierarchies of advantage among racial groups, these groups ordered from best

---

80. I first encountered the adjective *ethnoracial* in Denise Kimber Buell's 2008 book *Why This New Race?*, though the term appears in medical and psychology texts as early as 1997 (e.g., National Research Council, *Racial and Ethnic Differences*).

81. In keeping with this viewpoint, I capitalize references to all ethnic peoples throughout this text.

82. Tatum, *Why Are All the Black Kids Sitting Together*, 86.

83. Sechrest and Ramirez-Johnson, "Race and Missiology," 13–16.

84. Omi and Winant, *Racial Formation Theory*, 84–88; cf. Omi and Winant, "Theoretical Status of the Concept of Race," 7–12.

to worst, White to Black, with other groups arranged in between. To illustrate this framework, we can adjudicate two simple racial projects. We can see the first example in the policy prescription: "Asian kids should be assigned to advanced math classes because they are naturally good at math." This racial project would be judged as a racist one since it sets an *a priori* policy outcome based on a biological explanation that ignores examination of individual preference, merit, or habitus. On the other hand, the statement "Let's develop a support group association for Black-owned businesses" is not a racist racial project because it does not essentialize or assume anything solely based on ethnoracial belonging. This policy prescription does nothing to reify existing racial hierarchies but instead seeks to undermine them by providing support for an area in which African Americans are underrepresented.

Racism manifests as personal or individual discriminatory action that confers advantages to one or more races over others. More commonly, racism is exhibited as institutional racism, also called systemic racism, which embeds discriminatory attitudes, emotions, habits, and practices in social institutions. *Institutional racism* is an extension of individual racism and facilitates the maintenance of an advantage for one race over other races by restricting the choices, rights, mobility, and access of different racial groups to needed social and material resources.[85] When examining institutional racism or racist policies,[86] one considers power imbalances, the accumulation of intergenerational wealth, and the long-term maintenance of significant socioeconomic deficits for other races as exhibited in society. Voter identification laws are examples of institutional racism that have come roaring back into American life in the wake of recent Supreme Court decisions. While Whites and others may think that such laws are reasonable in their demand for identification for access to the ballot, the differential access that emerges in the wake of these laws reveals that these laws are racist projects that privilege some while disadvantaging others. Most frequently enacted as a requirement to present a driver's license or other state identification to vote, we should note that these requirements require purchasing these identification cards, amounting to a poll tax. Those who think that driver's licenses are needed in everyday life are not reckoning with the practicalities of life in large urban centers where the most marginalized rely on public transportation and often don't even own cars. Added to the burdens on the poor and marginalized[87] in this situation, government offices that issue

---

85. J. M. Jones, *Prejudice and Racism*, 14.
86. See Kendi, *Antiracist*, 17–18.
87. The mention of "the poor and marginalized" in an argument about institutional racism

such cards are often hard to get to via public transportation and are generally only open during business hours. These obstacles require access to a job with paid time off, deepening the economic burden of obtaining these documents. Finally, there's the irony these laws require procurement of a government document before exercising a constitutional right, over and against the outcry against the idea of mandatory gun licenses as a prerequisite for exercising that constitutional right. We can't help but note that this discrepancy turns on the demographics underlying the group rights at stake. Differential access to the right to vote—including voter identification laws, fewer numbers of available voting machines in heavily minority districts, purges of voting rolls, obstacles to automatic voter registration, restrictions on absentee and early voting, and other such practices—is one of the most heavily practiced forms of institutional racism in this country, the lingering legacy of slavery and the Jim Crow regimes of segregation, social domination, and discrimination.

Privilege is another crucial concept in the study of race relations. Like other terms in this domain, it has become a flashpoint in conversations about race, used as a blunt weapon by some and rejected out of hand by others. At its core, the concept of privilege refers to the racialized system of advantage or disadvantage alluded to above. Privilege refers to the differential access to resources that subtly impact ordinary life among Blacks and other communities of color. It is a way of naming and concretizing the social power that attends life among better resourced society members. Some privileges are straightforward to enumerate and are positively correlated with socioeconomic status. While enjoyed by many Whites, some privileges may apply to people of color in much smaller numbers: Did your parents own their own home? Were they ever laid off? Were they professionals? Were you able to go to college, graduate without debt, and find a good paying job after graduation? Have you ever inherited money, or do you expect to someday? Are you able to avoid dangerous places? Do you have to rely on public transportation? Other privileges associated with Whiteness have to do with the presumption of innocence and the benefit of the doubt: Have you ever received the benefit of the doubt in

---

may lead some to think a practice isn't "racist" if it also targets poor Whites and others. The sad truth is that discriminatory practices aimed at reducing Black flourishing often also negatively impact the elderly and poor Whites and have ever since discrimination based on race became illegal with the passage of the Civil Rights Act of 1964. Jill S. Quadagno in her book *The Color of Welfare* documents erosion of support in the American social safety net once it was no longer possible to ensure that Blacks and other minorities could be excluded from these benefits; also see McGhee, *Sum of Us*. For more on the institutional racism associated with voter identification laws and other voter suppression tactics, see C. Anderson, *White Rage*.

an encounter with law enforcement? Have you ever been accused of loitering or being in the wrong place? Are you able to avoid being around people who do not look like you? When speaking with persons in authority, can you reasonably expect that the person will look like you? Are you fearful about encounters with the police?

It is important to note that though privilege is systemic and invisible, it is also highly dependent on context.[88] For example, as a heterosexual, married, cis-gendered New Testament professor and academic dean in a Christian seminary, I enjoy the privilege of authority in classrooms and committees. I never have to worry about my sexuality or marital status, and I belong to the dominant religion in the country. Nevertheless, as a Black woman, I have been the subject of an unwarranted search of my belongings and car, accused of being in the wrong neighborhood, building, or office, and am often questioned about my competence in my field of expertise. A casual conversation with other employees about vacations, homelife, and childhood lets me know that I have less access to *wealth* than those who work for me. I have less home equity, family property, and expectations about inheritance, even if I have advantages over them in terms of *income*. I have frequently been denied privileges associated with my rank as a professor by students, faculty, and staff because I did not "look the part." I know the terror of driving, jogging, and breathing while Black and have worried about whether I would survive a routine traffic stop because none of the privileges I have by way of education and employment show on my face. I know that less qualified Whites received the promotions I was denied because I didn't fit the elitist profiles of White leaders, notwithstanding that I have those same privileges from education, experience, and training.

Over the years of teaching these concepts to those new to racial and ethnic studies, I've found that one of the most helpful moments invariably comes when differentiating the concepts of prejudice and racism since they are often elided in common usage. Having already defined racism as an ordered system by which some ethnoracial groups in society enjoy advantages that others do not via policies and practices, the way is now clear to talk about personal attitudes

88. Weems, "Re-Reading for Liberation," 19, 32: "We women of color doing work in the Western Academy are likely to find ourselves constantly dangling between two realities: the diasporic, postcolonial feminist discourses of our Two-Thirds World sisters and the privileged, hegemonic, theorizing discourses of Western feminism. . . . I had to face the ways in which I belong both to a marginalized group of readers (African American women/womanists) and a privileged class of interpreters (Western/North American feminists), depending upon the context in which I find myself."

via the concept of prejudice. *Prejudices* are positive or negative attitudes held by individuals or groups generalized from beliefs about a group.[89] Varying kinds of prejudices occur across peoples and epochs influenced by stories, beliefs, emotions, and experiences with target groups. Media images, pictures, and words around us may subtly influence our thinking and feeling about other groups; thus, prejudice is almost an automatic response to living in a racialized society. Psychologist Beverly Daniel Tatum vividly uses the metaphor of smog to describe how it is impossible to be unimpacted by positive and negative prejudicial attitudes about various groups in American society.[90] In the United States, people of color are often assumed to lack the social values of hard work and industriousness and are thus viewed as being undeserving of full participation in White society. Many believe that individual members of ethnoracial groups are "all alike," thus transforming any encounter between individuals into an intergroup encounter. However, though any group or individual can harbor negative or positive prejudices about others, an act of racism requires the capacity to withhold or convey resources to the persons toward whom one has negative feelings. Hence, while prejudice is a universal phenomenon operating inside every human heart, racism applies when groups or actors have the ability or power to achieve biased outcomes. Both prejudice and racism are wrong and outside of God's will, but they are different phenomena. Prejudice may involve the will to act in a biased way, but racism and discrimination require the capacity to achieve biased outcomes conceived in a prejudiced imagination.

Stereotypes are the mechanisms that express the prejudices that reflect positive or negative attitudes about groups and function to exaggerate group differences. That is, stereotypes don't cause prejudices; they reflect prejudices. Stereotypes are powerful because they play an organizing function in perceptual processes, serving as a shorthand for gathering, sorting, and synthesizing information about phenomena in lieu of firsthand experience. Stereotypes often have a grain of truth in them but can be factually incorrect and illogical in origin. Since they sometimes substitute for firsthand experience, they become dangerous; they can actually *determine* what is seen versus simply organizing perceptual input. Let's consider, for instance, the commonly held stereotype about the enslaved, which still survives in modern times, that enslaved persons are lazy. This stereotype likely does have a kernel of related truth in it in that enslaved Black people quite understandably *did not want to work as enslaved persons under often inhumane conditions.* Yet the fact that they worked from before

---

89. J. M. Jones, *Prejudice and Racism*, 27.
90. Tatum, *Why Are All the Black Kids Sitting Together*, 87.

daylight until long after sunset under grueling conditions was still not enough of a contradiction in terms to undermine stereotypes about Black laziness. Today there is a similar catch-22 vis-à-vis this stereotype and Black unemployment. Black unemployment rises and falls with White unemployment and is subject to the same market forces, but why, many ask, are their unemployment rates double that of Whites? Institutional racism is a better explanation of the differential barriers to employment than some biased notion about a deficit in Black industriousness. Institutional racism in employment patterns involves forces like undereducation, undercapitalization in Black communities, more impoverished schools, and the school-to-prison pipeline mediated via a vicious cycle of overpolicing, mass incarceration, and discrimination against the formerly incarcerated. As an example of the pernicious effects of stereotypes, the one about laziness takes much less effort to process even though these other complexities have much better explanatory power.

Stereotypes are hence highly resistant to new information and are thus very resistant to change. In other words, it is tough to disprove a stereotype. To make sense of new discrepant data, we usually find a way to make the new data fit the perceptual schemas associated with stereotypes so that we are far more likely to process this information as an outlier and an "exception to the rule." So, on encountering hardworking Black folk on the job, a counter-evidential observation vis-à-vis a stereotype about Black laziness, those operating under the stereotype are more likely to regard the hardworking Blacks in the office as "not like the rest of them." Stereotypes are very elastic so that we often protect them vigorously and judge discrepant behavior more harshly when it violates the stereotype. This dynamic is why some of the violent reactions against Hillary Clinton and Barack Obama as public figures may be due to how they each violate stereotypes about women and Blacks.

Book Overview

With these remarks about critical concepts in race and ethnicity, we can now give an overview of the remaining chapters in this book. The chapters in this book are arranged in New Testament canonical order in terms of the biblical texts they engage, apart from the treatment of a contrast between Romans and Revelation in the last chapter. Each chapter develops an analogical rhyme between the contemporary and biblical horizons on some aspect of race relations. The chapters follow a similar pattern and begin with a short reflection on an issue in race relations that gives a general sense of how the selected topic rhymes with themes in the focal biblical text(s) in that chapter. The following section discusses the contemporary theory from racial and ethnic studies or a discipline that explicitly addresses ethnoracial identity or gender. The essays also contain an overview of the focal New Testament document examined and introduces elements from the historically embedded story from that New Testament document that undergirds the rhyme. Each essay builds out the poetics of the analogy by bringing a discussion about the details in the text into conversation with elements of the contemporary racial dynamics of interest. Other sections, including the final one, explore constraining or limiting factors in the analogical treatment, showing where complexities need to be addressed vis-à-vis ethics in contemporary life. These chapters can be read as stand-alone articles since they have little overlap and revisit critical theoretical concepts from racial and ethnic studies as needed. Nevertheless, this introduction will be a helpful preliminary to the interpretive framework and hermeneutical terminology that occurs throughout.

Chapter 2 complicates common but vague and anemic notions about the *agapē* love of the New Testament. "Neighbors, Allies, Frenemies, and Foes in the Gospel of Matthew" opens with a reflection on the Charleston massacre where White supremacist Dylann Roof murdered a small group of Black Christians at an evening Bible study, a moment in recent American race relations where gospel imperatives regarding the love of one's enemies collided with the evil of racist violence. Instead of reducing love to an idea that does violence to the notion of justice, this chapter explores what it means to give love as a Christian toward the Other by fleshing out the poetic shape of a rhyme between Jesus's encounters with the Other in the Gospel of Matthew and the contemporary notion of "allyship." I use analogical reasoning to interrogate the relationships between victims of oppression and those from other communities who wish to resist oppression as partners in justice.

Reflection on Luke-Acts, the longest books in the New Testament, elicit some of the most extended chapters in this book as well. Chapter 3 focuses on the Gospel of Luke, while chapter 5 takes on the Acts of the Apostles. Both chapters take on questions about how people of color move between dominant and minoritized subcultures, focusing on the process of assimilation in chapter 3 and the diametrically opposed process of ethnic identification in chapter 5. Chapter 3, "Assimilation and the Family of God in the Gospel of Luke," explores a rhyme between ethnic tensions in Luke's Gospel and modern observations about how assimilation and accommodation processes impact minoritized family dynamics and economic tensions around immigration. We look at how Jesus navigates tension and resistance to the idea that outsiders and Jews are being brought together in a new, blended, and maybe not-so-harmonious family. I discuss how these dynamics work in the context of White grievance about the "undeserving," as well as tensions involving immigrants, including those between African Americans and African immigrants.

Chapter 4 is entitled "Sex, Crime, and Stereotypes in the Gospel of John" and examines two texts from John's Gospel: the encounter between Jesus and the Samaritan in John 4 and the story of the woman caught in adultery in John 8. As the title might indicate, this chapter explores how stereotypes condition interactions with minoritized women, whether in encounters where sexual stereotypes hover in the background or in encounters where guilt and innocence are mediated. This chapter explores how both kinds of interactions are fraught with racialized and gendered stereotypes about "good" and "bad" women. In John 4, we examine a rhyme correlating the interpretation of the Samaritan woman with contemporary stereotypes about hyper-sexed, out-of-control foreign women. In John 8, we look at the implications of these stereotypes regarding how Black women and girls fare in the criminal justice system.

As mentioned above, the relationship between culture and identity is the focus in chapter 5, "Negotiating Culture in the Family of God in the Book of Acts." This chapter continues the exploration of how people of color move between dominant and minoritized subcultures. It focuses on the dangers of assimilation and the benefits of locating one's identity within an ethnoracial community of origin. The chapter looks at how the early Jesus movement affirms the incorporation of Gentiles without asking them to change their identity and how the "Jerusalem Decree" sets the terms for intercultural interaction in the church.

As mentioned above, students find it easier to use associative hermeneutics for moral reflection with biblical narratives than with the epistles, though *Race and Rhyme* does offer examples of the latter, more difficult task through the discussion of 1 Timothy 2:8–15 in this chapter and again in chapter 8 through consideration of Romans 13:1–7. However, extended interaction with the epistles occurs in chapters 6 and 7 through discussions of 2 Corinthians and Ephesians, respectively. Both epistles pose well-known difficulties in interpretation, making them among the most challenging discourses to use for illustrative purposes. The sixth chapter, "Privilege, Identity, and Status in 2 Corinthians," associates the contextually dependent concept of privilege with the way that Paul negotiates challenges to his apostolic authority. In this epistle, he sometimes trades on his proud and revered ancient lineage. Still, other times he adopts the humble mien of a broke-down pastor who imitates the suffering of Jesus, another down and out itinerant preacher. This chapter helps Black women resist messages to accept their own suffering for Jesus's sake by looking at how Paul navigates contradictory impulses to high self-esteem and imitation of Christ. Chapter 7, "Ligamental Leadership for the Household of God in Ephesians," explores the intergroup dynamics in Ephesians, a popular text for those interested in race relations in Christianity. Many argue that the epistle addresses Gentile Christians unsure about their place as they enter a movement composed of multiple minoritized ethnic peoples, a situation that rhymes with contemporary US society where multiple minority groups wrangle for power and position in a turbulent sociopolitical landscape. My reading of Ephesians 4:1–16 offers a model for intergroup leadership for the leadership challenges faced by women and people of color, especially Black women. This chapter encourages leaders to stay attached to minoritized subgroups within the community through prophetic truth telling. The chapter ends by examining models of Black female leadership in the contemporary context during the Black Lives Matter protests for racial justice during the summer of 2020.

Finally, chapter 8, "Waking Up on the Wrong Side of Empire in Romans and Revelation," explores a rhyme between Romans 13 and the social welfare state in the United States. A secondary analogy sees a correlation between resistance to the expansion of social welfare with the situation underlying the prophetic message in parts of Revelation 2–3 and 11 regarding what John sees as the demonic lure of economic security that leads to compromise with Empire and the structures and values that support it. This last essay is the only one that brings biblical texts from two different NT authors into conversation by contrasting Paul's more positive view of Empire in Romans 13 with the anti-imperial perspective in John's Apocalypse. I have found the tensions at the center of this synthesis enormously helpful in getting students to confront the idea that the Bible was not written as a cohesive work delivered from on high in one fell swoop. Instead, it emerged in bits and pieces, offering varying messages to communities facing different political situations. This last chapter asks readers to understand that the various texts in the Bible are sometimes in tension with one another, as these two are. Rather than treating this circumstance as an obstacle to be mourned, this chapter attempts to find contextually relevant liberative messages in each text while refusing to flatten the differences between them.

NEIGHBORS, ALLIES, FRENEMIES, AND FOES
IN THE GOSPEL OF MATTHEW

> *A Black woman and a white woman*
> *charter our courses close*
> *in a sea of calculated distance*
> *warned away by reefs of hidden anger*
> *histories rallied against us*
> *the friendly face of cheap alliance . . .*
> *In this treacherous sea*
> *even the act of turning*
> *is almost fatally difficult.*
>
> —*Audre Lorde, "Outlines"[1]*

Other-Regard and the Oppressed

In my interdisciplinary work at the intersection of critical race theory[2] and New Testament interpretation, I have become fascinated with the tension that modern life poses between ethnoracial identity[3] and Christian identity. This tension is not often understood or acknowledged by the vast majority of

---

1. From Lorde, *Collected Poems of Audre Lorde*, 361–66.

2. The study of race and ethnicity is a large and unwieldy matter, spanning multiple disciplines in the humanities and social sciences, such as cultural anthropology, sociology, literary studies, ethnic and racial studies, education, philosophy, and more. Technically, the discipline of Critical Race Theory (CRT) refers to the examination of race, ethnicity, and social justice within legal studies. I use the term CRT here as an umbrella term describing the study of race across all of these disciplinary areas, referring to this broad body of work in lowercase type as a way of differentiating it from the narrower concerns in legal studies. For more on CRT, see, e.g., Crenshaw et al., *Critical Race Theory*.

3. See the definition of the term *ethnoracial* in note 80 on p. 39 above.

scholars in the Christian academy, given the overwhelming whiteness of this corner of society. In the United States, whiteness is normed and thus invisible, but this is not so concerning the identities of people of color. Yet, as a womanist New Testament scholar who is well-read on the dynamics of race and gender in American society, I sometimes find that my engagement with critical theory in race and gender collides with what may be, for some, an uncomplicated embrace of the imperatives of the gospel. For example, how should a woman who is stereotyped as a nurturing Mammy who owes tender concern to her superiors embrace the sacrificial Other-regard of the gospel? Should she embrace the self-effacing stereotype even though it has been a form of oppression, or should she reject the forced subordination of her God-given agency and need for self-protection as someone created in the image of God? It is one thing to urge the privileged and comfortable to surrender their privileges on behalf of a lost humanity. It is an altogether different matter to charge the downtrodden with further abasement that ends up redounding to the benefit of the oppressor. Thus, the centrality of loving, cruciform suffering in the way of Jesus in the Christian message becomes enormously complicated for historically oppressed peoples. The juxtaposition of suffering and God-talk is especially fraught for those who have experienced one or more of the evils of racism, sexism, homophobia, genocide, colonialism, or imperialism, like Native Americans, African Americans, Latinx people, Jews, women, nonbinary folk, and others.

In American society, the word *racism* is culturally loaded. It evokes images of bigotry such as Wallace's legendary stand barring the doors of integration at the University of Alabama, Rush Limbaugh's in-your-face use of gangster stereotypes when describing the heavy concentration of African Americans in the NFL and NBA, and Don Imus's characterization of the Rutgers University women's basketball team as "nappy-headed ho[e]s."[4] Even though racism is embedded in culture and inhabits institutions in ways that implicate every sector of society, if you are not using a fire hose to rebuff peaceful demonstrations for civil rights, then in this country you are not a racist. When Dylann Roof executed nine Black people on June 17, 2015, at Emanuel African Methodist Episcopal (AME) Church in Charleston, South Carolina, he instantly became an iconic image of White supremacist racism. Thus, a singular example of the conflict between the suffering center of Christian Other-regard and a lived

---

4. For Rush Limbaugh's use of stereotypes, see Maloy, "Worst Racial Attacks Limbaugh's Advertisers Have Sponsored." For the quote by Don Imus, see Faber, "CBS Fires Don Imus Over Racial Slur."

history of racism, sexism, and other forms of oppression exists in the various responses to the Charleston massacre.

In the immediate aftermath of the shooting, one typical response involved speculation about Roof's mental health on the reasoning that only someone who has mental illness could have gunned down Christians at prayer in a house of worship after spending an hour with them in a Bible study.[5] On the one hand, this response can give rise to a helpful discussion about the inadequacies of American institutions for mental illness. Still, on the other hand, it raises questions about why the media eschews alternate and more appropriate characterizations of the Charleston killer that better reflect Roof's stated motivations—for example, labels like "terrorist" or "White supremacist."[6] Another kind of response reached back into the psalms of Israel to pray imprecatory prayers about the massacre born out of overwhelming grief. Undoubtedly the most astounding response was one born of the gospel of Jesus Christ as some members of the victims' families forgave Dylann Roof when they had the chance to face him in a bond court hearing, at a time when their pain at the wrenching shock of the murders was still raw (cf. Matt. 18:21–22). Yet another response from Black church leaders in South Carolina attempted to straddle the gulf between lament and forgiveness: "You cannot be the thing you hate. You cannot become the evil you seek to eradicate. Forgiveness is not the same as ignoring the facts. We want justice."[7]

This last response illustrates the tension between an uncompromising love of enemies representing the apex of Christian ethics in Matthew 5:43–48 and the cries of the suffering wounded who find in that same gospel succor for a persecuted and trampled *imago Dei*. How should the downtrodden *give love to enemies*, and how should the dominant *be loving as enemies* in times of ever-increasing racial tension? In this chapter, I pursue a rhyme between concepts of love from the Gospel of Matthew and a thick notion of allyship; that is, the relationships between victims of oppression and those from other communities who wish to resist oppression as partners in justice. It turns out that it will be helpful to look at how Jesus's enemies are depicted in the gospel and observe how these interactions demonstrate enemy-love. Here we will focus

5. Lysiak, "Charleston Massacre."

6. Some saw the early framing of Roof's actions in terms of mental illness as a refusal to admit to racial motivation or as a way of exonerating or mitigating the heinousness of the crime, but such compassionate framing seems less frequent when the actions of people of color are perpetrators of crimes. See Butler, "Shooters of Color."

7. Goodwyn, "Shooters of Color." For a survey of Christian responses to the Charleston massacre, see Shellnutt, "Lament for Charleston."

not so much on Jesus's actions but more on the character of his enemies' inter-actions with him. To flesh out the poetic shape of the rhyme, we will examine Matthew's depictions of Jesus's enemies to help imagine how we might be transformed from enemies to friends. In other words, we will use analogical reasoning to construct a Christian ethic of allyship from the Gospel of Matthew. I begin with a survey of scholarship about being allies before looking at Gentiles as enemies in the Gospel of Matthew.

"Love" in Other Words—From Enemies to Allies

It is not surprising to learn that there is little discussion involving explicitly Christian ideas about loving one's enemy in the theoretical literature about race and racism; such categories are simply not deemed relevant outside of an explic-itly Christian worldview. Indeed, the *rarity* of acts of love toward enemies in the public conscience perhaps explains the swift and decisive action of those who lobbied to remove the Confederate flag from statehouses across the South in the wake of the Charleston massacre. The astonishing act of forgiveness offered to Dylann Roof after he went into that AME church to find Blacks he could kill in fulfillment of his White supremacist delusions acted as a moral prod. Their forgiveness undermined a revisionist history that had for decades successfully painted the Confederate flag as a symbol of Southern culture instead of the battle flag of a republic that fought and lost a war for the right to enslave Blacks.[8] Yet, one area of inquiry that may serve as an approximation of this kind of discourse in critical theory discusses the identity and habitus of allies for racial justice. Allies are those from dominant or privileged groups who engage in activism in support of social justice by helping to dismantle systems of oppression and unfair advantage in favor of increasing access to social goods for all.[9]

The term *ally* may have originated in LGBT activism against heterosex-ism in the 1990s,[10] but it also appears in discourse about social justice work

---

8. An interesting fact that emerged in the daylight of the renewed debate to take the Confederate flag down from state houses in the South was that the flag became a symbol of Southern culture almost a hundred years after the end of the Civil War, notably, as a backlash to the Civil Rights movement in the 1950s and 1960s. See Philips, "Why Is the Confederate Flag Still a Thing?"

9. Broido, "Development of Social Justice Allies." A participant in a study of White female anti-racist allies suggests that an ally is "someone who had reflected on being called a racist and admitted personal racial shortcomings." See Case, "Discovering the Privilege of Whiteness," 84.

10. Broido, "Development of Social Justice Allies," 3.

and critical whiteness studies.[11] A frequently cited definition of a social justice ally describes this activist as "a person who is a member of the 'dominant' or 'majority' group who works to end oppression in his or her personal and professional life through advocacy with and for oppressed peoples."[12] These activists acknowledge their unearned privileges and the power that their social identities grant them as they act to dismantle the structures in society that support privilege and power. They may be motivated to be allies by intimacy with others who have personally experienced oppression, as well as a sense of responsibility that acknowledges their own privilege.[13]

When it comes to being a social justice ally, there is broad agreement that the first consideration involves ownership of one's identity as a racial being, a step that is nonnegotiable for Whites and a considerable obstacle inhibiting broader White participation in social justice work.[14] In interviews, these activists insist that someone must admit to their own racism and privilege before becoming an anti-racist activist, and that "without that essential piece, you are living in denial" and without real hope that any authentic change can occur.[15] As with alcoholism, "the first step to recovery is admitting you have a problem. . . . [R]ecognition of White privilege [is] absolutely essential for White anti-racism and . . . some form of self-work on racism [is] needed" to make a beginning,[16] because, according to Ibram Kendi, "denial is the heartbeat of racism."[17] This step is foundational because of the way that whiteness is invisible in our racialized society. Whiteness as a norm allows Whites who do not have a critical consciousness to assume the universality of whiteness as

11. Patel, "Inclusive Model of Allyship," 78–81.

12. Washington and Evans, "Becoming an Ally," 195. Also see, for example, Neumann, "Being a Social Justice Ally," 65.

13. Neumann, "Being a Social Justice Ally," 65. This last motivation, personal experience with oppression, may be significant since anecdotal evidence suggests that lesbians and Jews are overrepresented in anti-racism work; see Eichstedt, "Problematic White Identities," 449–50.

14. See, for instance, Neumann, "Being a Social Justice Ally," 68; Alcoff, "What Should White People Do?," 21; Lewis, "What Group?"; Titone, "Educating the White Teacher as Ally"; Eichstedt, "Problematic White Identities"; and Reason and Evans, "Complicated Realities of Whiteness" who write of a racially cognizant self "that encompasses an understanding of guilt, power, and privilege yet avoids the paralysis and victim perspectives that some Whites assume" (71). Similarly, Kim Case finds that understanding the concept of White privilege is a precursor of White anti-racist activism; see "Discovering the Privilege of Whiteness," 79.

15. Case, "Discovering the Privilege of Whiteness," 84.

16. Case, "Discovering the Privilege of Whiteness," 84.

17. Kendi, *Antiracist*, 8.

the standard of human experience, something denied to people of color who are assumed to have narrow perspectives constrained by race or ethnicity.[18]

Akin to recognizing White racial identity as the precursor to anti-racism work is exploring the psychological, intellectual, moral, and material costs of racism for Whites.[19] To maintain racialized inequality, Whites must psychologically condition themselves for their place in the social order. They must adopt the ideology and rationalizations that reinforce thinking and behavior that perpetuate injustice and diminish all humans.[20] Thus, whiteness exacts psychological costs, though they are by no means equivalent to those that people of color experience. Accordingly, disorientation from a new experience of "feeling White" combined with a desire to repudiate White privilege can disable Whites' positive self-image and connection to community and history.[21] Thus, while we must never forget that these effects are not comparable to those faced by people of color, the psychological effects are nevertheless real, even if they in no way constitute "oppression."[22] As Paolo Freire succinctly puts it, "As oppressors dehumanize others and violate their rights, they themselves also become dehumanized."[23] According to Freire, "Dehumanization, which marks not only those whose humanity has been stolen, but also (though in a different way) those who have stolen it, is a distortion of becoming more fully human."[24]

---

18. DiAngelo, "White Fragility," 60. DiAngelo also exposes the similar operation of "individualism" as a strategy by which Whites deny complicity in racist structures and the implications for wealth and access to resources, etc. I frequently encounter versions of these universalist ("We're all in the image of God") and individualist perspectives ("Each person must be accountable to God") when I teach about race and racism in theological education. These two perspectives thus become a Christian version of the secular defensiveness manifest in such comments as "My family never did anything racist therefore I don't have responsibility for racism." Chanequa Walker-Barnes narrates similar interactions in which her White students resist reckoning with White racial identity; see *I Bring the Voices of My People*, 131–33.

19. For more on this topic see the series of psychological studies that develop an instrument to measure the psychosocial costs of racism to whites, e.g., Spanierman, Todd, and Anderson, "Psychosocial Costs of Racism to Whites"; Sifford, Ng, and Wang, "Psychosocial Costs of Racism to Whites"; Spanierman, Poteat, Beer, and Armstrong, "Psychosocial Costs of Racism to Whites"; and Poteat and Spanierman, "Further Validation of the Psychosocial Costs of Racism"; Walker-Barnes, *I Bring the Voices of My People*.

20. Frankenberg, *White Women, Race Matters*, 121.

21. Alcoff, "What Should White People Do?," 7.

22. Similarly Walker-Barnes, *I Bring the Voices of My People*, 124; and Goodman, *Promoting Diversity and Social Justice*, 103–4.

23. Freire, *Pedagogy of the Oppressed*, 42.

24. Freire, *Pedagogy of the Oppressed*, 28.

Diane Goodman's description of the psychological, social, moral/spiritual, intellectual, and material/physical costs of whiteness is helpful for situating this accounting of the adverse effects of whiteness and contributes to the cultivation of a critical White identity.[25] The psychological costs of whiteness involve diminished emotional and empathetic capacity and compromised mental health as Whites are socialized to conform to rigid standards of behavior constrained by gender and class. For instance, White women may be constrained by stereotypes that lock them into infantile, subordinate, and diminished agency, just as White men may be imprisoned by expectations of aggressive, competitive, success-at-any-cost behaviors.[26] Students in my classes that deal with race also report negative costs from being stereotyped as racists in encounters with some people of color. Studies show other negative health implications from pressure to achieve and maintain the success that is stereotypical of White status in a competitive environment. Areas with high income disparity also correlate with higher death rates for both the rich and the poor. Whites are inhibited by debilitating fears, both unconscious and conscious: fears of the Other, of racial discomfort, of losing privileges and entitlements, and of retaliation. There may also be fears for the well-being of intimate friends and family in dominated groups. "People from dominant groups tend to develop unhealthy psychological mechanisms (such as denial, false justification, projection, disassociation, and transference of blame) to deal with their fears of minorities or people from oppressed groups."[27] They can become weak with an inability to deal with discomfort, pain, or challenge.[28]

To these psychological costs, we could also add the social costs of isolation from being stereotyped by people of color as racist, rapists, elitist snobs, paternalistic, callous to human suffering, selfish, biased, spoiled, entitled, and untrustworthy.[29] Whites sometimes face ostracism within their own group for their anti-racist postures or actions in confrontations with family, friends, or coworkers. The moral and spiritual costs of whiteness also include loss of integrity and feelings of guilt and shame. Embarrassed and guilty about having more than others, Whites sometimes resort to "blaming the victim"

25. Unless otherwise noted, information in this paragraph comes from Goodman, *Promoting Diversity and Social Justice*, 105–9.

26. See Durik et al., "Ethnicity and Gender Stereotypes of Emotion," 430–31 and the scholarship cited there. Also see P. H. Collins, *Black Sexual Politics*, 58; hooks, *Yearning*, 57–64.

27. Also see Fernandez, "Impact of Racism on Whites in Corporate America," 109.

28. DiAngelo, "White Fragility," 54; DiAngelo, *White Fragility*.

29. Material in this paragraph comes from Goodman, *Promoting Diversity and Social Justice*, 109–19.

as a response or retreat into defensiveness. Whites often are ignorant of their own ethnic culture, heritage, and history and have a distorted or limited view of other cultures and their contributions to humanity, thus becoming out of touch with reality with an impoverished worldview and constrained exposure to different ways of living. Again, these disadvantages are not comparable to the sometimes lethal physical and material costs of racism to people of color like Native Americans, Blacks, and Latinx. Yet, there are indeed direct and indirect material and physical costs of racism for Whites in addition to the aforementioned psychological, social, and intellectual damages. Whites experience the indirect and direct costs of social unrest from protests about injustice, poverty, and disenfranchisement from societal benefits. Whites can become virtual prisoners in gated communities with stunted social networks because of fears about safety, having to spend time, money, and energy trying to protect themselves and their belongings.

White Christians can especially experience an integrity compromise when they experience difficulty doing the right thing and risking the disapproval of friends, family, or neighbors or succumb to social pressure in decision making. There is pain from knowing that one participates in falling so far short of God's will.[30] Chanequa Walker-Barnes's discussion of moral injury expands on this theme. In *I Bring the Voices of My People: A Womanist Vision of Racial Reconciliation*, she explores whiteness as a condition of moral injury into which Americans are socialized as they daily participate in reinforcing White supremacy and undermining social justice. For Walker-Barnes, whiteness is not something that people possess that can be given up, unlearned, or leveraged; instead, it possesses them and is bestowed upon them based on their presumed distance from blackness and access to racial power. She shows how the institution of slavery produced conditions ripe for moral damage since it affected all Whites and not just those who owned slaves since "the pre–Civil War American economy was dependent upon slavery, and the maintenance of slavery depended upon White acquiescence."[31] Here she quotes White ally theologian Jennifer Harvey who maintains that "as long as the system [of slavery] could rely on [White] people to choose not to be a safe haven when African peoples ran away, and to choose to serve as overseers, to mill the cotton that moved from South to North, to rely on wages earned in that production to feed their families, and on a myriad of other similar behaviors that ensured

---

30. Goodman, *Promoting Diversity and Social Justice*, 109–19.

31. Harvey, *Dear White Christians*, 54; quoted in Walker-Barnes, *I Bring the Voices of My People*, 121.

slavery functioned, it did not matter that most whites did not themselves own slaves."[32] With a thorough discussion of the horrors of slavery in hand, Walker-Barnes then opens up a discussion about moral injury by posing the question, *How does it affect a person to participate in a system that that person knows or believes to be evil?"*

According to Walker-Barnes, moral injury involves the impact of actions that violate our beliefs that arise from situations of moral dissonance when people behave, think, and feel in ways that run counter to their beliefs, ethics, and values.[33] Her synthesis of the persistent effects of slavery on White culture and epistemic frameworks is worth quoting at length:

> The moral injuriousness of slavery is not merely that to participate in, acquiesce to, or condone it was to commit a moral failing. Rather, it was that committing such a moral failing in the first place required one to distort one's cognitive and moral processing, one's "Christian imagination," as Jennings has argued. Further, the very act of participation intensified the distortion that enabled it to begin with. At its most basic level, slavery was enabled by the beliefs that White people were superior to all other peoples, that Black people were inferior to all others, and that human beings could be treated as property to be exploited, bought, and sold. Endorsing and acting upon these beliefs further intensified them; it also opened the door for committing countless other moral failings in order to sustain the original sin of enslavement. In the midst of this vicious cycle, the entire cognitive structure of White Americans was distorted.
>
> The justification and maintenance of a slave economy required the construction and defense of an elaborate cultural system . . . in order to maintain a brutal and utterly unnatural system. . . . This enculturation did not end post–Civil War; rather it continued in some capacity through the dismantling of legalized segregation and racial discrimination. . . . [M]any people stopped using overtly racial language, but the culture into which they were assimilated remained the same in every other way."[34]

Walker-Barnes goes to great lengths to differentiate the moral injury of whiteness from Whites as victims of trauma as some would identify them.

32. Harvey, *Dear White Christians*, 54; quoted in Walker-Barnes, *I Bring the Voices of My People*, 120–21.
33. Walker-Barnes, *I Bring the Voices of My People*, 133.
34. Walker-Barnes, *I Bring the Voices of My People*, 133–34.

Leaning on the *Diagnostic and Statistical Manual of Mental Disorders* (DSM-5), she notes that *trauma* involves sexual violence, exposure to a perceived threat to self or others, or witnessing harmful acts. At the same time, *moral injury* develops through a moral conflict that occurs when one's actions or the actions of peers or leaders are demonstrably inconsistent with one's own moral code. She utterly rejects the use of trauma as a category that characterizes White racial identity because of how such usage implies a false symmetry between the effects of slavery and racism on Blacks and Whites.[35] As a womanist theologian and clinical psychologist, Walker-Barnes avoids the language of "mental illness" in her discussion. Instead, she discusses the ways that White epistemological frameworks have been impacted by the moral injury of White supremacy, even as she explores how US cultural influences and institutions construct a system built to confirm the morally impaired epistemological patterns of White people and the ways that their cognitive frameworks render invisible to them the moral harms that emanate from White supremacy.[36]

Beyond owning one's identity as a racial being and understanding the ways that White supremacy inflicts psychological, social, and epistemological harm, next in importance in anti-racist activist development is gaining knowledge about oppression through formal and informal educational experiences and interpersonal relationships with other activists and people of color. It may be that growth in this area is spiral in that one may not take even the first step of understanding one's White social location in development as an activist without having had prior exposure to the facts of ethnoracial oppression; further growth emerges out of a continuing cycle of reflection on these concepts. Yet, a related theme in activist literature and scholarship is the idea that anti-racist Whites must be careful to avoid communicating an expectation that people of color are responsible for educating Whites about oppression, a posture that compounds and extends the paternalism of racial hierarchies.[37]

Activists report that maintaining one's commitment in the face of questions about credibility and lack of support from other White peers and significant others, including supervisors, friends, and family, is one of the most challeng-

---

35. Walker-Barnes, *I Bring the Voices of My People*, 136.

36. I should mention that Walker-Barnes also addresses how internalized racism involves epistemic harm for Blacks and other people of color as they absorb the powerful cultural messages around them.

37. Neumann, "Being a Social Justice Ally," 68; Broido, "Development of Social Justice Allies," 4. For a popular discussion of the dynamics of self-education for allies see Utt, "So You Call Yourself an Ally."

ing aspects of anti-racist work.[38] Robin DiAngelo suggests that this dilemma may emerge at least partially from what she calls "White fragility." According to DiAngelo, racial privilege builds expectations for racial comfort among Whites and lowers their ability to tolerate racial stress.[39] White fragility is defined as a state in which even a minimum amount of such stress triggers a range of defensive behaviors that function to reinstate a tolerable White racial equilibrium; behaviors including argumentation, silence, flight, and emotional outbursts of anger, fear, and guilt.[40] This fragility may be manifest in response to several challenges:[41]

1. *The challenge to White objectivity* happens if someone suggests that a White person's viewpoint comes from a racialized perspective.

2. *The challenge to White racial comfort* occurs when people of color express perspectives on race in ways that do not protect White sensibilities by couching ideas in polite and subdued terms and without any show of emotional upset. When Whites respond in ways that position themselves as victimized, blamed, attacked, or treated unfairly, and demand that attention be directed away from people of color and back onto White comfort, they become responsible for associating a lack of comfort with an explicit discussion of race with a lack of safety in a way that plays into racist tropes of people of color as aggressive and dangerous.

3. *The challenge to White solidarity* takes place when a fellow White person refuses to concur with another White person's perspective.[42]

4. *The challenge to meritocracy* exists when Whites refuse to countenance the idea that there is unequal access to resources.

5. *The challenge to White authority* may explain much of the virulent opposition to Obamacare on the right, especially since the policy is nothing more than a national adaptation of a Republican governor's health care solution. This challenge occurs in cases where Whites encounter a person of color in a position of leadership.

6. *The challenge to White liberalism* can occur when Whites who think they understand racism receive the feedback that their behavior or words had a racist impact.

38. Neumann, "Being a Social Justice Ally," 72.

39. DiAngelo, "White Fragility," 55.

40. DiAngelo, "White Fragility," 54–55.

41. DiAngelo, "White Fragility," 61–65. DiAngelo revisits and expands upon these themes in her later book *White Fragility*.

42. Compare this idea to the "advantaged-to-advantaged horizontal oppression" described in Patel, "Moving toward an Inclusive Model of Allyship," 83–85.

Overcoming fragility and maintaining one's commitment in the face of so-cial isolation may be aided by contact with others who have similar perspec-tives in White affinity groups.[43] Such a group provides a safe space to explore such issues as White guilt, sustaining anti-racist activism, and the positive con-struction of White identity.[44] It is a place wherein Whites process information about racism without hindering people of color in multiethnic conversations who are further along the trajectory of anti-racist activism by virtue of their experience.[45] Whites can practice talking about race with transparency in af-finity groups, asking possibly ignorant questions, challenging themselves to do better, and examining and reflecting on privilege more critically.[46] On the other hand, a White affinity group can be critiqued because "Whites may fail to detect much of the racism that people of color could easily pinpoint. White anti-racists struggling to deconstruct racism face the possibility that they lack the skills necessary to even properly identify racism."[47] Still, such groups are valuable as public declarations of White anti-racism and, more importantly, offer a space where Whites may educate themselves in a way that doesn't place undue burdens on people of color.

Fourth, allies must take action in their own communities, especially under the leadership of people of color when possible, resisting the impulse to jump in and take control.[48] These actions certainly include participating in public demonstrations such as attending marches and rallies, writing editorials, etc. But more commonly, anti-racist action involves interrupting the racist com-ments of family, friends, and coworkers, teaching about racism in classrooms and presentations, and advocating for diversity in everyday settings by hiring, advocating for, or mentoring people of color in the workplace.[49] Taking action also means rejecting "covert racism," such as tacitly supporting the activities of power holders who discourage connections with people of color or who are disapproving when others bring attention to matters of race in all-White

---

43. Broido, "Development of Social Justice Allies," 4. Also see especially Michael et al., "Becoming an Anti-Racist White Ally." This article describes a group of White students at the University of Pennsylvania in a group called White Students Confronting Racism (WSCR). Also see the description of White Women Against Racism (WWAR) in Case, "Discovering the Privilege of Whiteness."

44. Michael et al., "Becoming an Anti-Racist White Ally," 56.

45. Michael et al., "Becoming an Anti-Racist White Ally," 57.

46. Michael et al., "Becoming an Anti-Racist White Ally," 57–58.

47. Case, "Discovering the Privilege of Whiteness," 91.

48. Michael et al., "Becoming an Anti-Racist White Ally," 58.

49. Case, "Discovering the Privilege of Whiteness," 87; Broido, "Development of Social Justice Allies."

settings.[50] Other "White distancing" techniques must also be rejected and/or confronted, including: active resistance or defensiveness (i.e., "I'm not racist"); nonverbal signals of disapproval such as the silent treatment; accusations of oversensitivity; attempts to end discussions of race; and flight.[51] Above all, it is critical to realize in this area of discourse that prophetic, candid, persistent, and constructive reflection on one's position and privilege as a White person is an important responsibility and form of action.

Finally, humility is essential in ally development because White allies can be an obstacle in social justice movements because of a perhaps unconscious belief in their own superiority and tendency to dominate the agenda. They can cultivate humility through self-reflection and by learning the perspectives of the Other by imagining themselves in those circumstances.[52] Some may find it counterintuitive to recognize that self-confidence is as important as humility in the process of internalizing the idea that Whites are the beneficiaries of privilege. One study found that "without confidence in themselves . . . participants were unwilling or unable to consider that their success was due in part to their dominant status in society, and the privilege they thereby incurred."[53] Thus, there is a need to balance humility and confident self-understanding, much like what we see in Jesus's model in John 13:3–5 (cf. Phil. 2:6–8).

While the idea of constructing an identity around being a social justice ally is potentially appealing for White Christians and others, there is a lively debate about the very notion of "allyship" among activists and people of color. For example, Beverly Daniel Tatum's widely read book *Why Are All the Black Kids Sitting Together in the Cafeteria?* briefly touches on the notion of White identity development by describing how Whites respond to racism in one of four ways: they may become overtly racist, colorblind, guilty, or develop as White anti-racist allies. According to Linda Martín Alcoff, Whites who come to see their whiteness while learning about the dynamics of race experience disorientation from "feeling White," which, when combined with a desire to repudiate White privilege, can result in a negative self-image and a fractured

50. Case, "Discovering the Privilege of Whiteness," 89.
51. Case, "Discovering the Privilege of Whiteness," 90.
52. Broido, "Development of Social Justice Allies," 4; Michael et al., "Becoming an Anti-Racist White Ally," 59–60.
53. Broido, "Development of Social Justice Allies," 7, 10–13. Contrast this emphasis on humility with Julie Greenberg's struggle to accept the leadership of people of color in Greenberg, "Beyond Allyship."

connection to community and history.[54] For these Whites, Tatum's "White anti-racist identity" becomes the only recourse.[55]

But there are problems embedded in this construction of identity. Suppose a negative construction of whiteness resulting from a racialized society makes it difficult to have a positive White identity. In that case, this outcome represents the wages that all pay in living in a racialized society, one that affects people of color with far more severe consequences. The problem is some might view the effort to apply the language of fluid, fractured, and multiple identities to Whites in a way that leaves room for their agency while recognizing the structural aspects of identity as an attempt to sidestep responsibility for ending racial oppression. Cynics could see in this attempt another instance of the trope of the fragile White victim who shifts attention away from the oppression experienced by people of color and onto the lesser problems surrounding White identity.[56] Another difficulty is that in combination with rampant individualism among Whites, an amorphous White anti-racist identity might allow Whites to distance themselves from the actions of their racial group and demand to be granted the benefit of the doubt in all cases. Thus, a corollary to such an amorphous and thus unracialized anti-racist identity is the White person who recognizes whiteness as real, albeit the individual problem of other "bad" White people.[57]

Moreover, we can critique White anti-racist identity discourse about allyship because it leaves aside the nuance that coalitions against racism require. This discourse needs to account for how various communities of color experience racism without overlooking the need for collaborative alliances with and among different communities of color.[58] More importantly, some activists think it is dangerous to talk about allyship as a status or identity independent of ongoing acts of solidarity.[59] The status versus process perspective can become troublesome, for instance, when a White activist responds to correction about a problematic racist comment or action by dismissing the feedback based on their past efforts—in effect invoking the "I marched with Martin Luther King Jr." defense. Hence, one should not proclaim one's identity as an ally; one should be claimed an ally by those whom one is seeking to support.

54. Alcoff, "What Should White People Do?," 7.

55. Also see Delgado and Stefancic, *Critical White Studies*.

56. Eichstedt, "Problematic White Identities," 448.

57. DiAngelo, "White Fragility," 59.

58. Patel, "Inclusive Model of Allyship," 78–81. Similarly Lee, *Great World House*, and Mio, "Asians on the Edge."

59. Utt, "So You Call Yourself an Ally."

These reservations are critical and need to circumscribe the contours and nature of allyship as practiced by Whites. Nevertheless, I think it is unwise to withhold the possibility of positive identity construction for anyone suffering from the trauma of being racialized; to do so would be akin to how conservatives unfairly critiqued the "Black is Beautiful" movement in the 1960s and the Black Lives Matter movement today. I am not saying that Whites' need for a positive way of being White is as urgent as the need experienced by Blacks and other oppressed groups. Instead, in keeping with the love ethic in Matthew 5:43–48, I suggest that Christians should not withhold a good from an enemy because of the chance for abuse. If praying for enemies represents the minimum ethical behavior in Matthew 5:44, the other verses show the boundlessness of Jesus's intention (5:45, 48). Thus, wisdom and love dictate that there should be possibilities for Whites to craft an identity characterized by trust, humility, unceasing anti-racist action, and solidarity with people of color. Further, we should create an analogous conversation about how communities of color can become allies in broader anti-racist coalitions. In the next section, we will look at depictions of enemies in Matthew's Gospel for help in fleshing out the poetic shape of Christian love for the Other as the allyship needed to build multiracial coalitions for justice.

Matthew and the Nations

Much like the tensions in the Old Testament with respect to ancient Israelite ethnocentrism on the one hand and a welcome of outsiders through conversion on the other hand, the Gospel of Matthew, sometimes called the most "Jewish" gospel, displays ambiguity that also expresses these tendencies.[60] Nothing could scream ethnicity more than Matthew's addition of a Jewish genealogy to the Marcan account of Jesus's ministry and passion. The genealogy traces Jesus's descent from Abraham, the Israelite patriarch, on through David, the people's ideal king. Yet, there is also ambiguity as it mentions Jesus's Canaanite and non-Jewish forebearers—the latter of which are all depicted

60. On Matthew's Jewishness, see for instance M. J. Brown, "Gospel of Matthew" and Nolland, *Gospel of Matthew*, 17. On Matthew's ambiguity regarding Gentiles, see Caird, *New Testament Theology*, 393. Caird here speaks about the historical question regarding the continuity between the historical Jesus and the phenomenon of Gentile mission in the early Christian movement. For more on this question, see, e.g., E. P. Sanders, *Jesus and Judaism*. Michael Bird notes that this tension between inclusivism and exclusivism can sometimes appear side-by-side in Scripture and early Jewish literature: Isa. 66:15–21; Pss. Sol. 17.22–25, 30–31; 2 Bar. 72.2–6; t. Sanh. 13.2. See Bird, "Who Comes from the East and West?," 450.

as women. Womanist New Testament scholar Mitzi Smith maintains that the genealogy in 1:1–18 functions to identify Jesus as a mulatto/mixed-race Davidic messiah, born of the patriarchs and four Gentile women,[61] and captures Matthew's hybridized blend of universalism and particularism.[62]

In addition, the final scene in the Gospel contains the distinctive "Great Commission," verses that command the small band of devoted disciples to embrace a global teaching mission (28:19; cf. 24:14).[63] One would have to agree that this scene, emphasizing a worldwide Gentile mission at the end of the narrative, absolves this text of any charge of active racism or narrow ethnocentrism. Yet, we should note that the Great Commission also contains an embedded promotion of Jewish particularity.[64] What else could one conclude from the exhortation about "teaching [the nations] *to obey everything* that I commanded" in 28:20, when "everything" would surely include Jesus's teaching about doing Torah in 5:19? Such thinking prompts other scholars to see in the Great Commission less of an embrace of outsiders than an imperialistic program of conquest and domination, fodder for the later colonization of Africa and North America, baptized with a thinly veiled pretext of religiosity.[65]

Indeed, Matthew abounds with positive images of Gentile outsiders. For example, he narrates the arrival of the Magi, who seek to worship the new

61. M. J. Smith and Kim, *Toward Decentering the New Testament*, 61. Also see John C. Hutchison's discussion of the common approaches to understanding Matthew's inclusion of references to Tamar, Rahab, Ruth, and Bathsheba in Matt. 1:1–18 in his "Women, Gentiles, and the Messianic Mission"; likewise see Keener, *Gospel of Matthew*, 78–81.

62. Similarly, Michael Joseph Brown notes the "constant tension between the universal and the particular" in the Gospel of Matthew: "Matthew appears to be telling us that the universal is found and cultivated in our concern for the immediate issues in our life setting. . . . African Americans understand that every advance for human liberation has come one act at a time within specific settings in history" ("Gospel of Matthew," 86).

63. See Mitzi Smith's critical interrogation of the role of naming this pericope the Great Commission in "Knowing More Than Is Good for One." According to Smith, this naming has created an interpretive trajectory that obscures the social justice elements of Jesus's ministry while elevating an (over)emphasis on teaching.

64. Most scholars agree that Matthew was ethnically Jewish (e.g., Keener, *Gospel of Matthew*, 40). Matthew's emphasis on Jewish practice has even led some scholars to suggest that Matthew himself was not only Jewish, but also a Pharisee as well (Culbertson, "Reclaiming the Matthean Vineyard Parables"). Jennings and Liew appeal to Matt. 23:15 to point out that "there is little apprehension in Matthew's narrative world about the interaction between ethnic Jews and ethnic Gentiles," but perhaps go a bit further than the text when they insist that Matthew's Jesus "has no trouble associating with Gentiles" in light of 15:23–26. See Jennings and Liew, "Mistaken Identities," 481.

65. Dube Shomanah, *Postcolonial Feminist Interpretation*.

king of Israel in a scene that many read as proleptic of the Gentile mission (2:1–12).[66] Along with the passages that commend the faith of a Roman centurion and a Canaanite woman (8:5–13; cf. 15:21–28),[67] scholars note a positive posture toward Gentiles in the mention of a global eschatological banquet (8:11) and the exorcism of the two Gadarene demoniacs (8:28–34, though see below). Matthew also contains two citations of universalistic themes from Isaiah: the line from Isaiah 42:1, "He shall proclaim justice to the Gentiles," and the allusions to Isaiah 9 in the description of Jesus's ministry in "Galilee of the Gentiles" (4:15–16; 12:18–19). The kingdom parables of 21:28–22:14 hint at a Gentile mission, especially 21:43 where Jesus talks of giving the vineyard, that is, the people of Israel, to a people who produce fruit of the kingdom.[68] Finally, there is the confession of the Roman soldiers in 27:54 ("Truly this was the son of God") and the command to love one's enemies (5:44) written in the shadow of devastating war with the Romans and functioning as the pinnacle of altruism and the apex of Jesus's radical program of inclusiveness over the entire New Testament.[69]

66. See LaVerdiere and Thompson, "New Testament Communities in Transition"; W. Carter, "Matthew and the Gentiles"; Sim, "Gospel of Matthew and the Gentiles," 19–21; Sim, *Gospel of Matthew and Christian Judaism*; S. Brown, "Matthean Community and the Gentile Mission"; Senior, "Between Two Worlds"; Keener, "Matthew's Missiology"; Bird, "Who Comes from the East and West?," 445.

67. A number of scholars point out the interesting similarities between these two passages. Both appear to involve long-distance healings, both involve Gentiles who implore Jesus on behalf of a weaker same-sex member of their households, and both potentially underscore Jesus's hesitation about involving himself in ministry outside of the "lost sheep of the house of Israel" (cf. 10:5–6). The discussion below will explore the similarities and differences between these passages in more detail.

68. Some see evidence of a *tertius genus* motif in which Jews and Gentiles combine to form a new third race in 21:43 (Hagner, *Matthew*, 2:623). Though the third race motif does occur in the New Testament (e.g., 1 Cor. 10:32; Eph. 2:11–15; 1 Pet. 2:9), the common metaphorical imagery of the vineyard in Jewish thought and the larger context of Matthew favors an understanding that the vineyard itself is not being replaced in this parable, but only the *vine-growers* who tend the vineyard. Thus, the parable does not anticipate a new and differently constructed people of God, but a new set of leaders for the people of God. In 21:43, ἔθνος refers to a small, differentiated caste or group—here a group of leaders—as it sometimes does in other Greek literature of the period. For more on uses of ἔθνος in the period and the third race motif in Paul, see Sechrest, *Former Jew*. For more on vineyard imagery as a Jewish metaphor, see Culbertson, "Reclaiming the Matthean Vineyard Parables."

69. Thomas E. Phillips's survey of the contours of explicit love commands in the New Testament suggests that Matt. 5:43–48 and the parable of the Good Samaritan in Luke 10:25–37 represent the clearest and least parochial statements of love for others in the New

Nevertheless, the Gospel does contain evidence of stereotypic portraits of Gentiles that combine to create more ambiguity than is often acknowledged.[70] Gentiles are ethnocentric, hostile to outsiders (5:47), and they heap up empty words in prayers that vainly seek the attention of remote and distant gods (6:7).[71] Gentiles strive to accumulate meaningless material things (6:32), and they are known as brutal and arrogant tyrants (20:25). The saying at 7:6 about giving holy things to dogs and casting pearls to swine may be a derogatory reference to Gentiles. The command to "go nowhere among the Gentiles" in the missionary discourse explicitly excludes Gentiles from the disciples' ministry, a sentiment also reiterated in the passage about Jesus's encounter with the Canaanite woman (10:5–6; cf. 15:26).[72] Finally, in 18:17, we learn that Gentiles are stubborn, hard-hearted outsiders who refuse to bow to the community's will. The love command in 5:44 towers as a pinnacle of Christian ethics, promoting the love of enemies and prayerful concern for one's persecutors. Yet, it contains ambiguity about Gentiles by suggesting that Gentiles function as a negative foil for the Jewish righteousness commanded therein: "For if you love those who love you, what reward do you have? . . . And if you greet only your siblings, what more are you doing than others? Do not even

---

Testament, finding that commands to love in Revelation, the Epistles, and the other Gospels are strikingly inwardly focused. My own work on the parable of the Good Samaritan suggests that it falls more into this latter category than the former, leaving Matt. 5:43–48 as perhaps the lone explicit command of this type in the New Testament. I am grateful to Professor Phillips for allowing me to have a copy of his paper "Loving Neighbor, Loving One Another, and Loving Enemies: Three New Testament Ethics of Love," which was presented in the SBL "Ethics, Love, and the Other" Consultation in Atlanta, GA, in November 2010.

70. While many of these passages are dismissed as strange holdovers from the tradition that do not reflect Matthew's pro-Gentile viewpoint, it is true, as David C. Sim shows, that both retention of source material *and* deletion, additions *and* modifications, all communicate the editor's viewpoint ("Gospel of Matthew and the Gentiles," 29–30; *Gospel of Matthew and Christian Judaism*, 231). Sim's conclusion that the Gospel of Matthew is *anti-Gentile* (see Sim, *Gospel of Matthew and Christian Judaism*, passim) has not proven persuasive to most Matthew scholars, foundering mainly on its inability to account for 28:19 (cf. Donald Senior's thorough critique in "Between Two Worlds"). Sim's observations nevertheless do provide firm support for the fact that there is real ambiguity in the Gospel's portrait of Gentiles; cf. S. Brown, "Matthean Community and the Gentile Mission." See also see M. J. Brown, *Gospel of Matthew*, and Jennings and Liew, "Mistaken Identities," 480n37.

71. Nolland, *Gospel of Matthew*, 284, esp. n. 307.

72. It is interesting that Schuyler Brown thinks that the context of 10:5–6 nevertheless indicates the existence of a separate or parallel (yet concurrent) Gentile mission, since 10:18 indicates that the persecution of the missionaries will be a testimony to Jews and Gentiles. See S. Brown, "Mission to Israel."

the Gentiles do the same?" (Matt. 5:46–47 AT). Some point to the Separation of Sheep and Goats passage (25:31–46) as an example of an ethic of concern for the poor and marginalized, but others insist that it merely develops an inwardly focused ethic wherein Matthew holds the nations accountable for how they have treated "the little ones" in his movement.[73] What is commonly known as the "Gentile feeding narrative" in Mark 8:1–10, which symbolizes Jesus's abundant provision of salvation for the Gentiles, seems to have been moved back into Jewish territory in Matthew 15:32–39.[74] Further, Jesus's encounter with the Canaanite woman in Matthew 15:21–28 triggers a firestorm of protest about sexism, hierarchy, and ethnic discourse.[75] Interpreters recoil at the evangelist's portrait of a woman who seems to participate in her own denigration. At the same time, other readers resent the subtle anti-Semitism that emerges when critics label Jesus's behavior as racist and then suggest that it was somehow typical of Jewish thought of the time.[76]

Is the Gospel of Matthew "anti-Gentile" or "racist" in today's terms?[77] It is impossible to read a passage like the Canaanite woman episode today without thinking about racism and sexism in light of the hierarchical relations between groups in modern US society. However, a judgment about the character of Matthew's Gospel would also have to account for the numerous positive and inclusive tendencies in the Gospel as well. In settling this question, we need to consider carefully the historical and literary contexts of the Gospel of Matthew that gave rise to the ambivalence toward the outsider that we are discussing.

First, consider the kinds of pressures in Matthew's historical milieu that would give rise to the hostile polemics in the context. Written after the fall of Jerusalem during the Jewish War with Rome (AD 66–73), Matthew participates in the ensuing debates within Judaism about the people's future in terms

73. Cope, "Matthew XXV:31–46."

74. In Mark 7, Jesus invalidates food laws just prior to his encounter with the Syrophoenician woman, and in Mark 8, the second miraculous feeding of Gentiles abuts the encounter with the woman and becomes a narrative that symbolizes subsequent Gentile participation in a messianic banquet. Yet Matthew's changes to the Gentile feeding narrative in Mark 8 have so blurred the identities of the attending crowds that it is unlikely that Matthew envisioned this as a Gentile group, making it more likely that the scene functions as a climax in the mission to Israel. See Cousland, "Feeding of the Four Thousand Gentiles."

75. E.g., Guardiola-Sáenz, "Borderless Women"; Levine, "Matthew's Advice to a Divided Readership."

76. Levine, "Matthew's Advice to a Divided Readership," 25.

77. Stephanie Buchanan Crowder describes Jesus as the "perpetrator of . . . [the] classist and racist ideologies" at work in this text (*When Momma Speaks*, 88). On the other hand, it is more accurate historically to talk about the evangelist as the perpetrator of these tropes.

of their worship, society, and leadership. Matthew's conflict with the emerging rabbinic movement in the aftermath of the war is evident in his critique of Pharisees, as they became the dominant force in the fragmented remnants of Jewish society (cf. 5:20; 21:43–45; 23:1–36).[78] Matthew was likely writing in the city of Syrian Antioch. There is also evidence that Matthew's community faced persecution and rejection on a second front.[79] Following the Jewish war against Rome, the Gentiles of that city initiated violent anti-Jewish mob action, followed by repeated petitions to Rome to strip the Jews of all of the civil rights that the Romans had previously guaranteed them.[80]

But settled in an area where the Jesus movement was already pursuing a Gentile mission, Matthew's community possibly also faced positive pressure toward inclusivism within the Christian movement. The book of Acts documents Syrian Antioch as the center of an energetic mission to Gentiles from dedicated missionaries who wanted the community to welcome these Gentile converts and others beside them.[81] The Gentile mission might have increased

78. Davies and Allison, *Matthew*, 3:692–704. According to Daniel J. Harrington, Matthew is one of three post-70 AD responses to the fall of Jerusalem: apocalyptic Judaism (e.g., 4 Ezra, 2 Baruch), rabbinic Judaism, and Jewish Christianity. See "Polemical Parables in Matthew 24–25," 288–90.

79. Though complete certainty is impossible at this historical distance, many think that Syrian Antioch (also known as Antioch-on-the-Orontes) fits the hints about provenance that emerge from the text and from other early Christian sources. Antioch was an urban center with a sizable Jewish population and its location in Syria comports with Matthew's emphasis on locations in that region. As a known center of the mission to Gentiles in Paul's day, it would have had a population of Gentile converts. It might also be a likely place for the preservation of traditions about Peter in Matthew, given evidence that Peter was a frequent visitor there (e.g., Gal. 2:11–12). Finally, some of the earliest references to the Gospel appear in the letters of Ignatius of Antioch, which, with the links between the Gospel and the Didache, also connect Matthew to that city. Though some are more guarded, there is wide agreement about this city as the likely location for Matthew's community. See Keener, *Gospel of Matthew*, 41–42, and the scholars cited there. Cf. Hagner, *Matthew*, 1:lxxv, who is a bit more cautious.

80. For a more detailed reconstruction of the situation in Syrian Antioch, see also Sim, *Matthew and Christian Judaism*, 166–86, and Meeks and Wilken, *Jews and Christians in Antioch*, 1–54, esp. 4–5, 18. Sim sees evidence of this conflict with Gentiles in Matt. 10:17–22; 24:4–14, and especially 24:9 ("hated by *all* nations"; see his *Gospel of Matthew and Christian Judaism,* 30–38). Sim maintains that all but two of the prophecies in 24:4–14 contain descriptions that pertain to the community's historical situation. Also see Warren Carter's discussion of the complicity of the Jewish leaders with the Romans and the Gospel's anti-Roman polemic in his "Matthew and the Gentiles," 261–64, 271, and similarly his "Resisting and Imitating the Empire."

81. Sim, *Matthew and Christian Judaism*, 188–213.

the likelihood of opposition from the Pharisees, who may have ridiculed the Matthean community for being less observant, thus prompting Matthew's stress on meticulous law observance. Those promoting a mission similar to that of the apostle Paul, known for his active work among Gentiles in Antioch, would have only exacerbated the situation.[82] Thus, any Gentile mission in Matthew's community would have likely only proceeded on strictly Jewish terms (5:17–20; 7:15, 22; perhaps 24:11).[83] That is, a Matthean Gentile mission would have been a Torah-observant mission in its teaching and practice. In short, Matthew's ambiguity toward Gentiles may emerge from the fact that his group faced pressure on three fronts: active Gentile persecution in Antioch, hostility from Pharisees in the aftermath of the Jewish War,[84] and internal pressure within the Christian movement to accept local Jesus-believing Gentiles. It is no wonder that we see ambivalence in the posture toward outsiders in this gospel in such a context. Matthew insists on both Jewish priority and higher righteousness (10:5–6; 5:17–20), while at the same time embarking on a Gentile mission—but only so long as that mission is commensurate with "all that Jesus commanded" about piety and practice (28:19–20).[85]

When read in light of the historical forces underlying the universalistic-particularistic dialectic in Matthew, the love command and emphasis on forgiveness are nothing short of stunning. I think that Matthew's milieu was such that he and his readers *were* the oppressed in post-war late first-century Palestine. Having been thoroughly defeated by the Romans in the homeland

82. Sim, *Matthew and Christian Judaism*, 199–213.

83. Note that here I discuss the *terms* of a Matthean mission and not a Matthean *antipathy* to a Gentile mission as some have suggested on the basis of 10:5–6 (e.g., Meier, *Marginal Jew*, 3:544). Cf. Richard Bauckham's foreword to James LaGrand, *Earliest Christian Mission*.

84. The source of the persecution and hostility is debated. For instance, Schuyler Brown ("Matthean Community and the Gentile Mission," 216–17) suggests that the persecution emerged from the Jewish community and reads 10:5–6 as a concession to members of the Matthean community who were not in favor of a Gentile mission (218). Alternately, David Sim focuses on Gentile persecution in *Matthew and Christian Judaism*, 188–213.

85. Similarly, see Senior: "What I am suggesting here is that Matthew was attempting to bridge more than one divide at once. First of all, he was fending off attacks about his community's essential Jewish character from other factions within the Jewish community, but with equal conviction he wanted to communicate that heritage to a new generation of Christians, Jewish and Gentile" ("Between Two Worlds," 21; cf. 18). Somewhat similar is Schuyler Brown's conclusion: "The difficulty in finding a satisfactory theological explanation for the contradiction between Jesus' restriction of the mission to 'the lost sheep of the house of Israel' (Matt 10:6) and his extension of the mission to 'all nations' (28:19) suggests that the gentile mission may have been an object of current controversy within the evangelist's community" ("Matthean Community and the Gentile Mission," 193).

and humiliated by Syrians in Antioch, this community would have completely understood the difficulty of enemy-love from the underside. Given the questions with which we began, I suggest that when we imagine the fraught nature of love for one's conquerors when considering Matthew's Gospel, we also need to pose questions about what Matthew might have had in mind when he wrote about enemies. We will examine this question by looking at the rhetoric about and encounters with enemies in several passages in Matthew. Below we'll briefly look at (1) animal metaphors for Gentile enemies in 7:6; (2) Jesus's encounter with the Gadarene demoniacs in 8:28–34; and (3) the healings of the centurion's boy and the Canaanite's daughter in 8:5–13 and 15:21–28, respectively. What we'll see is that the depiction of Jesus's enemies in these passages functions analogously to a modern discussion of the nature of allyship in multiple directions beyond the Black-White binary, allowing us to do Christian reflection on what it means to be a loving enemy.

Gentiles, Pigs, and Dogs (Matthew 7:6 and 8:28–34)

The logion in Matthew 7:6 advises discretion when it comes to interaction with dogs and pigs, particularly when it comes to offering what is precious, in this case, "holy things" and "pearls":

> Don't give holy things to dogs, and don't throw your pearls in front of pigs. They will stomp on the pearls, then turn around and attack you. (CEB)

The verse uses figurative language since it is hard to imagine scenarios where one would literally offer pearls to barnyard animals. Still, there is some debate about how to understand the language. Is Matthew using ethnic epithets wherein the dogs and pigs in this verse represent Gentiles? For some, the unambiguous reference to non-Jewish outsiders as dogs in Jesus's encounter with a Canaanite in 15:26–27 is decisive on this question (cf. 2 Pet. 2:22) so that on this reading 7:6 contains the use of dehumanizing imagery about Gentiles.[86]

Yet, it may help to proceed from surer ground to the rockier terrain by examining the symbolic use of "pearl" in this text since the word appears elsewhere in Matthew. In 13:44–51, three parables appear in which the center parable uses "pearl" figuratively for the kingdom of heaven (13:45–46). If we

---

86. For a discussion about evidence that "dog" was a polemical reference to Gentiles, see Taylor, *Mark*, 350. Contra Nolland, *Gospel of Matthew*, 634; Levine, "Matthew's Advice to a Divided Readership," 32.

interpret these three parables as a set like other parable triads in Matthew, then the first two describe people who understand that the kingdom is unexpected, treasured, and costly. In the third, the common and unworthy live alongside the joyful and discerning until a final sorting between the evil and the righteous. Thus, the treasure finder of 13:44, the pearl merchant of 13:45, and the evil and righteous of 13:49 represent people with different attitudes toward the kingdom. If 7:6 is analogous, then we would say that the pearls in this saying represent the treasures of the kingdom and the pigs represent people with a negative disposition regarding the kingdom. Since holy things are parallel to pearls in 7:6, both seem to be a way of speaking of evangelism and discipleship through the proclamation of the kingdom.[87] A verse in the well-regarded early Christian text known as the Didache confirms this conclusion through an allusion to Matthew 7:6, implying that the dogs and pigs in the logion refer to those outside of the Christian movement (i.e., the unbaptized):

> Let no one eat or drink of your Eucharist, except those who have been baptized into the name of the Lord; for, indeed, the Lord said concerning this matter, "Do not give holy things to dogs." (Did. 9:5 AT)

In Jewish literature, pigs often function to mark the distinctively "un-Jewish," representing the basal measure of what is unclean. The Torah describes pigs as unclean (Lev. 11:7; Deut. 14:8) and in Jewish narratives abstinence from touching or eating swine is a distinctive marker of Jewish religion (Isa. 65:4; cf. Isa. 66:3; 2 Macc. 6:18–7:42; Josephus, *Ant.* 12.253 and *Ag. Ap.* 2.141).[88] Given

---

87. The adjective "holy" is grammatically neuter in the Greek text of Matt. 7:6, translated literally as "holy things." Aside from its somewhat ambiguous use in this verse, the adjective "holy" is applied to several other entities in Matthew: the Holy Spirit (neuter: 1:18, 20; 3:11; 12:32; 28:19); the holy city (feminine: 4:5; 27:53); the temple (e.g., "the holy place" [masculine] in 24:15); and holy people (masculine plural: 27:52). Thus, the grammar supports the idea that in this verse the "holy things" are those things that pertain to the Holy Spirit of God. In Matthew, the Holy Spirit gives life (1:18, 20), animates ministry by anointing and affirming (3:11, 16), directs (4:1), inspires (10:20; 12:1; 22:43), and exorcises evil (8:16; 10:1; 12:28). Since the Holy Spirit is God-given, it is more likely that the giving of holy things mentioned in Matt. 7:6 is a way of speaking of evangelism and discipleship through the proclamation of the kingdom.

88. Josephus, *Ant.* 12.253 (trans. Whiston): "And when the king had built an idol altar upon God's altar, he slew swine upon it, and so offered a sacrifice neither according to the Law, nor the Jewish religious worship in that country. He also compelled them to forsake the worship which they paid their own God . . . and made them . . . raise idol altars . . . and offer swine upon them every day." Josephus, *Ag. Ap.* 2.141 (trans. Whiston): "for the histories say that two things were originally committed to their care by their kings' injunctions. . . .

that their status as unclean caused domesticated pigs to be banned from Jewish regions, swine (especially wild boars as in 2 Sam. 17:8 LXX) also came to be associated with Gentiles, as attested in Matthew 8:30–32.[89] First- and second-century Jewish-Christian texts also make explicit this association between unclean swine and those who do not worship God according to Torah:[90]

> [8] Another commits adultery and fornication, and *abstains from meats,* and when he fasts, he does evil, and by the power of his wealth he overwhelms many; and despite his excessive wickedness he does the commandments: this, too, has a twofold aspect, but the whole is evil. [9] *Such men are wild pigs, hares; because they are half-clean,* but in truth they are unclean. [10] For God in the tablets of heaven has so declared. (T. Ash. 2:8–10; emphasis added)[91]

> [1] Now, wherefore did Moses say, "Thou shalt not eat the swine, nor the eagle, nor the hawk, nor the raven, nor any fish which is not possessed of scales"? . . . [2] Moses spoke with a spiritual reference. [3] For this reason he named the swine, as much as to say, *"Thou shalt not join thyself to men who resemble swine."* For when they live in pleasure, they forget their Lord; but when they come to want, they acknowledge the Lord. And [in like manner] the swine, when it has eaten, does not recognize its master; but when hungry it cries out, and on receiving food is quiet again. . . . [9] Moses then issued three doctrines concerning meats with a spiritual significance; but they received them according to fleshly desire, as if he had merely spoken of meats. [10] David, however, understands the knowledge of the three doc-

---

Accordingly, these priests are all circumcised, and abstain from swine's flesh; nor does anyone of the other Egyptians assist them in slaying those sacrifices they offer to the gods."

89. Matt. 8:30–32 (see parallels in Mark 5:11–16; Luke 8:32–33): "Now a large herd of swine was feeding at some distance from them [in the country of the Gadarenes; see 8:28]. The demons begged him, 'If you cast us out, send us into the herd of swine.' And he said to them, 'Go!' So, they came out and entered the swine; and suddenly, the whole herd rushed down the steep bank into the sea and perished in the water." A similar dynamic appears at Luke 15:15–16, where a Jew's proximity to swine also adds a note of reproach and humiliation.

90. The dating and authorship of the Testaments of the Twelve Patriarchs is uncertain. Scholars debate whether this is a Jewish collection with Christian interpolations originally written in the first or second century BC, or an essentially Christian document written sometime in the second century AD. While the larger part of the Testament of Asher appears to reflect Second Temple thought, some might see a Christian redaction in 7:2–3. Likewise, the Epistle of Barnabas was most likely written between the first and second Jewish Wars with Rome and is thoroughly Christian in outlook and possibly anti-Jewish at points (e.g., 4:7).

91. Translated by Craig Evans, *Pseudepigrapha.*

trines, and speaks in like manner: "Blessed is the man who hath not walked in the counsel of the ungodly . . . *and hath not stood in the way of sinners," even as those who profess to fear the Lord but go astray like swine.* (Barn. 10:1, 3, 9–10; emphasis added)[92]

The first-century AD Jewish philosopher Philo describes dogs as wild animals that are vicious and ravenous (*Giants* 35; *Decalogue* 114).[93] It may be that this perspective on canine nature is what makes them suitable as descriptors of outsiders in his *On the Contemplative Life* 40, where he contrasts those who hold the Sabbath in perfect holiness (36) with the raucous and rude drunken banquets of others in this verse:

in opposition and contrast to the banquets of others, when they drink strong wine . . . or even the most formidable thing which can be imagined for driving a man out of his natural reason, rage about and tear things to pieces like so many ferocious dogs, and rise up and attack one another, biting and gnawing each other's noses, and ears, and fingers, and other parts of their body, so as to give an accurate representation of the story related about the Cyclops and the companions of Ulysses, who ate, as the poet says, fragments of human flesh. (*Contempl. Life* 40)[94]

92. Translated by Roberts and Donaldson, *Apostolic Fathers.*

93. *Giants* 35: "Let not then our appetites rush eagerly in pursuit of all the things that are pleasant to the flesh, for the pleasures are often untameable, when like dogs they fawn upon us, and all of a sudden, change and bite us, inflicting incurable wounds. So that by cleaving to frugality, which is a friend to virtue, in preference to the pleasures akin to the body, we shall defeat the numerous and infinite multitude of irreconcilable enemies. And if any occasion should seek to compel us to take more than what is moderate or sufficient, let us not yield; for the scripture saith, 'He shall come near to him to uncover his nakedness'" (trans. Yonge). In this case wildness is associated with the figurative enemy of immoderate cravings.

Decalogue 1.114: "but in this case I shall be constrained to use an entirely opposite language. You who are men, are imitators of some wild beasts. Even the beasts have learnt and know how to requite with service those who have done them service. Dogs [formerly wild but now domesticated] who keep the house will defend their masters, and encounter death for their sakes when any danger suddenly overtakes them. And they say that the dogs employed among flocks of sheep will fight on behalf of the flocks and endure till they either obtain the victory or meet with death, for the sake of protecting the shepherds themselves from injury" (trans. Yonge).

94. Translated by Yonge. Similarly, in his treatise *That Every Good Person Is Free* 90, Philo writes: "others again having converted their barbarous frenzy into another kind of wickedness, practicing an ineffable degree of savageness, talking with the people quietly, but through the hypocrisy of a more gentle voice, betraying the ferocity of their real dis-

The same thing may be going on in Psalm 22:16, where the parallelism suggests that the psalmist describes the "company of evildoers" encircling him like a pack of dogs (cf. Ps. 59:6, 14). Moreover, the Book of Dream Visions found in the second-century BC Jewish apocalyptic work 1 Enoch also exhibits this motif. The largest section of the Book of Dream Visions retells Israelite history as an animal allegory where sheep represent the Israelites and pigs and dogs represent the Edomites and Philistines, respectively:

> [42] And the dogs began to devour the sheep and the boars . . . until the Lord of the sheep raised up one ram from the sheep. [43] And this ram began to gore and pursue with the horns, and it charged into . . . the boars: and it destroyed many boars, and after them, it injured the dogs.
>
> [46] And he proceeded to it, and he spoke to it alone in secret, and he raised him up into a ram and into a leader and into a leading one of the sheep; and the dogs because of all these things were troubling the sheep. [47] And the first ram pursued the second ram, and he fled from his presence; then next I was observing the first ram until he fell in front of the dogs. . . . [49] And the sheep grew and were multiplied; and all the dogs . . . fled from him and were becoming frightened of him. (1 En. 89:42–49)[95]

In this text, both dogs and wild boars represent those who tend to "trample" or to "turn and maul," and this suggests that Matthew 7:6 isn't so much about dehumanizing the Other as it is about issuing a warning about the danger inherent in making peace with enemies—Romans and perhaps Syrians as well in Matthew's case. In 7:1–5, Matthew counsels caution in making hasty judgments out of self-deception, while 7:6 warns against taking this cautious counsel too far in making judgments. Taken together, 7:1–6 instructs believers to exercise discernment when sharing the holy things of the kingdom with those who may be violent or who cannot discern the value of the precious gospel treasure. Indeed, if, as we have supposed, Jesus represents an oppressed, marginalized, and defeated people, then maybe this warning is counsel for those engaged in the Gentile mission, in another note of ambivalence as noted above.[96] The text describes a way of approaching potential friends who are or

---

position, fawning upon their victims like treacherous dogs, and becoming the causes of irremediable miseries to them, have left in all their cities monuments of their impiety, and hatred of all mankind, in the never to be forgotten miseries endured by those whom they oppressed" (trans. Yonge).

95. Translated by Craig Evans, *Pseudepigrapha*.

96. Similarly see Guelich, *Sermon on the Mount*, 353; France, *Matthew*, 144; and Hag-

have been enemies. One must approach judiciously and carefully, lest one gets trampled and mauled. One must have compassion that grows out of a rejection of self-deception (7:1–5), but we must season compassion with a dignity that may withhold what is precious in order to avoid likely harm.

It may be that Matthew 8:28–34 offers a live illustration of the wisdom in 7:6 in Jesus's encounter with the Gadarene demoniacs. The story represents one of Jesus's few incursions into Gentile territory in Matthew and thus is relevant to our discussion about the nature of the Christian's engagement with the Other. The story describes an encounter with Gentiles placed virtually on the heels of Jesus's successful engagement with a Roman centurion. Here, instead of being greeted with faithful deference, he is confronted with two demon-possessed men who live amid concentrated Gentile impurity—both corpse impurity given that they live among tombs, and food impurity given they live close to swine herds. The men are agitated and fiercely violent, presumably so much so that they cannot live in the community (8:28). The violence of the demons becomes apparent after the exorcism when Jesus transfers the demons from the men to the herd of pigs. The animals immediately rush to their death in the sea, apparently driven to suicide by the demons.

The passage thus depicts these Gentiles as impure, unfit for the community, and highly dangerous. In other words, Jesus's exorcism exposes the dangers inherent in association with Gentiles, alluded to in Matthew 7:6. More interesting for our purposes, the passage also raises questions about the demeanor of the Gentile community that receives Jesus's gift of healing.[97] Instead of eliciting faith, service, or gratitude (cf. 8:9–10, 13–15), this exorcism only prompts rejection in a way that shows the wisdom of the discretion counseled in 7:6. The entire community, which had just received their own back from (living among) the dead, would rather reject Jesus than deal with the person who brings gifts of deliverance. What was it about Jesus that prompted such a seemingly incomprehensible response from the townspeople? There is no direct evidence in the passage that they objected to his message—could they have been focused on simply rejecting his person despite the gifts that he brought? Was Jesus "not their kind" somehow, and if not, what was it about his person

---

ner, *Matthew*, 1:171–72, notes the possibility that the logion prohibits the Gentile mission and concludes that the caution applies to both Jewish and Gentile evangelism. On the other hand, my interpretation emphasizes that this logion cautions those involved in the Gentile mission.

97. Nolland (*Gospel of Matthew*, 374) likewise suggests that the story's emphasis is on the response of the townspeople: "Matthew is not interested in the experience of the demoniacs (only in Jesus' act and the reaction of the townsfolk)."

that was so objectionable? Though Jews could not be reliably differentiated from Gentiles by physical appearance, it might be that Jesus was demonstrably Jewish in his dress.[98] Michael Brown suggests that they wanted no part in Jesus's boundary-transgressing mission.[99] Building on this idea, I suggest there is an undertone of ethnic conflict in the story, especially as it appears in Matthew's source in Mark with its less-than-subtle references to Roman legions (Mark 5:9, 10, 15, and perhaps 17a). I propose that Matthew's abbreviated version has retained these elements of ethnic conflict between Jesus and the Gadarenes, though in a more attenuated and nuanced way. Indeed, as an adaptation of the parallel account in Mark 5:1–20, Matthew's story may reflect interest in communicating that one must be *very careful* when engaging with Gentiles. Does the single demon-possessed man of Mark 5 that has become a pair of men in Matthew 8 subtly insinuate that one is more likely to encounter Gentiles like these violent and possessed men than the respectful and humble individual Gentiles in Matthew 8:5–13 and 15:21–28?[100] In our final analysis, it may be that Matthew wants to say that Gentiles do not all approach Jesus with the respect and deference that characterizes the centurion and the Canaanite and that the wise evangelist would do well to keep that in mind when taking the gospel to the nations.

The Centurion and the Canaanite (Matthew 8:5–13 and 15:21–28)

Jesus's encounters with two other Gentiles will provide additional insight on the theme of encountering enemies. There are four stories in Matthew where a parent or guardian seeks healing for a son or daughter, and in addition to the main characters, there are other similarities among them (8:5–13; 9:18–26; 15:21–28; 17:14–21). For instance, the healings of the (synagogue) leader's daughter and the centurion's boy-child potentially involve Jesus's travel to the patient (cf. 8:7; 9:19), and the epileptic's father and the Canaanite mother both plead for mercy (cf. 17:15; 15:22). Further, there are similarities between each of these four episodes and other healing narratives in the Gospel. For example, the centurion's child suffers paralysis as does the patient of 9:2 (cf. 8:6); and Peter's kinswoman and the leader's daughter both rise at Jesus's touch (cf. 8:15;

98. Jennings and Liew, "Mistaken Identities," 491n59.

99. M. J. Brown, *Gospel of Matthew*, 97.

100. Similarly, Nolland notes that the doubling of the demon-possessed characters here over Mark 5:1–20 "probably represent[s] nothing more than an insistence that the incidents were not 'one-offs' but part of a larger pattern" (*Gospel of Matthew*, 375).

9:25). But to my eye, no two of these accounts have more in common than the healings of the centurion's boy-child and the Canaanite's daughter in 8:5–13 and 15:21–28, respectively.

As in these other narratives, the centurion and Canaanite request healing for a dependent who is not present; the centurion for his boy-child, and the Canaanite for her daughter.[101] Both exhibit urgency about their need for Jesus's intervention on behalf of their dependents. The Canaanite woman repeatedly asks for help, overcoming repeated rebuffs from the disciples who want her to cease her petitions.[102] The pleading of the centurion reveals his urgency, accompanied by a vivid description of the boy-child's torment. But what is especially striking about these two stories is that both of the supplicants

101. There is a great deal of ambiguity in the use of the word παῖς in 8:5–13. In favor of the translation "son": (1) Matthew uses δοῦλος in 8:9 when the centurion describes his authority over others; (2) παῖς refers to children vs. servants the three other times it is used in Matthew, outside of the OT quotation in 12:18 (= servant): child/children (21:15); male children (2:16); and son (17:18; note υἱός [son] is used as a synonym for this person in an earlier verse). Some suggest that Matthew uses the more ambiguous term παῖς because of the possibility that the child was illegitimate due to the ban on marriage for Roman soldiers during the empire (e.g., Jennings and Liew, "Mistaken Identities," 470–71), but this ban did not apply to officers like the centurion (see Saddington, "Centurion in Matthew 8:5–13"). Perhaps influenced by the parallel account in Luke 7:1–10, other scholars adduce that παῖς refers to a servant (e.g., Plummer, *Matthew*, 196), though others wonder about the "deep emotional attachment" enacted by the centurion for a mere slave (e.g., Derrett, "Law in the New Testament," 174). Appealing to Roman military culture and a well-known use of παῖς to designate the passive partner in a same-sex relationship, Jennings and Liew suggest that the παῖς is the centurion's youthful "boy-love" in a pederastic relationship (Jennings and Liew, "Mistaken Identities"). However, D. B. Saddington questions the relevance of the authors' heavy appeal to the "love triangle" of the first century BC Latin author Tibullus, as described in his poetry (see *Tib.* 1.1.53–58), while also pointing out that the passages Jennings and Liew cite regarding homosexuality among centurions actually refer to rape instead of the kind of emotional intimacy proposed in the biblical text (Saddington, "Centurion in Matthew 8:5–13," 140–42). It is probably best to render the word "boy" in a way that captures the ambiguity as I have here and recognizes those who think that either term is possible, such as Derrett ("Law in the New Testament," 174), who says it is deliberately ambiguous; similarly see Bultmann, *Synoptic Tradition*, 38–42; Keim, *Jesus of Nazara*, 219; Sparks, "Centurion's παῖς"; Levine, *Matthean Social History*, 108, 119; Luz, *Matthew 8–20*, 8, 10n17.

102. In the context of a discussion about intersectional class tensions between African American women who work inside the home versus those who work outside of the home, Stephanie Buchanan Crowder describes the Canaanite as analogous to a working mother. She defines work as "the consistent, conscientious act of pursuing those in power and challenging authority for survival, healing, health, wholeness, and future security" (Crowder, *When Momma Speaks*, 85, 88).

are Gentiles, like the Gadarenes in Matthew 8. They are the only Gentiles in the Gospel who have dialogue with Jesus.[103] Though the epileptic's father addresses Jesus as "Lord," the fact that these two Gentiles acknowledge his Lordship and accord him dignity and authority is much more surprising (8:6; 15:22).[104] In fact, the particular identities of the Roman and the Canaanite raise the stakes on confessing the superiority of this wandering rabbi. The Roman represents the oppressive military force that had, within living memory of the community receiving this Gospel, devastated the Jewish people, their temple, and capital city, inflicting horrific losses that threatened to crush the very heart of the people. The Canaanite represents a different kind of enemy but one no less potent. She embodies a deep-rooted, long-standing, and entrenched hostility intertwined with a peculiar kind of intimacy that is anchored in shared life, shared land, and even shared ancestry.[105]

No doubt, this aspect of their interactions with Jesus contributes somewhat to his commendation of them for their faith, but both go even further.[106] Even as the centurion manifests a healthy sense of his own agency, he also exhibits

103. However, neither episode represents a Gentile mission per se, especially in view of 10:5–6. In my judgment these episodes help prepare the terms of the Gentile mission that Jesus calls for in 28:18–20, by helping the earliest disciples identify those Gentiles who will be likely to respond to the gospel. On a different note, while both are Gentiles, it is important to note that this episode also represents the first time that a woman speaks directly to Jesus in the Gospel of Matthew. See Crowder, *When Momma Speaks*, 87.

104. Kingsbury, "Miracle Chapters of Matthew 8–9," 566.

105. The Canaanite addresses Jesus as Lord, as does the centurion and the epileptic's father, but she adds to her confession the idea that she sees him as the "Son of David." On her lips the phrase seems to be a particularly *Israelite* appellation that alludes to the opening genealogy of Matthew, which includes a reference to another Canaanite woman (1:5). For more on the connection between the Canaanite women of the genealogy and the Canaanite woman of Matt. 15:21–28, see Hutchison, "Women, Gentiles, and the Messianic Mission" and especially Levine, "Matthew's Advice to a Divided Readership," 26, 36–37. Further, we should reflect on the fact that Jesus's Canaanite ancestry problematizes the racial purity aspect of the ethnocentric message in Matt. 10:5–6. Just like the findings of modern genetics that renders the idea of pure races dubious, Matthew's genealogy suggests that the icon of Judaism, the Davidic Messiah-King Jesus, is himself "mixed race" or mulatto; see Smith and Kim, *Toward Decentering the New Testament*, 61–62.

106. Kingsbury's observation that Jesus's response in these miracle stories sometimes closely parallels the language of the original request seems to hold up in this case (ἰαθήσεται ὁ παῖς μου, Matt. 8:8; cf. ἰάθη ὁ παῖς [αὐτοῦ], Matt. 8:13). According to Kingsbury, this helps identify these people as models of faith. It is also interesting that while the Canaanite and the centurion are both commended for their faith, the faith of the leader's father in 9:18 who believes that Jesus can restore his dead daughter to life goes unremarked. This narrative detail may give further confidence to the idea that Matthew intends a more deliberate

belief in Jesus's ability to do what he cannot (8:8). For her part, the Canaanite exhibits extraordinary agency and persistence in the face of the disciples' overt obstructionism and Jesus's more passive distancing silence and active rebuff (15:3–5).[107] Some think that Jesus's apparent reluctance in the encounter with the Canaanite also manifests with the centurion. Though there is debate about Jesus's reluctance to engage the centurion in 8:5–13, it emerges most surely in those interpretations that understand 8:7 as a question versus a statement,[108] as seen in the difference between "Shall I come and heal him?" (NIV) and "I will come and heal him" (NRSV and many others).[109] Others see a reluctance in the use of the emphatic pronoun in 8:8 ("Shall I myself [ἐγὼ ἐλθὼν] come . . ."), which might signal Jesus's aversion for entering Gentile territory (cf. 8:28–34) or a Gentile's domicile (cf. Acts 10:28). But in any case, the Canaanite and the centurion are enemies who reach out to Jesus for grace across the lines of

---

contrast between the centurion and Canaanite stories. See Kingsbury, "Miracle Chapters of Matthew 8–9."

107. For more on the woman's agency see Guardiola-Sáenz, "Borderless Women."

108. Almost all of the more than one hundred and sixty questions in Matthew contain some word or syntactical construction that indicates the presence of a question. Of the relatively few that do not contain a marker of this kind, most are clearly questions based on the surrounding context. For instance, only nine verses without a clear word or phrase in the context result in different translations among the seven major English versions: NRSV, CEB, NASB, NET, NIV, NJB, and NLT, and only in 8:7 is there a significantly different meaning in the resulting translations. Though it is more likely that 8:7 is a statement rather than a question (e.g., see the analysis in Jennings and Liew, "Mistaken Identities," 478–80), one may, however, still detect a level of reluctance in this verse on other grounds. If 8:7 is not a question, then there must still be something in the verse that invites the centurion's response about not needing Jesus to travel to the patient in 8:8–9 (see Levine, "Matthew's Advice to a Divided Readership," 30). The need to connect Jesus's statement in 8:7 with the centurion's response in 8:9 is satisfied by translating the former with the fairly common interpretation of the adverbial participle in 8:7a (ἐγὼ ἐλθὼν) as a conditional: "If I come, I will heal him." For more on the conditional adverbial participle see Wallace, *Greek Grammar*, 632.

109. For a defense of understanding 8:7 as a question see Levine, "Matthew's Advice to a Divided Readership," 30, who says that the question "foreshadows the conversation with the Canaanite" in 15:21–28 and also offers a basis for the centurion's counterproposal in 8:8–9. Jennings and Liew ("Mistaken Identities," 482n40), on the other hand, think that it is a mistake to let parallels with 15:21–28 drive the exegesis of 8:7, and ask "why is it not equally valid to argue that Jesus' response to the centurion must parallel his . . . [receptivity] to the paralytic's friends in 9:1–7 because both sufferers are paralyzed?" My own position is that the parallels with 15:21–28 are absolutely appropriate in light of the numerous indications about Matthew's ambivalence about Gentiles as described above, so that the narrative thus invites comparison between these two actual encounters with Gentiles, which share more similarities than any of the other healing stories considered.

profound enmity. They demonstrate their desire to be connected to Jesus and receive his grace and mercy, overcoming understandable resistance from him considering the past they share with him. They are humble, respectful, and deferential. They believe Jesus, they trust Jesus, and they have confidence in his ability to meet the presenting needs.

Yet, there are interesting differences between these two stories, some of which will prove helpful for our consideration of Jesus's encounters with those who represent Israel's enemies. The most salient difference involves gender, which likely also has implications for the interpretation of these scenes. The centurion is among the most powerful males in the given social context. At the same time, the Canaanite is an isolated, utterly abject, and helpless female, and the ways that the gender of the dependent aligns with the gender of the protector only amplifies this difference. Modern readers may be especially troubled by these differences, especially as they seem correlated with the postures that Jesus takes vis-à-vis the man and the woman. For though we may see reluctance in Jesus's interaction with the centurion, nothing in this interaction approaches the scandalous exchange in his dialogue with the woman.[110] In 15:24–26, Jesus expresses his unwillingness to violate his exclusive mission to Israel in a metaphor that likens the woman and her sick child to dogs. Some interpreters try to dismiss or soften the scandal by describing the dog as a puppy,[111] the situation as a test of the woman's faith,[112] or teasing humor in a spectacularly unfunny moment.[113] The most sensitive interpreters will agree that none of these interpretive attempts prove satisfactory in the end.[114]

Though we cannot explore the many interesting issues for race relations in the episode with the Canaanite, the angle that is most salient for our purposes is the woman's response to something analogous to a racialized stereotype.[115]

---

110. For an extended consideration of how this text might function in a biblical approach to race and racism see Sechrest, "Humbled among the Nations."

111. Derrett, "Law in the New Testament," 163; but compare with Levine, "Matthew's Advice to a Divided Readership," 32: "As feminists frequently remark, being called 'little bitch' is no improvement to being called 'bitch.'" Also note Harrisville, who finds no justification for reading "dog" as a house pet, since rabbinic materials see dogs as despised wild beasts ("Woman of Canaan," 283).

112. E.g., Derrett, "Law in the New Testament," 162.

113. Mounce, *Matthew*, 153; McNeile, *Matthew*, 31; and France, *Matthew*, 247; critiqued by Boring, "Gospel of Matthew," 336n343.

114. See Nolland, *Gospel of Matthew*, 633–35, for a thoughtful discussion of the problems in this text for modern readers.

115. For more on this passage and the woman's apparent internalization of a negative stereotype see Sechrest, "Humbled among the Nations."

In 15:26, Jesus characterizes Israelites as children and outsiders as dogs, and this corresponds to the symbolism of the images of swine and dogs in Matthew 7:6 discussed above and amounts to constructing Gentiles as ferocious, ravening beasts like those Jesus met in 8:28–34.[116] Yet, instead of resisting the categorization, the woman accepts the image to channel it in a way that advances her plea.[117] If it is possible to characterize this acceptance as something akin to internalized racism, a more generous understanding is that she recognizes that the label is a part of the cost of seeking a relationship with a longtime enemy. She understands that she lives in a world that she did not construct and that does not facilitate the relationship she seeks. Her only way forward is to *trust that Jesus's love can transform the terms of this encounter.*

The construction of a relationship between Jesus and these former enemies is even more explicit in the episode with the centurion, who knew he was entering into a patron-client relationship based on the request for healing.[118] Suppose patronage happens in Roman culture when people seek extraordinary resources from individuals who possess them or control them. In that case, the centurion's decision to approach a leader from a despised religious sect is remarkable from the soldier's viewpoint as well as the Lord's perspective.[119] There is no explicit mention or detail that would suggest that the centurion saw himself as Jesus's social equal. On the contrary, his use of the word "lord" constitutes an acknowledgment of Jesus's superior power as a patron. But when the centurion calls attention to how he and Jesus both command power, it demonstrates his understanding of the honor owed to a superior, even as he begs for grace as a client on behalf of someone for whom he has both responsibility and affection.[120]

But perhaps the most crucial difference between the two episodes for our purposes is the difference in the kind of enemies that the centurion and Ca-

---

116. Note that while the available data does not support the conclusion that the dog was a common stereotype for Gentiles in the period, this construction does appear valid within the narrative world of Matthew. Cf. Nolland, who notes that dogs function as a negative metaphor for Gentiles in later rabbinic materials, rightly disputing the idea that the imagery is a common one for Gentiles in the period (*Gospel of Matthew*, 634). This same tactic is implicit in my discussion about the imagery, though Nolland neglects to reckon with how the imagery functions in Matthew (e.g., in considering 7:6; 8:28–34; and 15:21–28 together) as I do here.

117. On the way that the woman uses trickery to accomplish her goal, see Guardiola-Sáenz, "Borderless Women."

118. Jennings and Liew, "Mistaken Identities but Model Faith," 483, though see Saddington's rebuttal in "Centurion in Matthew 8:5–13."

119. DeSilva, *Honor, Patronage, Kinship and Purity*, 96.

120. DeSilva, *Honor, Patronage, Kinship and Purity*, 95–119.

naanite woman represent. Although the centurion is a more recent enemy associated with the raw aftermath of the war with Rome, the Canaanite woman is from a people with a long-standing record of hostility and strife. Musa Dube notes that the characterization of the woman as a "Canaanite" thus marks her as a foreign woman from a land that "must be invaded, conquered, annihilated."[121] Therefore, differences in the level of tension with the two supplicants may also result from the fact that it is sometimes easier to reconcile with a new enemy than to make peace with one with whom one shares a centuries-long fraught and complicated history of aggression. Perhaps that is why there is also a slight difference in the commendations that they receive from Jesus: the centurion has a faith not seen elsewhere in Israel, but the faith and humility of the Canaanite woman are exemplary of the greatest in the kingdom of heaven (15:28; cf. 18:1–4).

Loving the Other: Neighbors, Allies, Foes, and Frenemies

A synthesis between our consideration of Jesus's interaction with his enemies in Matthew and our earlier review of allyship begins by acknowledging the framework of love for enemies established in 5:43–48. No less important, however, is his caution regarding the approach to enemies in 7:6. Through analogical reasoning, we are attempting to imagine ourselves in the posture of those who began as enemies toward Jesus in the Gospel of Matthew, either through their own circumstances or through the intrusion of the history of nations, a history that can and often does transform one-on-one interactions into intergroup tension. Accordingly, in trying to take our cues about enemy-love from these characters, we find that the Gadarenes, the centurion, and the Canaanite represent possible ways of entering into a discussion of allyship. Of course, these stories are first and foremost about how these outsiders encountered and demonstrated faith in the Son of the God of Israel. We need to remember that Jesus was a Jew and from a people who had experienced oppression from some and had conflict with others. By doing so, we can also model our approach in the modern world on analogy with theirs when approaching others who have previously experienced violence and oppression.

The centurion and the Canaanite illustrate what it might look like to be loving enemies or allies. At the same time, the episode with the Gadarenes demonstrates the importance of discernment in undertaking work with enemies. In seeking to find and be allies, it is essential to remember that, stereo-

---

121. Dube Shomanah, *Postcolonial Feminist Interpretation*, 147.

types aside, individual members from groups with whom there is or has been conflict will vary in their willingness and capacity for relationships. Some like the centurion and the Canaanite will have the character and awareness of their history and identity to inhabit humility and demonstrate love. In contrast, others like the Gadarenes will be hostile, resistant, and callous. We should also note that the faith of the boy and girl who needed healing was irrelevant. It was the faith of those who advocated on their behalf who provided the crucial link, yet another way of recognizing the critical contributions and limitations of individual agency *and* group identity.[122] Similarly, Crowder defines the work that the Canaanite does as a working mother in a way that captures how advocacy for self and the Other is at the heart of allyship:

> Work is the consistent, conscientious act of pursuing those in power and challenging authority of our survival, healing, health, wholeness, and future security. It is relentless advocacy. To work . . . is not only to seek my welfare but the well-being of persons in my family, my community, and the world. . . . It is what I/we do, not what is done to me/us. . . . Work is thus more than a reluctant, "I've got to go to work": it is an intense, focused, determined "I've got work to do!" because life and soul are at stake.[123]

The humility of the Canaanite and centurion allies stands out, and though their unusual deference to Jesus was first and foremost rooted in their recognition of his status as the Messiah of Israel and theirs as outsiders, it is not too much of a stretch to imagine that their understanding of their social history also played a part in their demeanor. The narrative world of the Gospel of Matthew makes this possibility more likely given the clarity of Jesus's mission to Israel (10:5–6; 15:24). In other words, here we get hints of some of the same issues that drive the literature on allyship. Allies start with the recognition of one's own identity and social location. One adopts a posture of humility by acknowledging one's shortcomings (8:8a). We exercise agency by foregrounding urgent and necessary action (15:22–27), and we return to work among our own people as a key ingredient in forming relationships with the Other. Above all, the exemplary allies in the Gospel of Matthew exhibited full confidence in Jesus's ability to do what was needed because they knew who he was. Analogously, we need to recognize that communities of color are endowed by their Creator with all the resources of agency and co-regency in creation when it

122. Derrett, "Law in the New Testament," 183.
123. Crowder, *When Momma Speaks*, 89.

comes to leading work that participates with Christ in bringing justice and healing to earth as it is in heaven. Good allies will trust in these God-given talents and submit to the leadership initiatives by people of color instead of succumbing to narratives of imputed inferiority and stereotypes.

Our discussion of these texts also examined the differences in the depictions of these enemies, and these distinctions will also be fruitful for our construction of the nature of Christian allies. We've already noted that Matthew reveals that we can expect some who with deference and honor will invite the creation of community, while others will prove dangerous and discriminatory. But we have also noted differences in engaging enemies directly related to the intensity and proximity of the opposition. The Romans were intense but recent enemies to Jews; Canaanites were long-standing, bitter enemies from the past; and the Gadarenes perhaps represent the local active hostilities that Matthew's community might have faced in Syrian Antioch. Accordingly, it is possible to see a different way of being a biblically shaped ally in each of these narratives. Below we'll discuss "Neighbors," "Allies," "Foes," and "Frenemies" in light of these and other texts.

We see in the Roman centurion the "Neighbor" who represents allyship among communities of color, an area that we saw was underdeveloped in the literature on allies. As mentioned above, the centurion exhibits a respectful demeanor when he engages Jesus. One reading of the centurion's situation can help us envision this as a posture to help communities of color ally with other oppressed communities. According to Robert Bertram, the centurion's situation involves a problem with autonomy, unworthiness, and co-enslavement, and each of these circumstances adheres when Neighbors enter into allyship with other people of color.[124] Like other disadvantaged communities, Neighbors experience diminished capacity in their autonomy because of the effects of racism and other forms of discrimination. Just as the centurion experienced the limits of his autonomy when he was unable to relieve the boy's pain and urgently sought help, so too must people of color learn to develop alliances with others who understand something of the pain of disenfranchisement and constraint.

Much of the literature on allyship focuses on White anti-racist identity construction. As mentioned earlier, it emphasizes that White allies must first overcome the invisibility of whiteness and grow awareness of how their identities have been racialized as White. Here we emphasize that something analogous is also necessary for the Christian Neighbor, who as a person of color also

---

124. Bertram, "Complete Centurion."

needs to learn about the nature and processes of racialization experienced by other oppressed communities. As exemplified by the centurion of Matthew 8, Neighbors must acknowledge their "unworthiness" regarding the experiences in different communities of color by learning about these differing experiences of racialization through research, interpersonal contact, and co-labor in co-alitions for justice. As Neighbors who draw their cues from the demeanor of Matthew's centurion, they too will take their agency in hand and act in a manner that befits the urgency to relieve the suffering of those with whom they are co-enslaved. Like all allies, however, they will be characterized by epistemic humility. When it comes to issues that directly affect the communities with whom they want to ally, Neighbors will acknowledge the superior knowledge in these communities and follow their lead, doing unto others just as they would like others to act toward themselves. People in these alliances must do all they can to avoid an "Oppression Olympics" where coalition members compare and measure their pain and suffering in a futile effort to outdo one another as "most oppressed."[125]

The Canaanite represents the White "Ally," who is the subject of most scholarship on White anti-racist identity development. The Canaanite is the perennial enemy of the Jewish people, analogous to the relationship between Whites and people of color, especially Blacks. In light of the broader narrative in Matthew, the Canaanite helps establishes the truth found in contemporary race relations that it is virtually impossible to live in isolation and that one's enemy always constrains one's life in some way or another. Indeed, the author of the Gospel did not or could not even describe Jesus's ancestry without also talking about Canaanites, and something similar is at work with Blacks and Whites, especially in the South. The protracted and entangled history of conflict between Canaanites and Jews possibly bears on the woman's portrait in the Gospel.[126] Though gender dynamics are clearly at work in this text, I suggest

125. Martinez, "Seeing More Than Black and White."
126. Matthew's changes to the earlier, milder version of the episode in Mark 7:24–30 remove several features that in Mark communicate a greater welcome to Gentiles. Matthew eliminates Mark's mention that Jesus actually enters a Gentile home and possibly eats there by placing the meeting outside, after the woman has come out to him to make her request (cf. Matt. 15:17–20; Mark 7:19). Just prior to the passage in Mark 7, Jesus invalidates food laws, and afterwards the miraculous feeding of Gentiles in Mark becomes a narrative that symbolizes Gentile participation in a messianic banquet. Yet Matthew's version of this feeding narrative from Mark 8 has blurred the identities of the attending crowds so that it is unlikely that Matthew envisioned this as a Gentile group. Matthew also deletes the phrase from Mark 7:27 "Let the children be satisfied first," removing the implication from the Marcan account that Gentiles will eventually receive the benefits of Jesus's mission. Matthew

that her submissiveness is even more pronounced than the centurion's because trust issues come to the forefront. Similar considerations will complicate interactions between White anti-racist activists and especially African Americans. The woman's position of profound humility and lowliness out of the spotlight is an acknowledgment that the relationship she seeks will generally not have room for a focus on her needs and desires because her reception by Jesus is bound up in the history of conflict between their peoples. Likewise, White anti-racists must learn what it means to be imprisoned by stereotypes of White bigotry that, while damaging, represent only the merest fraction of the material, emotional, and spiritual harm endured by those wounded by centuries of institutional racism. White allies like the Canaanite must squarely face the lack of trust and conflict bequeathed on them by history but must nonetheless dare to imagine the new creation that Jesus represents. This work demands the cultivation of a character that imitates their Lord, where they do "not wrangle or cry aloud, nor will anyone hear [their] voice in the streets" (Matt. 12:19–20). They listen and learn, and like the Canaanite, they engage deeply with what the oppressed say, even when it hurts. "When criticized or called out, allies listen, apologize, act accountably, and act differently going forward."[127] In solidarity with those who have no respite from racism and prejudice, allies are endlessly persistent and refuse to back down, take breaks, or retreat into privilege.[128]

In Matthew's version of the conflict at Gadara, the exorcised men and the townspeople represent "Foes" in the work of social justice. Though it is clear that Jesus loves these people as he has loved any in the narrative, sharing the mercy of God with them in freeing them from their oppression, these people prove by their actions that they are not yet ready for community. The exorcism of the demon-possessed Gentiles in Gadara illustrates the warning in 7:6 against offering holy things and pearls to those with volatile tempers or destructive tendencies. The demons leave the men, enter a herd of pigs, and drive the herd to their deaths, which powerfully reveals the forces that may be unleashed when attempting to establish relationships with former enemies

---

changes Mark's identification of this woman from "Syrophoenician" to "Canaanite," which identifies her as an archenemy of the ancient Israelites. The woman's response in Matthew is more submissive, with her references to the "master's table" (Matt. 15:27; cf. Mark 7:28), and her explicit confession that Jesus is Lord (Matt. 15:22; cf. Mark 7:26). In Matthew, Jesus initially refuses even to acknowledge her request and possibly even her presence. When finally consenting to respond to her in 15:26, Jesus implies that the woman and all such Gentiles are dogs who should not receive the blessings reserved for the house of Israel.

127. Utt, "So You Call Yourself an Ally."

128. Utt, "So You Call Yourself an Ally."

in the arena of race relations. These forces may also inhabit our context. We can see racism as a spiritual power of evil that exercises control beyond the ken of a single individual as it inhabits institutions and cultures, blanketing our society like smog.[129] When Jesus breaks off contact with this inhospitable and isolationist community, it is a decision that the Gadarenes ultimately bring on themselves.

We cannot end this consideration of Jesus's enemies in Matthew without an abbreviated look at the Pharisees, the group with whom he has the most intense conflict of all. However, the Pharisees are better described as "Frenemies," the enemies that one finds right in one's household, rather than those typifying encounters with the ethnic Other.[130] Though it is beyond the scope of this chapter to examine the numerous interactions between the Pharisees and Jesus in Matthew, we will keep with the theme of animal metaphors and touch on the three passages where Jesus calls the Pharisees "snakes" and a "brood of vipers" (3:7–12; 12:34; 23:33).

In biblical and postbiblical literature, snakes and other serpents function to signal sin (Gen. 3:1–15), deception (4 Macc. 18:8), and death by poison. In the Testament of Abraham, the true, frightening personification of Death takes on the vivid form of a viper and other snake imagery, while other texts also combine these motifs.[131] For instance, Sirach 21:2 combines poisonousness with sin ("Flee from sin as from a snake; for if you approach sin, it will bite you . . . and can destroy human lives"), and in Psalm 58:3–4 [57:4–5 LXX], the venom of the snake is a metaphor for the lies of wicked sinners (cf. Ps. 140:3 [139:4 LXX]). Thus, when Matthew introduces the Pharisees in 3:7–12 by call-

129. Tatum in *Why Are All the Black Kids Sitting Together* describes racism as a smog that affects everyone in a racialized society.

130. For more information on the nature of the sibling rivalry-like conflict between Jesus and the Pharisees see E. P. Sanders, *Jesus and Judaism*.

131. T. Ab. 17:12–14: "Then Death put off all his comeliness and beauty, and all his glory and the form like the sun with which he was clothed, [13] and put upon himself a tyrant's robe, and made his appearance gloomy and fiercer than all kind of wild beasts, and more unclean than all uncleanness. [14] And he showed to Abraham seven fiery heads of serpents and fourteen faces, (one) of flaming fire and of great fierceness, and a face of darkness, and a most gloomy face of a viper, and a face of a most terrible precipice, and a face fiercer than an asp, and a face of a terrible lion, and a face mixed and snake-like" (trans. Evans, *Pseudepigrapha*).

Cf. T. Ab. 19:14–15: "I showed you also the poisonous wild beasts, asps and basilisks, leopards and lions and lions' whelps, bears and vipers, and in short the face of every wild beast I showed thee, most righteous one, because many men are destroyed by wild beasts, [15] and others by poisonous snakes, serpents and asps and cerastes and basilisks and vipers, breathe out their life and die" (trans. Evans, *Pseudepigrapha*).

ing them a brood of vipers, he describes them as conveyors of the poison of deception, sin, and death, a characterization that shares some of the characteristics of the Gadarenes. They are told that they must produce fruit of repentance in word and deed (3:8; 12:34), exhortations that echo the emphasis on reflection and action in the literature on building alliances. Matthew's Pharisees are hypocrites who teach one thing but do another (23:3). They seem to care only about status and the accoutrements of religious status: fringes, phylacteries, good seats, and fancy titles (23:2–3, 5–12). They are puffed up and puff themselves up, forgetting that we are all siblings under God (23:5–12). Instead of a clear-eyed vision of their posture vis-à-vis the emerging Christian movement, the Pharisees rely on their ancestry and completely miss the opportunity present in the historical moment (3:9; cf. 23:30–33). As such, the Pharisees are the "Frenemies" represented by the vast majority of White Christians who remain in blissful ignorance about the suffering and oppression experienced by their siblings of color. But rather than build a problematic analogy between contemporary White bigotry and the ancient Pharisaic precursors of rabbinic Judaism, I would rather reflect on the way Jesus and the Pharisees were bound together in deeply engaged debate about issues that mattered. Would that the debate about race relations in the church mimicked Jesus and the Pharisees, where they could not escape the other in real life. Each was constantly testing the ideas of the other, desperately fixated on understanding God's will for the whole community.

In this consideration of Matthew's depiction of enemies, we began with a tentative reconstruction of Matthew's social location so that we might adequately contextualize the depictions of those who were Jesus's enemies. By exploring the probable setting for Matthew's composition in post-war Syrian Antioch, we were able to identify at least three social pressures operating at that time of the Gospel's composition. There was Gentile persecution from the Romans and Syrians, both remembered and locally active; hostility from Pharisees in the aftermath of the Jewish War; and internal pressure to welcome local Jesus-believing Gentiles. We imagined that these pressures might have given rise to Matthew's ambivalence about Gentiles. Sometimes he describes them positively and leans into the idea of a Gentile mission, and sometimes he describes them in negative terms, likening them to vicious animals, urging a more careful and distant posture. We then examined the postures of various enemies depicted in Matthew. We saw the blinded and recalcitrant Pharisees as "Frenemies" within the household of faith. Likewise, we saw the violent Gadarenes who are forever frozen in our minds as demon-possessed, violent, and unpredictable as inhospitable "Foes" of social justice. We considered the thoughtful centurion, who actively engages with Jesus on behalf of a valued friend as a "Neighbor" to other oppressed communities, and we described the strategic Canaanite who as an "Ally" acknowledges that the world is not structured in a way that makes room for her needs and desires, but who nonetheless dares to imagine the new community that Jesus represents.

The goal of allyship is not retaliation. I have no desire to see allies in privileged groups shamed or punished or allies in adjacent groups demonized or further marginalized. Instead, allyship is collective action that tries to eliminate the conditions that dehumanize us all, to restrain evil in our midst, and to seek our common good. Each one of us needs to be able to see what *and who* has been previously invisible as we cautiously move toward inhabiting the kinds of relationships that give honor to the gospel, risking pain but persisting in our desire to build the Beloved Community.

3

ASSIMILATION AND THE FAMILY OF GOD
IN THE GOSPEL OF LUKE

. . . remember
for the embattled
there is no place
that cannot be
home
nor is.

—*Audre Lorde, "School Note"*[1]

Apples, Bananas, Coconuts, and Oreos

In his keynote address to the Democratic National Convention in 2004, Barack Obama invoked his personal narrative as a way of characterizing the amazing possibilities inherent in the American Dream: "In no other nation of the world is my story possible." As the story of a product of a White woman from the upper Midwest and a Kenyan father studying on a scholarship in US schools, Obama's account of his rags to riches journey was inspiring and uplifting. Without a doubt, this speech started him on the path to the White House a mere four years later. Yet, one line in the address was particularly memorable for many middle-class African Americans and others familiar with their dilemmas. Obama spoke of eradicating "the slander that says a Black youth with a book is acting White."[2] This line would resonate with Black parents who daily fight the influence of a particular Black subculture that maligns education as a

---

1. From Lorde, *Collected Poems of Audre Lorde*, 276.
2. Transcript: Illinois Senate Candidate Barack Obama at Democratic National Convention, 27 July 2004, http://www.washingtonpost.com/wp-dyn/articles/A19751-2004Jul27.html, accessed 13 August 2010.

sellout to whiteness. "Acting White" is a phrase that would also stimulate painful discussion across generational lines among immigrant families, as revealed by hurtful epithets commonly used in minority youth-culture contexts: apple, banana, coconut, and Oreo cookie, each describing how those Indigenous peoples, Asian Americans, Latinx Americans and Black Americans belong to their respective minoritized communities in looks only—and how these people aren't *truly* members of their cultures of origin on the inside where it really counts. Parents and others ask how behaviors that promote well-being and engagement with other cultures beyond African American culture can become signifiers of disloyalty and loss of particularity. This vignette illustrates the complicated tangle of identity, assimilation, and the negotiation of in-group and out-group loyalties that we engage in this chapter.

At the center of this book is reflection on the implications of a conviction found in early nineteenth-century New Testament scholarship that the presence of Jews and Gentiles in a single community gathered around Jesus as Christ was a problem that permeated theological reflection in the early church.[3] This book suggests that theological reflection on the relationships between Jews and Gentiles in the New Testament is generative for thinking about race relations in the contemporary scene. As a group, the New Testament writings depict varied theological engagement on the problem of mixed communities of Jews and Gentiles in early Christian churches, and nowhere is the contemplation of this fraught relationship more apparent than in Luke-Acts. Likely third among the four Gospels,[4] Luke is concerned about the

---

3. See the analysis of nineteenth-century scholarship in Tyson, *Luke, Judaism, and the Scholars*. Though I disagree with the anti-Jewish tone of this nineteenth-century scholarship, I do think that the basic proposition stands, that the early church wrestled with issues emerging from the incorporation of Gentiles into an essentially Jewish community. To one degree or another, many New Testament authors grapple with tensions emerging around the incorporation of Gentiles, whether in dealing with the tensions within their communities around these issues like Paul and Luke, or whether the problems emerged around sectarian theology which highlighted intra-ethnic group tensions as in Matthew, the Johannine literature, Hebrews, Ephesians, and James.

4. This study assumes the priority of Mark as a source used by Matthew and Luke but rejects the Q hypothesis as an explanation for the verbatim similarities between Matthew and Luke (i.e., the so-called double tradition). Instead, with a growing number of scholars, I think that these verbatim similarities emerge from Luke's direct literary dependence on a version of the Gospel of Matthew. For more on this approach see Goulder, *Luke*; Sanders and Davies, *Studying the Synoptic Gospels*; Franklin, *Luke*; Goodacre, *Case against Q*. Redaction criticism, however, comprises only one of the methods that animate this study, along with literary, historical, and cultural methods. Though my critical perspective on the solution to

significance of Jesus for relationships between the center and the marginalized in Israel. In addition, there is focus on tensions among Jews that emerge from the incorporation of Godfearers and other Gentiles into early Christianity. Luke's Jesus tries to prevail over racial and ethnic conflict by modeling an inclusive, blended, and harmonious family.

The relationship between Judaism and Christianity is an important topic in the interpretation of Luke-Acts, mainly because of the debate about the degree to which these documents exhibit anti-Jewish views.[5] Armed with rich information for analysis, scholars struggle to synthesize disparate evidence. Specifically, interpreters must reconcile the more positive references to Jews and Jewish religious institutions in Luke and the early part of Acts with the much more negative portraits of angry, rioting Jews in the latter part of Acts. The thrice repeated declarations of Paul in Acts 13:46, 18:6, and 28:25–28 that seem to describe an outright abandonment of the mission to Jews cause many to think that Luke's theology is completely supersessionist. If, on the other hand, we understand Luke as Jewish, others might question whether Luke is "Jewish enough." The best solutions to the dilemma will reconcile this disparate data in a way that makes sense of Luke's theological agenda and perhaps clarifies his narrative purposes. But on any definition of ethnic tension, the

---

the Synoptic problem will become apparent at one or two points, the major conclusions in this analysis stand regardless of one's approach to the Synoptic problem.

5. Tyson's *Luke, Judaism, and the Scholars* helpfully surveys the history of scholarship and the range of opinion on the question of anti-Judaism in Acts, and an earlier 1988 edited volume on the subject allows several of these scholars to describe their findings in a succinct medium that facilitates comparison (Tyson, *Luke-Acts and the Jewish People*). Tyson's own influential readings can be found in Tyson, *Images of Judaism in Luke-Acts*. Nineteenth-century scholarship virtually ignored ancient Jewish sources in forming their reconstructions of early Judaism; see, e.g., Baur, *Paul*; Harnack, *Acts of the Apostles*; Harnack, *Luke the Physician*. More recent influential interpretations include Jacob Jervell's description of Luke as a Jew who is at pains to demonstrate that Israel, the heir to the promises of God, is composed of the most pious Jews and righteous God-fearing Gentiles; see Jervell, *Theology of the Acts of the Apostles*; Jervell, *Luke and the People of God*; Jervell, "Church of Jews"; cf. Tyson, *Luke, Judaism, and the Scholars*, 91–109; and Rhamie, "Whiteness, Conviviality and Agency." According to Jack Sanders, Luke sees the Jewish people as intransigent and hostile to the early Jesus movement, a position that imputes a certain amount of anti-Jewish sentiment to the author of Luke-Acts. See J. T. Sanders, "Jewish People in Luke-Acts"; J. T. Sanders, *Jews in Luke-Acts*. Robert Tannehill's reading of Luke-Acts as tragedy also merits attention; see Tannehill, "Israel in Luke-Acts"; Tannehill, "Rejection by Jews and Turning to Gentiles." Contextualized readings of Luke-Acts are also noteworthy: see Liew, "Acts"; Upkong, "Luke"; Smith and Kim, *Toward Decentering the New Testament*; Crowder, "Gospel of Luke"; and D. K. Williams, "Acts of the Apostles."

intergroup clashes between the apostles and Jewish and Gentile unbelievers in Acts qualify as parade examples.

Modern social theorists almost unanimously affirm the idea that ethnicity is socially constructed around a variety of criteria. Different groups will uphold varying identity elements in their self-definition with similar constructions of identity in antiquity. If some privilege putative ancestry and geographic origin, other definitions of group identity will focus on appearance, language, religion, or access to critical social resources such as material wealth. Intergroup conflict can often expose the differing valuations and constructions of identity among groups. It can even form an important aspect of self-identity since some groups may simply understand themselves as a group based on some long-standing opposition to another group. We shall see that the Third Gospel emphasizes the familial aspects of the new community, while Acts narrates the widening breach in the extended family as it becomes more diverse.

While most scholars assume either a Jewish mission or a Gentile one in early Christianity, I would maintain that Luke-Acts represents neither. Instead, the two-volume work describes a Christianity where Gentiles keep parts of the law in deference to its Jewish constituents, but not all of it (cf. Gal. 5:3).[6] In other words, Luke's project is the creation of a blended family with elements of both the old and the new. Suppose at the end of Luke-Acts the goal of a blended mission and community fails as some maintain. In that case, it is a failure that continues in modern social life, given the political fragility of blended multiracial coalitions even today. Notwithstanding the tragic outcomes of Luke's hope for harmony in the context of an extended family as they appear in Acts, we shall see that the Third Gospel depicts the full flower of those hopes since the movement of Acts provides a framing for the ethnic conflict and brokenness that prevailed in Luke's community. While this chapter will focus on the hope of reconciliation that Luke describes in his first volume, chapter 5 will focus on Acts and explore the strategies that Luke deploys in negotiating the painful divisions that were appearing as fissures in the new movement.

This chapter explores analogical rhymes that correlate tensions between Gentile Christians and Jews inside and outside the Christian movement, with modern observations about assimilation, accommodationist cross-cultural or intercultural integration, and the economic tensions that complicate these dynamics. We shall see that Luke's narrative grapples with issues of acceptance and rejection and the stakes involved in the movement between Gentile and

---

6. Cf. Slater who notes the blended or hybrid nature of the missionary project described in Acts. See *Ephesians*, 18.

Jewish cultures. It seems that Luke was no stranger to the painful economic choices faced by the outwardly leaning assimilator or the hurt experienced by the inwardly focused guardian of the hearth and protector of its resources. In Luke-Acts, the principles of loyalty are centrifugal, stretching outward toward the constitution of a new and extended family, yet also centripetal, reaching inward in the sharpened focus of the loyalties and responsibilities that prevail inside of the newly emerging family construct. Below, I explore some of the intergroup dynamics that prevail in assimilation and acculturation processes before engaging three key passages in Luke that showcase his concerns about interfamilial group conflict: the Prophecy of the Broken Family embedded in the sermon at Nazareth in Luke 4:14–30; the Parable of the Broken Family (a.k.a. the Prodigal Son) in 15:11–32; and the Parable of the Trickster (a.k.a. the Unjust Steward) in 16:1–9. In a final section, I discuss how these dynamics work in the context of White grievance about "undeserving" immigrants and people of color, and I explore tensions between African Americans and African immigrants. The moral lapses in all these contexts and stories stem from an inability to imagine or countenance intimacy with outsiders as members of the same family.

Assimilation: Opportunity and Peril

In some respects, the United States is built atop a quixotic ideal since the concept of "a nation of immigrants" holds within it a deep irony. Synonymous in many contexts with the terms people, ethnicity, ethnic group, and race, the nation is usually composed of primarily homogenous people who organize themselves within a shared territory. Anthony Smith, a leading scholar in the study of the origins of nations, suggests that modern nations are the evolutionary progeny of ancient *ethnie*. They, in turn, represent the ancient antecedents of ethnic communities that supplied the raw material for the construction of the state.[7] While some *ethnie* developed into nations through the horizontal integration of peoples in outlying regions proximate to a territorial homeland, others evolved through a vertical mobilization of culture wherein a privileged class politicized the religious or traditional culture of the lower classes.[8]

---

7. Here Smith uses the French term *ethnie* for the English phrase "ethnic group" (A. Smith, "Origins of Nations," 340). *Ethnie* is equivalent to the Greek ἔθνος, and the French terminology is very widely used in ethnic studies literature, likely as an attempt to escape accretions from folk concepts about ethnicity in contemporary use.

8. A. Smith, "Origins of Nations," 340.

Nation-states are thus the result of the structural organization of ethnic groups that added governing structures to a belief in common ancestral origins, one that lives in a land with well-defined territorial borders. The nation-state is the most common result of the social-historical evolution of *ethnie* in modern global politics. Yet, the United States, a territorially bounded nation composed of many ethnic peoples who each have their separate narratives of ancestry, culture, and ancestral homeland, is likely the parade example of the exception that proves the rule. As a nation founded as the colonizing extension of an Anglo-Saxon empire, its history is one in which the tensions between peoples who are resident, forcibly relocated, or attracted to its territory are constantly being tested. US culture, like any culture, is a self-sustaining and self-reproducing system of meanings, beliefs, values, and norms that guide behavior and condition identity.[9] Yet, as a multiethnic and multiracial nation, it is also true that US culture is constantly being renegotiated and contested in search of a unifying identity construct. Who are the *real* Americans?

Cross-cultural engagement, or intercultural adaptation, may be viewed as a composite of four subprocesses: (1) the process of being socialized into one's home culture (*enculturation*); (2) acquisition of communication competency in a new environment (*acculturation*); (3) the process of adopting new cultural norms while simultaneously adjusting one's initial enculturated competency (*deculturation*); (4) the point at which enculturation and deculturation achieve an equilibrium (*assimilation*).[10] Within the US context, then, *acculturation* refers to processes associated with involvement in and movement between a subculture of origin and majority White culture, and we can identify high levels of majority White culture involvement with "assimilation" and high levels of culture of origin involvement with "ethnic identification."[11] In US race relations, assimilation is a process by which an individual from a minority culture of origin begins to acquire the beliefs, values, and practices of the dominant White cultural milieu with the hope or expectation that the

9. Geertz, *Interpretation of Cultures*; Lyttle, Barker, and Cornwell, "Adept through Adaptation." "Culture" is a difficult term that has been defined in at least one hundred and sixty different ways according to Andrea Moore in "Confused or Multicultural."

10. Lyttle, Barker, and Cornwell, "Adept through Adaptation," 687–88.

11. Smokowski, Roderick, and Baccalao use "acculturation" as an umbrella term for the group of processes that concern the movement between two cultures; see "Acculturation and Latino Family Processes," 295. LaFromboise, Coleman, and Gerton, on the other hand, use the term "acculturation" to refer to one of five models of cultural involvement; in particular the kind of cultural involvement associated with second culture acquisition; see "Psychological Impact of Biculturalism," 397.

dominant White culture will accept the individual as a bona fide member of that culture.[12] Though assimilation is often depicted as the preferred cultural outcome for marginalized US subcultures or third culture internationals, researchers studying these phenomena consistently report that the opposite process achieves better results. In other words, there is a positive relationship between self-esteem and high levels of ethnic identification among African Americans, Latinx, and Whites alike, a result that flies in the face of assimilation as a social "ideal."[13]

In measuring assimilation, some researchers assess whether a minority group is similar or dissimilar to the majority culture in terms of language use, employment patterns, intermarriage, naturalization, and residential location, and they correlate these similarities with personal, familial, and community stress levels.[14] Once considered the ideal, the "melting pot" image for society in the United States has become increasingly problematic for many, and people who advocate for assimilation as a strategy for race relations in modern society are increasingly isolated.[15] Today, more and more theorists reckon that assimilation, which assumes a fundamental sameness between the assimilator and the receiving community, entails a loss of identity for the individual. Therefore, assimilation also undermines how minority group identities preserve the group's distinctive history and heritage.[16] If *e Pluribus Unum* ("out of many comes one") remains the motto inscribed on the great seal of the

12. Nagel, "Rethinking Geographies of Assimilation," 400.

13. Smokowski, Roderick, and Baccalao, "Acculturation and Latino Family Processes," 297. It is important to add, however, that identity construction is much more complex for global multicultural persons who have had deep exposure to multiple international cultures, and who may experience a sense of cultural homelessness. See Hanek, Lee, and Brannen, "Individual Differences"; Tanu, "Toward an Interdisciplinary Analysis."

14. Nagel, "Rethinking Geographies of Assimilation," 402.

15. E.g., McWhorter, "Getting over Identity"; McWhorter, *Losing the Race*; Cosby and Poussaint, *Come On People*.

16. Salomone, "Transnational Schooling," 385. Later in the same essay, Salomone describes two important concepts debated in current literature: segmented assimilation and transnational citizenship. Segmented assimilation refers to the global observation that some immigrants experience upward assimilation into a White-dominated middle class, while others assimilate downward into a minority-dominated underclass (see pp. 402–3). Transnational citizenship refers to a new form of identification that is not possible without a global economy and technological and economical improvements in transportation and communication. This kind of citizenship and assimilation pattern involves thick "multi-stranded" connections between the former and new contexts, up to and including dual citizenship—some estimate that up to half of all nations recognize this possibility—allegiances that are manifest most concretely in monetary remittances to the former context (pp. 388–90).

United States, the romanticism of that sentiment now leaves many marginalized communities cold. A desire for unity is no doubt a worthy aspiration when it comes to policy and other goals of statecraft. While this goal may have the best economic interests of those communities at the forefront, it represents the death of identity for many considered the Other. Even if minority communities long to participate in the American dream to gain economic and social parity with members of the dominant White culture, this dream stands at the site of a deep ambivalence if lost identity is the cost of access to that dream. As Kendi puts it, "Assimilationist ideas are racist ideas."[17]

For example, some investigators report a high negative association between acculturation and the degree of family conflict.[18] Assimilators often face the hostility of contemporaries, both those who reject the idea that the host culture is or should be normative and those who cannot see any "goods" worth having in the host culture.[19] Assimilators have lower levels of self-esteem in comparison with those with high levels of ethnic identification. Further, research shows high levels of stress, isolation, and alienation associated with failure to assimilate due to hostility coming both from within the culture of origin and from the dominant White culture. With skin color so determinative of status in public discourse, many people of color find that they *cannot* ultimately assimilate. Persons who desire assimilation and who seek to be accepted by the White culture may be only partially accepted or even ultimately rejected by that culture due to the barriers posed by ethnicity, skin color, language, or speech patterns.[20] Assimilators experience excessive stress while learning the new behaviors of the dominant White culture and shedding behaviors associated with the culture of origin. Stress manifests in decreasing levels of family cohesion and familism[21] as adolescents turn from the family of origin to peers in the dominant White culture as reference points.[22] Thus, assimilation causes rifts in families as the elders lament what appears to them to be a cavalier rejection of revered and honored traditions and ways of relating by younger people who adopt the practices and values of the dominant culture.

---

17. Kendi, *Antiracist*, 29.

18. Smokowski, Roderick, and Baccalao, "Acculturation and Latino Family Processes," 297.

19. LaFromboise, Coleman, and Gerton, "Psychological Impact of Biculturalism," 397.

20. LaFromboise, Coleman, and Gerton, "Psychological Impact of Biculturalism," 396.

21. *Familism* has to do with the primacy of the family over the individual, as famously articulated by Mr. Spock of Star Trek fame: "The needs of the many outweigh the needs of the few." See Smokowski, Roderick, and Baccalao, "Acculturation and Latino Family Processes," 297.

22. LaFromboise, Coleman, and Gerton, "Psychological Impact of Biculturalism," 397.

Elders find it difficult to countenance the youths' penchant for an outward-looking focus on being accepted by the dominant White culture at the expense of cultural traditions.

The benefits of assimilation are understandable in terms of improved economic conditions, living standards, and the possibility of being accepted by most of one's peers. However, many find that the high costs of assimilation in terms of personal identity and affiliation with one's elders, extended family, and cultural traditions are ultimately not worth the gains associated with dominant White culture acceptance, especially given the barriers that inhibit full acceptance and economic gains that are promised but never fully materialize. It is tragically easy these days to disrupt the assimilation of new immigrants and people of color. All it seems to take is one racially charged event in the media to overset years of intentional assimilation that result in people being lumped together into crude bins. Indeed, the rise of hate crimes and racial animus during the Trump presidency can be understood as a backlash in the wake of the election of the first African American president, along with the gender and ethnic diversity of his cabinet, advisers, and high court nominees. Similarly, the Asian American community, long regarded as a "model minority" by those idealizing the assimilationist ideal, also became the unwilling target of increased hostility and hate crimes during the COVID-19 pandemic. President Trump's racist penchant to label the novel coronavirus "the China Flu" contributed to a toxic environment for the pan-Asian community, as he tried to deflect blame for a situation that was spiraling out of control.

Some in minority communities accept the assimilationist ideal as the only rational response for achieving happiness. However, more and more people are beginning to conclude that "successful" integration into the dominant culture in the United States must be accompanied by a sense of personal identity rooted in the history and culture of ethnic particularity to survive the stresses of a sometimes hostile majority White culture. Paradoxically, ethnic particularity and a strong sense of ethnic identification need to precede total or partial assimilation into majority culture norms and customs. Today there is an increasing emphasis on the hybridity and mixedness of bicultural attachments.[23] Scholars working in racial and ethnic studies stress the political value

23. Biculturalism can be defined as a process of acculturation between assimilation and ethnic identification. This process describes a posture held by minority groups vis-à-vis a dominant culture that is marked by a moderate to high level of involvement in both the culture of origin and the target culture. Biculturalism is characterized by affirmation of blended traditions, foods, norms, and languages from minority and majority cultures. While biculturalism is one possibility that may result from multi-ethnic ancestry, processes of

of transgressing oppressive boundaries. Such an emphasis also builds a holistic identity for the outwardly focused would-be assimilator as well. It is becoming more common for immigrants and other people of color to reject assumptions about the desirability of assimilation and call for revisions in the definition of "mainstream" and the normalization of White middle-class society as the target of assimilation.[24] Such activists reject the notion of sameness implicit in assimilation and call for greater tolerance for cultural diversity in the public sphere. More recent studies find that previous assumptions about the eventual triumph of assimilation processes in US civil society have underestimated the dual allegiances and tendencies toward biculturalism within US minoritized subcultures. The same is true of multicultural identity vis-à-vis the "third culture" transnational attachments of other immigrants.[25]

In some ways, the advent of mixed congregations of Jews and Gentiles in early Christianity has analogies with the American myth of a "nation of immigrants." Many scholars hypothesize that the author of Luke-Acts was a Gentile, possibly like the Godfearers mentioned in Acts who were attracted to Judaism but had not become proselytes.[26] By contrast, Gifford Rhamie reads the author of Luke-Acts as a Jew. Rhamie identifies Luke as a nonrabbinic Afroasiatic diasporic Hellenistic Jew who was "in the imperial world, but not of it" and who writes with a "double consciousness" and "use of imperialist's tools" that should not be taken as indicative of solidarity with Rome's politics.[27] In Rhamie's reading, Luke was a cosmopolitan with international interests in multiple peoples, politics, and religious discourses, likely from the urban con-

bicultural acquisition may also apply to people who self-identify with a single ethnic group when they acquire dominant culture characteristics while also maintaining high levels of involvement with their culture of origin.

24. Nagel, "Rethinking Geographies of Assimilation," 401, 403.

25. Nagel, "Rethinking Geographies of Assimilation," 400–407; Salomone, "Transnational Schooling," 388–90. For more on third culture identity see Hanek, Lee, and Brannen, "Individual Differences"; Lyttle, Barker, and Cornwell, "Adept through Adaptation"; Moore, "Confused or Multicultural"; Navarrete and Jenkins, "Cultural Homelessness."

26. E.g., for Luke as a Gentile see Keener, *Acts*, 1:1–247, 402–6; for Luke as a Jew see Jervell, *Theology of the Acts of the Apostles*, 5–6. For more on this topic see Rhamie, "Whiteness, Conviviality and Agency," 192n529.

27. Rhamie, "Whiteness, Conviviality and Agency," 202–9. Rhamie identifies Luke as an *Afroasiatic* Hellenistic Jew to highlight the multiple cultural influences extant within the geographic region generally referred to by biblical scholars as the ancient Near East (ANE), which encompasses the peoples in West Africa, North Africa, East Africa, Ethiopia down to the Horn of Africa, all of Arabia, Palestine, and Syria. Following Cain Hope Felder's usage, Rhamie deploys the term politically to center and deepen the epistemic impact on students of the period of the profound cultural and social interconnection of these African peoples in the period of interest; see "Whiteness, Conviviality and Agency," 25n94, 61–63.

text of Antioch-on-the-Orontes in Syria. Through that location, he would have been exposed to many Jewish subcultures and thus more willing to receive these more marginalized groups as authentically Jewish, as well as those thoroughly fluent in the Greco-Roman literary and political discourse:

> Luke writes with the . . . anticolonial sensibility. . . . But Luke's theology, I argue, is written . . . from the perspective . . . of a Hellenised Syrian, Jewish initiate of The Way. It is difficult to tell the extent of his generational descent as Jewish. Perhaps that is not important. What is perceivable is a social location that is of an educated artisan who is probably subordinate to an elite patron such as Theophilus. Yet, if he writes from the margins of a subcultural Jewish adherent, then his Hellenised, diasporic gaze could likely antagonise the centrality of the Jewish cultic institution. . . . However, in the process, all Jews—Judaeans, Samaritans, proselytes and diasporans—are reclaimed by Luke as Jews; and all Graeco-Roman Gentiles—including Godfearers—are extended the same hand of fellowship. . . . It is an ethnoreligious reclamation, an invitation of unification, where all the people groups (or nations) are persuaded to come to the Hebrew God.[28]

In other words, Luke is, in Rhamie's eyes, a bicultural denizen of the period, equally at home in non-rabbinic Afroasiatic Hellenistic Judaism as he was in well-educated Greco-Roman society. He had a posture characterized by an affirmation of blended traditions, foods, norms, and languages from minority and majority cultures. No matter how one understands Luke's origins as an author, his writing possesses a sincere interest in cultivating bicultural sensitivities, manifested in his command of the scriptures of Israel on the one hand and his deep familiarity with Greco-Roman culture, literary conventions, and politics on the other. In chapter 5, we will explore the strategies that Luke uses to promote biculturalism in Acts, but in this chapter, we will explore some of the implications of acculturation processes as they appear in the gospel narrative. I suggest that the Third Gospel was written for Gentiles and diasporic Jews to navigate unfamiliar Pharisaic and emerging rabbinic Jewish cultures. Specifically, the Messiah's mission to regather dispersed Jews along with the anticipation of the outwardly focused mission to Gentiles prompts something analogous to the pain of interfamilial stress associated with assimilation processes. As an earnest, acculturated, bicultural cosmopolitan, Luke may not have completely understood the bitterness of Jesus's contemporaries toward the mission to the outcast. However, we can discern how this anger mimics

---

28. Rhamie, "Whiteness, Conviviality and Agency," 201–3.

the stress and sense of betrayal that families feel when one of their own has an interest in outsiders that is like a cultural defection. We shall see that the hostility of Jesus's close associates in Nazareth in Luke 4:14–30 rhymes with the high negative association between assimilation and family conflict, and the economic tensions bubbling up beneath this conflict. Next, we look at the parable of the Broken Family in Luke 15:11–32, traditionally known as the parable of the Prodigal Son. We will see that this story revisits the pain of families strained by the pressure of receiving back those who have wandered off into a flirtation with a foreign majority culture. We shall see that this story has economic implications as well. In both episodes, Luke's interest in affirming his dominant Jewish culture prevents a wholesale disparagement of that culture, a goal that he achieves through careful appeal to the idea of "family" as the operative framework. Finally, a brief look at similarities between the parables of the Broken Family in 15:11–32 and the Trickster Steward in 16:1–9 ends the next section and highlights the economic dynamics that complicate discussions about assimilation, identity, and resistance.

The Prophecy of the Broken Family (Luke 4:14–30)

Traditionally known as the Sermon at Nazareth, many agree that the prophecy of the Broken Family in Luke 4:14–30 represents Luke's version of a similar scene from Mark 6 that has been augmented with material from his independent sources.[29] This episode forecasts the manner and reception of Jesus's ministry while also bringing together several other Lukan thematic interests: the radical reversal where the mighty are brought low and the lowly are exalted; an interest in help for the poor; the similarity of Jesus's prophetic ministry to episodes in the Elijah/Elisha narrative; and Luke's concern for the Gentile mission.[30] The programmatic, liberative nature of this episode is well known, but few have understood the full extent of its prophetic significance.[31]

---

29. Bultmann, *Synoptic Tradition*, 32–33; Fitzmyer, *Luke*, 1:526–27; Evans, *Luke*, 266–75; and Tannehill, "Mission of Jesus," 66. Others see this episode as originating from Luke's use of unique material in L: e.g., Kimball, "Jesus' Exposition of Scripture"; P. D. Miller, "Luke 4:16–21," 418; I. H. Marshall, *Luke*, 177–80; Tuckett, "Luke 4,16–30, Isaiah and Q." See I. H. Marshall, *Luke*, 179–80 for a summary of many of the views held by the above scholars.

30. Kolasny, "Luke 4:16–30," 69. The Jubilee imagery also hints at Lukan interests in the plight of the poor and the use of wealth.

31. On the programmatic nature of the episode see Conzelmann, *Theology of St. Luke*, 31–37, 221; Bornkamm, *Jesus of Nazareth*, 75; Tannehill, "Mission of Jesus"; Tiede, *Prophecy and History in Luke-Acts*, 19; Hill, "Rejection of Jesus at Nazareth," 161; J. A. Sanders, "From

Though many consider 4:14–15 transitional and not really a part of this pericope, these verses establish Jesus's presence in the district of Galilee and indicate that his ministry there was well received and accompanied by the same kind of miracles that will continue to mark his activity in the rest of the Gospel beyond this episode. More significantly, the careful mention of Jesus's spreading fame in Galilee in 4:14–15 also hints at the importance of the contrast between Jesus's positive reception in Galilee with the tense conflict in Nazareth. Still, other features in Luke's redaction communicate his focus on the intimacy of the setting. For example, the striking use of the language in 4:16 to describe Jesus's hometown is much more vivid than the simple reference to a "homeland" in Matthew and Mark. Where Mark 6:1 and Matthew 13:54 mention Jesus's return to his "hometown,"[32] Luke adds the longer phrase "Nazareth, where he was nurtured"; another reference to Jesus's hometown appears in 4:23 as well.[33] These touches help us understand Luke's emphasis on the intimacy of this setting, a context in which Jesus is interacting with bros and homies—that is, friends, family, and well-known neighbors.

One major issue in 4:17–22 concerns the presence or intensity of Jubilee imagery in the Isaiah quotation in verses 18–19. Some think Jesus has proclaimed the dawning of the great day of economic liberation from debt and realignment of capital based on how the Jubilee imagery has been added to the quotation from Isaiah 61:1, blending Isaiah 61:1–2 with Isaiah 58:6. On the other hand, some scholars reject the idea of an added emphasis on the Jubilee concept and alternately suggest that these verses convey that the oppressed are now free from sin versus free from debts, the former of these themes appearing often in Luke-Acts.[34] Since the rest of the gospel narrative is an exposition of how Luke

---

Isaiah 61 to Luke 4," 104; Siker, "First to the Gentiles," 75. According to Fitzmyer, "Luke has deliberately put this story at the beginning of the public ministry to encapsulate the entire ministry of Jesus and the reaction to it" (*Luke*, 1:529). For a general overview of how the programmatic character of Luke 4:16–30 is worked out in the rest of Luke-Acts, see Stanton, *Gospels*, 90–95, and Kimball, "Jesus' Exposition of Scripture," 180.

32. The English "hometown" being a translation of the Greek πατρίδα αὐτοῦ.

33. The marked use of a perfect periphrastic in 4:16 adds emphasis and heightens attention to Jesus's return to his hometown: "Nazareth where he had been nurtured" (Ναζαρά, οὗ ἦν τεθραμμένος).

34. Luke replaces the phrase "to heal the brokenhearted" from Isa. 61:1 with "to send away the oppressed in freedom" (ἀποστεῖλαι τεθραυσμένους ἐν ἀφέσει; Luke 4:18), a phrase which seems to be a reference to the day of Jubilee from Isa. 58:6. Because the deleted reference to healing the brokenhearted fits well with the gospel narrative, the substitution of phrases was probably motivated by the desire to include a phrase containing the word ἄφεσις, meaning "release" or "freedom," which is used frequently in Luke with reference to

saw Jesus's ministry as an interpretation of this quotation, I suggest that Luke blends a metaphorical and literal understanding of these issues. Luke seems to adopt a more metaphorical approach concerning the Jubilee idea of freedom from captivity and oppression. The particular words *prisoners* and *oppressed*[35] used in 4:18–19 make no further appearance in Luke-Acts. However, a different word for oppression appears in Acts 10:38, where the idea is spiritualized when the text says that Jesus healed "all who the devil oppressed." On the other hand, the Jubilee imagery is manifested in Luke's preference for the plight of the poor. Luke concretizes the beatitude about the blessings on the "poor in spirit" from Matthew 5:3. He illustrates this blessedness in terms of ultimate salvation and implied rewards in the stories about Lazarus and the rich man and the widow's offering (16:19–31; 21:1–4), as well as in calling for the wealthy to administer concrete aid to the poor (14:13, 21; 18:22; 19:8). Though Luke contains only one episode involving the healing of a blind man (18:35–43), references to these kinds of miracles also appear in summary statements that point to the idea that salvation involves material and physical conditions as well as spiritual ones (7:21–22; 14:13; cf. 14:21).[36] Thus, Luke's concern for lifting spiritual and physical burdens from the poor and marginalized is clear. In Luke 4:18–19 then, Jesus inaugurates an era of Jubilee thinking with both horizontal economic implications and vertical spiritual components.

A major puzzle in 4:14–30 concerns the origin of the tension that boils over into the Nazarethites'[37] murderous rage at the end of the pericope in 4:28–29. Jeremias famously focused on the question in 4:22 ("Is this not Joseph's son?") as the first indication of hostilities toward Jesus and a rejection of Jesus's mes-

---

the forgiveness of sin. In the LXX the word ἄφεσις appears frequently in connection with the Jubilee laws, which, though never practiced in ancient Israel, were meant to restore the fortunes of the poor, eradicate accumulated debt, and realign the distribution of capital so that ancestral lands would return to their original owners every fiftieth year. Interpreters who do see Jubilee imagery concretely present in Luke include Hertig, "Jubilee Mission of Jesus"; Kimball, "Jesus' Exposition of Scripture," 186–88; P. D. Miller, "Luke 4:16–21," 419–20; contra L. T. Johnson, *Luke*, 81. Darrell L. Bock, however, affirms the presence of Jubilee imagery while still maintaining that the primary referent is spiritual release for sin in the context of Jesus's ministry; see Bock, *Luke*, 1:406–10.

35. Prisoners: αἰχμαλώτοις; oppressed: τεθραυσμένους.

36. The similarity of 7:22 to the quotation in 4:18–19 is especially significant, in that 7:22 seems to point to a narrative fulfillment of the miracles prophesied in the inaugural sermon.

37. Throughout, I use the term *Nazarethites* when referring to Jesus's hometown residents, distinguishing them from *Nazarenes*, a term often associated with believers in the early Jesus community.

sianic status.[38] For Jeremias, the townspeople express doubt about Jesus's ministry in 4:22. He focuses on the ambiguity in the phrase "they were testifying about him and marveling"[39] in 4:22 and thinks that the words convey negative attitudes toward Jesus's ministry. Contrary to Jeremias, however, Luke's use of these verbs "testifying" and "marveling" is actually always positive or neutral elsewhere in Luke-Acts, a fact that led other interpreters to discount Jeremias's interpretation that the townspeople are hostile in 4:22 and to look elsewhere for the cause of the friction between Jesus and the people in his hometown.

Noting that Luke's account deletes the explicit interpretation about the people's anger as in Mark 6:3 that "they were offended at him," more recent interpreters pointedly see Jesus as the provocateur in Luke's account in 4:23. In Luke, there is no explicit mention of the townspeople's anger until after Jesus gives an interpretation of the proverb. This interpretative trajectory is evident in the NLT translation of 4:23, which renders Jesus's words thus: "You will undoubtedly quote me this proverb: 'Physician, heal yourself'—meaning, 'Do miracles here in your hometown like those you did in Capernaum.'" In context, Jesus's use of the proverb suggests that a messianic ministry rejects the favoritism that a miracle worker might be expected to show his hometown friends and closest kin. In this exchange, Jesus says that his ministry is not limited to an inward focus on Nazareth but may include healings and miracles for others, including even traditional enemies (4:23–27).[40] Immediately thereafter, the townspeople erupt in anger in 4:28–29, where the people drive Jesus out of town with the intention of tossing him off a cliff.[41] It is difficult to avoid

---

38. Jeremias, *Jesus' Promise to the Nations*, 44. Jeremias's interpretation exploits the fact that "testifying" (μαρτυρέω) can be positive or negative depending on context, though the word is never negative in Luke-Acts. Instead, throughout it is either neutral (Acts 10:43; 13:22; 14:3; 15:8; 22:5; 23:11; 26:5) or outright positive (Acts 6:3; 10:22; 16:2; 22:12). See also Bock, *Luke*, 1:413–15; Hill, "Rejection of Jesus at Nazareth," 164; I. H. Marshall, *Luke*, 178; Siker, "First to the Gentiles," 79–80. Cf. Hertig, "Jubilee Mission of Jesus," 170.

39. Testifying: ἐμαρτύρουν αὐτῷ; Marveling: ἐθαύμαζον.

40. Kimball, "Jesus' Exposition of Scripture," 196–98.

41. That the crowd does not react negatively until after v. 27 has been recognized by Bajard, "Péricope de Nazareth," 166; Koet, *Interpretation of Scriptures in Luke-Acts*, 39–41. Other scholars likewise resist the idea that the crowd is angry in Luke 4:22 as they are in the parallel episode in Mark. Flender rightly regards Jeremias's exegesis as "highly artificial" (*St. Luke*, 152–53). Emerson B. Powery notes, "There is no exegetical evidence that the audience's question [in Luke 4:22] is spoken negatively" (*Jesus Reads Scripture*, 204n59). I might add further that if there are allusions to Jubilee imagery in Jesus's sermon as some maintain, it is difficult to understand why these Nazarethite peasants would reject a sermon preaching a year of Jubilee, however literal or metaphorical these references to remission

the conclusion that the people's anger is triggered by the idea that the bounty of Jubilee blessings is to be extended beyond the borders of Israel. It may be that the Nazarethites resent the possibility that Israel's Jubilee resources will be shared with outsiders.

Bridget Green's womanist reading of a different passage in Luke suggests a fruitful direction for our exploration of Luke 4:14–30. Green explores Mississippi civil rights activist Fannie Lou Hamer's proto-womanist hermeneutic found in her 1971 speech entitled "Nobody's Free until Everybody's Free." The speech was one that Hamer delivered at the founding of the National Women's Political Caucus. Green leverages Hamer's interest in poverty-relieving initiatives for children of all races as an interpretive prism for understanding Jesus's focus on children in Luke 18:15–17, where Jesus teaches about the sociopolitical shifts in the kingdom of God that value and protect those who are the most marginalized.[42] Both Jesus's message and Hamer's message work in their respective political realities by envisioning a social landscape where everybody is free, including those not usually included in such spaces.[43]

But there are also associative linkages between Hamer's speech and Jesus's sermon at Nazareth regarding this theme of prophetic inclusiveness. At one point in Hamer's speech, she reflects on the irony of the language in the US Constitution that proclaims that American society is based on the consent of the governed. She says that she laughs whenever she thinks about the phrase "with the people, for the people, and by the people" because it's just not true, and for Hamer, it never has been true.[44] This irony forms a strong counterpoint with Hamer's convictions that her problems as an excluded citizen are similar to those of White women, though she implies that Black women have a longer-standing understanding of the nature of their oppression than the White women of her day do. Jesus's interaction with the Jews at Nazareth seems to involve a similarly limited horizon. Their enthusiasm about the prospect of Jubilee blessings and their prospective liberation is inwardly focused and does not seem to be extended with generosity toward the other conquered Semitic peoples on their borders who were likewise crushed by Rome. The Nazarethites are not concerned about the oppression beyond their borders, and neither do they understand how their own oppression is linked to it. As Green puts it: "shared

---

of debts would eventually prove. Kimball thinks the crowd is unfavorable as a result of the Elijah/Elisha comments (Kimball, "Jesus' Exposition of Scripture," 196–97).

42. B. A. Green, "'Nobody's Free until Everybody's Free.'"

43. B. A. Green, "'Nobody's Free until Everybody's Free,'" 291.

44. Hamer, "Nobody's Free until Everybody's Free," 136.

racial [or ethnic] oppression does not guarantee solidarity or consideration for shared justice."[45] Thus, Hamer's speech and the Nazareth episode both exhibit a prophetic, expansive concern for the Other. Jesus emphasizes concern for the outsiders adjacent to his community when he alludes to episodes where God lavishes mercy on outsiders like the widow of Zarephath and Naaman the Syrian in 4:25–27. These allusions are apparently so striking that they prompt a fit of immediate and violent anger from the Nazarethites in 4:28. Similarly, Hamer's speech is replete with her boundary-spanning inclusiveness and a concern for poverty-relieving initiatives for all children and multiracial political action:

> The changes we have to have in this country are going to be for liberation of all people because nobody's free until everybody's free.[46]

> I couldn't say today that I'm fighting for equal rights. . . . I've passed equal rights and I'm fighting for human rights, not only for the black man, for the red man, but for the white man and for all the people of this country.[47]

By expanding her sphere of concern to other ethnic groups, Hamer risks the same kind of exclusivist backlash from her own people that Jesus encounters in Luke 4. Perhaps she anticipates this reaction when she makes it clear that she is in no way trying to disassociate herself from her people: "And I'm not fighting to liberate myself from the black man in the South because, so help me, God, he's had as many and more severer problems than I've had." So Hamer's commitment to solidarity with other oppressed communities in no way diminishes her identification and concern for her own people.

I suggest that the placement, programmatic function, and details of the episode in Luke 4 anticipate the possibility of backlash to Jesus's inclusive vision of family that reclaims marginalized Jews while adding new Gentile siblings. Thus, I read the episode as a prophecy about responses to Jesus's ministry in Israel that will occur later in Luke-Acts. After Jesus's short sermon in 4:17–21, the Nazarethites are understandably excited because they, like we, heard the echoes of the Old Testament Jubilee ideal of canceled debts and a redistribution of capital to alleviate structural poverty. This reaction is not dissimilar in tone from the reports about praise for Jesus described in 4:15. Excited about Jesus's understanding of the prophets and proclamation about fulfilling these

---

45. B. A. Green, "'Nobody's Free until Everybody's Free,'" 305.
46. Hamer, "Nobody's Free until Everybody's Free," 136.
47. Hamer, "Nobody's Free until Everybody's Free," 137.

promises, these villagers who had long been intimate with him and his family eagerly anticipate receiving the fruit of Jesus's newly manifest authority (4:14). Jesus's use of the proverb about a physician's hometown obligations indicates that he detects in their marvel and excitement a readiness to ask for special favors based on the intimacy of their relationship with the homegrown prophet. In other words, Jesus doesn't provoke the anger of the Nazarethites so much as he anticipates and prophesies their resistance to his message.

Others have noted the way that Elijah imagery operates in this programmatic text and throughout Luke-Acts. For example, the story of Elijah's visit to the widow of Zarephath (1 Kings 17) mentioned by Jesus in his "inaugural" sermon in Luke 4:25–26 occurs at the very outset of Elijah's ministry in the narrative in 1 Kings. Similarly, Elisha's healing of Naaman, a Gentile military attaché dispatched to the Israelite court (2 Kings 5:1–14), is discussed in 4:26 and parallels Peter's ministry to the God-fearing Roman centurion named Cornelius in Acts 10–11. Besides Jesus's inaugural sermon in Nazareth, the widow of Zarephath narrative is referenced elsewhere in Luke-Acts. Notably, Elijah's healing of the widow's son (1 Kings 17:17–22) is paralleled by Jesus's raising of the widow's son in Luke 7:12–15.[48] More subtly, the famine alluded to in the widow of Zarephath story finds an analog in Acts 11:28 where, as with Elijah and the widow, a famine brings Jews and Gentiles into fellowship when the Gentile Christians in Antioch send Paul and Barnabas to the church in Jerusalem with money for food.[49] Indeed, a reprise on this famine motif may also be at work in the conversion of Cornelius in Acts 10–11. Peter's hunger in Acts 10:10 accompanies the opening vision of clean and unclean food that prepares Peter for his contact with Cornelius. Further, we will see below that this motif of famine and hunger as motivation for healing divisions will appear again in the Luke 15 parable.[50]

Most interpreters recognize the fact that Jesus's mention of Elijah and Elisha anticipates Luke's interest in the Gentile mission, and some see the rejection of the Nazarethites as a prophecy that anticipates the rejection of the gospel by the Jews and the turning to the Gentiles narrated in Acts.[51] Yet this

48. Crockett, "Luke 4:25–37." Siker notes that 4:18–30 is fulfilled in 7:1–23 when Jesus's miracles mimic the Elijah and Elisha miracles referred to in Luke 4:25–27. See "First to the Gentiles," 86–89.

49. Crockett, "Luke 4:25–37," 181.

50. See Judette Kolasny's extension of Crockett's thesis in "Luke 4:16–30."

51. Anderson says the rejection in Luke 4:28–29 is fulfilled by the rejection by the Jewish people at the end of Acts, but goes too far in saying that Jesus is the one rejecting the people ("Broadening Horizons," 272). Cf. I. Howard Marshall who suggests that Nazareth begins

episode functions prophetically not only regarding the Gentiles; more importantly, it also prophesies the breach in Israel. In Luke 4:32, we see how Jesus's reception in Capernaum forms a vivid contrast with his rejection at Nazareth in 4:28–29. The Capernaumites' desire to have Jesus stay (4:42) could not be more striking when compared with the Nazarethites' willingness to kill him and throw him out of town (4:30). There is a deliberate contrast between the Nazarethites' parochial focus on their own town and what Jesus has done for those beyond the confines of his homeland in Capernaum and the other cities in Galilee, a reversal of what might be generally expected concerning duty to family and intimate associates versus one's responsibilities to outsiders, as indeed Jesus's citation of the physician proverb indicates.[52] Thus, this pericope not only forecasts Jesus's rejection by the people at the end of the gospel,[53] but it also prophetically illustrates the divisions in Judaism that will become apparent in Acts.

The emphasis on the intimacy of the setting in Luke 4:14–30 suggests that we should construe the Nazarethites' anger as analogous to the sense of betrayal that minority communities feel when one of their own rejects them in favor of a fascination for outsiders who are, after all, still hostile. After Jesus's short sermonic interpretation of Isaiah 61, the villagers in Nazareth are understandably excited about the possibility that in Jesus they have a prophet proclaiming the advent of an era of Jubilee release from debt, sin, and suffering.[54] Yet, Jesus's use of the proverb about a physician's hometown obligations indicates that he detects in their marvel and excitement a readiness to ask for special favors based on the intimacy of their relationship with him. Jesus's words prompt the hometown crowd to anger and resistance, a microcosm of a later breach in Israel that will divide those who eagerly participate in the new community gathered around him and those who resist it.[55] The Nazarethites'

---

to symbolize the Jewish nation in this pericope in Jesus's implied threat to them that others would be more responsive to the gospel message than they (*Luke*, 178). It is better to see here an example from Israel's history regarding the danger involved in rejecting a prophet and his message. For more on this interpretation see Bock, *Luke*, 1:417–18.

52. See, e.g., Fitzmyer, *Luke*, 1:528; Siker, "First to the Gentiles," 84–85. While I agree with Siker that this episode does participate in the reversal theme in Luke, I do *not* concur with his later suggestion that this reversal signals that Jesus's mission means that the Jewish mission is secondary to the primary mission to Gentiles.

53. H. Anderson, "Broadening Horizons."

54. See especially J. B. Green, *Luke*, 211–13. For more on the Jubilee imagery, especially the issue of release from debt, see Ringe, "Luke 4:16–44."

55. So also Siker, "First to the Gentiles," 83. Siker adds that this reaction epitomizes Israel's expectation that they are the immediate beneficiaries of Jesus's ministry. This fits with

anger is analogous to the stress that families feel when one of their own has an interest in others that seems to be nothing short of a cultural defection. Though the correspondence is not perfect, modern stress about assimilation may reflect sentiments similar to the Nazarethites' tangled emotions about intimate betrayals and scarce economic resources, as economic pressures drive the assimilation and perceived betrayals among immigrants in the first place. Yet, as we will see below, the parable of the Prodigal Son powerfully demonstrates that fear of scarcity makes it possible to exclude the Other even when we know them to be members of the family.

The Parable of the Broken Family (Luke 15:11–32)

If the Nazarethites' anger mimics some of the stress and sense of betrayal that families feel when one of their own seems to engage in cultural defection, the parable of the Broken Family vividly illustrates this pain. It includes the strain that families can experience under the pressures of assimilating the marginalized, the righteous indignation that can greet the perpetrator of a cultural betrayal, and the unwavering hope to preserve the family and restore loyalty to it. Below I will consider the passage in its context and review the prominent literary features in the parable.

Luke 15:11–32 is one of the best-known passages in the New Testament. As the longest parable in the New Testament, this Christian favorite still generates a surprising amount of debate about some of its particulars, especially regarding the parable's function in its Lukan context. Traditionally known as the parable of the Prodigal Son, many interpreters focus on the first half of this two-part story, virtually ignoring the mention of *two* sons at both the beginning and end of the parable (15:11, 32). Variously designated the parable of the Waiting Father,[56] the Forgiving Father,[57] the Compassionate Father and

---

the overall trajectory of Luke-Acts, and accounts for the tension between Gentile Christians and Jews both inside (Acts 15:1–23) and outside of the Christian movement (Acts 13:45; 14:1, 19; 17:5, 13; 21:27; 25:7–8, 18–19). Below, we shall see that this interpretation also fits with the posture of the elder son in Luke 15.

56. Easton, *Gospel*, 241.

57. Bock, *Luke*, 2:1295. Bock's comment that an even better title might be something like "A Father and His Two Different Sons" (2:1306) captures the spirit of the interpretation offered here.

his Two Lost Sons,[58] and the parable of the Father's Love,[59] each of these titles indicates a choice among at least three possible interpretive trajectories that focus on the younger son, the father, or the eldest son respectively. The parable's traditional title corresponds to a relatively common overemphasis upon the younger son,[60] despite the suggestion made long ago that the interpretive accent properly falls on the latter section in two-part parables.[61] Titles such as "The Waiting Father" or "The Father's Love" reflect the selection of the second of the three interpretive options mentioned above. While the idea of "Two Lost Sons" does well in trying to hold both halves of the story together, I would question the judgment it makes about the elder son based on the details of the story.[62] My preference for the title "The Parable of the Broken Family" for this story communicates my vision about how both halves of the story function in Luke's two-volume narrative.

There are early allegorical interpretations of this parable by Jerome, Ambrose, and Augustine where the two brothers either represent Jews and Gentiles respectively or, in the case of Ambrose and Augustine, portraits of the "ostensibly just" and the "penitent sinner."[63] Most modern scholars downplay the allegorical correspondences between the sons, the Jews, and the Gentiles in favor of limiting the scope of the analogy to the Pharisees versus the tax collectors and sinners in the immediate context. Yet, interpretations that rule out more extended allegorical correspondences in an *a priori* fashion ultimately fail. The confrontation between Jesus and the Pharisees in the literary context virtually demands that we inquire about how the characters represent groups in the narrative world of Luke-Acts.[64] In other words, approaches that completely dismiss allegorical readings sunder the parable from its context in Luke's Gospel; they go too far by ruling out the correspondence between the sinners and tax collectors and the younger son in 15:11–24, and that between the Pharisees and the eldest son in 15:25–32. On the one hand, the simple correspondence between the Pharisees, sinners, and the elder and younger

---

58. Snodgrass, *Stories with Intent*, 117; cf. "The Parable of the Lost Son" per I. H. Marshall, *Luke*, 604.

59. Jeremias, *Parables of Jesus*, 128–31.

60. Price, "Luke 15:11–32," 64.

61. Jeremias, *Parables of Jesus*, 131; Snodgrass, *Stories with Intent*, 30.

62. Evans, *Luke*, 589–90; Jeremias, *Parables of Jesus*, 131.

63. Snodgrass, *Stories with Intent*, 127–28.

64. Wendland in "Christ's Parables of the Lost" suggests that the stories in Luke 15 form a single parable.

brothers is itself an allegorical move.[65] Further, Acts ends on an open-ended note of conflict similar to that which concludes the family's story in Luke 15, suggesting that this parable participates in a broader network of theological themes beyond the immediate narrative context and functions as a building block in the overarching structure of the work.

N. T. Wright's allegorical interpretation of this parable casts the story as a recapitulation of the exile and restoration of Israel.[66] In this reading, "Israel goes off to a distant land, becomes a slave, then is brought back to her own land," and the thrust of the story is on the people's exile and restoration as the people of God through the ministry of Jesus.[67] This story is paradigmatic for Wright in that it depicts Jesus engaged in the retelling of the story of restoration from exile in new and exciting ways.[68] According to Wright, the Pharisees and elder brother represent those Jews who never left the land and opposed the returning people; that is, the Pharisees and the elder brother are, in effect, Samaritans![69] He notes the parallels between Luke 15 and Acts 15 where the Pharisees grumble about welcoming outsiders and sees a connection between Israel and the church in Acts 15:16–17. Luke crafts the appeal to Amos 9:11–12 in Acts 15 to highlight how the restoration of Israel *initiates* the welcome of Gentiles.[70] Thus, for Wright, the climax of the parable is in Luke 15:18 where the younger son confesses his sin after having returned from "exile" in repentance.[71] Yet, here as with other interpretations mentioned above, the interpretation ignores the second half of the parable and only addresses the part played by the eldest son obliquely, calling him "implicitly condemned."[72]

Another major interpretive issue is whether the parable emphasizes the idea of repentance found in the first half or whether the emphasis should be on the second half of the parable, where the concept of celebration is at the forefront. Tradition favors the former proposal, but attention to various details in the discourse supports the idea that the emphasis is on the latter part of the parable. Perhaps interpretation has lingered on the first half because of the strangely unsatisfying ending of the story in the second half. Yet, instead of

---

65. See especially Snodgrass, *Stories with Intent*, 136, on this point; similarly Bock, *Luke*, 2:1306.

66. Wright, *Jesus and the Victory of God*, 125–31, 242, 254–55.

67. Wright, *Jesus and the Victory of God*, 126.

68. Wright, *Jesus and the Victory of God*, 242.

69. Wright, *Jesus and the Victory of God*, 127.

70. Wright, *Jesus and the Victory of God*, 128.

71. Wright, *Jesus and the Victory of God*, 254–55.

72. Wright, *Jesus and the Victory of God*, 130.

mourning the missing reconciliation scene at the end of the parable, we might accept Luke's invitation to imagine the end of the story: Will the dutiful son relent and rejoice in the return of the prodigal, or will he leave home in turn? It may be that the larger arc of the narrative in Luke-Acts hints or comments on the open-ended nature of this beloved parable.

Several grammatical and literary features support the impression that the intended emphasis rests on the latter half of this parable. A look at the Greek morphology in the second half of the parable finds that its verb forms are 20 percent more heavily marked than those found in the first half, even though the first half is longer.[73] We can also note that the verses in 15:1–2 that provide the narrative setting are among the most prominent verses in this chapter. This syntax, which confirms the idea that it is Jesus's act of gathering the marginalized and eating with them that prompts the grumbling of the Pharisees and scribes, provides the occasion for the three stories.[74] Literarily, this grumbling is directly addressed only by the attitude of the eldest son in the latter half of the two-part parable. Though lostness is undoubtedly a principal element in the discourse in chapter 15, the inclusio established by the Pharisees' and elder brother's grievances suggest that these attitudes are the major issues that unify the message of the chapter. Thus the grievance theme contrasts with the themes of celebration and joy that run across each story and binds all segments into an artfully arranged literary whole.[75] Each of the stories in the chapter-long parabolic discourse[76] nuance the theme of celebratory restoration: the first introducing the movement away from and back toward unity and wholeness (15:4–7), the second highlighting the effort required for restoration (15:8),

73. Here I am appealing to verbal aspect as a way of measuring markedness by noting that present/imperfect and perfect/pluperfect tense forms are more marked than aorist inflections. For more on verbal aspect see Porter, *Verbal Aspect.*

74. The opening periphrastic in 15:1 in the imperfective aspect (Ἦσαν δὲ ... ἐγγίζοντες πάντες οἱ τελῶναι καὶ οἱ ἁμαρτωλοὶ) is one of the two most marked grammatical constructions in the chapter. For more on periphrasis and verbal aspect see Porter, *Verbal Aspect,* 441–78, especially p. 460 on Luke 15:1.

75. Wendland, "Christ's Parables of the Lost"; Fitzmyer, *Luke,* 2:1075. Snodgrass's interpretation, which has the advantage of focusing equally on both parts of the concluding story, determines that the focus of the parable is on the "lostness" of the sons, one because of sin, and the other because of hardheartedness and that it functions climactically with reference to the parables of the Lost Sheep and Coins. Yet even Snodgrass, who names 15:11–32 the parable of the Lost Sons, notes that "celebration and joy are the dominant motifs in the chapter" (*Stories with Intent,* 95); see also I. H. Marshall, *Luke,* 597.

76. I. H. Marshall, *Luke,* 600.

and the third gathering all these ideas and setting them within the context of familial brokenness and reunion.[77]

There is little attention in scholarly literature to the mention of the famine, the resource scarcity, which drives the profligate son to seek employment with a Gentile, but this Lukan literary device also signals an interest in the restoration of wholeness to this divided family.[78] Though the famine device elsewhere in Luke-Acts seems focused on Jesus's mission to incorporate Gentiles into the people of God (Luke 4:25; Acts 7:11; 11:28), its use in this parable suggests that this device also applies to Jesus's mission to regather the dispersed of Israel (Luke 3:23; Acts 1:8; 13:46–47; cf. 28:28).[79] For Luke, famine is a force that overcomes the centripetal forces of fragmentation to bring disparate peoples together, whether separated by great geographic distances or simple household dinner tables.[80] The observation that the severe famine (see 15:14) is an important issue in the first half of the parable is implied by attention to the verbs in the account of the prodigal's adventure in verses 13–20. The narrative does highlight the fact that the younger son lived riotously, thus viewing his lifestyle from the perspective of the Jewish traditionalist. Still, all of the other actions in the foregrounded present tense are connected to the idea of famine: the feeding of the pigs,[81] the eating of the pigs,[82] the son's longing to eat,[83] the fact that no one gave him food,[84] the abundance of food elsewhere,[85] and

77. Green discusses the intensification that occurs across these stories—from one lost sheep out of a hundred, to one lost coin out of ten, to one lost son out of two—as well as the emphasis on the necessity of celebration as a consequence of restoration. See J. B. Green, *Luke*, 572–73, 575–76.

78. For more on the way that famines function in Luke-Acts, see Crockett, "Luke 4:25–37."

79. Crockett, "Luke 4:25–37." Also see Judette Kolasny, who builds on Crockett's interpretation by showing that Acts 10–11 is a further fulfillment of the famine motif and prophecy in Luke 4:26–27. See Kolasny, "Luke 4:16–30," 70.

80. Against a strong tendency in scholarship on the gospels, E. P. Sanders disagrees with Jeremias and the legacy handed down by him and argues that the Pharisees did not equate the people of the land with sinners. The conflict between Jesus and the Pharisees was not, according to Sanders, over table fellowship with the common folk nor the associated issue of ritual purity. The conflict arose because of Jesus's willingness to include sinners in the kingdom of God apart from the requirements of the ceremonial law, if they responded to his message. See E. P. Sanders, *Jesus and Judaism*, 174–211. This issue is far from settled in New Testament scholarship.

81. To feed the pigs: βόσκειν χοίρους (15:15).

82. The food that the pigs were eating: κερατίων ὧν ἤσθιον οἱ χοῖροι (15:16).

83. The son's longing to eat: ἐπεθύμει χορτασθῆναι (15:16).

84. No one gave him food: οὐδεὶς ἐδίδου αὐτῷ (15:16).

85. The abundance of food elsewhere: περισσεύονται ἄρτων (15:17).

his perishing in the famine.[86] These details in the story support the idea that famine drives the prodigal's return from foreign lands and the possibility of healing the divisions in the family.[87]

Many are puzzled by the fact that part of the prodigal's rehearsed speech is dropped when he appears before his father (i.e., 15:19b: "Make me like one of your laborers"). Yet, we should not fail to note the great tragedy expressed in the part of the speech that does appear twice in these three verses—that the son no longer feels worthy of claiming his relationship with his family. The father's undignified run and the signs of honor heaped on the returning son, including the ring, robe, and feast, add depth to this touching scene of family reconciliation,[88] and the verb forms in this section confirm the emphasis on the motif of celebration. First, in verse 20, we see that the reconciliation begins while the prodigal is still far distant ("And while he was still far distant[89] the father saw him and had compassion on him"). Second, verse 23 emphasizes the famine motif through the father's order to bring in food ("Bring the fatted calf and let us eat and celebrate").[90] Finally, Luke emphasizes the communal celebration of the lost son's return in verse 24 by accenting the son's lostness[91] and the rejoicing of the village.[92]

A great deal of ink has been spilled on whether the younger brother's speech in 15:21 communicates genuine contrition since his rehearsed speech in 15:18–19 differs from what he tells his father when they are face-to-face, omitting the phrase "Make me like one of your laborers."[93] What interpreters have not seemed to notice, however, is that omitted literary details (shown in italics below) appear elsewhere in the chapter as well:

---

86. The son's perishing in the famine: λιμῷ ὧδε ἀπόλλυμαι (15:17; lit. "Here I am dying of hunger").

87. For more on the debate about whether the prodigal repents, see Jeremias, *Parables of Jesus*, 130; Forbes, "Repentance and Conflict," 217; and Snodgrass, *Stories with Intent*, 138, who are all in favor of this idea. Contra Evans, *Luke*, 590–91; Petzke, *Lukas*, 140–41; Scott, *Hear Then the Parable*, 116; Bailey, *Finding the Lost*, 129–33; Juel, "Strange Silence," 10.

88. Cf. Jeremias, *The Parables of Jesus*, 132.

89. Note the imperfective aspect in the phrase "And while he was still far distant" (μακρὰν ἀπέχοντος; 15:20).

90. Bring the fatted calf and let us eat and celebrate: φέρετε τὸν μόσχον τὸν σιτευτόν, θύσατε, καὶ φαγόντες εὐφρανθῶμεν (15:23).

91. "Because he has been lost" in the emphatic stative perfect participle (ὅτι . . . ἦν ἀπολωλὼς; 15:24).

92. "They began to rejoice" is phrased with a bulky periphrastic with a present infinitive: ἤρξαντο εὐφραίνεσθαι (15:24).

93. "Make me like one of your laborers": ποίησόν με ὡς ἕνα τῶν μισθίων σου (15:19). Bock is in favor of reading this as an example of genuine repentance, despite the omitted phrase in the prodigal's speech (*Luke*, 2:1314). Contra Juel, "Strange Silence."

Pair 1

"Just so, I tell you, there will be more joy in heaven over one sinner who is repenting *than over ninety-nine righteous who have no need for repentance*." (15:7)

"Just so, I tell you, there is joy in the presence of the angels of God over one sinner who is repenting." (15:10)

Pair 2

"Rising, I will go to my father and I will say to him, 'Father, I sinned toward heaven and before you. No longer am I worthy to be called your son. *Make me like one of your laborers*.'" (15:18–19)

"Then the son said to him, 'Father, I sinned toward heaven and before you. No longer am I worthy to be called your son.'" (15:21)

Pair 3

"'Let us eat and celebrate because this *son of mine* was dead and lives again, he had been lost and was found.'" (15:23c–24)

"'But we had to celebrate and rejoice, because this *brother of yours* was dead and lives and having been lost he was found.'" (15:32)

In each case, the incomplete repetition calls attention to the omitted phrase. In the first case, the omitted comparison ("than over ninety-nine righteous who need no repentance"; 15:7) shows that the comparatively greater joy over the repentant sinner is a key issue that connects the two shorter parables in the discourse, and not the fact of repentance per se. The modified phrases in the third pair ("son of mine"/"brother of yours"; 15:24, 32) confirms the judgment that it is the eldest son's unwillingness to celebrate the restoration of the younger that is a focal issue. In addition, it is the repetition in the verse pairs above that binds the two halves of the last parable together. The theme of lostness connects the third parable to the first two parables, just as the repetition in the first pair binds those two short parables together.

The omitted phrase in the second pair ("Make me like one of your laborers"; 15:19) has undoubtedly received more scholarly attention. Yet when viewed in connection with the other two uses of this literary device, it may be more prudent to focus on what the omitted phrase tells us about the contrast between the two sons rather than the possibility that the phrase gives insight into the youngest son's state of mind. In other words, the omitted phrase in 15:19 calls attention to the similarity between the youngest son's reflection that he *should* be one of the father's common laborers and the eldest son's self-portrait in just those terms ("for so many years I have been serving you"; 15:29). This comparison highlights the fact that family relationships are of significance in this discourse.

In Luke 15:29–31, the son's anger and the father's response may hint about the division in Israel that this episode predicts. In the son's speech, we see that the use of "never" in 15:29 is carefully balanced by the words "always" and "all" in the father's responses (15:31). To the son's first assertion in 15:29, "I've *never* transgressed a commandment," the father responds by saying, "You are *always* with me," thereby connecting the elder son's obedience with the unbroken fellowship between them. To the son's accusation that the father had "*never*" given him even so much as a goat (15:29), the father responds by saying, "*All* I have is yours" (15:31). The father's answer likewise affirms the value that the father places on the eldest son. It implies that measuring giving and taking is meaningless within the context of their unbroken union. Indeed, when contrasted with the robe, ring, and feast given to the younger brother, the phrase "all I have is yours" points to God's abiding generosity with infinite resources. God's abundant wealth is more than adequate to redress the brother's implicit economic fears about sharing a now diminished inheritance with an unworthy sibling. Thus, economic pressures are latent in the emphasis on famine scarcity in this story and potentially underneath the elder's worry about his diminished inheritance. We'll see these themes come into greater focus in the next section when we look at the adjacent parable in 16:1–9.

Despite the father's generosity, the eldest's hurt is evident in verse 30. Bitterly pointing out to the father that "this son of yours" had devoured the father's living with prostitutes, his statement exaggerates the younger brother's moral deprivation beyond what is explicit in the narrative. In essence, the eldest son fractures the family by refusing to acknowledge his relationship with his brother and, in the process, explicitly affirms the younger son's sentiment that he no longer deserved to be part of the family. The eldest brother's rhetorical attempt to fracture the family is not so subtly rebuked by the additional changes to the repetition between 15:24 and 32. In these verses, the father shifts talk about "this son of mine" (15:24) to the phrase "this *brother* of yours" (15:32). Having already registered that the rejoicing at the restoration of the prodigal is conspicuously absent in the scene between the eldest and the father, we note that the narrator never tells us whether the eldest son ultimately goes into the celebration or whether he finally refuses to be restored. When we recall that Luke's two-volume work ends on this same open-ended sense of broken communion in Acts 28:28, we thus expose the fact that the plea for the restoration of the family stands at the center of Luke's theological agenda.

The Parable of the Trickster Steward (Luke 16:1–9)

Complementary themes and motifs drive the rhetorical concerns in the adjacent parable of the Unjust Steward in Luke 16:1–9, renamed as the parable of the Trickster Steward. This parable explores questions about praiseworthy actions embedded in the context of financial exploitation and a rigged labor system.[94] Although the parable is addressed to Jesus's disciples rather than the Pharisees (16:1; cf. 15:1–2), it is possible that Luke's use of subversive stories and coded rhetoric slyly continues a concern with the interfamilial conflict in the preceding chapter. That said, this parable also picks up and highlights the economic concerns that are more muted in the preceding chapter.[95] The steward is more like the younger sibling than the elder in Luke 15. For example, both the youngest son and the steward are sympathetic characters in their respective parables, facing destitution. Both characters misuse wealth and are engaged in financial shenanigans at the beginning of each story. The prodigal son demands a cash-out of his inheritance and then wastes his father's wealth (15:13), and the tricky prodigal steward busily squanders his employer's wealth (16:1). More interesting is the observation that readers of the parable of the Trickster Steward experience a moral outrage at this story that is comparable to the elder brother's anger at the reinstatement of the prodigal. We say, "How

94. Crowder, "Gospel of Luke," 175–76.

95. Green likewise sees the parable in 16:1–9 as a continuation of themes in chapter 15: "In fact, the theme of this narrative section concerns the appropriate use of wealth to overstep social boundaries between rich and poor in order to participate in a form of economic redistribution grounded in kinship" (J. B. Green, *Luke*, 589). On the use of subversive rhetoric, Stephanie Buchanan Crowder's interpretation of Luke is also helpful as she calls attention to an analogy between Luke's use of coded and subversive rhetoric, and the code-switching and coded messages embedded in the Negro spiritual songs of the slave era (Crowder, "Gospel of Luke," 159). For Crowder, examples of this motif in Luke include the status reversals in the Magnificat, the address of the work to "Theophilus," and Jesus's words to the sinful woman in 7:36–50, which may in fact be also intended for Simon Peter. I suggest that this latter case serves as a model for the coded messages in the parable of the "Unjust Steward" in Luke 16:1–9 with dual messages for the disciples and the Pharisees.

can Jesus commend this crooked steward?" just as the elder brother accuses his father of injustice: "When this son of yours devoured your living with prostitutes . . . you killed a fatted calf."[96] By juxtaposing the parable of the Trickster Steward with the parable of the Broken Family, Luke turns from a rebuke of the Pharisees upset at the inclusion of unworthy sinners to a story that addresses the sense of offense that the Pharisees and other faithful Jews might be feeling at a generous welcome for an "unworthy" brother. The stern reckoning of the householder connotes the appropriateness of the sense of moral outrage in both stories.

The concern for restoration appears in the parable of the Trickster Steward and the longer parable of the Broken Family, signaled in the former by the steward's hope that he might eventually be received into the homes of his clients (16:4). In this parable, Jesus praises the use of wealth to foster intimacy with those burdened by heavy debts and then ties such action to heavenly approbation ("welcome you into eternal dwellings" [16:9]). The parable in Luke 16 about the servant makes a point similar to the one made in Luke 15 about the two brothers. The father's generosity and the master's affirmation form a vivid contrast with concerns about the wealth squandered by the steward and younger brother. More importantly, the juxtaposition of these parables acknowledges the unsavory actions of the steward and youngest son while simultaneously recognizing the survival exigencies that drive them to desperate straits.[97] In one sense, Luke 16:1–9 suggests that if it is commendable for a crooked steward to use wealth to gain a reception into the homes of friends under threat of destitution, it is even more likely that the faithful will gain the favor of heaven when they use wealth to make friends among the marginalized in their own communities. Thus, famine drives restoration and reconciliation in the broken family of 15:14–24, just as the threat of deprivation drives the receptions mentioned in 16:4 and 9 in the parable of the steward.

96. For a summary of readings that attempt to wrestle with the interpretation of this parable and the moral problems in the steward's actions, see Bock, *Luke*, 2:1326–43. Bock ultimately favors an interpretation that is similar to the one herein, viewing the parable as "an exhortation to use money wisely and generously so as to enter heaven" (2:1332–33, 1338). Differences between my interpretation and his largely concern our decisions about where the parable ends and the extended application begins: Bock sees 16:1–8a as a unit while I think the section includes 16:9, given the similarity of 16:4 (δέξωνταί με εἰς τοὺς οἴκους αὐτῶν) to 16:9 (δέξωνται ὑμᾶς εἰς τὰς αἰωνίους σκηνάς) and the use of forms of δέχομαι in 16:4, 6, 7, and 9.

97. Green notes the fearfulness of losing status and shelter that seem to motivate the steward in 16:3–4 against the backdrop of the economics of the role of ancient stewards (J. B. Green, *Luke*, 590).

Both stories relate to Luke's concern about regathering the marginalized in Israel and restoring breaches in the community.[98]

Yet, in another way, the parable of the trickster steward has a particular resonance in the African Diaspora. The steward's shrewd actions are analogous to the stories of Anansi the Great Spider, the folk hero from the Asante people of Ghana in the West African region formerly known as the Gold Coast. "Anansi" means "spider" in the Twi language spoken by the Asante people and symbolizes wisdom.[99] Though some identify Anansi as a deity, there is evidence that he has more in common with other indigenous trickster figures such as Br'er Rabbit (i.e., Brother Rabbit), who originated from the folklore of the Bantu-speaking peoples of South, West, and Central Africa.[100] In traditional Asante religion, Anansi was a mediator bringing stories and wisdom from the divine realm to the human realm on the one hand, but also bringing chaos and disrespect for social hierarchies on the other hand. By telling Anansi stories of how the trickster poked fun at powerful elites, the function of these stories in their Asante setting was

> to aid the harmony of the Asante social system as a whole. Both philosophical and comical commentaries on life, they were used as a medium for negotiation and as a temporary release from a controlled environment. As the release was temporary and only acceptable in certain contexts it tested the limits of Asante codes of behaviour but in doing so redefined and strengthened its boundaries. Rather than having a "blind faith" in their social structures, through the medium of Anansi the Asante incorporated scepticism into their belief systems, and by doing so made them both more resilient and profound.[101]

With the transatlantic slave trade in the nineteenth century, Anansi trickster stories migrated to the West Indies via Ananci stories and to the American South via Br'er Rabbit stories. A shapeshifter, he sometimes appeared as a

---

98. For more on the interpretation of the Trickster Steward/Unjust Steward, see Hiers, "Friends by Unrighteous Mammon."

99. E. Z. Marshall, "Liminal Anansi." According to anthropologist John Mbiti, the association between wisdom and God may be seen in the title for God *Ananse Koroko* among the Asante, which means the Great Spider, that is, the "Wise One." Mbiti, *African Religions and Philosophy*, 51.

100. E. Z. Marshall, "Liminal Anansi," 31.

101. E. Z. Marshall, "Liminal Anansi," 38. Also see Vecsey, "Exception Who Proves the Rules."

man, woman, or god. However, as a spider, Anansi represented a liminal figure whose dwelling in the rafters of homes symbolized his suspension between earth and heaven.[102] Br'er Rabbit and Br'er Anansi (or Anancy) stories were prized and even emulated among slaves for the way that their trickery and deception allowed them to defeat their larger enemies and secure the food and privileges they needed to survive.[103] "Br'er Rabbit and Br'er Anancy were no models of virtue—they were greedy and deceitful and often immoral and vindictive, even vicious at times. But given the nature of their conditions and the savagery of their enemies . . . their behavior was understood, applauded, and emulated in the slave communities."[104] As Emily Marshall writes:

> Using Anansi tactics the slave implemented methods of survival and psychological and physical resistance; finding ways to do less work, eat more food, trick and steal from Massa and generally using brains over brawn. It is said that the escaped slave Paul Boggle shod his horse back-to-front to deceive British soldiers in pursuit of his trail, and the Maroons used Anansi tactics to hide, outwit and terrify their pursuers. . . . In his Jamaican setting, Anansi was breaker rather than tester of the chains. He becomes a symbol of creative chaos and longed for freedom in a tyrannical and coercive order.[105]

Against this backdrop, the steward resembles the function of the Br'er Rabbit and Br'er Anansi stories in the African diaspora. When read as a resistance story that takes on and wins against a stacked system of economic exploitation, the trickster steward of Luke 16 comes closer to dismantling the master's house with the master's tools than many could have imagined.[106]

Assimilation and Threat

The parable of the Broken Family in 15:11–32 uses the conflict between siblings as an allegory for the tension between the Pharisees and the marginalized in Israel and anticipates the conflict in Acts between Jews in the early Christian movement and Jews in other sectarian and non-sectarian groups. However, several aspects of the story invite comparison with dynamics associated with the processes

102. J. A. Johnson, "Anansi."
103. Dance, *From My People*, 2. Br'er Anansi stories appear in the US South as Br'er Rabbit stories and vice versa.
104. Dance, *From My People*, 2–3.
105. E. Z. Marshall, "Liminal Anansi," 39–40.
106. Lorde, *Sister Outsider*, 110–13.

of acculturation and their impact on relations within and between ethnoracial groups. For example, the two brothers in the story represent two postures for persons struggling to reconcile involvement in their culture of origin with participation in the majority culture. In the younger son, we see a person who has immersed herself in an alien culture only to find that the immersion has come at the cost of self-esteem and deprivation externally and division in the community of origin internally. This person may be the parade example of someone who experiences the stress, isolation, and alienation associated with the failure to assimilate to a hostile dominant culture and the hostility within the culture of origin because of their attempted involvement with the dominant culture.

In the parable of the Broken Family, the eldest son's exaggeration of the younger sibling's sins suggests that the elder finds the younger unworthy of embrace given the younger's attraction to alien habits in far-off venues. This disdain is vividly manifest when the elder sibling refuses to acknowledge the younger as a member of the family (15:30). There might also be a sense of betrayal that emerges at the implied criticism in 15:29 ("I have never disobeyed your command"). Either the younger should never have left in the first place, or at the very least, he should not have participated in sexual immorality or violations of Torah while among the Gentiles (15:30). This dynamic rhymes with the traditionalist's posture, who resists the allure of alien practices in the first place, but who also stubbornly fails to acknowledge the exigencies of survival that drive cultural accommodation. In addition, the story also manages to convey a sense of outrage that while survival may have been at stake in some of what happened to the younger sibling, that sibling's misuse of the wealth and squandered family money is morally problematic, a question not engaged directly until Luke 16:1–9. Most intriguing of all is the idea that the father, the central figure in this narrative, represents a bicultural mediator. On the one hand, he welcomes the marginalized assimilator back to the family fold and restores his dignity, while on the other hand, he also honors the traditionalist's steadfast loyalty. While morally ambiguous acculturation actions are never affirmed outright, Luke 15 and 16 both explicitly rebuke division in the community and celebrate reconciliation and restoration in the aftermath of cultural accommodation.

We've also seen that the eldest son's anger in the story of the Broken Family reiterates the anger of Nazarethites after Jesus's inaugural sermon, and together they predict aspects of the division in Israel later in Acts. Jesus's mission to gather the dispersed in Israel ironically ends by dividing the people of God even further. Luke 4 anticipates the division appearing in Acts, and Luke 15 and 16:1–9 stand as value-laden and pragmatic pleas to avoid that outcome. Thus, the passages we've examined in Luke-Acts not only speak to group dynamics within an ethnic group vis-à-vis varying postures toward the majority culture, but they also speak to tensions *within a family*. After all, the discourse containing intensifying parables involving lost sheep, coins, and sons in Luke 15 begins with grumbling among the Pharisees, those loyalists who are angry that Jesus is fraternizing with sinners and the traitorous tax collectors colluding with Rome in the economic exploitation of the people.

Indeed, both passages hint at economic tension simmering beneath the anger of the Nazarethites in Luke 4 and the elder son in Luke 15. In Luke 4, the echoes of the Jubilee laws heighten the Nazarethites' expectation of economic relief. Their anticipation turns to anger at Jesus's suggestion that outsiders will share in messianic beneficence. Likewise, in Luke 15, the financial tension resonates between the premature demand by the younger son for his inheritance and the reluctance of the elder to see his part of the inheritance further eroded by the returning wastrel, and these economic themes are made even clearer in the adjacent parable in Luke 16. But what if it is God's *preference* to spread wealth and mercy upon those that most people think of as unworthy? What if that was just the kind of ministry in which the Lord delights? What if we were to imagine Jesus as the Great Liminal Anansi who mediates between heaven and earth, upending the regimes of hierarchy and economic exploitation that bedevil our society, earning the master's praise for using the tools of exploitation to the benefit of the debt-burdened?

When I give students an open-ended assignment to reflect on the significance of Luke 15:11–32 for modern race relations, some White students identify with the elder brother in the prodigal parable. They imagine Blacks and contemporary minorities as the "sinful" younger brother and themselves in the part of the (self-)righteous older brother. Quite possibly, these students exhibit implicit bias by associating minorities with the negative state of being sinful. They also often identify a rhyme between the elder brother's anger and White racial grievance that resents social programs disbursed to "undeserving" immigrants and Blacks.[107] Whether politically correct or not, these students seem to have difficulty resisting the notion of unworthiness that attaches to members of minority cultures, in all likelihood reacting to the barriers of skin color, culture, and language that inhibit assimilation and full participation in society.

For these students, there are several issues discussed in this chapter that could serve as helpful correctives. First, Luke 15:11–32 and 16:1–9 suggest that approval, approbation, and social credit do not represent the terms of a zero-sum

---

107. See chapter 8 for more on the politics of grievance and social welfare in the United States.

game. In Luke 15:31-32, the father's insistence that "all I have is yours" poignantly illustrates how little one needs to seek favor that is already accrued as social advantage; the parable insists on God's impartial care and regard for both siblings. The story suggests that judgments about unworthiness are not the prerogative of the traditionalist. While values may complicate reconciliation between the brothers in the parable, no considerations of this kind inhibit the father's welcome, who only acts to restore whatever honor and esteem have gone missing. Likewise, in the second half of Luke 15:11-32, the interaction between the elder brother and the father affirms the emphasis on the goals of ethnic identification by approbation for the brother who persists in devotion to the community. Both the Broken Family and the Trickster Steward parables insist that the providence of God moves inexorably through famine and deprivation toward restoration. These stories boldly encourage actions that disburse wealth beyond parochial concerns to promote reconciliation in broken communities.

Yet, no analogy is perfect, and here as well there are limits for a modern appropriation of the intra-group dynamics in this parable. The first and most crucial limit concerns the imperfect correspondence between the sinfulness of the prodigal's actions and the efforts of minorities or transnationals to fit into majority culture. However much traditionalists might disagree with attempts to adopt elements of White majority culture, such activities are not violations of divine standards of conduct. Similarly, our reading of the trickster steward in Luke 16:1-9 hints that social capital, however acquired, is valuable and necessary for survival, a posture that encourages generosity on occasions when an assimilationist posture is engaged as a last resort.

However, the trickster presents us with a new take on the assimilator and offers the possibility to discard our moral ambivalence about assimilation as a survival strategy. Like an Anansi/Br'er Rabbit story in the context of the slaveholding and Jim Crow South, the Trickster Steward receives commendation for trickery that redounds to his own benefit and also the benefit of his compatriots. This approbation valorizes ethnic belonging through its attention to folk facing similar conditions. It comports with social science research about how a sense of belonging to an ethnic community is a key resource for navigating a hostile dominant culture.

The Trickster Steward cultural image also helps us to move from an assimilation-survival framework to a resistance-survival framework. Within a society that prioritizes cooperation and the common good like that of the Judeans of Jesus's day or the nineteenth-century Asante of Ghana, tricksters like the steward serve as a creative outlet that tests the social order even as it reinforces it. But in settings that strangle human dignity and discipline difference, the rhyme between Br'er Rabbit stories, Anansi stories, Luke 16:1-9, and the dynamics of assimilation represent a fresh angle on the problem of assimilation. Rather than viewing the fact of assimilation as a deplorable but sometimes necessary act of survival, the Trickster Steward of Luke 16 reframes assimilation as an act of resistance in its own right. The trickster is a revolutionary who turns the values of Empire upside down, disbursing wealth to co-sufferers in deprivation in ways that increase everyone's chances of survival. The trickster performs economic solidarity in ways that adapt and bend the tools of financial exploitation from the hostile surrounding culture to serve the interests of the marginalized and their minoritized communities of origin.

Another vital limit for these rhymes focuses on the intimate images of hometown and family that are centered in these stories. What are the limits of a family? What is its extent, and who gets to be inside the circle of intimates? These stories resonated with my students as a fruitful place for reflection on race relations precisely because their tensions easily aligned with tensions in contemporary race relations. The grievance at being decentered, the anger at "unworthy" outsiders, the sense that blessings that "properly" belong to insiders are being disbursed to others all found leverage in their lives. White grievance about sharing social goods with minorities who are stereotyped as unworthy, dangerous, subhuman, invisible, and uncivilized is at the center of the dynamics roiling US society today. But the solution found in the biblical situation only works to the degree that the analogy holds regarding the governing metaphors that set the context. When the actors in the contemporary scene cannot recognize each other as members of a common humanity, much less the same community or family, the father's climactic statement that "all I have is yours" is only another reason for anger. In other words, the stories only work insofar as the factions can recognize each other as members of the same family.

Modern economic exigencies are vastly more complex than the relatively simple financial transactions pictured in these parables, as are the difficulties in navigating ethnic particularities even inside the color line. The family's wealth and the eldest son's security render the disparagement of his destitute brother morally offensive. Likewise, modern disparagement of assimilation may be a privileged luxury for those who indulge in purist notions of culture and identity and are especially fraught for immigrants. For immigrants, assimilation is the only rational alternative for minorities seeking to survive in a frequently hostile American culture. These considerations rhyme with tensions between African immigrants and African Americans who may also find it difficult to see each other as members of the same family.[108] It is not

---

108. See for example Guenther, Pendaz, and Makene, "Impact of Intersecting Dimensions of Inequality."

uncommon for African immigrants to use techniques to distance themselves from Blacks that White immigrant ethnic groups repeatedly deployed at other moments in American immigration history. Many African immigrants find themselves sorted into the dangerous racial hierarchies besetting Blacks while also navigating entry into an immigrant-hostile society. While first-generation African immigrants face predictable barriers to assimilation from anti-Black bias in the larger society, many second-generation American-born children of African immigrants face many stresses of accommodation and assimilation described here. They must balance respect for ethnic heritage with a desire or need to assimilate to African American values and frameworks.[109] With an eye on improving the recognition of family across the African diaspora, African immigrants should not overlook findings about the protections of ethnic identification in the US context. For their part, African Americans at odds with these immigrants could do well to cultivate an understanding of the assimilationist's dilemma.

Notwithstanding the gulf between the economic arrangements in these parables and those in contemporary society, the relatively simple financial solutions presented here may still be helpful. The Broken Family and the Trickster Steward parables that sanction the use of wealth to restore the community may nevertheless offer a moral compass for cultivating a Christian posture toward public policies that seek to promote economic justice. The US economy lacks the infinite resources that the God figure has in the story, and realistically modern communities have to contend with sharing a finite pie. Nevertheless, it may be that policies that promote economic justice and give greater access to economic opportunity for minorities are really only those that *shrewdly* serve to enlarge the pie and further the long-term interests of the broader society. Denying these resources for greater economic opportunity to people of color works against society's economic interests at large.[110] Such values may, in fact, conflict with the capitalist motivations that subordinate the public good over the private accumulation of wealth. Still, it may be on just that point that the biblical stories continue to exercise their transforming power.

109. Guenther, Pendaz, and Makene, "Impact of Intersecting Dimensions of Inequality."
110. Unlike other western democracies, the US economy is able to grow despite labor shortages caused by an aging population and shrinking birthrates, in part due to its high rates of immigration—both legal and illegal. For a book-length treatment of how denying resources to minorities impoverishes everyone, see McGhee, *Sum of Us*.

4

SEX, CRIME, AND STEREOTYPES IN
THE GOSPEL OF JOHN

When I speak of the erotic, then,
I speak of it as an assertion of
the life-force of women;
of that creative energy empowered,
the knowledge and use of which
we are now reclaiming.

—Audre Lorde, "Uses of the Erotic:
The Erotic as Power"[1]

Judging Bodies, Judging Flesh

Let's begin with a story about something I experienced as a Black female high school student when I was placed in an internship with a middle-aged White male judge on the municipal court of Philadelphia.[2] Imagine observing a case involving a young Black female defendant in court at a bench trial that unfolded without witnesses except the White police officer performing the arrest. I remember concluding that the defendant was innocent as the trial proceeded, and I was initially shocked when the judge handed down a guilty verdict. A second shock came hard on the heels of the first as the case turned to sentencing. Barely a moment after the judge banged the gavel and rendered the verdict, the court clerk handed up a set of documents which the judge, with no evident surprise, proceeded to read aloud regarding a rather long history of the defendant's prior arrests and prosecutions. To my later shame,

---

1. This essay appears in Lorde, *Sister Outsider*, 53–59 (quote on p. 55).
2. This encounter is based on real life, though details have been changed or obscured.

I remember thinking at the time that I'd been wrong about the defendant's innocence in light of all the offenses on that rap sheet.[3]

If you were in my place and were told that judges have no access to records of prior encounters with law enforcement until after the verdict, would you have been tempted to think that the judge had correctly discerned the woman's guilt? After all, if that rap sheet was accurate, the young woman was likely guilty, right? Now, with decades of experience observing bias in our justice system, I know that even rap sheets need to be contextualized. I know that her prior record may represent nothing more than the tragic accumulation of charges, arrests, and convictions from an unjust and discriminatory school-to-prison pipeline that feeds a prison industrial complex. Though that judge had years of experience informing his judgment, another Black woman hearing the same facts might be more willing to give the defendant the benefit of the doubt, as I did initially. When the judge's opinion swayed me, there were good reasons to suspect that both the judge and I might have been guilty of judging "according to the flesh," or, as one translation puts it, judging "by outward appearances" (John 8:15 NET). If he misjudged her because of racial and gendered stereotypes about Black women, my younger self was likely deferring to his authority according to different stereotypes about White men.

This chapter will explore how stereotypes are gendered and racialized through engagement with the stories of the Samaritan woman in John 4, the woman caught in adultery in John 7:53–8:11, and the apocryphal story of Susanna and the Elders. The story in John 4 will help us discern how gendered assumptions about sexual immorality operate vis-à-vis the trope of the foreign woman and the influence of such tropes on cross-cultural intimacy. By contrast, the stories of Susanna and the woman in John 7:53–8:11 will help us explore gendered racialized images associated with the criminal justice system. To prepare to engage these texts, first I shall explore the nature of racialized and gendered stereotypes for women of color.

Foreign Women and Racialized Gender Stereotypes (John 4)

In modern society, the belief that females are weaker and more emotional than males has been one of the most enduring gender stereotypes.[4] The trope of the

---

3. A rap sheet is a colloquial expression for a document called a "Record of Arrests and Prosecutions" (i.e., RAP).

4. See the scholarship cited by Durik et al., "Ethnicity and Gender Stereotypes of Emotion," 430–31.

helpless White women reveals residual values from Victorian culture still present in modern European and American gender typecasts. Contemporary gender norms dictate scripts in which authoritative, strong, and competent White men protect pure, childlike, and passive White women.[5] By contrast to the Victorian ideal for European and American women, Jezebel imagery has become associated with the femme fatale in contemporary American culture. Jezebel imagery depicts women as sensual, foreign, and dangerous. [6] The images of the Jezebel and the Virgin are archetypes that play out in recognizable ways among ethnoracial minorities as these tropes appear in stereotypes of many women of color.

Womanist Hebrew Bible scholar Wil Gafney helpfully excavates the biblical roots of the Jezebel imagery, whose story extends from 1 Kings 16 until 2 Kings 9. Noting how today her name is a cross between a taunt and a slur,[7] Gafney describes her as a foreign queen of tremendous agency who effectively ruled Israel through her husband, Ahab.[8] Gafney characterizes Jezebel's piety to her god and goddess, Baal and Asherah, as an embarrassment to the biblical writers and editors when describing her religious devotion. While Israelite devotion often falls short of equal fervor, nothing "on earth could get [Jezebel] to forget, abandon, or betray her identity and culture."[9] Although her worship of Baal and Asherah becomes a framework for the criticism of idolatry, Gafney points out that Jezebel's worship of the goddess Asherah was shared by many in Israel in the period. For Gafney, Jezebel's story and the stereotypes that grew up around her are a way of disciplining the agency of women and critiquing and controlling their behavior, especially Black women's behavior. Though Black women are regularly constructed as Jezebels, the imagery is more rooted in how Jezebel exemplifies the danger of the foreign woman than in any substantive appeal to the biblical narrative. With her gruesome death narrated in epic detail, her fate is a warning to both women who seek to usurp power and men who marry foreign women.[10]

According to Patricia Hill Collins, the negative stereotypes of the Mammy and the Jezebel for Black women both originate from the dysfunction and

5. Durik et al., "Ethnicity and Gender Stereotypes of Emotion," 431.

6. Pippin, "Jezebel Re-vamped," 222–23.

7. Gafney rightly identifies the use of the name Jezebel in Rev. 2:20 as a slur (*Womanist Midrash*, 239). For more on this usage, see chapter 8 below.

8. Gafney, *Womanist Midrash*, 239–44.

9. Gafney, *Womanist Midrash*, 240.

10. Gafney describes this death narrative as one without peer in the Hebrew Bible, occurring in four acts: 1 Kings 21:14–24; 22:34–40; 2 Kings 9:4–10; and 9:30–37 (*Womanist Midrash*, 243).

rationalizations of slavery. The Mammy "house slave" ideal imagines Black women as strong, obese, nurturing, ugly, and overwhelmingly loyal to Whites. This is exemplified in Hattie Daniels's beloved (by White audiences) character in *Gone with the Wind*. Collins sees an appeal to this figure when some Black male comics in drag portrayed the African American woman as an ugly, masculinized mother figure.[11] The Jezebel, on the other hand, was the antithesis of the paradoxically neutered Earth Mother Mammy.[12] As the other side of the same coin, the Jezebel was a hypersexualized, morally loose man-eater.[13] There has also been the suggestion that the Jezebel image may have evolved somewhat from the forced oppression of slavery.[14] Black women were forced to disrobe in auctions and could not help but expose their limbs when forced to do backbreaking labor in the fields. Equally, however, the ideology of casting Black female slaves as loose women also served as a rationalization for rape by their White male owners since such offspring increased the assets of that owner. By labeling the Black female slave as a Jezebel, slave masters also justified their sexual abuse and economic exploitation on the logic that it is impossible to rape an oversexed promiscuous woman.[15]

The Sapphire is a third stereotype applied to Black women and articulates the most common one used to denigrate them today through the image of the Angry Black Woman (ABW). Sapphire was a character in a 1940s vintage television show called *Amos 'n' Andy*.[16] Married to one of the featured Black male characters, Sapphire was an emasculating, harassing, overbearing Black wife who sought total control over her husband. We shall see that this pernicious trope has had devastating effects on the lives of Black women in US society in the era of mass incarceration. Almost any emotion exhibited in public becomes

11. P. H. Collins, *Black Sexual Politics*, 125.

12. Patricia Hill Collins centers the images of the mule and the whore in her exploration of racialized gendered stereotypes rather than those of Mammy and Jezebel (*Black Sexual Politics*, 53–85). Despite the slightly different imagery it is easy to see that all of these authors are referring to the same social phenomenon.

13. Morton, *Disfigured Images*, 9.

14. White, *Ain't I a Woman?*, 27–61, esp. 49 and 56.

15. Morton, *Disfigured Images*, 9–10, 33; White, *Ain't I a Woman?*, 27–61, esp. p. 46; P. H. Collins, *Black Sexual Politics*, 58–59; similarly Schüssler Fiorenza, *Revelation*, 135. As Ibram Kendi notes, the racialized justifications *followed* the economic self-interest (*Antiracist*, 42).

16. The radio show was conceived by White comics Freeman Gosden and Charles Corell and ran from 1928 to 1953 (Mance, "Sapphire," 772). The show had White title actors, before Black actors briefly played the title characters on television from 1951 to 1953 (Clayton, "Amos 'n' Andy"). Essentially, then, the mostly third-person characterization of the Sapphire character was a construct of White male comedy.

associated with anger for Black women. The angry Black woman is the foil for the White-normed Anglo-Saxon *sang-froid* (lit. "cold-blooded") stereotype. At best, this older French expression captures the European ideal of the man who is imperturbable under strain; at worst, this image represents emotionally vacant cold-bloodedness in public life.

Asian Americans are often perceived or portrayed as quiet, submissive, good at math, hard-working, and nerdy."[17] Through the Geisha image, Asian American women are fetishized as exotic,[18] hypererotic, desirous of sexual domination, and the ideal gratifiers of Western neocolonial libidinal formations.[19] As an antidote to visions of liberated career women, the Asian Pacific Lotus Blossom stereotype "disciplines" White women, just as Asian Pacific Americans, in general, are used against their non-model minority counterparts, African Americans.[20] When seen through the colonial mindset, Asian American women are stereotyped as having compliance and complacency that caters to their harassers' belief that Asian Pacific American women will not fight back. The stereotyping holds that they will be receptive to sexual advances and will make "good" victims.[21]

Just as African American stereotypes of women involve both asexual and sexually promiscuous modes, so too do Asian American stereotypes, as seen in the contrast between the Mammy and Jezebel on the one hand and the Lotus Blossom and the Geisha on the other. A third prominent stereotype of Asian women occurs in the image of the Dragon Lady, popularized recently in the so-called Tiger Mom. It is not hard to see that the assertive, bold initiative of the Asian American Tiger Mom who fights for her children also appears in stereotyped depictions of the Jewish mother and other White immigrant mothers. Likewise, we can see that these images connect organically with the Sapphire

---

17. Okazaki, "Teaching Gender Issues," 44–45.

18. In one study, an investigator conducted internet interviews with nine White men who posted ads "seeking an Asian female." One man responded that he wanted to diversify his experience in dating women from other ethnic groups. Another suggested that a quid pro quo dynamic prevailed: unattractive White males can win with Asian females because such women are seeking White males because they are "superior . . . with more money . . . and more power." On the other hand, over three quarters of the respondents referenced the [sexual] submissiveness and exotic beauty of Asian women as the source of their desire to date Asian women exclusively, the classic terms of the Geisha/Suzie Wong/Madam Butterfly fetish. See Kim, "Asian Female and Caucasian Male Couples," 235–37; cf. Said, *Orientalism*, 92–103.

19. Cho, "Converging Stereotypes," 191.

20. Cho, "Converging Stereotypes," 191.

21. Cho, "Converging Stereotypes," 191.

trope for Black women. In other words, the denigration of assertive minoritized women subtly points to how these women are racialized, ridiculed, and dismissed for behavior associated with success when attributed to White men.

Concerning Latinx stereotypes, gender stereotypes center around *machismo* and *marianismo*. The masculine ideal of *machismo* expects men to be authoritative, aggressive, and dominant, and the feminine ideal of *marianismo* typecasts women as loving, asexual, passive, emotional, weak, subservient, and thus vulnerable to mistreatment and abuse.[22] Similar to the dichotomy of the Mammy and the Jezebel in African American stereotypes, Hispanic stereotypes of women are likewise divided into the "good woman" and the rebellious "bad woman."[23] The Marianista perspective sees women as hyperfertile mothers, nurturers, and caregivers, while the "Hot Latina" is exotic, sexually available, and more motivated by physical and sexual pleasure than White women.[24] It may be that the Latina maid has replaced the Mammy in the White American imagination as the stereotyped beloved house servant.

Just as Black women and other women of color are chained to stereotypes that depict them as aggressive, hypersexualized, and nurturing, so too White women have to contend with living in prisons of passivity and weakness and confinement to feminized and thus devalued spaces.[25] Accordingly, the discourse on Jezebel, refracted through the colonial mind as the image of the foreign, dangerous, and seductive woman, is also deployed against Southern women who break with tradition.[26] As we'll see in the next section, the colonial prism is the invisible subject of interpretations of the Samaritan woman in John's Gospel. We will see that interpretations of the Samaritan woman episode are performances that have "sex on the brain" and illuminate the problem of racialized feminine stereotypes.

Sex on the Brain: Sex and the Samaritan Woman (John 4:1–42)

[1]Now, when Jesus learned that the Pharisees had heard that Jesus is making and baptizing more disciples than John, . . . [3]he left Judea and started back to Galilee.[4]But he had to go through Samaria. [5]So he came to a Samaritan

22. Durik et al., "Ethnicity and Gender Stereotypes of Emotion," 431; Espin, "Sexuality in Hispanic/Latin Women."

23. Lopez, "Perspectives in HRD," 102.

24. Lopez, "Perspectives in HRD," 101–2; Beltran, "Hollywood Latina Body," 82.

25. Morton, *Disfigured Images*, 9; also see Minrose C. Gwin's comment: "Just as black women were forced to be strong, white southern women often were compelled to appear weak" (*Peculiar Sisterhood in American Literature*, 46; also see 4, 11, 14).

26. Pippin, "Jezebel Re-vamped," 230.

city called Sychar. . . . [6]Jacob's well was there, and Jesus, tired out by his journey, was sitting by the well. It was about noon.

[7]A Samaritan woman came to draw water, and Jesus said to her, "Give me a drink." [8](His disciples had gone into the city to buy him some food.) [9]The Samaritan woman said to him, "How is it that you, a Jew, ask a drink of me, a woman of Samaria?" She said this because Jews do not share things in common with Samaritans. [10]Jesus answered her, "If you knew the gift of God, and who it is that is saying to you, 'Give me a drink,' you would have asked him, and he would have given you living water." [11]The woman said to him, "Sir, you don't have a bucket and the well is deep. Where would you get this living water? [12]Are you greater than our ancestor Jacob, who gave us the well . . . ?" [13]Jesus said to her, "Everyone who drinks of this well water will be thirsty again, [14]but those who drink of the water that I will give them will never be thirsty. The water that I will give will become in them a spring of water gushing up to eternal life." [15]The woman said to him, "Sir, give me this water so that I may never be thirsty or have to keep coming here to draw water!"

[16]Jesus said to her, "Go, call your husband, and come back." [17]The woman answered him, "I have no husband." Jesus said to her, "You are right in saying, 'I have no husband'; [18]for you have had five husbands, and the one you have now is not your husband. What you have said is true." [19]The woman said to him, "Sir, I see that you are a prophet. [20]Our ancestors worshiped on this mountain, but you all say that Jerusalem is the place where people have to worship." [21]Jesus said to her, "Woman, believe me, the hour is coming when you will worship God neither on this mountain nor in Jerusalem. [22]You worship what you do not know; we worship what we know, for salvation is from the Jews. . . ." [25]The woman said to him, "I know that Messiah is coming who is called Christ. When he comes, he will proclaim all things to us." [26]Jesus said to her, "That's who I am, the one who is speaking to you now." [27]Just then, his disciples arrived and were shocked that he was talking with a woman, though no one asked, "What do you want from her?" or "Why are you talking with her?"

[28]Then, leaving her water jar, the woman went back to the city. She said to the people, [29]"Come and see a man who told me everything I have ever done! Could he be the Christ?" [30]They left the city and were on their way to him. . . . [39]Many Samaritans from that city believed in him because of the woman's testimony, "He told me everything I have ever done." . . . [41]Many more believed because of his word. [42]They said to the woman, "It is no longer because of what you said that we believe, for we have heard for ourselves, and we know that this is truly the Savior of the world." (AT, slightly abridged)

In *Men and Women in the Fourth Gospel*, Conway argues that the women in the Fourth Gospel are depicted as full participants in God's will and Jesus's mission.[27] They provoke Jesus into engaging his mission (Jesus's mother in John 2), model the apostolic calling (the Samaritan in John 4) and faithful discipleship (Mary in John 12:1–8), and appear in crucial scenes like the hour of revelation and the hour of his death. Thus, the depiction of women in the Fourth Gospel is much more positive than in the other gospels. Women in John are prophets, apostles, and seekers of truth.[28]

Though the Samaritan woman episode is one of the longest in the New Testament in which a woman appears, many interpreters come to very different conclusions about this woman. I suggest that interpreters with sex on the brain interpret the marital symbols in the text through a preoccupation with stereotypes of the foreign woman. These interpreters describe her as despised and morally outcast with public shame; she is a husband-hunting liar with a morally messy life.[29] Even the kindest interpreters who pick up on the courtship imagery note her lack of suitability as a bride for Jesus.[30]

Not surprisingly, the exchange where Jesus describes the woman's multiple partners creates much of the backdrop for the oversexed interpretations. When Jesus asks the woman to fetch her husband (4:16), her reply is taken as deliberate obfuscation regarding the immorality of her social situation. The exchange confirms what some see as the inappropriate nature of her brazen interaction with Jesus. Others, noting the repeated references to water and gushing springs, explore how such imagery has a long history in biblical materials as a metaphor for sex.[31] The mention of gushing springs in association with women symbolizes intercourse and becomes, in some interpretations, cause for blaming the woman for soliciting Jesus as a partner. However, if we read it this way, it seems to me that one would have to blame Jesus for introducing the water/sex theme in verses 13–14.

The passage also inflames the "sex on the brain" condition through the ethnic tensions in the story. The woman in John 4 is unnamed and recogniz-

27. Conway, *Men and Women in the Fourth Gospel*. Others dispute this positive characterization of the depictions of women. For example, Lynn St. Clair Darden argues that the text often undermines the positive depictions in subsequent passages about the women in question. See "Womanist-Postcolonial Reading."

28. Raymond Brown suggests that Mary of Bethany is a prophet, an implication of Brown's interpretation of the anointing episode in John 11; see R. E. Brown, *John*, 1:454.

29. "Morally outcast with public shame" and "a morally messy life": Carson, *John*, 216–17; "a husband-hunting liar": Brant, "Husband Hunting," 215.

30. Brant, "Husband Hunting," 215; cf. O'Day, "John."

31. See Josh. 15:19; Prov. 5:15–20; 9:13–17; and Song of Sol. 4:13–15.

able only by her ethnic membership in a people with a long history of conflict with the ancient Israelites.[32] The narrator heightens the ethnic conflict in the story with the woman's first spoken words in 4:9: "How is it that you, being a Jew, ask me for a drink since I am a Samaritan woman?" The explanatory gloss in that verse, "For Jews have no dealings with Samaritans," only adds to the dramatic tension. A reading of this text with attention to ethnic dynamics must also remark on the exclusivity of Jesus's claim in 4:22 that "salvation comes from the Jews." Further, in an ancient parallel of modern anxiety about inter-ethnic mixing, Jewish leaders accuse Jesus of being a demon-filled Samaritan in John 8:48. Here the author indicates that Jesus's ethnic identity seems to have been compromised by his association with Samaritans. If true, then the charge of demon possession in the verse might signify the extent of the horror over alliance with the ethnic Other.

However, Lynn Cohick's work on women in early Christianity can be helpful here.[33] Some think that Jewish marriages were presumed to end in death and not divorce. [34] Analysis of early second-century AD Jewish marriage documents reveals that death was a frequent cause for the ending of many marriages.[35] However, Cohick points out that the numerous disputes about divorce in the New Testament and rabbinic writings made it likely that divorce was a contested issue for Jewish and early Christian families.[36] She suggests that the Samaritan woman was not necessarily immoral, so much as desperately unlucky. This woman might have been widowed several times, as was common given the short life expectancies of men and the tendency for women to marry while they were young. Indeed, in the early second century, Rabbi Akiba's stance that a man could divorce a woman for any reason at all opens the possibility that the Samaritan woman could well have been *sinned against* because of a casual approach to divorce.[37] While she was unlikely to

---

32. Though I give attention to the Pericope Adulterae below and maintain that the story is early and belongs alongside other historical episodes in Jesus's life, I recognize, with the consensus among biblical scholars, that it is likely a very late addition the Fourth Gospel. In other words, the Samaritan woman may have been the only unnamed woman in the autographs of John.

33. Cohick, *Women in the World of the Earliest Christians*, 122–28.

34. Instone-Brewer, "1 Corinthians 7," 228–29.

35. Cohick, *Women in the World of the Earliest Christians*, 117–19.

36. Cohick, *Women in the World of the Earliest Christians*, 116.

37. In her analysis, Cohick mentions the possibility that the permissiveness of Beth Hillel on the subject of divorce ("Even if she spoils his broth") may have represented hyperbole, in that the rabbis knew that the exorbitant *kettubah* (i.e., marriage contract payment) of two hundred denarii to a divorced wife puts divorce out of the realm of the practical for the ordinary Jewish male. Likewise, the possibility exists that the tradition about this encounter

have been widowed five times, it is not beyond plausibility that she had five husbands through an unlucky combination of being divorced several times and widowed several times. Since Jewish law gave the right to divorce only to men and not to women, it is unfair to assume the woman's immorality contributed to her situation.[38] From the perspective of the woman herself, it is no wonder that she longs to end her visits to the local watering hole, which may have functioned something like a trope for mating rituals in modern bars: "Sir, give me this water so that I may never be thirsty or have to keep coming here to draw water!" (4:15).[39]

Of course, many commentators link the assessment of the woman's immorality to the information that Jesus gives when he describes her current situation in 4:17–18: "You are right in saying, 'I have no husband' . . . and the one you have now is not your husband." On this head, Cohick lists several plausible situations that show that immorality assessments about her are possibly too harsh, in addition to the possibility considered above that she is desperately unlucky through death and divorce. She could have been the second wife in a polygynous marriage recognized by her peers though not by Jesus, who disapproved of bigamy.[40] She might also have been a concubine because the man involved was a Roman citizen who could not legally marry beneath his social rank. Similarly, her partner may have refused to marry her to prevent any children she might bear in the relationship from inheriting his wealth.[41] To these scenarios, we could also add Gail R. O'Day's speculation that the situation might reflect the custom of levirate marriage, where the last male in line refused to marry her (cf. Gen. 38; Luke 20:27–33).[42] Some might raise questions about the woman's morals in agreeing to continue in a relationship under such circumstances, but the merciful would note that in this period a woman without a husband or father to protect or provide for her was in a precarious state. Thus, it is better to refrain from condemning her more than Jesus himself does in the text.[43] Even in a different case where Jesus extends

---

between Jesus and a woman who had had five husbands was likewise crafted to hint at the damage done in such a permissive atmosphere for divorce.

38. Cohick, *Women in the World of the Earliest Christians*, 124.

39. I associate a visit to a watering hole with participation in a marriage market due to the number of interpreters who note the number of biblical patriarchs who found their wives at the local well. For more on this see Alter, *Art of Biblical Narrative*, 47–62.

40. Cohick, *Women in the World of the Earliest Christians*, 125–26.

41. Cohick, *Women in the World of the Earliest Christians*, 125.

42. O'Day, "John," 567.

43. Similarly, Marianne M. Thompson writes: "That she is currently living with a man outside a legally contracted marriage indicates to some commentators her immorality, but to others also her desperation. She needed the protection and support of a husband, but

mercy to a woman "caught in the very act" of sin, his explicit command to the woman to "sin no more" has no analog in the dialogue with the Samaritan (see discussion regarding John 7:53–8:11 below).

Some male scholars argue that the woman's solo appearance at the well at high noon in the heat of the day indicates that other women shunned her for her sinful past. More persuasive are Lynn St. Clair Darden and others who note that the high noon setting for the encounter contrasts Jesus's earlier encounter with Nicodemus, a Jewish leader, in the dead of night (John 3:2; cf. 4:6).[44] Indeed, we might wonder if the townspeople would have trusted her testimony about Jesus if they were used to thinking that she lacked moral scruples (4:29–30, esp. v. 39).[45] Darden's womanist reading suggests that Jesus's interaction with the Samaritan signals that he regards her as equal in authority to his disciples. He sits and talks with her about spiritual matters. She performs acts similar to them when she, like they, drop all earthly labor to attend to the more urgent religious roles to which Jesus has called them.[46] Leaving her water jar as she goes off to spread the good news to her people is the Johannine equivalent of Jesus's call to disciples elsewhere in the Jesus tradition (John 4:28–29; cf. Matt. 4:19–21; Mark 1:17–20; Luke 5:4–10). You could even say that the woman's comment about how Jesus knew all about her history in 4:28–29 plays a role similar to Peter's exclamation, "I am a sinful man!" in Luke 5:8. Yet, it is interesting to note how the Lukan episode does not provoke angst among interpreters about Peter's unworthiness, similar to what we find regarding this woman's past. Darden's comment that the Samaritan is "totally unconcerned with what Jesus revealed to her about her life" is particularly apropos.[47] Indeed, given the deliberate contrasts between the Samaritan and Nicodemus regarding setting, the character of their respective interactions with Jesus, and the evangelistic results, we should conclude that the Samaritan was the true religious leader in these chapters where Nicodemus was not.

No doubt, another aid to interpretations emphasizing the woman's sinful hypersexuality has been the reading of this text against the backdrop of the OT betrothal type scene, especially since the publication of Robert Alter's *The Art of Biblical Narrative*. According to Alter, a type scene is a narrative in which stock elements communicate the story's overall arc in ways easily recognizable

---

had settled for what she could get. Jesus calls attention to her problematic situation, but he does not condemn her. Subsequently commentators and preachers have hastened to fill the void!" See Thompson, *John*, 103.

44. Contrast Keener, *John*, 584–633, with Darden, "Womanist-Postcolonial Reading," 99.
45. Cohick, *Women in the World of the Earliest Christians*, 128.
46. Darden, "Womanist-Postcolonial Reading," 98–99.
47. Darden, "Womanist-Postcolonial Reading," 99.

to readers/hearers in a given culture.[48] He identifies four betrothal scenes in the Old Testament that are instances of these narrative types (Gen. 24:10–61; 29:1–20; Exod. 2:15b–21; the book of Ruth) and other more allusive references in 1 Samuel 9:11–12 and Judges 14. The narrative in John 4 has most of the elements of the general betrothal type scene described by Alter and seems mainly to evoke the Isaac-Rebecca betrothal narrative in Genesis 24. In type scenes, a bridegroom or surrogate journeys to a foreign land as Isaac's surrogate does in Genesis 24:48, having been sent by Isaac's father Abraham (cf. John 4:4). Next, the protagonist meets a woman at a well, and one of them draws water from it, which creates a bond between the two. Third, the woman rushes home in excitement to bring news of the stranger's arrival. Finally, a betrothal takes place after the stranger has been invited to a meal.

Though the basic features of the type scene are recognizable, John 4 creatively reworks at least three elements from Genesis 24 to serve the theological interests of this gospel: the abundance of water, the kinship alliance, and the betrothal meal. First, there is an abundance of water involved in the original encounter between Abraham's agent and Rebecca. When Rebecca offers to water the servant's ten camels (24:10) until they've had enough to drink (24:19), she is essentially undertaking the chore of hauling over three hundred gallons of water for the animals.[49] Yet in John 4, Jesus is the one who offers to provide abundant water, not the woman. Though she is sure that liquid abundance is available from her ethnic heritage via "our father Jacob's well" (4:11–12), the abundant water that Jesus offers is first a metaphor for the Holy Spirit (4:34). Still, given the betrothal motif, the plentiful water also represents the abundance of offspring that will emerge from a fertile union. The children just off the horizon in John 4 are not the natural children born to Jesus and the woman, but rather new Samaritan children of God who are Jesus followers (1:12). Depicted lavishly as a plentiful crop in fields that are ready for harvest (4:35), these children are the many Samaritans who will come to believe through the woman (4:39) as well as those believing through their own encounter with Jesus (4:41–42).

Second, the betrothal episode in Genesis 24 stresses the need to find a bride from within the patriarch's kinship network (Gen. 24:4, 15, 27). Indeed, this element appears to be the biggest twist in the reworking of the scene for

48. Alter, *Art of Biblical Narrative*, 47–62.
49. Mukasa-Mugerwa, *Camel*, 43–44. According to *National Geographic*, "camels are famous for their ability to travel as many as 100 miles (161 kilometers) without water. They retain their body moisture efficiently, but they do not function without water. In fact, a thirsty camel can drink as many as 30 gallons (135 liters) of water in about 13 minutes." See *National Geographic*, "Animals Photo Ark: Arabian Camel."

this Johannine narrative where ethnic tension abounds precisely *because* Jesus transgresses by engaging the Samaritan woman at all, much less in daring to imagine her as a suitable bride.[50] The woman, though initially wary of the interethnic contact (4:9, 12), quickly loses her reserve and becomes excited about her rising awareness about her interlocutor's identity (4:19–25), rushing to take the news about his arrival back home (4:28; cf. Gen. 24:28). Most significantly, whereas Rebecca goes to her immediate family home to announce her encounter, the Samaritan makes her announcement to all the people of her city. This shift demonstrates that the ethnic component of the story—that is, the making of new children for God—is among the crucial emphases for John. Echoing 1:12, Jesus creates a new family by giving the Samaritan woman the power to become a bride of worth and distinction through her recognition of Jesus's messianic status (cf. Nicodemus in 3:1–2, 9–10). Jesus's seemingly random command to fetch her husband initiates this empowerment. His recognition of her past and her discernment of his prophetic standing is the currency in this transfer. This exchange rhymes, as we said above, with Peter's confession after the miracle of the nets in Luke 5:8–9.

Third, the author has evocatively reworked the betrothal meal from the Rebecca story in Genesis 24:51–54 to return to the theme of abundance. In John 4:30, the Samaritans do not simply offer Jesus a meal; they show him two days of hospitality. In addition, we should consider whether Jesus's conversation with the disciples in 4:30–35 about the food is also a twist on this element of the type scene. The disciples find Jesus's certainty about food inexplicable. On the other hand, Jesus himself operates with a clear expectation of a meal since he is aware that a betrothal is in process.

Someone might question whether a marriage occurs, even if granting the influence of a type scene on the passage. One of the arguments offered against the idea of a completed betrothal in this passage is the proximity of bridegroom language that refers to Jesus in 3:29. If Jesus is the groom, then the irregularity of the woman's marital history presents an obstacle for a wedding for some interpreters, although only for those interpreters who are married to the idea of her immorality. Suppose the narrator wants to show that Jesus's forgiving nature accepts the woman despite her checkered history; wouldn't

50. Note, however, that in using the Isaac-Rebecca scene, the author of John subtly insists that Samaritans have a kinship relationship with Jews. In the original, the patriarch's servant is bound to come home with a wife from within the family. By alluding to Gen. 24, John depicts Samaritans as kinspeople, a move that resists all attempts to depict them as outsiders from the Jewish family.

that call for a more forthright discussion of her sin? This passage lacks any explicit discussion of sin. If, on the other hand, the woman has been sinned against, then she is suitable as a bride. But that begs the question about the lack of an explicit marriage in the scene.

I think the bridegroom imagery on the cusp of this episode in 3:29 and the symbolic offspring discussed above attest to a fruitful union, notwithstanding the lack of more literal markers of a wedding. For those troubled by this lack, some help may come from recognizing that the intertextual allusions between this scene and the traditional scenes are via the Rebecca narrative in Genesis 24 and not the Jacob and Rachel narrative in Genesis 29. In the latter passage, the protagonist instantly falls for the girl, whereas the story in Genesis 24 involves an agent who seeks a bride. Thus, Jesus searches for a bride as the agent *who has been sent on behalf of the groom* in John 4. The frequent and prominent theme throughout John about Jesus as sent by God supports this interpretation.[51] Nevertheless, it may be worth a closer look at the discomfort raised by the idea of Jesus's marriage to the Samaritan.

Jesus and Interracial Marriage

As a piece of literature, the primary accent in John 4 is its Christology, as the passage teaches about Jesus's identity and mission. After all, Jesus openly confesses his identity as the Messiah to the unnamed woman in this passage when he denies this privilege to the Roman prelate (4:26; cf. 18:33–37). Furthermore, through the betrothal metaphor, the passage reveals Jesus's peculiar mission as the agent of God who seeks a people who will worship God in spirit and truth (4:23). Thus, John 4 testifies about Jesus's relationship to God: Jesus is a broker whose "food is to do the will of God" (John 4:34).[52]

Notwithstanding the christological and theological significance of the passage, I contend that this stylized encounter between Jesus and an ethnic female outsider stimulates anxiety about intermarriage among western interpreters, especially among those interpreters who are sensitive to the influence of the author's use of the betrothal type scene. The stereotypes about ethnic women discussed above are like smog in the air that hinders every interpretive breath, with the result that these interpreters have an unspoken but palpably horrified fascination with the possibility that Jesus consorts with an ethnic woman upon

51. See John 3:17, 34; 5:36, 38; 6:29, 57; 7:29; 8:42; 10:36; 11:42; 17:3, 8, 18, 21, 23, 25; 20:21; cf. Neyrey, "'I Am the Door.'"
52. Neyrey, "'I Am the Door.'"

whom they have heaped racialized stereotypes.[53] After all, Jesus is also described as the bridegroom in the verses immediately preceding the discourse with the Samaritan (3:29) and later describes himself as someone who is one with God (10:30).

Although growing in frequency, the relatively small number of interethnic and interracial marriages in this country and other western nations may indicate that the general population is still uncomfortable with interracial relationships.[54] It may be that interracial marriages and relationships represent a threat to the dominant social order, as suggested by some. In that case, the specter of an even symbolic embrace of the ethnic woman by Jesus represents a supremely destabilizing prospect among these interpreters.[55]

Interrogating the logic of White supremacist culture is one way of exploring how western imaginaries view the embrace of foreigners as implicitly destabilizing. Writing to advance a strategy that sidesteps a figurative "Oppression Olympics" that disrupt multiracial coalitions, Andrea Smith explores the question of whether a Black-White binary excludes consideration of how White supremacy racializes all peoples of color.[56] Rather than trying to minimize any one element of this ideology, Smith identifies three racialized binaries that are always at work in White supremacy: a Black-White binary built on slavery that puts Blacks at the bottom of American socioeconomic hierarchies; a Native-White genocidal colonial binary that seeks to eliminate claims to lands coveted by settlers by eliminating Indigenous peoples; and an Orientalist-White binary

---

53. Beverly Daniel Tatum's metaphor about racism as a smog that affects all who live in US society is applicable here as well with respect to racialized gendered stereotypes in the West. See Tatum, *Why Are All the Black Kids Sitting Together*.

54. It is true that interracial and interethnic marriage is increasingly popular in the United States. According to the US Census bureau, 11 percent of whites, 18 percent of blacks, 27 percent of Hispanics, and 29 percent of Asians were married to someone outside of their ethnic or racial group in 2015. Despite the increased rate of growth in intermarriage across all demographics, however, the sheer number of such marriages is still relatively low, constituting a new high of 17 percent of all marriages in 2015 (in 1980, that share was just 3.2 percent). Intermarriage rates are highest among Asian women at 36 percent and Black men at 24 percent. See the 2017 Pew Research Center study by Livingston and Brown, "Intermarriage in the U.S." as well as Garcia et al., "Latinos' Perceptions of Interethnic Couples," 350; Dalmage, "Discovering Racial Borders"; and Wu, "Changing Face of America."

55. Garcia et al., "Latinos' Perceptions of Interethnic Couples," 352.

56. "Oppression Olympics" is a phrase coined by Martinez, "Seeing More Than Black and White." It refers to dynamics in which communities of color figuratively compete for attention regarding their particular oppressions, leading to a fracturing of coalitions against injustice.

that performs hostility against all "exotic" newcomers.[57] Smith's three pillars of White supremacy show how these logics are embedded in rhetoric that seeks White separation from the ethnic other. Thus the prospect of Jesus's intimacy with the ethnic woman may animate fear of lost power vis-à-vis the Black-White binary, fear of lost property along the Native-White binary, and fear of lost purity along the axis of the Orientalist-White binary.

There is no question that this story draws attention to ethnic particularity and questions about union with the ethnic other. First, the narrator reminds the audience that Samaritans and Jews share a single ancestral lineage: while the main character in the story is unnamed, the patriarchs taken together as Jacob and Joseph are mentioned four times by name. Second, we cannot fail to notice that both Jesus and the woman take pride in their ethnic heritages. In verse 12, the Samaritan woman explicitly and proudly compares Jesus to her great patriarchal ancestor, expressing doubt that some ordinary Jew could measure up or provide her with resources as great as those bequeathed to her and her people. On the other hand, Jesus's bold declaration that "salvation comes from the Jews" (4:22) shows that his ethnocentrism is just as strong, if not stronger, than hers. Since Rome defeated all the peoples of the Levant in this period, we can see both of their sentiments as a determination to preserve ethnic distinctiveness amid defeat. Even more interesting is that both Jesus and the woman express their ethnic pride on the precipice of creating a new family. To notice the ethnic pride at such a moment is to note how the story resists the notion that an interethnic marriage requires the dilution of ethnic identification for either partner.

The fact is, Jesus considers this woman a worthy bride for God and ma- triarch of a new people for God, notwithstanding a hard-luck history that likely includes abandonment and rejection via death and divorce. The woman doesn't dupe Jesus into thinking that she is worthy; he simply seeks and affirms the truth of her condition. Above all, the text signals a shift in the criterion for creating a family. It is no longer based on ethnic membership or patriarchial gender norms but only on coming to and joining oneself to God in Christ.

I suspect that the history of interpretation for this passage includes a tor- tured if subliminal fear of intermarriage, evidenced by those interpreters who notice the betrothal imagery and reject the idea that Jesus joins with a for- eign woman. Opponents of interracial marriage sometimes use the language of colorblindness but then proceed to scapegoat "society" for its hostility to such unions. That the biblical writer uses marital imagery to depict Jesus's

57. A. Smith, "Settler Colonialism."

encounter with a woman from a different ethnic group should have profound implications for resistance to interracial marriage in the church. In this biblical story, the bride is a full-grown woman(ist) and not the virgin of Israel's founding narratives. This Samaritan bride who brings the good news to her people reveals herself to be every bit as desirable as the matriarch Rebecca, in ways that go beyond outward beauty and the fearful logic of domination. Jesus refuses to engage her as a Jezebel or an erotic freak. He gives her the same dignity given to Israel's matriarchs *because of* his understanding of her past, not despite it. She is not a Geisha or a Jezebel or a hot Latina, but a person of remarkable resilience in the face of multiple hardships. This compassionate gaze sees beyond stereotypes about promiscuity, with eyes seeing trauma, rejection, and abandonment instead. This optic will be vital as we look next at how these stereotypes imprison marginalized women and girls in contemporary life.

Metaphorical and Material Prisons

This section serves as a prelude to considering Jesus's posture toward crime and punishment by connecting these themes with our earlier discussion of stereotypes. By looking at Black women and girls in the prison industrial complex and the school-to-prison pipeline, we can engage some of the real-world consequences of racialized gendered stereotypes. We'll start with an overview of how Black women fare in the prison industrial complex before considering the plight of Black girls in the school-to-prison pipeline. We'll end this section by looking at how the racialized stereotypes reviewed earlier in this chapter result in overscrutiny and excessive discipline for Black women and how these regimes of control are beginning to focus on using White female bodies to feed the rapacious economic engines of mass incarceration. All of this will prepare us for a final reflection on women vis-à-vis three ancient texts: the unnamed woman caught in adultery in John 8:11, the lead character in the apocryphal work Susanna and the Elders, and the Samaritan's story explored above.

Race, Gender, and the Prison Industrial Complex

With over two million people behind bars in federal and state prisons and local jails, the United States incarcerates more people than even the most repressive countries in the world, outpacing regimes in China, Russia, and Iran (figure 4.1).[58] The so-called War on Drugs began in 1971 in President Richard Nixon's

58. The United States outstrips other countries in lifetime sentences as well. A 2012

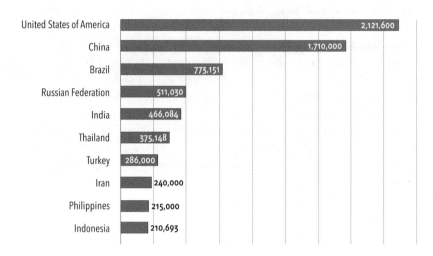

Figure 4.1. Ten Countries with the Largest Imprisoned Populations (June 2020)
Data retrieved from Institute for Crime and Justice Policy Research 2020

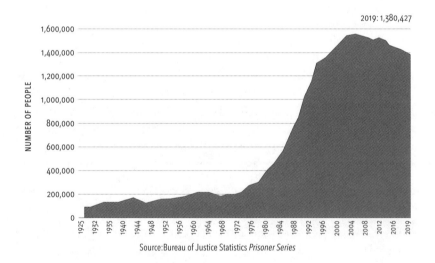

Figure 4.2. US Prison Population (1925–2019)
Data from the Sentencing Project 2021

address to a special session of Congress.[59] Congress issued their first salvo enjoining the war with the passage of the 1986 Anti-Drug Act during the Reagan administration. This law focused on punishment rather than treatment by establishing mandatory sentencing minimums, and it introduced the disparate 100:1 ratio in sentencing for crack versus powder cocaine, which fueled racially disparate results since Whites are more likely to use powder cocaine.[60] Another cause of skyrocketing imprisonment rates was prosecutors' increasing use of plea bargaining as an instrument to force defendants to plead guilty, in effect punishing defendants who choose to go to trial.[61] Defendants who choose to go to trial get sentences that average eleven years longer than the sentences given to defendants who plead guilty.[62] The War on Drugs uses a myriad of strategies—rulings by the US Supreme Court extending the power of police and prosecutors, long sentences, mandatory minimums, three-strikes laws with mandated minimums, aggressive policing, a focus on custody over rehabilitation in prisons, the piling up of collateral consequences, and increased reliance on fees and fines to fund state criminal justice systems—to produce a situation where millions are imprisoned with broad, generational community impacts.[63] As a result, the United States has increased the incarcerated population by nearly 500 percent over the last forty years (figure 4.2).[64]

Since Whites and minorities use drugs at roughly the same rates, the War on Drugs should have yielded incarceration rates roughly aligned with their population proportions. In other words, if drug arrests transpired on terrain

---

study by the Sentencing Project ("Parents in Prison") estimates that one of every seven people in prison is serving a life sentence. According to Tiffany Simmons, "The rationale behind life sentences without or with parole makes little sense from a penological perspective since inmates tend to age out of offending. Reducing prison sentences for serious offenders runs into strong political opposition. . . . [Further,] almost six million individuals, many of them African American, are barred from voting despite having completed their sentences. [By contrast, in] many European nations, inmates can vote while they are serving sentences. Court rulings in Europe have made wholesale bans on voting a violation of human rights. Canada, Israel and South Africa similarly have found bans on voting based on conviction of criminal offenses unconstitutional." See Simmons, "War on Drugs on Black Women," 740.

59. Jones and Seabrook, "New Jane Crow"; Simmons, "War on Drugs on Black Women," 731.

60. Simmons, "War on Drugs on Black Women," 723.

61. Simmons, "War on Drugs on Black Women," 731.

62. According to Tiffany Simmons, 97 percent of drug convictions were concluded through plea bargains in 2012 ("War on Drugs on Black Women," 731).

63. Simmons, "War on Drugs on Black Women," 735.

64. The Sentencing Project, "Trends in U.S. Corrections."

aligned with drug use, more Whites would have been victims of mass incarceration.[65] Thus, the actual over-incarceration of Blacks and Latinx people point, above all, to the results of police discretion in law enforcement. Michelle Alexander's 2010 book, *The New Jim Crow*, does an excellent job describing mass incarceration in the US as a prison industrial complex that exerted renewed draconian state-mandated control as a backlash to new Civil Rights legislation in the 1960s to 1970s. Alexander documents how the so-called War on Drugs of the 1980s and 1990s wreaked devastation in a new period of social control over Black, Indigenous, and Latinx bodies that acts as a virtual renewal of the Jim Crow era.[66] Her book has effectively changed the conversation about US corrections and has helped bring about desperately needed reforms that have slowed imprisonment rates over the last ten years (figure 4.2).[67]

The effects of mass incarceration are well known (figure 4.3), with Black men born in 2001 having a one in three chance of being imprisoned at some point in their lifetimes (figure 4.4). However, the plight of women is much less visible, especially regarding Black women (figure 4.5). As described earlier in this chapter, gendered stereotypes for Black women are metaphorical prisons, and this section describes some of the real-life consequences of these metaphors for African American women and girls. Though imprisonment rates have declined in recent years for Black women, in 2019 the rate for African American women was still 70 percent higher than for White women, and the rate for Latinas was 30 percent higher (figure 4.6).[68] Likewise, girls of color aged 12–17 are more likely to be incarcerated than White girls. Black girls are three and a half times more likely to end up in a juvenile justice facility than White girls, while Indigenous girls are four times more likely to be imprisoned.[69]

Marissa Alexander's treatment in the criminal justice system illustrates its continuing inequities even during the current period of declining incarceration rates for Black women. This account from *Essence* magazine was pieced together from an exclusive interview with author Jeannine Amber, which was published in 2015:

65. Simmons, "War on Drugs on Black Women," 736.

66. Alexander, *New Jim Crow*, 123: "Although the majority of illegal drug users and dealers nationwide are white, three-fourths of all people imprisoned for drug offenses have been black or Latino."

67. For example, in 2014 and 2015, forty-six states enacted laws, issued executive orders, or passed ballot initiatives designed to reform the criminal justice system, per Simmons, "War on Drugs on Black Women," 737–38.

68. The Sentencing Project, "Incarcerated Women and Girls."

69. Brock, "Women of Color behind Bars."

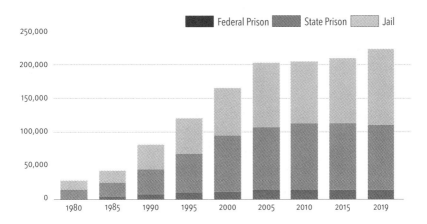

Figure 4.3. Mass Incarceration in the United States (1980–2019)
Prison figures are from year-end 2019 while jail figures are from year-end 2018, the latest available data from the sources used. From the Bureau of Justice Statistics: Historical Corrections Statistics in the United States 1850–1984 (1986); Prison and Jail Inmates at Midyear Series (1997–2018), Prisoners Series (1986–2019), Washington, DC.

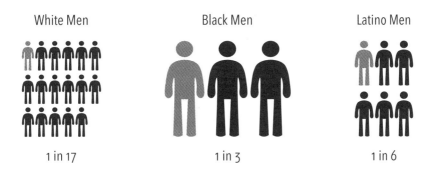

Figure 4.4. Lifetime Likelihood of Imprisonment for US Men Born in 2001
Data from the Sentencing Project 2021

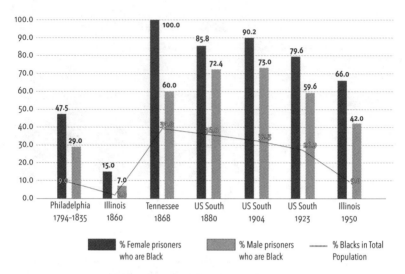

Figure 4.5. *Historical Trends in Black Female Incarceration*
Graph constructed from data described in Gross, "African American Women, Mass Incarceration," 27–28; and Gibson and Jung, "Historical Census Statistics"

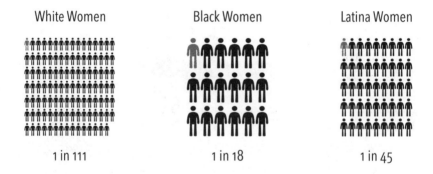

Figure 4.6. *Lifetime Likelihood of Imprisonment for US Women Born in 2001*
Data from the Sentencing Project 2021

On July 31, 2010, Alexander, then a 29-year-old mother of three, returned to the Jacksonville, Florida, home she once shared with her estranged husband, Rico Gray, to collect some belongings. Gray, who had been arrested three times in the past on charges of domestic violence, showed up unexpectedly with his two sons from previous relationships.

According to Alexander, Gray flew into a rage and threatened to kill her after seeing some text messages on her phone. Alexander says she ran to her truck, but was unable to leave because the garage door was broken. She then retrieved her gun from her vehicle's glove compartment, went back inside and fired a warning shot into the kitchen wall. Gray left the house and called 911, telling the operator that Alexander had shot at him and his children. Alexander, who had given birth to the couple's daughter only nine days before the incident, was subsequently charged with three counts of aggravated assault.

Four months after the event, Gray gave a sworn deposition to the state's prosecutors in which he admitted to a history of physically abusing Alexander and other women with whom he'd had relationships. "I got five baby mamas and I put my hand on every last one of them except one," he said under oath. "The way I was with women, they was like they had to walk on eggshells around me. You know, they never knew what I was thinking or what I might do. Hit them, push them."[70]

Alexander was convicted of aggravated assault charges in 2012 for firing a warning shot during a confrontation with her estranged, abusive husband, a man against whom she had a restraining order.[71] Her conviction, carrying a twenty-year mandatory sentence, transpired despite a Stand Your Ground law in Florida that allows for the use of deadly force in self-defense with no duty to retreat when a violent intruder breaks into a home or car. A judge denied that defense, citing a "factual dispute" about whether the law applied when prosecutors noted that the bullet went into the wall behind her husband rather than into the ceiling, asserting that she fired "out of anger."[72] On the other hand, the same Florida Stand Your Ground law was a factor in George Zimmerman's acquittal after fatally shooting Trayvon Martin, an unarmed black teenager.[73]

70. Amber, "In Her Own Words."
71. Gross, "African American Women," 25.
72. Hauser, "Florida Woman."
73. According to Christine Hauser, the Stand Your Ground law was not an explicit factor in Mr. Zimmerman's defense because his lawyers argued he shot in self-defense. But Stand

In other words, Alexander, a battered Black mother who had neither hurt nor killed her abuser, was unable to invoke the same legal protections accessed by Zimmerman, an overzealous neighborhood watchman who had killed a harmless Black teenager carrying Skittles.

While awaiting a new trial in November 2014, Alexander accepted a plea deal to serve an additional sixty-five days in jail followed by two years of probation under house arrest with a surveillance monitor. Her case also illustrates the plea bargain tactic that drives longer sentences described above: she agreed to these terms instead of facing new charges that could have changed her sentencing from the twenty years she'd already received to sixty years. In other words, *nine days after childbirth* this new mom fired a warning shot at the man she had a court order against, a sworn abuser, and consequently had to worry about charges leading to *sixty years* in prison. Something is terribly wrong with this situation. As Kali Nicole Gross puts it:

> Alexander's case reflects the legacies of an exclusionary politics of protection whereby black women were not entitled to the law's protection, though they could not escape its punishment. . . . Without institutional safeguards, black women seeking security or justice would have to create those circumstances for themselves, which often placed them on the receiving end of harsh sentences from the same legal system that failed them. . . . The elephant in the room is that black women have had to be better prepared to defend themselves against partner violence because it is well-known that the criminal justice system will not protect them.[74]

Overall, the United States accounts for 5 percent of the world's population and 25 percent of the world's inmates, but imprisons 30 percent of women incarcerated globally.[75] According to the *New York Times*, the number of incarcerated women increased by more than 750 percent between 1980 and 2019, a rate twice that for men.[76] Two-thirds of incarcerated women in the United States are women of color.[77] Though this receives less attention in the media, Black women are also subject to aggressive policing. When taking women into custody, male officers may not conduct searches, which female police officers

---

Your Ground was part of the jury's instructions and played a role in the way the police approached the initial investigation. See Hauser, "Florida Woman."

74. Gross, "African American Women," 25–26.
75. Simmons, "War on Drugs on Black Women," 742.
76. Levin, "Primal Wound."
77. Brock, "Women of Color behind Bars."

do, but they may complete street-level frisks. So when stopped in street encounters, Black women are subject to the same humiliation as Black men but suffer different kinds of abuse, including sexual molestation.[78]

More than 60 percent of women in state prisons and nearly 80 percent of those in jail are the primary caretakers of minor children.[79] One in fifteen black children, one in forty-two Latinx children, and one in 111 White children had a parent in prison in 2007.[80] However, once incarcerated, mothers often have very little to no contact with their children, usually because state prisons are often located more than one hundred miles away from urban areas, and federal prisons are even more remote. Compounding the distance between home and the prison facility is the high cost of transportation and collect calls as call recipients are typically charged exorbitant rates, another dimension of the prison industrial complex.[81]

The history of women's prison experiences has always been racialized. As shown in figure 4.5 above, there is a long history of Black female trauma in unjust US justice systems. A 1662 Virginia law incentivized rape to produce more slaves, decreeing that the children of enslaved Africans and Englishmen would be enslaved or free according to the mother's condition, changing a legal practice that had up until then comported with English law focused on the father's status.[82] Colonial rape laws compounded their subjugation by excluding recognition of sexual assault for Black women.[83] Limited almost exclusively to domestic service and agricultural work, Black women were vulnerable to sexual harassment in White homes and accusations of theft—whether real or imagined.[84]

In the nineteenth century, Black women received longer sentences and less rehabilitation training.[85] While drug crimes form the bulk of arrests for women today, larceny constituted the lion's share of Black women's criminal arrests in the eighteenth and nineteenth centuries. Jones and Seabrook examine the

78. For instance, Mitzi Smith describes the case of Oklahoma City police officer Daniel Holtzclaw, who sexually assaulted and raped poor Black women. In December 2015 a jury convicted Holtzclaw of eighteen counts of rape and sexual assault and he was later sentenced to 263 years in prison. See M. J. Smith, *Womanist Sass*, 63.

79. Simmons, "War on Drugs on Black Women," 741.

80. The Sentencing Project, "Parents in Prison."

81. Jones and Seabrook, "New Jane Crow," 136.

82. Gross, "African American Women," 26.

83. Gross, "African American Women," 26.

84. Gross, "African American women," 28.

85. Brown and Chesney-Lind, "Women's Incarceration in the United States," 129.

antebellum, eugenics, and mass incarceration eras to demonstrate how a Jane Crow set of laws and practices have inhibited Black women in mothering their children across time, thereby disrupting the social cohesion of the Black community. Slave breeding programs became institutionalized after Congress passed a prohibition on importing slaves that went into effect in 1808. Slave breeding enacted a system of punishments and rewards that sold, punished, or separated Black women from their families if they were infertile or recalcitrant.[86] In the first half of the twentieth century, the eugenics movement attempted to eradicate undesirables like Black women by preventing pregnancies among those considered unfit or unintelligent through birth control and sterilization programs, which the Nazis later used as models.[87] White female rehabilitation characterized twentieth-century thinking about incarceration for women, though reforms failed to improve conditions for Black women.[88] Yet, in the twenty-first century, more punitive attitudes have emerged, with less focus on rehabilitation and increased emphasis upon the rise of mandatory sentencing and get-tough policies.[89] At the height of the War on Drugs from the mid-1980s through 1991, the number of Black women incarcerated for drug crimes increased by 828 percent. This increase was nearly twice that of Black men and three times the number of White female drug offenders."[90]

Girls and Women Scrutinized, Stereotyped, and Punished

When we learn that schools suspend Blacks students at three times the rate of Whites, we can conclude that this discipline-and-punish form of social control exempts no part of African American life. Schools that impose harsh, zero-tolerance disciplinary measures for minor offenses increase the likelihood that students will become ensnared in the criminal justice system. Along with the use of police officers to maintain order and reliance on courts for in-school infractions, these tactics form the basis of a "school-to-prison pipeline."[91] A landmark study on how Black girls are affected by this school-to-prison pipeline opens with stories that illustrate these dynamics:

86. Jones and Seabrook, "New Jane Crow," 139.
87. Jones and Seabrook, "New Jane Crow," 141.
88. Brown and Chesney-Lind, "Women's Incarceration in the United States," 130.
89. Brown and Chesney-Lind, "Women's Incarceration in the United States," 130.
90. Brown and Chesney-Lind, "Women's Incarceration in the United States," 132.
91. Crenshaw, Ocen, and Nand, "Black Girls Matter," 52–53; Dukes, "Overlooked Link."

In 2014, a 12-year-old girl faced expulsion and criminal charges after writing "hi" on a locker room wall of her Georgia middle school, and a Detroit honors student was suspended for her entire senior year for accidentally bringing a pocketknife to a football game. In 2013, an 8-year-old girl in Illinois was arrested for acting out, and a 16-year-old girl in Alabama who suffers from diabetes, asthma, and sleep apnea was hit with a book by her teacher after she fell asleep in class. The student was later arrested and hospitalized due to injuries she sustained in her interaction with the police. Also in 2013, a 16-year-old in Florida was arrested when an experiment she tried on school grounds caused a small explosion, and a 12-year-old girl was threatened with expulsion from an Orlando private school unless she changed the look of her natural hair. In 2007, a 6-year-old girl was arrested for having a tantrum. Later that year, a 16-year-old girl was arrested in a California school for dropping cake on the floor and failing to pick it up to a school officer's satisfaction.[92]

Recent examples of this excessive treatment of Black girls attest to the fact that these patterns are ongoing: an upstate New York police officer pepper-sprayed a nine-year-old Black girl in January 2021; in May 2020, a Michigan judge had a fifteen-year-old Black girl arrested and incarcerated because she didn't complete her online schoolwork; in August 2020 Denver police handcuffed and detained four Black girls, ages six, twelve, fourteen, and seventeen, at gunpoint when police wrongfully suspected the car they were riding in was stolen; and in September 2019, police arrested and fingerprinted a six-year-old Black girl for kicking a staff member during a tantrum at her school in Orlando.[93]

There is evidence that teachers interpret transgressions more critically when children of color exhibit them. One 2011 study found that educators punish African American and Latinx students more severely than Whites for the same or similar behavior, conclusions reaffirmed in an experiment in 2021.[94] Research in 2015 implied the operation of implicit bias in school discipline when it found a "punishment gap" wherein African American students are punished primarily for subjectively assessed infractions such as disobedience

92. Crenshaw, Ocen, and Nand, "Black Girls Matter," 5.
93. Nuamah, "Police Killed a Black Teenage Girl"; Slevin and Nieberg, "Colorado Officers Won't Be Charged."
94. Nuamah, "Police Killed a Black Teenage Girl."

or defiance.[95] A 2017 study examined detailed school discipline records for a diverse urban school district in Kentucky and found significant disparities in punishment for Black girls.[96] They were three times more likely than White girls to receive an office referral and received them for subjective infractions such as disruptive behavior, dress code violations, disobedience, and aggressive behavior. By contrast, more severe infractions associated with less ambiguous offenses such as truancy, theft, substance use, and possession of a weapon show either no effect of race or found White students more likely to be in violation.[97] In other words, educators disciplined African American girls for assertive behavior interpreted as loud and overbearing. Latina and White girls in the same school did not receive similar admonishments to behave like "ladies," even when they exhibited comparable behavior and wore similar clothing.[98] Thus, the authors concluded, "school discipline penalizes African American girls for behaviors perceived to transgress normative standards of femininity."[99]

Stereotypes of Black women and girls impede their life outcomes in innumerable interactions in everyday life in commerce, school, employment, and more. This section has shown that these stereotypes have a toxic influence, particularly when these women and girls engage regimes of discipline and punishment. Stereotyped as poor, uneducated, and unable to identify their own best interests, they are seen as bad, unfit mothers and disproportionately have their children taken from their custody in encounters with the criminal justice system.[100] Imagined as oversexed Jezebels, they are prey for sexual assault from police officers and jailors in macabre echoes from the Jane Crow and the slaveholding past. The Angry Black Woman (ABW) trope is partially a relic of slaveholders' insistence that Black women didn't suffer physical pain as White women do, so they could perform the same backbreaking labor as Black men. We've seen that this image affects the lives of Black girls even before they attain full maturity as women, resulting in disparate punishment for minor infractions that push them ever closer to the carceral state. Depicted as loud and

95. Skiba et al., "Race Is Not Neutral"; Forsyth et al., "Punishment Gap."

96. Morris and Perry, "Girls Behaving Badly?" The Kentucky school district in question had twenty-two grade 6–12 schools where Whites were 64 percent of the total population, Blacks were 24 percent, Latinx were 8 percent, and Asians were 4 percent. These demographics were roughly representative of the southeastern US location of the district.

97. Morris and Perry, "Girls Behaving Badly?," 18.

98. Morris and Perry, "Girls Behaving Badly?," 3.

99. Morris and Perry, "Girls Behaving Badly?," 1.

100. Jones and Seabrook, "New Jane Crow," 141, 146, 148.

aggressive with an "attitude," they are recipients of force tactics incommensurate with their ages or the seriousness of the minor offenses they commit.

Both the Jezebel and ABW phenomenon were vividly on display in the viral video involving Eric Casebolt and Dajerria Becton.[101] In 2015, Casebolt body slammed fifteen-year-old Dajerria Becton, clad in a two-piece bathing suit, into concrete as he handcuffed her at a pool party in a private, predominantly White subdivision. Casebolt, a White cop twice her size, kneeled on her back as she called for her mother, dynamics both eerily similar and yet horrifically twisted from the video that launched a thousand mass demonstrations in the wake of George Floyd's murder. Becton eventually won a $148,000 settlement with the City of McKinney, TX, but the threat to Black women and girls from the ABW stereotype screams from this account of the aftermath of the encounter:

> The settlement announcement came shortly after McKinney mayor George Fuller referred to Becton as "a verbally abusive, disobedient girl" in an email to Dominique Alexander, a local activist. . . . "He was the one who was verbally abusive," Dajerria's attorney, Howard University School of Law grad Kim T. Cole, tells Teen Vogue, referring to Casebolt. "You're not afraid of white people who pose an actual threat, who walk out of shooting up a church or a school without a scratch on them, but you are afraid of a Black girl and her 'tone'?" Cole says. "Watch the video—she never used a cuss word, never talked back to him—all she did was repeatedly ask someone to call her mama," the lawyer says.
>
> Mayor Fuller's comments reflected the position taken by the city and Casebolt in their pleadings in Dajerria's lawsuit: *that by speaking in Casebolt's direction, Dajerria ostensibly posed a threat to the officer*, a perceived threat that justified grabbing the then 15-year-old by the hair, throwing her facedown on the ground, and straddling her with his knees to her back. (emphasis added)[102]

The collision between the ABW-Sapphire stereotype and the carceral state most likely also figures in Marissa Alexander's story and the critical decision that banned her use of the Stand Your Ground defense. Legal scholar Sharon Angella Allard maintains that the stereotype influences whether a "battered wife syndrome" defense is accessible to Black women accused of violence against abusive partners as in Alexander's case. According to Allard, the legal theory rests

---

101. Dukes, "Overlooked Link," 55.
102. Ritchie, "Dajerria Becton."

on the idea that battered women suffer from "learned helplessness" adopted to help them live with the constant fear of battering rather than focusing on trying to escape the situation.[103] To access this defense, a battered woman needs to convince a jury that she is "normal," where "normal" derives from stereotypes about White women imagined as weak, passive, and fearful. Impeded by stereotypes of Black women as angry and impervious to harm, juries may find their stories of battering less credible because they believe their situation doesn't fit that of the stereotypical battered woman.[104] Since the battered women theory is based on stereotypes of White women, Allard finds that the theory does not apply to women of color.[105] In order "to present a successful defense to a charge of killing her batterer, the woman must not appear angry," a standard that has tragic implications for Black women who are subject to the ABW-Sapphire stereotype.[106] In other words, Marissa Alexander didn't stand a chance once the prosecutors argued that she fired her warning shot "in anger."

There is an aphorism in the Black community that says something to the effect that if White America has the sniffles, Black America has pneumonia. We saw that play out in the pandemic, where underlying poor health, lack of access to health care, and overrepresentation in lower-wage jobs placed them in essential worker categories requiring routine interaction in public, resulting in catastrophic COVID deaths among Black, Latinx, and Indigenous populations. Yet, students of racial and ethnic studies have long understood that the dysfunctions heaped on the backs of Blacks and other people of color eventually take a toll on White victims as well.[107] There is some evidence that Whites are beginning to experience the tragic costs of a punitive approach to drug addiction, which has for decades decimated the Black community even in an era of reform where incarceration rates are declining. It appears that law enforcement is sweeping up rural, low-income White women in the drug war at higher rates than had previously been experienced by urban Black women. Though there are still two to three times as many Black women imprisoned as White women, the incarceration rate between 2000 and 2019 went up for White women by 41 percent, while the rate for Black women declined by 60 percent.[108] Some or

103. Allard, "Rethinking Battered Woman Syndrome," 192.

104. Allard, "Rethinking Battered Woman Syndrome," 193–94.

105. Allard, "Rethinking Battered Woman Syndrome," 197.

106. Allard, "Rethinking Battered Woman Syndrome," 197.

107. See for instance McGhee, *Sum of Us*; Quadagno, *Color of Welfare*; Metzl, *Dying of Whiteness*.

108. The Sentencing Project, "Incarcerated Women and Girls"; Brown and Chesney-Lind, "Women's Incarceration in the United States," 132–33.

all of the change can perhaps be explained as drug enforcement policy shifts from a focus on crack cocaine to methamphetamines. Likewise, in urban centers where Blacks are concentrated, criminal justice reform is speedier, while whiter, rural communities retain the status quo.[109] Similar declines are evident in the imprisonment rate for Black men as well: Between 2000 and 2015, the rate of black men dropped by more than 24 percent, while the White male rate increased slightly. So even though the racial disparity between Black and White is declining, as legal scholar John Pfaff at Fordham University has put it, "the racial disparity remains so vast that it's pretty hard to celebrate. How exactly do you talk about 'less horrific'?"[110] In the text that follows, we'll look at how the situation of women of color in the prison-industrial complex rhymes with biblical stories about women caught in judicial proceedings.

Susanna, the Samaritan, and the Women Who Were Caught (John 7:53–8:11 and Susanna and the Elders)

Then each of them went home, [8:1]while Jesus went to the Mount of Olives. [2]Early in the morning, he came again to the temple. All the people came to him, and he sat down and began to teach them. [3]The scribes and the Pharisees brought a woman they had caught in adultery and making her stand before all of them [4]they said to him, "Teacher, we caught this woman in the very act of committing adultery. [5]In the Law, Moses commanded us to stone such women. Now what do you say?" [6]They spoke this way to test him to have a charge to bring against him. Jesus bent down and wrote with his finger on the ground. [7]When they kept on questioning him, he straightened up and said to them, "Let anyone among you who is without sin be the first to throw a stone at her." [8]And once again, he bent down and wrote on the ground. [9]When they heard it, they went away, one by one, beginning with the elders, and Jesus was left alone with the woman standing before him. [10]Jesus straightened up and said to her, "Woman, where are they? Has no one condemned you?" [11]She said, "No one, sir." And Jesus said, "Neither do I condemn you. Go your way, and from now on, do not sin." (John 7:53–8:11 AT)

The pericope in John 7:53–8:11 was almost certainly not a part of the autographs of the Gospel of John, in that no version of it appears in manuscripts

109. Hager, "Mass Incarceration Mystery."
110. Hager, "Mass Incarceration Mystery," 2.

from before AD 400. While the passage usually appears after John 7:52, other biblical manuscripts attach the story in different places in the narrative: after 7:36, 7:44, or 21:25.[111] There are even a few manuscripts in which the story is inserted in the Gospel of Luke after 21:38.[112] Despite the near unanimity that it was added to the gospel late, most scholars regard the passage as an authentic and early piece of the Jesus tradition by the usual canons of historical analysis. The story likely circulated in oral history long before it was attached to gospel manuscripts.[113] As such, we often see the passage printed in Bibles at John 7:53, though marked off with some indication of its textual uncertainty. Although the passage is regarded as canonical by the Catholic and Orthodox confessions within the church, most Protestant Bibles have indicators that signal its secondary status relative to the surrounding biblical text.

But what is less well known about the passage is its similarity to the first-century BC story of Susanna and the Elders (hereafter "Susanna").[114] The Susanna story, shown below, is counted as an apocryphal story for Protestants, but it is included in the canonical scriptures of the Roman Catholic and Eastern Orthodox churches.

[1]There was a man living in Babylon named Joakim. [2]He married a woman named Susanna, daughter of Hilkiah, who was very beautiful and God-fearing. [3]Her parents were also righteous and taught their daughter according to the Law of Moses. [4]Joakim was very wealthy and had a garden attached to his house. The Jews came to him because he was most honored overall. [5]That same year two elders were appointed from the people as judges. About these men, the Master had said, "Lawlessness comes from Babylon, from elders who were judges who were supposed to govern the people." [6]And they stayed in Joakim's house, so anyone having lawsuits came to them there.

[7]And it happened that when the people left at midday, Susanna would walk in her husband's garden. [8]Daily, the two elders saw her going into the garden and walking around; they lusted after her. [9]They corrupted their thinking and avoided looking toward Heaven or remembering their duty to judge rightly. [10]They were both riveted by her, but they did not want to tell each other of their affliction. [11]They were ashamed to talk of their lust because they wanted to have sex with her. [12]Day after day, they eagerly spied on her.

111. Metzger, *Greek New Testament*, 188–89.
112. Metzger, *Greek New Testament*, 189.
113. Metzger, *Greek New Testament*, 189.
114. Clanton, "(Re)Dating the Story of Susanna."

[13]And one day, they said to each other, "Let us go home now because it is time to eat." And they left, separating from each other. [14]But turning back, they each came back, meeting at the same place. Pressing each other for a reason, they confessed their lust and then plotted together for a time about when they could get her alone. [15]As they were watching for a suitable day, she entered the garden with only two girls like she'd done the day before and the third day before that. She wanted to bathe in the garden because it was hot. [16]There was no one there except the two elders who were hiding so that they could watch. [17]And she said to the girls, "Bring me oil and perfume and shut the door of the garden so that I can bathe." [18]They did as she asked and shutting the door of the garden, they left by the side door to bring the things she ordered them to get. They did not see the two elders because they were hiding.

[19]When the girls left, the two elders rose and ran over to her. [20]They said, "Look here, the doors of the garden are shut, and no one sees us. However, we are lusting for you, so give your consent and have sex with us. [21]If you don't, we will swear against you that you were having sex with a young man, which is why you sent the girls away from you." [22]Susanna sighed deeply and said, "I'm trapped. If I do this, they will kill me for adultery, and if I don't consent, I still won't be able to escape you. [23]I choose not to do this. I'd rather fall into your hands than sin before the Lord." [24]Then Susanna screamed loudly, and the two elders shouted out too, [25]one of them running to open the door of the garden. [26]When the people in the house heard the shouting in the garden, they rushed out of the side door to see what had happened to her. [27]When the elders told their story, the slaves were mortified because no one had ever said something like this about Susanna.

[28]The next day, when the people gathered at Joakim's house, the two elders came with the devious intention of putting Susanna to death. [29]They said in front of everyone, "Send for Susanna, the daughter of Hilkiah, who is the wife of Joakim." So the people sent for her, [30]and she came with her parents, her children, and her relatives. [31]Now, Susanna was very voluptuous and stunning in appearance. [32]Because she was covered up, those lawless elders ordered her stripped because they wanted to get satisfaction by looking at her beauty. [33]Then those who were with her and everyone who saw her wept.

[34]Rising, the two elders placed her in front of everyone and laid hands on her head [35]while the weeping woman stared up into heaven, for her heart trusted in the Lord. [36]Then the elders said, "While we were walking alone in the garden, she came in with two female slaves and shut the doors of the

garden and sent the slaves away. Then a young man came to her who had been hidden, and he went to bed with her. ³⁸Since we were in the corner of the garden watching this lawless deed, we ran to them, and, ³⁹although we saw them having sex, we were not able to capture him because he was stronger than us. He opened the door and rushed out. ⁴⁰We grabbed hold of her and asked her who the young man was, ⁴¹but she did not want to tell us. This concludes our testimony." The assembly believed them because they were elders and judges, so they condemned her to death.

⁴²Then Susanna cried out loudly, "O Eternal God. You know what is hidden, and you see all things before it happens. ⁴³You know that their testimony against me is false. Look, I am about to die but haven't done any of the things in their wicked charges against me!" ⁴⁴Then the Lord attended to her voice. ⁴⁵Just as they were leading her away to execute her, God stirred up the holy spirit in a young boy named Daniel. ⁴⁶Daniel shouted out, "I want nothing to do with shedding this woman's blood!" ⁴⁷All the people turned to him and said, "What are you talking about?"

⁴⁸Standing among the people, he said, "You foolish Israelites! Are you going to judge a fellow Israelite woman without knowing the facts or making an inquiry? ⁴⁹Go back to court; these men have lied in their testimony against her." ⁵⁰So all the people hurried back, and the other elders said to him, "Sit with us and tell us what gift of insight God has given to you." ⁵¹Daniel said to them, "Separate them far from each other, and I will cross-examine them." ⁵²After being separated, he summoned one of them and said, "You evil, dirty old man with an evil past, now your past sins have caught up with you. You were making unjust verdicts, condemning the innocent, and exonerating the guilty, all while the Lord decreed that you should not kill the innocent or righteous." Then he said to him, "If you saw them being intimate, under what kind of tree did you see them with each other?" And the elder said, "Under a mastic tree." ⁵⁵Then Daniel said, "Truly you are lying through your teeth! The angel of the Lord has already received a sentence from God to cut you in two." ⁵⁶Then turning from that elder, he ordered them to bring the other one. He said to him, "You are a Canaanite and not a true Judahite. Beauty has seduced you, and lust has corrupted your heart. ⁵⁷You did the same thing to the Israelite women, but they gave in and slept with you in fear. But a Judahite woman did not put up with your wickedness. ⁵⁸So now tell me, under what kind of tree did you catch them being intimate with each other?" The elder said, "Under an evergreen oak." ⁵⁹Daniel said to him, "Truly you are lying through your

teeth. The angel of God stands holding a sword to slice you in two and utterly destroy you both."

[60]Then, the whole assembly shouted out with a loud noise and blessed the God who saves those who keep hope in God. [61]They arose against the two elders because Daniel got them to exhibit their lying from their own mouths. Then they did to the two elders what they wickedly planned to do to their neighbor. [62]They did what the law of Moses required and killed them; that day, innocent blood was saved. [63]Hilkiah and his wife praised God for their daughter Susanna, with Joakim, her husband, and all their relatives, because she was not found guilty in this matter. [64]Daniel became greatly admired among the people from that day onward. (AT)

Amy-Jill Levine's feminist critique analyzes the narrative through the prism of colonial strategies of resistance, highlighting several pertinent issues. First, she notes that the story focuses on controlling Susanna's sexuality in a way that rhymes with Michelle Alexander's discussion of mass incarceration as social control of Black and Latinx bodies. Using some of the same categories as found in Alexander's discussion of the prison industrial complex, Levine discusses the intersection of identity, representation, and control in Susanna. She notes how male writers used women as metaphorical representatives of the community, depicting their relationship to external and internal threats through stories featuring women as virgins, whores, and widows. Control over external threats or control over the community, as in Susanna's case, is figured through trauma inflicted on their bodies or through their bodies.[115] Susanna's assault is analogous in some ways to the plight of Black women who are abused and punished by the same systems that are allegedly established to protect them. The elders in the text are analogous to the predatory police officers who sexually assault the women they are supposed to protect.

Susanna reasons that she is in a no-win situation. She will be sentenced to death by Torah for adultery if she gives consent under pressure and essentially consigns herself to their control in an abusive relationship. Yet, she also realizes that withholding consent is not viable since they can either overpower her or falsely accuse her, both of which still likely leave her condemned of adultery and subject to execution. But Susanna uses her knowledge of the situation and the law to do what she can to protect herself. In verse 24, when she decides to refuse the elders pressuring her into sex she cries out in a loud voice, re-

---

115. Levine, "Hemmed in on Every Side," 318; cf. 309–10; Alexander, *New Jim Crow*, passim.

flecting knowledge of Deuteronomy 22:23–27, which exonerates the woman who cries out for help when sexually assaulted in an urban center like Babylon (cf. v. 3).[116] In this action, Susanna resists her attacker rather than submitting to the abuse. She reminds us of Marissa Alexander at this point, who tried to seek the protection of the law against her abuser. Having already secured a restraining order against him, Alexander wanted to protect herself via Florida's Stand Your Ground law when engaging her abuser, believing she had a legal right to resist her abuser in her own home. Unfortunately, Alexander is unlike Susanna in that she did not receive the protections of full citizenship and the presumption of innocence that Susanna received through Daniel's advocacy. Just as the Deuteronomistic code assumes that innocent women will behave in prescribed ways when under assault, so too does our justice system think that there is only one stereotypical framework of action for a battered woman. This legal framework left Marissa Alexander unprotected and imprisoned for morally just actions because prosecutors saw her as a Jezebel or Sapphire and not as someone like Susanna, a woman presumed innocent and worthy of legal protection. Susanna's self-advocacy is similarly judged less harshly than Black girls caught in discriminatory discipline at school. She screams while being pressured into rape (Sus. 24), she shouts out loud, defending herself and protesting the elders' lies rather than cowering in abject silence (vv. 42–43). In this, she is analogous to the Black girls who have nothing for their defense but their own loud voices and an I'm-not-gonna-take-it-anymore attitude.

Susanna's demeanor during the confrontation with the elders before the community is also worth noting. She enters the gathering accompanied by her parents and relatives, in effect "bringing the voices of her people" with her as she enters the arena where her life will be at stake.[117] This solidarity may not have affected the outcome, but the display of support was likely striking. One wonders what it was about the tableau that convinced Daniel of her innocence when so many in her own household were duped (Sus. 46–48; cf. vv. 26–27). My translation also heightens the humiliation in the scene after the elders summon her. Verse 31 makes plain the elders' prurient interest in Susanna's appearance by translating it as "very voluptuous," a phrase that other versions domesticate by rendering "great refinement" (NRSV), "very graceful" (NJB), and "elegant" (CEB).[118] Crazed with ungovernable lust at the sight of

116. M. J. Smith, *Womanist Sass*, 66.
117. Here I am deliberately echoing the evocative title of the book by Chanequa Walker-Barnes, *I Bring the Voices of My People*.
118. My translation of the word τρυφερὰ as "voluptuous" (Sus. 1:31) suits the broader context of lust and sexual assault in the larger story as well as the local context of an unwarranted

her curves, the elders order her stripped to gain a peek of what she'd denied them earlier. Maybe this action is what stimulated Daniel's insight into their character and defense of Susanna. The humiliation that she suffered by their command is profound, reducing her and her whole family to copious tears, even provoking the most hardened onlookers to compassion (v. 33).

We can note several correspondences between the Susanna story and the one in John 7:53–8:11. First, both stories involve judges and elders who bring accusations of adultery against a woman.[119] Second, both stories allege that the woman was "caught in the very act." Though the Susanna story is explicit about the salacious interest of the elders who plot to rape her and expose her face and body to the community, there may also be something scandalous in the Johannine story. Does the insistence that the elders caught her in a sex act in John 8:4 imply that this unnamed woman sits shamefully uncovered (in contrast to the elders who force Susanna into this pretense)? Third, while the women are brought before their respective communities to face the death penalty, they both escape punishment, in one case through acquittal and in the other through clemency. Fourth, in both cases, the woman is accused of adultery, but neither partner is available for judgment. Finally, the women are similarly rescued from the death penalty through a righteous man's mediation.

The similarities between the two stories suggest that the author of the Johannine-situated pericope may have intentionally shaped the story to call attention to the apocryphal story of Susanna. The intertextuality between the two stories may explain the otherwise odd detail that Jesus inexplicably bends down to write in the dirt with this finger two times (John 8:6, 8). Though interpreters have puzzled over the significance of this detail endlessly, it may be a Danielic allusion to another famous story about the deity's writing finger (Dan. 5:5). Of course, the Susanna story itself echoes other stories in the canon. The portion of the story that takes place in her husband's garden may echo Eve's story in Eden.[120] Allowing for the inverted genders of the main characters, the

---

strip search to humiliate a prisoner. "Voluptuous" is also one of the primary associations of the Greek as described in Liddell-Scott (s.v. τρυφερὰ).

119. The leading accusers in Susanna are the two judging elders (v. 5: "and they appointed two elders . . . as judges") while the scribes and Pharisees are the main accusers in John 8:3. Note, however, that it is the elders who are the first to leave in John 8:9 ("one by one beginning with the elders") after Jesus challenges the crowd to reckon with their own sin before stoning the woman. It is interesting to speculate if this detail reflects a narrative detail in verse 5: "Two elders among the people had been appointed as judges that year. It was about them that the Lord had spoken: '*Lawless disorder has come out of Babylon, from elders, from judges who were supposed to guide the people*'" (Sus. 5 CEB). Does John 8:9 reflect the emphasis on the elders' wickedness shown in Sus. 5?

120. Levine, "Hemmed in on Every Side," 316.

Susanna story also powerfully evokes the storyline of the conflict between Potiphar's wife and Joseph, where the wife pressures Joseph into adultery and subsequently falsely accuses him of rape when he refuses to sin.[121]

Readers who can see the similarities between Eve and the serpent, Potiphar's wife and Joseph, and Susanna and the Elders will be well-positioned to discern how these stories rhyme with the plight of Black women caught in the prison industrial complex or the school-to-prison pipeline. These scenarios involve overly scrutinized women, pressured or tempted into sin, and subsequently punished or threatened with punishment. I suggest that the sense of entrapment that prevails across these literary vignettes also exists among men of color caught in cycles of poverty, even when, like Eve, these people succumb to the lure of using illegal drugs. For Black and Latinx women and men, figurative entrapment is quickly followed by entanglement in the prison industrial complex, with all of the incentives in the system to supply bodies for the big business of corrections, bodies that lack the political and economic clout to protest or intervene. Like Susanna and the adulterous woman in John, they are overscrutinized and publicly humiliated when dragged before judges and magistrates. The situation further aligns with the woman in John, given that their partners in crime are not policed with the same rigor. White male illegal drug users are two to seven times less likely to be arrested, indicted, and incarcerated than their Black and Latinx counterparts. One nationwide study found that Black and Latinx drivers were more likely to be searched than White drivers, though they were less likely to be carrying contraband than White drivers.[122]

Just as Susanna is a more sympathetic figure than the woman in John 8, so too are the White opioid abusers in recent years treated more compassionately than the Black crack addicts of the 1990s.[123] As one writer noted, "the heroin epidemic shows that how we respond to the crimes accompanying addiction depends on how much we care about the victims of crime and those in the grip of addiction. White heroin addicts get overdose treatment, rehabilitation, and reincorporation . . . Black drug users got jail cells and 'Just Say No.'"[124]

The people in these ancient literary and contemporary scenarios are all materially harmed by public accusations and the shame and humiliation that attend

121. Levine, "Hemmed in on Every Side," 316.
122. See the results of the Stanford Open Policing Project (Pierson et al., "Large-Scale Analysis of Racial Disparities in Police Stops"). The Portland, OR, police department found that while Blacks and Latinos were twice as likely to be searched for contraband (drugs, weapons, etc.), Whites were more than 20 percent more likely to have banned material when searched (Theriault, "Playing a New Race Card").
123. Yankah, "When Addiction Has a White Face."
124. Yankah, "When Addiction Has a White Face."

them. All of them need righteous mediators who can intercede with the powerful forces arrayed against these hapless defendants. People of color need trusted mediators like Daniel, who comes from within the community and speaks with insight about the power of gendered and racialized effects of racism and discriminatory stereotypes. They need knowing and potent mediators who can advocate for clemency and point out the sin that lives among the accusers.

Thus, like Jesus in John 8, Christians need to speak into the American jurisprudence system and advocate for mercy. Christians, especially Black and Latinx Christians, need to be agents on behalf of those caught in the criminal justice system, just as Christ was an agent for God and advocated for the woman charged with adultery. We need to act on behalf of those muzzled by plea deals in a system that sweeps up the guilty and innocent alike, or those who, at a minimum, are no more guilty than many others. Christians *could* insist that we should equally condemn all who violate drug laws to loss of voting rights, loss of liberty, and vanishingly low job prospects by demanding that Whites get incarcerated for drugs at the same rates as Blacks. It would be better to advocate to "ban the box" in employment screening, decriminalize marijuana, repeal felony disenfranchisement, and increase funding for rehabilitation programs instead of prisons and jails. As these reforms take hold in both urban *and* rural centers, Christians can make sure Blacks and Latinx peoples can access these reforms at the same rates as Whites, guarding against repeating the disparate treatment of Black women in past prison reform efforts.

Yet, the possible literary relationship between the Pericope Adulterae and Susanna indicates that there might be some ambiguity concerning the Johannine woman's guilt. In the Susanna story, the reader knows that the charges are false because the alleged partner in adultery doesn't exist, raising questions, at least in my mind, about the guilt of the woman in John 8, given all the other similarities. When we recall that Susanna and the Elders clearly show that the heroine is the victim of false charges, we might begin to wonder if the missing male partner in John 8 suggests that the accusations are false in this case as well. Are Jesus's words to the woman something short of outright condemnation (8:10–11)? It's hard to say since the pronouncements of the Johannine Jesus are sometimes oblique ("If you are the Christ, tell us plainly"; 10:24) and sometimes not (the woman said, "'I know that . . . Christ is coming.' . . . Jesus said, 'That is who I am'"; 4:25–26). Perhaps the main point is that Jesus is less interested in her guilt than her restoration to the community.

The intertextuality of John 8 with Susanna and the Elders operates as a cautionary tale for Christians who are cultivating a posture about crime and punishment given the unequal justice for Blacks, Indigenous peoples, and the Latinx community. Susanna's case forces us to acknowledge that sometimes all is not as it seems and that someone who "looks" guilty may be the product of unbearable pressure on the most vulnerable. It prompts us to ask questions about those *not* appearing before the judge. It reminds us to inquire about how physical characteristics like the gender and race of the accused color perceptions of guilt and innocence. Susanna is similar to the Samaritan woman, and perhaps both are similar to the woman in John 8. Both Susanna and the Samaritan are not precisely what they appear to be. Given this, we begin to ask questions about the woman in John 8 accused of adultery but not punished for it by an all-knowing Jesus.

By reading the Johannine stories alongside earlier Jewish stories, both women seem less like sinners and more like those sinned against. In the case of the Samaritan woman, intertextuality with Genesis 24 shows her analogous to the exemplary woman who is God-ordained marriage material like Rebecca. Like the women of old, the Samaritan is worthy; she does good on her own initiative and guards the honor due to her people and forebearers. Indeed, we saw that internal contrast between John 3 and 4 point to the possibility that Jesus sees her as a true religious leader in a new ingathering of Israelites. In the case of the woman caught in adultery in John 8, intertextuality with the story of Susanna in the apocryphal legends of Daniel shows that she is analogous to Susanna. If Susanna is a virtuous woman whom criminals unjustly accuse as a consequence of their ungovernable lust and political agenda, perhaps we should question whether the elders in John 8 have accused that woman unjustly, in furtherance of their political aims (8:6).

For some readers, the analysis here has not wholly exonerated from sin the women in these stories in John. Further, these women may all exercise too much agency to be commended by males of the period. Nevertheless, these stories illustrate the difficulties of judging according to the flesh and according to appearances, and these texts play an important role in developing this theme in the Gospel. Through these stories, we see the problem of racialized and gendered stereotypes more clearly, particularly as these images imprison the minds and bodies of women and men of color in their sweeping logic. Jesus is the one trusted to judge with right judgment, who judges with the insight of God in contrast to human decisions that focus on appearances. Likewise, may we all seek the mind of Christ.

NEGOTIATING CULTURE IN THE FAMILY OF GOD IN THE BOOK OF ACTS

If we do not stop killing
the other in ourselves,
the self that we hate in others,
soon we shall all lie
in the same direction.

—*Audre Lorde, "Between Ourselves"[1]*

Beyond Diversity 101

Columbia Seminary, situated in the Atlanta metropolitan area, is one of the oldest seminaries in the United States with a vibrant, accomplished, and diverse faculty and student body. In many ways, it is a community that has progressed beyond basic conflict about inclusiveness and representation at the "Diversity 101" level, as it leans toward Martin Luther King Jr.'s Beloved Community ideal—even though that concept too is a complicated one.[2] Upon joining the community, I almost immediately found my expectations about it confirmed in both wonderful and sobering ways. When I looked for the inevitable scars that bear witness to the complicated messiness of a pursuit of justice, they were everywhere evident because life in a diverse community is hard work. Nevertheless, the scars left behind by attempts to manifest diversity, equity, and inclusion are, to me, a thing of beauty.

One of the challenges of living in this particular diverse community is the challenge of trying to be faithful to the seminary's long and rich Presbyterian heritage while also embracing, including, and empowering a host

---

1. From Lorde, *Collected Poems of Audre Lorde*, 323–25.
2. E.g., Burrow, "Beloved Community."

of non-Presbyterian community members at all levels of the institution, among trustees, administrators, faculty, staff, and students. The ongoing challenge is to create a blended community of Christian siblings where its members honor a particular long-lived heritage, but which also includes and embraces other heritages and differing visions about how to live out and engage the dominant inheritance. Does faithfulness to the heritage mean that it must be preserved as bequeathed? What happens to the legacy when newer members live out the heritage in innovative ways? Is there room for outsiders, and if so, for how many? Will newcomers have a stake in adding to the legacy, or is there a limit beyond which change can't be tolerated? Questions in this register abound whether one is concerned with family dynamics in the blended family, with generational or cultural differences in immigrant communities, or with the changing demographics in southern Presbyterian seminaries.

Some psychologists say that the desire to fit in is one of the most compelling human drives. This desire plays out in our national community and smaller community settings like Columbia Seminary. The American dream is that anyone could immigrate to this country and succeed if they work hard, sacrifice, and play by the rules, but the truth is that the United States has never been a welcoming society. In back-to-back cases in the 1920s, the Supreme Court denied petitions for citizenship by two Asian immigrants: one-and-a-half generation Japanese American Takao Ozawa in 1922 and Indian immigrant Bhagat Singh Thind in 1923.[3] Though Ozawa and Thind had played by the rules and tried to fit in, in both cases the court ruled against their US citizenship because they weren't White. The story of a different Indian immigrant, Vaishno das Bagai, demonstrates the heartbreaking impacts of these decisions. Bagai and his wife and three sons had done everything they could to "pass" as Americans and be accepted as citizens based on being a "free White man" with his family.[4] They completely assimilated into American culture by wearing American suits, speaking fluent English, adopting Western manners, and opening Bagai's Bazaar, a small family business. In the pain of being denaturalized after the 1923 *United States v. Bhagat Singh Thind* Supreme Court decision, Bagai committed suicide, leaving a note addressed to the *San Francisco Examiner*:

3. Lee and Bean, "Reinventing the Color Line."

4. At the time that Bhagat Thind petitioned for naturalized US citizenship in 1922, the 1906 Naturalization Act held that only "free white persons" and "aliens of African nativity and persons of African descent" could become United States citizens by naturalization.

I came to America thinking, dreaming, and hoping to make this land my home. Sold my properties and brought more than twenty-five thousand dollars (gold) to this country, established myself and tried my very best to give my children the best American education.

In year 1921 the Federal court at San Francisco accepted me as a naturalized citizen of the United States and issued to my name the final certificate, giving therein the name and description of my wife and three sons. In last 12 or 13 years we all made ourselves as much Americanized as possible.

But they now come to me and say, I am no longer an American citizen. They will not permit me to buy my home and, lo, they even shall not issue me a passport to go back to India. Now what am I? What have I made of myself and my children? We cannot exercise our rights, we cannot leave this country. Humility and insults, who is responsible for all this? Myself and [the] American government.

I do not choose to live the life of an interned person; yes, I am in a free country and can move about where and when I wish inside the country. Is life worth living in a gilded cage? Obstacles this way, blockades that way, and the bridges burnt behind.[5]

Today, not fitting in can still cost you dearly. Some people will insult minorities, harass them, and even shoot them dead for entering spaces that have been constructed as belonging to Whites. But as we discussed in chapter 3, if you can pull it off, "passing" or assimilating can result in a higher income and better educational outcomes for immigrants. On the other hand, the pressure to assimilate can be downright oppressive. It can be soul-killing to conform to a pattern created for Whites that does not have minoritized persons in mind. Keeping some traditions amid rising new imperatives is an urgent question in a divided society that seems to unravel just a little more every day.

I contend that the book of Acts grapples with similar dynamics. This chapter will supplement our discussion about assimilation and threat in chapter 3 by leveraging biculturalism as a framework for creating blended communities that honor the old ways while making room for new arrivals. After a brief survey of the theme of biculturalism in Luke-Acts, I'll examine what two extended passages in Acts say about the ethnic composition of the family of God. Acts 8–11 shows that the author's biculturalism emphasizes Jewish and Gentile ethnic identification that affirms the benefits of locating one's identity within an ethnoracial community of origin. Next, we will see that Acts 15 is the

5. From the testimony of Bagai's granddaughter Rani Bagai in "Bridges Burnt Behind."

centerpiece of the author's pragmatic intercultural compromise at the nexus of respect for family heritage and welcome to the outsider. This chapter will show that biculturalism in Luke-Acts eschews the assimilation ideal by insisting on allegiance to heritage even while making space to embrace the newcomer.

Biculturalism and Family Dynamics

As discussed in chapter 3, acculturation is the overall process of cultural involvement around two foci: (1) retention of culture-of-origin involvement, and (2) a degree of host or dominant culture involvement.[6] At least two theoretical frameworks describe the processes of acculturation in the United States: assimilation theory and alternation theory. Both frameworks focus on retaining the culture of origin identity and a positive relationship with the dominant society, though they differ concerning the end state of the acculturation process.[7] As described in chapter 3, assimilation theory holds that the subgroup will cease to identify with the culture of origin.[8] On the other hand, alternation theory, emphasizing biculturalism and an intercultural dimension of culture change, holds that the group or individual will retain the culture of origin while establishing a positive relationship with the dominant White culture.[9] Bicultural or intercultural skills empower people to choose the manner, timing, and intensity of affiliation with a culture of origin or a second or third culture situationally.[10] Theorists predict that biculturalism reduces the adverse outcomes associated with assimilating to a new culture and decreasing contact with the culture of origin. Specifically,

6. Smokowski, Roderick, and Bacallao, "Acculturation and Latino Family Processes," 296. LaFromboise et al., on the other hand, do not use acculturation as a broad term signifying second culture acquisition. They also differentiate acculturation from assimilation by recognizing that acculturation will maintain the culture of origin after becoming competent in the target culture, but they also emphasize its involuntary nature (LaFromboise, Coleman, and Gerton, "Psychological Impact of Biculturalism," 397–98). That is, acculturation refers to the cultural acquisition needed to survive economically in the new culture, but these individuals do not necessarily acquire the values and worldview associated with the target culture. For these scholars, acculturated individuals never lose the identity associated with the culture of origin, and experience all of the negative psychological effects inherent in that rejection. In other words, this model is the holding place for the "failures" of the assimilation paradigm, containing the people who might want to assimilate but who can't because of the barriers in the dominant culture.

7. Smokowski, Roderick, and Bacallao, "Acculturation and Latino Family Processes," 296.
8. Smokowski, Roderick, and Bacallao, "Acculturation and Latino Family Processes," 296.
9. Smokowski, Roderick, and Bacallao, "Acculturation and Latino Family Processes," 296.
10. LaFromboise, Coleman, and Gerton, "Psychological Impact of Biculturalism," 399–400.

there seem to be greater levels of family cohesion and lower levels of family conflict when aspects of the origin and host cultures are blended.[11] Further, bicultural skills offer greater emotional and cognitive functioning, enabling individuals to withstand the stresses associated with second culture acquisition.[12]

It is important to emphasize that I do not intend the investigation of biculturalism or intercultural competency in this chapter to normalize or valorize a Black-White binary that overlooks how other minority groups are racialized.[13] Though interculturalism signifies a capacity to function effectively in multiple other cultures rather than just one different culture, both interculturalism and biculturalism involve rootedness in one's own culture and positive relations with other cultures.[14] The emphasis on biculturalism here is from the perspective of a minoritized person in the United States who is navigating between their own culture of origin (whether internal or external to the United States) and dominant White culture. Racialization unfolds differently across minoritized groups as they each experience the harms of White supremacy in variegated ways. I hope that exploring the benefits and costs of biculturalism as a way of navigating between the particular and the dominant will rhyme with how some minoritized groups and individuals navigate White supremacy en route to intercultural competence. Some might offer a criticism that a conversation framed around biculturalism still centers White supremacy rather than provides a way of thinking that calls all communities to reimagine ways of being outside of the racialized structures in the United States.[15] I would respond that analogical reasoning around biculturalism in Acts nevertheless constructively advances discussions about racism by offering an explicitly situated standpoint that avoids so-called objective and disinterested hegemonic discourse on the one hand, while also inviting conversation about where this strategy for navigating racism vis-à-vis White supremacy works and where it doesn't.

Bicultural competency involves the capacity to appreciate and internalize the basic worldview and social mores of a particular culture while also interacting with members of the dominant culture.[16] Theorists label this competency

---

11. Smokowski, Roderick, and Bacallao, "Acculturation and Latino Family Processes," 296.

12. LaFromboise, Coleman, and Gerton, "Psychological Impact of Biculturalism," 399–400.

13. For more on a critique of a Black-White binary framework for race relations in the United States, see Alcoff, "Latino/as, Asian Americans, and the Black–White Binary"; Goto, "Beyond the Black–White Binary"; Perea, "Black/White Binary Paradigm of Race" (1997); Perea, "Black/White Binary Paradigm of Race" (1998).

14. Neuner, "Socio-Cultural Interim Worlds," 48–49.

15. E.g., Goto, "Beyond the Black–White Binary."

16. LaFromboise, Coleman, and Gerton, "Psychological Impact of Biculturalism,"

culture frame switching,[17] which refers to the ability to link culture-specific knowledge (i.e., cognitive knowing) with cross-cultural sensibilities (i.e., behavioral doing).[18] Bicultural competence can include a broad range of skills.[19] Still, fundamental to biculturalism is a deep knowledge of the cultural beliefs and values of both the culture of origin and the dominant culture. Bicultural people can relate to persons in the majority culture and the minority culture and likewise maintain a positive attitude toward people in both groups. Again, biculturalism involves cultural efficacy in the culture of origin as well as the ability to be efficacious in the dominant culture. Where there are linguistic or dialectal differences between the two cultures, biculturals are fluent in both settings. Bicultural competence also includes comfort with a broad repertoire of social roles: the ability to inhabit social, occupational, and political roles in either culture even when there are significant differences between the role structure in the majority culture and the same structures in the minority culture.[20] Perhaps most importantly, bicultural or intercultural capacities do not operate in isolation but include rootedness in the culture of origin.[21] In other words, inherent

---

403. The authors also note that people don't have to hold the two cultures in equal regard, though there is an assumption that both cultures are regarded positively, and no attempt is made to order them hierarchically (p. 404). I guess the issue is that Jesus has a positive value on Gentiles' lives. Paul demonstrates an ability to live competently in both cultures (cf. the speech at the Aeropagus in Acts 17 with temple visit in Acts 21).

17. Hong, "Bicultural Competence," 95.

18. Hong, "Bicultural Competence," 102. Hong also theorizes that biculturals possess a high degree of cultural metacognition, giving them skills to be able to identify and select which culturally sensitive behaviors should prevail over other cultural values in a given social setting. Metacognition selects which cultural practices should prevail in ambiguous multicultural situations. Hong also notes that frequent frame switching increases biculturals' sensitivity to context when decoding communication, because values, norms, and interpersonal cues are context dependent. Thus, they more readily comprehend the need for cross-cultural sensitivity. For example, a Korean businesswoman decides to shake hands with her more senior western male counterpart, making a decision to select the western values of her more powerful male colleague versus those prevailing in her culture of origin.

19. LaFromboise, Coleman, and Gerton, "Psychological Impact of Biculturalism," 403. There is currently lack of a broadly accepted definition of bicultural competence; see Hong, "Bicultural Competence," 95–96. Hong defines bicultural competencies as: (a) culture-specific knowledge, (b) cross-cultural abilities, including behavioral adaptability (ability to appreciate and detect culture-specific aspects of social behavior) and cross-cultural communication skills (including verbal and non-verbal), and (c) cultural metacognition, that is, the ability to transfer culturally specific knowledge into transcultural principles ("Bicultural Competence," 96–97).

20. Smither, "Human Migration," 64.

21. LaFromboise et al. maintain that "groundedness" is required for successful bicultural

in biculturalism is a strong sense of ethnic identification[22] that empowers one's capacity to negotiate a second culture successfully. Biculturalism is foundational for the intercultural competence needed for navigating multicultural spaces in which a dominant White culture prevails over other subcultures.

Without a doubt, the processes of acculturation are complicated. A study by Smokowski, Roderick, and Bacallao found data that support both the assimilation and alternation/biculturalism paradigms. The study suggested that for all the advantages of biculturalism, the assimilation paradigm also permits a measure of success. As discussed in chapter 3, assimilation can be a cultural asset that contributes to positive life outcomes, including high family cohesion, familism, and lower family conflict, not to mention higher education levels and family incomes. However, with assimilation, family cohesion and adaptability to the new environment decrease with time and ultimately undermine family dynamics. This decrease may be due to increased acculturation stress, including experience with discrimination from the majority culture and poor coping behaviors.[23] Similarly, as for support for the alternation/biculturalism paradigm, a different study found that biculturalism was positively associated with familism, strong family cohesion, and family adaptability.[24] Yet, it is challenging to acquire deep efficacy in a second culture, meaning that even if biculturalism offers clearer positive outcomes, these capacities may be more difficult to acquire.

The concepts of double consciousness and liminality are in some ways adjacent to the idea of biculturalism, and all three include consideration of the cost

---

identity that can positively negotiate the stress of bicultural identity, that it cannot be done on one's own, and that one needs social support systems in both cultures (LaFromboise, Coleman, and Gerton, "Psychological Impact of Biculturalism"). Yet, oddly, they support this conclusion by citing work that suggests that African American and Native American cultural resilience emerges from dependence on strong extended family networks, and not, as they insist, on cultural networks in both the culture of origin and majority culture. For instance, they cite F. M. Baker who argues that the African American reliance on extended family networks provides resources to avoid acculturation stress on mental health and other negative life outcomes such as crime, single-parent households, attempted suicide, substance abuse, and post-incarceration adjustments (Baker, "Afro-American Life Cycle"). Such extended family networks are also common resources in other communities of color in negotiating American systems of White supremacy. See, e.g., Red Horse, "Family Structure."

22. In chapter 2 we defined ethnic identification as an enculturation process that involves high levels of allegiance and involvement in the culture of origin.

23. Smokowski, Roderick, and Bacallao, "Acculturation and Latino Family Processes," 304, 306.

24. Smokowski, Roderick, and Bacallao, "Acculturation and Latino Family Processes," 302–7.

associated with living at the intersection of two cultures. W. E. B. Du Bois's concept of double consciousness refers to how African Americans invariably see themselves, as a survival strategy, both through their own eyes and through the eyes of a dehumanizing dominant culture.[25] Liminality, a term developed over one hundred years ago but popularized in Homi Bhabha's work,[26] refers to living in in-between situations and conditions characterized by a sense of isolation, dislocation, or uncertainty vis-à-vis established hierarchies and traditions. Some think these capacities may be assets for some people of color living in the interstitial spaces between minority and majority cultures. The critical thing to remember is that biculturalism emphasizes acquiring one culture while keeping a positive and grounded relationship with the culture of origin. Indeed, some studies even found that ethnic ghettos can function as a grounding social network for second culture acquisition.[27]

Early assumptions about biculturalism only highlighted the negative associations. The common, negative pop culture metaphors about such individuals—the Oreo, coconut, apple, and banana symbols for people who have colored skin on the outside but are said to be White on the inside—assume that bicultural individuals inhabit a marginalized status. Such individuals are said to suffer from confusion about norms arising from their cultural heritage and identity ambiguity, in all cases preferring White norms and values over those espoused by their ethnic communities.[28] However, later theorists have highlighted the overall benefits to society of intercultural contact. More recently, some evidence suggests that bicultural involvement was the best predictor of esteem and well-being. These studies indicate that bicultural individuals exhibit higher cognitive functioning and mental health status than monocultural, assimilated, or acculturated people. Unlike acculturation or assimilation, biculturalism posits a bidirectional relationship between an individual's culture of origin and the dominant White culture.[29]

---

25. Du Bois, *Souls of Black Folk*, 45: "It is a peculiar sensation, this double-consciousness, this sense of always looking at oneself through the eyes of others, of measuring one's soul by the tape of a world that always looks on in amused contempt and pity. One ever feels his twoness,—an American, a Negro; two souls, two thoughts, two unreconciled strivings; two warring ideals in one dark body, whose dogged strength alone keeps it from being torn asunder."

26. Horvath, Thomassen, and Wydra, "Introduction." Also see Bhabha, "DisseminNation"; reprinted in Bhabha, *Location of Culture*, 139–70.

27. LaFromboise, Coleman, and Gerton, "Psychological Impact of Biculturalism," 407.

28. LaFromboise, Coleman, and Gerton, "Psychological Impact of Biculturalism," 395.

29. LaFromboise, Coleman, and Gerton, "Psychological Impact of Biculturalism," 399.

In the final analysis, I don't think that the practice of biculturalism is as straightforward as one might conclude from this review. Those promoting the virtues of biculturalism may not have adequately captured the difficulties of life in liminal spaces. There is aching pain when biculturals are labeled with these colorful fruit-inspired metaphors or other hurtful epithets like "sellout" or "race traitor" by people in the culture of origin.[30] Further, the full embrace of double consciousness or liminality by building and maintaining networks in both communities sometimes carries a double cost. It is not uncommon for bicultural people to be simultaneously accused of racism by the host culture and selling out by the culture of origin. Indeed, even the positive information from chapter 3 adds a layer of complication. We recall that high levels of culture of origin involvement in ethnic identification result in higher self-esteem. I suggest that bicultural thriving involves a delicate dance that requires one to know where they come from and to be firmly rooted in the past while also having open arms toward the change concomitant with extending the blessings of intimacy toward others.

Biculturalism in Luke-Acts

Though scholars regularly treat the Third Gospel and Acts separately by convention, most agree that the same person authored this two-volume work. Although there are new narrative developments and emphases in Acts, many of the themes and concerns evident in the Gospel of Luke are carried over into Acts. For example, the prophecy-fulfillment motif in Luke 4:14–30 is also apparent in the second volume as the programmatic Pentecost narrative in Acts 2:1–21 prophesies the inclusion of the nations into the commonwealth of Israel. The motif about the split in Israel that we detected in the parable of the Broken Family in Luke 15:11–32 takes center stage in Acts as open hostilities emerge in the diaspora concerning the understanding of Jesus and the incorporation of Gentiles. Acts begins with the declaration that the ministry of Jesus must extend from Jerusalem to all Judea, Samaria, and the end of the earth (Acts 1:8). After that, the action moves progressively outward from concern about the community of disciples in Jerusalem and beyond as Luke's attention later shifts to the inclusion of the Gentiles, a theme occupying the latter half of the second volume.[31]

30. For a discussion of Paul and the race traitor themes in Acts, see Sechrest, "The Perils of Passing."

31. It is impossible to know for sure whether the author of Luke-Acts had access to or knew about the Pauline Epistles, yet I've also always thought that this narrative ordering could serve as the Lukan version of Paul's "To the Jew first, and also to the Gentiles" ideology (Rom. 1:16).

A necessary consequence of the widening mission among non-Jews is questioning about identity-forming practices that contribute to a common group identity. If the accent in the Gospel of Luke is on the reconstitution of Israel around the central figure of her Messiah, the emphasis in Acts is on the relationship between factions in the newly regathered Israel. I suggest that Luke's concern for the populations involved in the reconstitution of Israel amounts to a set of bicultural sensitivities as described above. We shall see that major themes and stories in Acts focus on negotiating differences among these various constituencies.

Even though the negotiation of difference receives the most development in Acts, it is apparent in the Gospel of Luke too, perhaps notably in the parable of the wineskins in Luke 5:36–39. Here the author works with two forms of the underlying tradition, one from Mark 2:21–22 and another from Matthew 9:16–17:[32]

> [21]"No one sews a piece of unshrunk cloth on an old cloak; otherwise, the patch pulls away from it, the new from the old, and a worse tear is made. [22]And no one puts new wine into old wineskins; otherwise, the wine will burst the skins, and the wine is lost, and so are the skins; but *one puts new wine into fresh wineskins.*" (Mark 2:21–22 NRSV)

> [16]"No one sews a piece of unshrunk cloth on an old cloak, for the patch pulls away from the cloak, and a worse tear is made. [17]Neither is new wine put into old wineskins; otherwise, the skins burst, and the wine is spilled, and the skins are destroyed; but new wine is put into fresh wineskins, *and so both are preserved.*" (Matt. 9:16–17 NRSV)

The Marcan version evidences little concern for the old garment, emphasizing the need to preserve the freshness of the gospel in wholly new containers.

---

32. This study assumes the priority of Mark as a source used by Matthew and Luke but rejects the Q hypothesis as an explanation for the verbatim similarities between Matthew and Luke (i.e., the "double tradition). Instead, with a growing number of scholars, I think that the double tradition emerges from Luke's direct literary dependence on a version of the Gospel of Matthew as well as Mark's Gospel. For more on this approach see Goulder, *Luke*; Sanders and Davies, *Studying the Synoptic Gospels*; Franklin, *Luke*; Goodacre, *Case against Q*. Redaction criticism, however, comprises only one of the methods that animate this study, along with literary, historical, and cultural methods. Nevertheless, though my critical perspective on the solution to the Synoptic problem will become apparent at one or two points, the major conclusions in this analysis stand regardless of one's approach to the Synoptic problem.

The Matthean version is interested in keeping the new wine but is also interested in protecting the old garment from further damage; likewise, it ends by opting to preserve both new wine and old wineskins. Luke reveals his interest in biculturalism by building on the Matthean approach. After affirming the desire to preserve and blend both old and new (vv. 36–37), he expresses concern for newcomers (v. 38), but ends by reinforcing the need to be anchored in the old (v. 39):

> [36]"No one tears a piece from a new garment and sews it on an old garment; otherwise *the new will be torn, and the piece from the new will not match the old.* [37]And no one puts new wine into old wineskins; otherwise the new wine will burst the skins and will be spilled, and the skins will be destroyed. [38]But new wine must be put into fresh wineskins. [39]*And no one after drinking old wine desires new wine, but says, 'The old is good.'*" (Luke 5:36–39 NRSV)

Note that the parable calls attention to the possibility of damage to both old *and* new. Luke's Jesus insists that the ancient practice of fasting is not outright rejected but only laid aside during a season for embracing the new (cf. 5:34–35).[33] Further, this passage emphasizes the importance of the new while leaving no doubt about the value of the old: "No one, after drinking the old wine, wishes for new; for he says, 'The old is good'" (5:38–39). In combination, then, Luke's emphasis on affirming the value of the new while remaining anchored in the old is analogous to the balletic moves in the dance of biculturalism.

In other words, Luke's interest in biculturalism emerges in the context of a blended family culture of Christian Jews and Gentiles, a family negotiating tension that had been forecast at the outset of the gospel in Luke 4:14–30, as we saw in chapter 3. Further, it is a family of a definitively *Jewish* character in which Jewish practices are the bedrock. Early in Acts, Luke describes the ideal family: it is a *diverse* family, encompassing members from all corners of the cosmos, and an *intercultural* one, supernaturally equipped to break boundaries of geography and culture (Acts 2:1–11). This is a family that cares for its own, that grows by its ability to transcend conflict (Acts 6:1–7), that prays in one accord, and that meets the needs of its members (Acts 2:42–47; 4:32–35; 5:1–11). Yet, like all families, this is a family that has to negotiate to accommodate its constituent members. Composed of Greek and Aramaic-speaking Jews and God-fearing Gentiles, it is a cross-cultural family that must learn to bridge differences and respect boundaries.

---

33. Carroll, *Luke*, 135.

This chapter looks at two potentially liberative passages in Acts oriented around the tensions between bicultural adaptation and ethnic identification with a community of origin. Looking first at Acts 8–11, we will see Luke's strong affirmation of marginalized Jewish groups as well as Gentile ethnic identification. Next, we will explore the dynamics of bicultural accommodation in Acts 15, focusing on how the "Jerusalem Decree" sets the terms for intercultural interaction in the church.[34]

Jewish and Gentile Ethnic Identification (Acts 8:1–11:18)

Gifford Rhamie's reconstruction of Luke's identity as a non-rabbinic Afroasiatic diasporic Hellenistic Jew comports with interest in the text in biculturalism and the desire to reclaim marginalized Jewish subpopulations in the mission to the diaspora that unfolds in this section of Acts. From chapter 3, we recall that Rhamie sees Luke as a cosmopolitan author exposed to many Jewish subcultures and marginalized groups even as he was also thoroughly fluent in the Greco-Roman literary and political discourse.[35] Luke's affirmation of blended traditions, foods, norms, and languages from minority and majority cultures positions him as a *bicultural* cosmopolitan. Attention to the structuring device of Acts 1:8 and the placement of key conversion narratives—the Ethiopian, Paul, and Cornelius—show his interest in reclaiming the Jewish ethnic identification of Samaritans and diaspora Jews in Acts 8–11 as well as the Gentile ethnic identification of proselytes later in Acts 15.

The citation of Isaiah 49:6 in Acts 1:8 helps us understand the literary function of Acts 8–9 and plays a vital role in preparing for the account of the first Gentile converts in Acts 10–11. Reflecting the programmatic nature of 1:8, I suggest that all the converts before Acts 10 are Jewish, and all of this prepares the way for the first Gentile convert in that chapter.

> "Rather you will receive power when the Holy Spirit has come upon you; and you will be my witnesses in Jerusalem, in all Judea and Samaria, and *to the end of the earth*."[36] (Acts 1:8 CEB)

---

34. Though each of these episodes in Acts 8–11 and 15 contain important questions about the historicity of Acts, these issues are not the primary concern in this study; rather I am concerned with the theological and literary significance of the intergroup dynamics depicted therein.

35. Rhamie, "Whiteness, Conviviality and Agency," 202–9; also see pp. 98–100 above.

36. "The end of the earth": ἕως ἐσχάτου τῆς γῆς.

And [the LORD] said to me, "It is a great thing for you to be called my servant so that you may set up the tribes of Jakob and turn back the dispersion[37] of Israel. See, I have made you a light of nations, that you may be for salvation *to the end of the earth.*"[38] (Isa. 49:6 NETS)

Isaiah 49:5–6 is an important Old Testament text for Luke. Beyond its use here in Acts 1:8, Luke associates this same text with Jesus through the confession of Simeon the Faithful who recites Isaiah 49:5–6 at the temple when Jesus is presented as an infant for his circumcision (Luke 2:32). Luke also links the text with Paul, who decisively quotes it in Acts 13:47 as a characterization of his own ministry. But what is more critical about Isaiah 49:6 is that the verse says that Gentiles are a part of the sweep of God's salvation. At the same time, Isaiah 49:5 also shows that a regathering of the dispersion of Israel precedes the gathering of Gentiles from the end of the earth. This temporal ordering rhymes with Luke's description of the mission from Jerusalem and the Jewish conversions in the first half of Acts as programmatically forecast in 1:8.

The Jewish Branch of the Family of God (Acts 8–9)

Acts 8–9 shows how the witness to Jesus expands beyond the confines of Judea to Samaria and to the end of the earth, as forecasted in Acts 1:8 and thus a symbolic fulfillment of that prophecy.[39] This section tells the story of three converts to the Christian movement, all of whom are Jewish broadly speaking: the Samaritan Simon Magus, the Ethiopian eunuch, and the Pharisee Paul of Tarsus. Each of these converts represents an important step that prepares for the Gentile mission that occupies the latter half of the book of Acts.[40] In the prelude to the three conversion stories, the narrator reports the start of persecution for the church in Jerusalem, harassment that will have the effect of rendering the Jerusalem leaders secondary in the growth of the church beyond Judea and scrambling to keep up with the spread of the gospel.[41] The

---

37. "The dispersion": διασπορὰν.
38. "The end of the earth": ἕως ἐσχάτου τῆς γῆς. See note 36 above.
39. Steffek, "Quand juifs et païens," 104–5.
40. Similarly Weiser, *Apostelgeschichte*, 1:212.
41. Tannehill, *Narrative Unity of Luke-Acts*, 102–4; contra Demetrius Williams who sees the Jerusalem church with a key role in overseeing the spread of the gospel: "Luke's emphasis is that the nature and spread of the gospel is coordinated by the Jerusalem church in the initial stages (cf. 8:14; 11:1, 22)." See D. K. Williams, "Acts of the Apostles," 230.

persecution scatters or disperses[42] the believers into the Judean countryside and Samaria (8:1). Philip, the hero of this section and one of the seven Hellenistic Jewish leaders chosen in Acts 6:1–6, is included in this dispersion and starts the mission to Samaria (8:4–5).[43]

The fraught relationship and hostility between Jews and Samaritans are well known. Yet in Luke 10:25–32, Jesus surprisingly casts a Samaritan as the hero of his parable in a place where one would typically expect to see a faithful Israelite. But a close reading of the preceding context of this story in Luke 10:1–12 depicts the gathering of seventy disciples for a worldwide mission to the diaspora. It suggests that the events immediately preceding this story may be read as Jesus recruiting disciples for this mission in 9:51–62, including people from the Samaritan villages described in 9:52–55. Taken together, these and other hints indicate that, according to Luke, Jesus thought of the Samaritans as Israelite insiders.[44] In context, Philip's ministry in Samaria in Acts 8:4–24 subtly adds a new node in that motif as Samaria receives news about the Messiah with unalloyed joy (8:5–8). The story of Simon Magus also recognizes a measure of the ambivalence about the Samaritans that possibly reflects the historic fractures in the relationship between the two Jewish factions (cf. Luke 17:18).

In Acts 8:9–13, Philip's proclamation and deeds of power in Samaria bear fruit so that even Simon the local magician is baptized along with many men and women. Interestingly, Philip's outreach to the Samaritans in this chapter requires no extraordinary angelic intervention in contrast to Peter's experience of being supernaturally urged to minister to Gentile outsiders. This contrast with Acts 10–11 indicates that the mission to Samaria, though initiated providentially and confirmed by the apostles through the reception of the Holy Spirit (8:5–25), was more like the mission in Judea than like the mission to the Gentiles. Despite this, there is nevertheless a note of ambiguity and ethnic tension in the story. While Philip felt no need to check in with the Jerusalem officials before offering baptism to the Samaritans, it is important

42. "Disperses": διεσπάρησαν (Acts 8:1).
43. "Dispersion": οἱ . . . διασπαρέντες (Acts 8:4).
44. For more on this interpretation see Sechrest, "Double Vision," 209–14; cf. Demetrius Williams who calls Samaritans "near kinfolk" of the Jews ("Acts of the Apostles," 225). When describing Luke's identity as a diaspora Jew, Rhamie suggests that Luke writes from the margins as "a subcultural Jewish adherent . . . [whose] Hellenised diasporic gaze could antagonize the centrality of the Jewish cultic institution" so that "in the process, all Jews—Judeans, Samaritans, proselytes and diasporans—are reclaimed by Luke as Jews" ("Whiteness, Conviviality and Agency," 202–3).

to note that these Jerusalem leaders did feel the need to inspect the outcome of this mission. Note that it was only after this verification by the apostles that the Samaritans received the gift of the Holy Spirit. Altogether, there does seem to be some ambivalence about the Samaritan mission. On the one hand, the author accepts Samaritans into the broader Jewish family, but on the other hand, he is also aware that his might be a minority opinion.

This ambivalence also manifests in the characterization of Simon Magus. The only named convert in this narrative is a corrupt and shady Samaritan—an "Othering" motif frequently found in descriptions of minorities (8:18–24). According to the text, Simon initially received salvation with enthusiasm and attached himself to Philip as a local companion (8:13). Yet after the visit from the apostles who prayed that the Samaritans might receive the Holy Spirit, Simon offers money to receive the same power as the apostles, that he too could see "the Spirit given through the laying on of hands"—that is, through *his* hands (8:18). In combination with the idea that the conversion of the Samaritans was "incomplete" until after the coming of the apostles from Jerusalem,[45] the story of Shady Simon, the corrupt convert, adds a note of discord to this family reunion scene, distancing the Samaritans as recipients of this new grace. Rejecting the racialized denigration of Simon, we nevertheless note that the text marginalizes him within a larger narrative arc that gives Samaritans a greater status as insiders than Gentiles like Cornelius occupy. Hence, in borrowing the logic we employed in chapter 2 on allyship, we note how difficult it is to turn the page when renewing relationships encumbered by long, tangled, and violent histories.[46]

By contrast, the Ethiopian eunuch of Acts 8:26–39 comes much closer to embodying the Lukan portrait of the ideal convert. He is high ranking and devout and comes onto the scene as he departs Jerusalem after making a long and thus expensive pilgrimage from Ethiopia to Jerusalem, probably for a major festival.[47] Even more, when Philip meets him, he is reading aloud from the scriptures of Israel. Consequently, while the piety of the Ethiopian is not in question, his identity is much more so. Today most interpreters see him as a Gentile, and though there is considerable debate about whether he is a proselyte, most end up rejecting this possibility too.[48] Those who see him as

45. Tannehill, *Narrative Unity of Luke-Acts*, 104.

46. See chapter 2 above, especially the section "Loving the Other: Neighbors, Allies, Foes, and Frenemies."

47. I. H. Marshall, *Acts*, 162.

48. In favor of viewing the Ethiopian as a Gentile, see I. H. Marshall, *Acts*, 160–65; Barrett, *Acts of the Apostles*, 1:424–25; Tannehill, *Narrative Unity of Luke-Acts*, 108–9; Keener,

a Gentile try to puzzle out why this episode recounting the first conversion of a Gentile receives so much less attention and space from our author than Cornelius's story does in Acts 10–11. As a Roman centurion, Cornelius is also a devout and high-ranking representative of an empire.[49] Still, where his story occupies seventy verses spread across three chapters, the Ethiopian receives a scant fifteen verses in Acts 8.[50] Is this another veiled affront that communicates the marginality of this group of dark-skinned converts similar to the rhetorical effect of depicting Simon as a Shady Samaritan?

In a rare break from modern scholars who carefully avoid any mention of the character's race, Demetrius Williams and Cain Hope Felder take the time to explore the Ethiopian's ethnoracial identity. Williams begins by raising a question about whether the tendency to relegate this episode to a subordinate role in the narrative is one that effectively elevates the conversion of the European Cornelius over the African eunuch.[51] Williams may be correct, but it is also possible that interpreters are wrestling with the emphasis on the Cornelius episode conveyed by the varying lengths of the episodes. Is it possible that Luke himself is the one who is "colorstruck" by emphasizing the lighter-skinned Cornelius over the Black Ethiopian?[52] While there may well have been color prejudice prevailing in Luke's milieu, we shouldn't forget that Luke's is the only gospel that mentions Black leadership in the influential Antiochene church (13:1; 11:20) as Cain Hope Felder reminds us.[53] Felder concludes that the omission of activity of the Holy Spirit in this story effec-

---

Acts, 2:1566–67; Gaventa, *Acts*, 142. Compare with Weiser, *Apostelgeschichte*, 1:209, 212, and 252, who says that Luke left the Ethiopian's identity deliberately ambiguous and with Rhamie, "Whiteness, Conviviality and Agency"; Haenchen, *Acts*, 312; and Wall, "Peter, 'Son' of Jonah," who says that the eunuch is Jewish or a Jewish proselyte (84).

49. Smith and Kim, *Toward Decentering the New Testament*, 99.

50. Smith and Kim opt for describing Cornelius as the first *significant* Gentile convert and call the episode about the Ethiopian one that is parallel to the conversions of Cornelius and Lydia; see Smith and Kim, *Toward Decentering the New Testament*, 99.

51. D. K. Williams, "Acts of the Apostles," 226.

52. "Colorstruck" is a colloquial expression among some African Americans that refers to the condition of being unduly influenced by colorism, or the tendency to assign greater social capital to African Americans (and other ethnicities as well) who have lighter skin tones, or the implicit understanding that it is better to look like a White person than to have a dark complexion. Similar dynamics prevail elsewhere in the African diaspora as well. For more on this topic see Chavez-Dueñas, Adames, and Organista, "Skin-Color Prejudice"; Glenn, *Shades of Difference*; Schwarcz, "Not Black, Not White," and especially the intersectional analysis in Hunter, *Politics of Skin Tone*.

53. Felder, *Race, Racism, and the Biblical Narratives*, 39. For more on color prejudice in antiquity see Byron, *Symbolic Blackness*; Snowden, *Before Color Prejudice*.

tively de-emphasizes this conversion compared to the Gentile conversions in Acts 10:44–45. He suggests that this "circumstantial de-emphasis . . . enables Europeans thereby to claim that the text of Acts demonstrates some divine preference for Europeans."[54] I agree that it is more likely that *contemporary* scholars are the parties blinded by color prejudice. The solution is to consider the Ethiopian's ethnoreligious identity more carefully without being blinded by his race. Felder finally rejects the possibility that the eunuch is the first Gentile convert because this would undermine the Lukan theme of the universal reach of the gospel to Gentiles, but he never really interrogates the possibility, left on the table, that the Ethiopian is another *Jewish* convert.

I think that the White gaze in the Eurocentric New Testament guild influences interpretations regarding the Ethiopian in Acts. The eunuch's conversion is a partial fulfillment of the universalism in Acts 1:8 because the Ethiopian represents *Jews* from one end of the earth (the other end in Rome), and interpreters seem scarcely able to countenance the possibility of a Black Hellenistic Jew. This possibility is precisely the direction pursued in Gifford Rhamie's compelling study of Acts 8:26–39.[55] Rhamie argues that the Ethiopian eunuch was more than likely a "black African Jew of nonrabbinic Hebrew stock" and that understanding his identity this way contributes to the programmatic force of Acts 1:8.

Beginning with the question, "Why cannot the Ethiopian eunuch in Acts 8:26–40 be conceptualised as a Jew in the British academy?" Rhamie proceeds to examine the question from several angles. He begins by interrogating the impact of whiteness on the biblical studies academy, hypothesizing that whiteness functioned as an epistemological force that privileged appeals to Greco-Roman literatures over "Afroasiatic" ones in historical-critical investigations. Whiteness and the epistemology of ignorance à la Charles Mills operate to erase the Ethiopian's Jewish identity and impede the production of knowledge about this matter. Noting that four out of five dissertations on the eunuch have not made it into published form, Rhamie critiques the Eurocentric gaze as "riddled with Cartesian blind spots . . . [that] are racialised, deodorised and clinicalised." According to Rhamie, the academy has failed to adequately interrogate the peculiar admixture of ethnicity, race, and religion in antiquity that allows for the possibility that the Ethiopian could be Black, African, and Jewish at the same time. Next, he moves on to a historical consideration of the early history of interpretation of the Ethiopian's identity. In one

---

54. Felder, *Race, Racism, and the Biblical Narratives*, 38.
55. Rhamie, "Whiteness, Conviviality and Agency."

section, he critically examines the *Adversus Judaeos* tradition in the writings of the church fathers Justin Martyr, Tertullian, Irenaeus, Pontius/Cyprian, Eusebius, Chrysostom, Jerome, Augustine, and others. Concluding that the earliest writers take the Ethiopian's Jewishness for granted, Rhamie identifies Eusebius as starting a decisive shift away from this understanding. With greater ambiguity about the Ethiopian's identity in Jerome and Augustine, Rhamie notes the accompanying rise of anti-Judaism and "*Adversus Judaeos* power politics."[56] The balance of the work explores the function of the episode in understanding the programmatic nature of Acts 1:8, similar to the discussion here, and offers a close reading of Acts 8:26–39.

To be sure, the question about the Ethiopian's ethnic identity is wrapped up in questions about his status as a eunuch, a point that is not stressed as much in Rhamie's work. Those who dismiss the idea that the Ethiopian is Jewish do so mainly because eunuchs were excluded from membership in Israel, according to Deuteronomy 23:1. Consequently, many see the eunuch's conversion as the fulfillment of Isaiah 56:3–8.[57] Yet there is significant evidence that Luke regarded the Ethiopian as a high-ranking official, another connotation of the word "eunuch" in antiquity, and not someone whose identity as a Jew was "compromised" by his sexual status. For example, the Septuagint—the Greek version of the Hebrew Bible—often contains the word "eunuch" as a synonym for a high official,[58] and the Greek of Acts 8:27 suggests that Luke is following the Septuagint's "high official" usage at this point:

56. Rhamie, "Whiteness, Conviviality and Agency," 185–87.

57. E.g., Barrett, *Acts of the Apostles*, 1:424; Tannehill, *Narrative Unity of Luke-Acts*, 109; (I. H. Marshall, *Acts*, 160–62; contra Rhamie, "Whiteness, Conviviality and Agency," 40, who sees "eunuch" as a title by synecdoche and, as above, more generally as an Afroasiatic non-rabbinic Jew. In view of the evidence presented here that associates "eunuch" with "official" in this narrative, I am often puzzled by the deference to the view that Luke couldn't have intended to communicate that the Ethiopian was Jewish because of Deut. 23:1. While it is true that there is a clear allusion to Isa. 56:3–8 (see the discussion about that text below), there is no textual indication in Acts 8:26–39 that Luke has Deut. 23:1 in mind. Specifically, that verse uses completely different words for someone who is a eunuch (εὐνοῦχος; "eunuch" in Acts 8:27; cf. θλαδίας καὶ ἀποκεκομμένος; "a castrated and cut off male" in Deut. 23:2 [LXX]). Further, it seems to me that Luke's free use of his sources in the Gospel and creative reworking of LXX traditions throughout the two volumes signals that he was entirely capable of excluding inconvenient information in the interests of advancing his theological agenda (e.g., see interpretive discussion in commentaries about Acts 5:1–11 [cf. Achan in Josh. 7]; Acts 8:26–40 [cf. the Emmaus narrative in Luke 24:13–27]; and the discussion about Luke 4:16–30 in chapter 3 above). This capacity to appeal to the tradition freely is even less remarkable if one identifies the author in ways similar to Rhamie's construction above. I think that the black skin of the Ethiopian is an (implicit/unconscious) obstacle to the idea that he could represent a Jew.

58. E.g., Gen. 37:36; 39:1; 40:2; 1 Sam. 8:15; 2 Kings 8:6; 2 Chron. 18:8; cf. Deut. 23:2; Isa. 56:3, 6.

Line 0 (8:27a): And behold (καὶ ἰδοὺ)

Line 1 (8:27b): a man, an Ethiopian eunuch, an official (ἀνὴρ Αἰθίοψ εὐνοῦχος δυνάστης)

Line 2 (8:27c): of Candace Queen of Ethiopia (Κανδάκης βασιλίσσης Αἰθιόπων)

Line 3 (8:27d): . . . who was over her entire treasury. (ὃς ἦν ἐπὶ πάσης τῆς γάζης αὐτῆς)

Note that the four Greek words in line 1 are all in the nominative case, indicating that the terms after the first word are all in apposition to that first word, "man" (ἀνὴρ). Thus the latter words function to describe in more detail the man who is the main character in the narrative: Ethiopian, eunuch, official. The three Greek words in line 2 are all in the genitive case (Candace, Queen, Ethiopia), and all three thus further define the nature of the office specified by the last nominative case noun on line 1 ("official"; δυνάστης). In other words, he is an official designated by "Candace," the Queen of Egypt.[59] Barrett translates these lines as: "There was an Ethiopian man, a eunuch and minister of Candace, Queen of the Ethiopians, who was in charge of all her wealth," thus interpreting the man as both a sexual minority and a high official.[60]

Further, Rhamie's interpretation of the first word in line 1, "man" (ἀνὴρ) adds another critical interpretive nuance. While some see the word as an assertion of the Ethiopian's masculinity, notwithstanding his so-called status as a sexual minority, Rhamie's investigation of the use of the Greek word elsewhere in Acts leads to a different conclusion. He notes that no other character in Acts is introduced with so much of a rhetorical flourish, indicated by the use of an exclamation, a long string of appositional nouns, and followed by another series of descriptive genitives. Rhamie goes on to suggest that the combination of the exclamation (ἰδοὺ) with the vocative use of "man" appears twenty-nine times in Acts. Where it does, it seems to connote the idea of a kinsman, fellow, or companion, as in the appellation "Fellow Galileans/Jews/Israelites" (see 1:11; 2:14, 22; 3:12; 5:35; 13:16; 21:28; cf. 17:22). With this in mind, we might translate the phrase "Look here—an Ethiopian eunuch kinsman, a court official of Candace, queen of the Ethiopians" as Luke's way of identifying the Ethiopian as an Afroasiatic Jew from the diaspora.[61]

59. Luke erroneously takes "Candace" as a proper name rather than more properly interpreting "Candace" as the title of the ruling queens of Ethiopia in the period.

60. Barrett, *Acts of the Apostles*, 1:419. Similarly Weiser: "In fact, however, the high officials at Oriental courts, especially among queens, were castrati" showing that the two interpretations, eunuch or sexual status, "are not mutually exclusive" (*Apostelgeschichte*, 1:212).

61. Rhamie, "Whiteness, Conviviality and Agency," 317–20, esp. 321.

Several factors favor the interpretation that Luke presents the man as a high-ranking official in the Jewish diaspora who represents the end of the earth ("an Ethiopian kinsman who is a eunuch, in other words, an official"). First, Ethiopia is mentioned twice in 8:27, which indicates that the emphasis is on the man's origins and reinforces the idea that he comes from very far away. Second, his role is also mentioned twice—that he is a high official and manages the queen's treasury. Third, the emphasis on his high rank also correlates with the mention of the chariot.[62] It's not that Luke didn't know about Deuteronomy 23:1—indeed Luke's comment that the Ethiopian was an "official" (δυνάστης) might indicate that he was intentionally crafting the story in such a way as to signal that "eunuch" means "official" as well as referring to his sexual status. A different question is whether the caveats in Deuteronomy 23:1 (or the history with Samaritans!) decisively shaped Luke's understanding of Israelite belonging.

Barrett suggests that there is a "measure of truth" in the idea that the Ethiopian represents another tradition about the start of the Gentile mission, one that Luke subordinated to the Cornelius story by "describing him as a pilgrim . . . reading the Bible . . . interpreting eunuch to mean official."[63] But Barrett has already dismissed the idea that the Ethiopian was Jewish,[64] missing the fact that for Luke, "eunuch" was a high-ranking official and a sexual designation. Barrett thinks that if Luke intended for this story to narrate the conversion of a non-Jew in fulfillment of Isaiah 56:3–5 and Psalm 68:31–32, then it is odd that there is no quotation or allusion to these passages.[65] However, Barrett doesn't reckon that Luke actually mentions that the Ethiopian was reading Isaiah—Isaiah 53:7–8 are the verses discussed in Acts 8:32–33—and that Isaiah 56:3–4 are the only verses in Isaiah that mention a eunuch. In other words, Luke regarded the Ethiopian as a Jewish eunuch from the farthest point of the diaspora. He saw the Ethiopian as having been already "joined to the Lord" (Isa. 56:3, 6), who had been brought to Jerusalem by the Lord to worship (Isa. 56:7). It is quite possible he categorized the Ethiopian, Simon, and himself as among the "dispersed of Israel" (Isa. 56:8; cf. Acts 8:1, 4).[66] In other words, the use of the words "Isaiah," "dispersion," and "eunuch" are enough to establish Luke's allusive style of reworking the LXX version of Isaiah 56.

62. Weiser, *Apostelgeschichte*, 1:210.
63. Barrett, *Acts of the Apostles*, 1:420.
64. Barrett, *Acts of the Apostles*, 1:424–26.
65. Barrett, *Acts of the Apostles*, 1:421.
66. "Dispersed of Israel" (Isa. 56:8 LXX): τοὺς διεσπαρμένους Ισραηλ (cf. διασπείρω in Acts 8:1, 4).

Luke alludes to Isaiah 56:3–8 not because it excludes certain sexual minorities from Israel, but because it talks about including eunuchs in the regathering of Israel's dispersion (τοὺς διεσπαρμένους Ισραηλ; Isa. 56:8 LXX). The eunuch observes sabbaths and festivals and has a name "better than sons and daughters" (Isa. 56:4–5), though he is now joined to a new "Lord." The descriptor "eunuch" anchors this present narrative to the oracle in Isaiah 56. Luke adds the double mention of the Ethiopian's office to signal that he is reworking the Isaianic tradition to focus on eunuchs as officials versus the exclusionary Deuteronomy 23:1, which is nowhere mentioned here.[67] He is one of the "outcasts of Israel" who are gathered by the Lord "besides those already gathered" (Isa. 56:8). In other words, the citation focuses on how Jesus now serves as the Lord spoken of in Isaiah 56, similar to the way the citation of Joel 2:28 works in Peter's speech in Acts 2:21. The Ethiopian's sexual status was not the same obstacle in Luke's cosmopolitan vistas of belonging as might have been the case among the rabbis.

To situate a briefer discussion of our final Jewish convert, Paul the Pharisee, we begin by noticing the envelope formed by the brief mention of Paul in Acts 8:1b–3 on one end, with the more extended narrative of Paul's conversion in chapter 9 on the other end. The odd introduction of Saul/Paul at the tail end of the Stephen narrative not only draws attention to the similarities of these two figures to each other and to Jesus,[68] but it also serves to identify all the intervening material as a prologue to Paul's more extended introduction in the next chapter. From a literary standpoint, Acts 8–9 represents the final stages in the focused mission to Israel before shifting focus toward the Gentile mission in Acts 10–11 and beyond. The mention of Paul enclosing intervening material about the conversion of Simon Magus and the Ethiopian show, symbolically, that there is a sense of fulfillment regarding the idea that all Israel, including Samaria and the furthest reaches of the Jewish diaspora, have had the chance to hear the word of the gospel. Afterward, the missionary focus shifts to the conversion of the nations (cf. Rom. 1:16). In other words, Paul's conversion as the crucial figure in the mission to Gentiles is another crucial preparatory step toward the inauguration of the Gentile mission in Acts 10–11.[69]

The account of Paul's conversion in Acts 9 has supernatural accoutrements. The narrative about Cornelius's conversion has supernatural paired visions that draw two parties to conclude that each has received the same divine message.

---

67. See note 58 above in this chapter.
68. Tannehill, *Narrative Unity of Luke-Acts*, 100.
69. So also Weiser, *Apostelgeschichte*, 1:253.

In both Paul's case and the Cornelius episode, these long narratives are subsequently retold on two other occasions, appearing a total of three times each across the whole of Acts,[70] and these features point to the importance of these episodes in Luke's overall literary purposes. Many suggest that the Cornelius story serves to recount the conversion of a paradigmatic Gentile convert. If so, then perhaps Paul's conversion story is likewise paradigmatic and serves as a climax to stories about the reception of the gospel among Israel. In Cornelius's case, his piety distinguishes him as the ideal Godfearer, and something similar may be true in Paul's case. The most pious Jews in the narrative world of Luke-Acts are the Pharisees, known for their meticulous observation of the law. In fact, in Luke-Acts the Pharisees have been portrayed in remarkably positive ways. There are friendly, non-Christian Pharisees that show up in the Gospel in several passages (Luke 7:36; 11:37; 13:31; 14:1; Acts 5:34–39; 23:10), and there is a complete absence of Pharisees in Luke's passion narrative. Even after his conversion, Paul describes himself as a Pharisee when defending himself in his speeches at the end of Acts before the Jewish authorities (Acts 23:6; 26:5). He speaks with pride about being from the sect of the Pharisees, which is the one that is the strictest and loves the law the most. Paul's rootedness in his Jewish heritage and particular identity as a Pharisee anchors his intercultural/bicultural work among the ethnic Other. In these situations, Paul's identity as a Pharisee works to solidify his credibility as a proponent of the gospel. If the most pious of those from Israel have been won over for the gospel, then surely that gospel will be winsome to the rest of Israel.

When read from the perspective of a diaspora Jew such as our author, we can see that all three of the converts discussed in this section would have had a higher claim to membership in Israel than would any Godfearer. Their proximity to Israel would have been compelling to readers like Luke, representing the target audience.[71] The length and repetition of Paul's conversion story and the sheer amount of space devoted to this character's actions suggest that Paul is a paradigmatic Jewish convert whose importance to the mission to Israel and the Gentiles cannot be underestimated. Hence, in its detail and repetition, Paul's conversion story is designed to persuade both Jews and non-Jews. Consequently, all of the stories in Acts 8–9 testify to the God-driven, relentless advance of the gospel and prepare for the major turn from an exclusive focus on Jews as the gospel goes to the nations.[72]

---

70. For the conversion of Cornelius the first Gentile see 10:1–43; 11:4–18; and 15:7–11. For accounts of Paul's conversion see 9:3–18; 22:6–16; and 26:12–18.

71. Tyson, "Jews and Judaism in Luke-Acts."

72. Similarly Weiser, *Apostelgeschichte*, 1:252, with reference to the baptism of the Ethiopian.

The Gentile Branch of the Family of God (10:1–11:18)

The first step in the Gentile mission occurs in Acts 10:1–11:18, which depicts the God-authorized conversion of the first Gentile converts by Peter, an apostle who has unquestioned credentials regarding his Jewish identity. This narrative in Acts 10–11 rhymes with the account of the descent of the Spirit in Acts 2. Though the idea is lost on some, we should note that the tongues of fire in Acts 2 only land on the diaspora Jews gathered together for Pentecost in Jerusalem. If you think of the Jews as a particular ethnic group, then Acts 2 is a scene that highlights the geographic diversity among these early Judaisms—not the ethnic diversity of the early Christian movement.[73] In other words, Acts 10–11 functions as a Gentile Pentecost and adds a new emphasis on ethnic diversity that affirms Gentiles as full members of the early Christian movement with equal access to the gift of the Spirit. As with all analogs, the association with the Acts 2 episode is clear though partial. The manifestation of the Spirit through speaking in tongues is a major similarity, though there is no wind or tongues of flames here (2:4; cf. 10:46). But in another critical respect, they are similar in that both scenes include a manifestation of the Spirit *without* an immediately preceding baptism, unlike many of the other conversion scenes narrated in Acts. The descent of the Holy Spirit in Acts 10 supernaturally attests that the Gentile converts are acceptable to God without a painful and perhaps lethal rite of circumcision for adult males. Circumcision had already proved to be an obstacle for potential adult male converts to Judaism and was thus a barrier to the Gentile mission and the creation of an inclusive community modeled on the blended family.[74] In addition, this long narrative unit justifies the Torah-light mission to the Gentiles described in the rest of Acts. For Luke, Gentiles do not need to become Jews (Acts 11:18), and they may enter Israel without fully adopting the law of Moses. However, we will see that Luke is not interested in abolishing the Jewish dietary laws and is less interested in the table fellowship between Jewish and Gentile Christians.[75] He is most interested in showing that Gentiles enter the people of God as Gentiles and do not need to convert to Judaism and undergo circumcision.

The main point in Peter's initial vision about the mingled clean and unclean animals in 10:9–16 is expressed three times by the heavenly voice: "What God has made clean, you must not call common" (10:15–16). Verse 28 describes a religious prohibition on assimilation when Peter explains to his Gentile compan-

73. Similarly D. K. Williams, "Acts of the Apostles," 218.
74. Smith and Kim, *Toward Decentering the New Testament*, 98.
75. Weiser, *Apostelgeschichte*, 1:266.

ions that "it is unlawful for a Jew to associate with or visit a Gentile." Whether accurately representing the range of opinions in the period or not, this prohibition is the kind of cultural practice that contributed to the persistence of Jewish identity through the ages. Yet, there is debate in our sources about whether it was strictly illegal for Jews to associate with Gentiles. It might be that we could render the word translated here as "unlawful"[76] instead as "indecent" or possibly "abominable" or "disgusting." This semantic range is a good proxy for the variety of opinions about contact with the Other among Jews in the period.

Clinton Wahlen engages this question, beginning with the idea that there was a widespread practice among Jews to avoid associating with Gentiles because they considered their idolatrous lifestyle to be defiling.[77] Whalen proposes three categories of food in this section instead of two, based on parallels in Jewish sources.[78] To the categories of "clean" and "unclean" in 10:14–15, Wahlen adds "common" as a category.[79] He defines common as indicating the temporary or potential defilement associated with people and things due to circumstances (such as intermingling or proximity) versus the inherent permanent defilement from unclean animals so defined by nature.[80] According to Wahlen, "the sight of unclean animals intermingling with the clean seems to have convinced Peter that the clean animals should be treated as 'common,' that is as potentially defiled and hence unacceptable as food."[81] Hence Wahlen interprets 10:15 as follows:

> "You must stop reckoning as 'potentially defiled' what God has declared 'clean'" [10:15]. . . . Peter finally understands the meaning of the vision: Just as the animals were to be reckoned as clean despite being mixed with the unclean, so Cornelius should be considered "clean" despite his remaining

---

76. "Unlawful" (Acts 10:28): ἀθέμιτός.

77. Wahlen, "Peter's Vision," 506–8.

78. Wahlen, "Peter's Vision," 510–15. Applicable Jewish sources include: 4 Macc. 7:6; m. Demai 2.2; 3.4; cf. 7.1–3; t. Tehar. 5.10–14; b. Pesah. 20b; 11QTª XLVII, 14, 18; LII, 18; Josephus, J.W. 2.150.

79. Category 1—clean (i.e., "what God has cleansed": ἃ ὁ θεὸς ἐκαθάρισεν; 10:15). Category 2—unclean (10:14; ἀκάθαρτον). Category 3—common (i.e., "profane, unholy, impure": κοίνου; 10:14)

80. Wahlen, "Peter's Vision," 511; later Whalen compares this idea of "unclean by nature" to the idea that Paul expresses in Gal. 2:15: "We ourselves are Jews by nature (φύσει Ἰουδαῖοι) and not Gentile sinners" (515n43).

81. Wahlen, "Peter's Vision," 514; similarly Bruce, Acts, 206n18.

uncircumcised. Peter now understands the impropriety of applying such categories to people.[82]

As mentioned earlier, Cornelius is paradigmatic of the non-Jewish convert who acts with righteousness and thus receives favor from God ("anyone who fears him and does what is right is acceptable to him"; 10:34). His praiseworthy actions include almsgiving and prayer, which are iconic deeds of righteousness in Jewish thought[83] (10:2; cf. 15:8), leaving no doubt that Cornelius is a "worthy" recipient of grace—he is definitely a "good Gentile."[84] God even chooses Cornelius to be the recipient of an angelic visitation (10:3–4, 34). We can view him as a righteous man who sees the value of the God of Israel but who has not renounced his own identity through conversion. The visions, the outpouring of the Spirit, and Peter's speech all testify that it is God who directs the expansion of mission, who attests to the equality of Jews and Gentiles in receiving the Spirit, and who affirms Gentile ethnic identification and universality of access and equality of standing:

"God shows no partiality, but in every nation, anyone who fears him and does what is right is acceptable to him." (Acts 10:35)

"Jesus Christ—he is Lord of all." (v. 36)

"Everyone who believes in him receives forgiveness." (v. 43)

The Holy Spirit fell upon all who heard the word. (v. 44)

---

82. Wahlen, "Peter's Vision," 515. Colin House makes a similar point, arguing that unclean and common are separate categories and that this distinction removes the conflict between Acts 10–11 and Acts 15: "The [divine voice in 10:15] stated what the Cross-Event had really done: removed 'the wall of separation,' thus allowing the 'clean' and 'unclean' creatures to associate freely again. Clearly the Jew was to remain ethnically a Jew, the Roman a Roman, the Greek a Greek, etc., but now the divine command illustrates that free association cannot defile." See C. House, "Defilement by Association," 150.

83. Wahlen, "Peter's Vision," 509n19, citing Tob. 12:8; Matt. 6:2–6; Acts 9:36; Weiser, *Apostelgeschichte*, 1:253, 263.

84. Robert Wall in "Peter, 'Son' of Jonah" suggests that Luke used the Jonah story to craft the details of Peter's encounter with Cornelius. The difference is that rather than evil Ninevites about whom there might be real worry as to whether they are "worthy" recipients of grace, Luke makes sure that the description of Cornelius rejects that notion.

"Can anyone withhold the water for baptizing these people who have received the Holy Spirit just as we have?" (v. 47)

The emphasis that this narrative receives in the overall work indicates that Luke knew that the welcome of Gentiles into the household of God on a fully equal basis with Jews was momentous, a potentially massive upheaval that rhymes with the backlash against the three Reconstructions in US history described in chapter 1. Recognition of this may help answer one of the puzzling features about the role of Acts 10–11 vis-à-vis Acts 15. In other words, it may be that Luke revisited the narrative in Acts 10–11 with its coordinated visions and cosmic signs to sanction the mission to incorporate Gentiles into this ancient people, providing the legal preconditions in Acts 15 to bolster the credibility and sanction for this mammoth shift in the culture. Acts 11:3 indicates that it is not Peter's action in baptizing Gentiles that stirred the Jerusalemites to anger, nor perhaps the idea that these Gentiles had also received the gift of the Spirit. Instead, they seem to have been disturbed by the idea of assimilation, that Peter had transgressed the norms of Jewish purity by staying at Cornelius's home and sharing food with him (10:23; cf. 10:6).[85] Indeed, much of early Christian history and most of the New Testament bears witness to the difficulty that the early Christian movement had in reconciling itself to the entrance of Gentiles into the ancient Jewish family. Awareness of the tectonic shifts in Jewish culture from the inclusion of the Gentiles may have prompted the length and repetition in these stories, not to mention the carefully chosen characters and carefully narrated supernatural accompaniments. Indeed, later episodes in Acts seek to rehabilitate and underline Paul's reputation as an authentically devout Jew (16:1–5; 21:17–40).[86] No doubt aware of Paul's compromised standing as a devout Jew because of his work with the ethnic Other, Luke selected stories that would best narrate and promote the Gentile mission. He must have also been aware that among the stories about Gentile conversion available to him, those featuring Peter would prove to be less controversial than those featuring Paul, especially since this aspect of the gospel was provocative to many.[87]

85. Steffek, "Quand juifs et païens," 105: "Étrangement, ce n'est pas le fait que Pierre ait baptisé des païens, que ceux-ci aient reçu l'Esprit, et le don de glossolalie, qui trouble les esprits des frères jérusalémites, mais bien le fait que Pierre ait partagé la nourriture avec eux. Cette . . . accuse Pierre d'avoir transgressé les norms de pureté juive, normes qui interdisaient aux juifs de fréquenter des incirconcis (donc des impurs) et de partager avec eux une nourriture qui devait probablement être impure elle aussi."
86. Sechrest, "The Perils of Passing."
87. John B. F. Miller's work adds support to this idea. Miller finds that the dream visions

We can read Acts 8–9 as the symbolic fulfillment of the idea that the gospel had been extended throughout the Jewish diaspora as far as the end of the earth. More importantly, we also see in the passage a conceptualization of the global and multiracial nature of the Jewish family as it adapts to receive and celebrate the Messiah of Israel. Provocatively, Luke insists that the departed and dispersed of Israel, Samaritan and Ethiopian respectively, are welcomed into the new movement before ever a word is spoken to an outsider. This motif, repeated throughout Acts where Paul speaks first in synagogues before preaching in Gentile marketplaces, is the Lukan version of Paul's refrain in Romans 1–2: that the gospel goes "to the Jew first and also to the Gentile" (Rom. 1:16; 2:9–10). Likewise, Acts 10–11 is a remarkable story with its clear emphasis on the idea that Gentile identity is preserved through a God-initiated and sanctioned conversion and a welcome into the people of God. By the end of this episode, the early Christian movement has moved from being a geographically dispersed phenomenon to one that is also ethnically diverse. The people have moved away from traditions that require a clear separation among people relegated into clean, unclean, and common categories. To those who might have been nervous about the implications of such a massive cultural change, Luke responds by painting a portrait of the ideal Gentile convert who was pious, obedient, and humbly grateful for the gift of grace. He portrays the Gentile Pentecost by emphasizing the degree to which God led humans through every step of the momentous change. Indeed, the preemptive bestowal of the Spirit on the members of Cornelius's household confirms that God fully accepts the Gentiles as they are. This sign above all others is the supracultural indicator that deems each of the cultures represented here as worthy of divine sanction.

---

in ancient narratives function as messages from God that serve to give new direction in a narrative, but that an interpretation of a dream vision gives the characters offering the interpretation the responsibility for the new direction. Miller suggests that Peter's lengthy and interpreted symbolic dream vision in Acts 10, the only interpreted symbolic dream vision in the New Testament outside of Revelation, reveals the deep measure of unease that this issue presents to the early church (J. B. Miller, "Symbolic Dream-Visions," 454–55). In support of this general understanding of the way that these vision sequences work is the observation that Peter's new insights about the significance of the visions don't actually come from the vision itself (Weiser, *Apostelgeschichte*, 1:255). In context, then, according to Miller, this dream vision plays two roles: First, it offers divine direction about the acceptability of Gentiles. Second, it places the responsibility for annulment of divinely ordained food laws on Peter's shoulders. If Miller is right about this literary function, then it seems that Luke was wise to have put this load on Peter's uncompromised shoulders than to put it on Paul's already burdened back.

Yet, there are discordant notes in these texts and among their interpreters as well. The global dispersion of the Jewish family in Luke is something less than one big happy family as ethnic Othering emerges rather stridently in the characterization of a featured Samaritan convert. Strangely, the Ethiopian seems to fare better in Luke's hands than in the hands of modern critical scholars, many of whom seem somehow reluctant to identify this dark-skinned noble as a Jew, even though he's depicted on an expensive pilgrimage to worship in Jerusalem (cf. 24:11 where Paul does the same thing) while poring over the scriptures of Israel. There is thus an implicit but dangerous ethnic hierarchy that can cause the unwary modern interpreter to stumble: greedy, grasping, shady Samaritans are ranked on the bottom; Blacks are sexually suspect just as they are today, but (European) Romans are best of all and especially the high-ranking military types. Worst is the unfortunate analogy between animals and humans at the center of the Cornelius narrative. These are precisely the kind of themes that lead some to conclude that some types of humans are bestial and others are "cleaner" than others, motifs that appear in all manner of hideous racist stereotypes.[88] Indeed, this trope is latent in the pandemic era racist anti-Asian rhetoric (e.g., "China Flu" as an epithet for COVID-19) that associates a disease-causing global health crisis with a particular ethnic group.

Even though these implicit and explicit hierarchies seep out of the narratives about the construction of the new blended family in the household of God, the main character in Acts—God—levels the ground and is a resource for positive, inclusive, universalizing rhetoric. The sign of tongues confirms and preserves identity by opening the door for movement across cultural borders while adding specific injunctions against hierarchies of belonging. Unlike the subtle indications in Acts 8–9 of ethnic hierarchies that rank the Palestinian Jew above the Samaritan or the Ethiopian constituents in the extended Jewish family, the sign of tongues emphasizes that all peoples have access to the same Spirit privilege. Taken as a whole, chapters 8–11 lean into the preservation of individual ethnic identities within the family of God.

88. These motifs are clear in contemporary anti-Black stereotypes, but the themes appear in other racist tropes as well. For example, Jessie Daniels describes Christian anti-Semitism in the medieval period as the pre-modern antecedent to modern anti-Black racism. Christian beliefs about Jews combined negative images of the Jewish body (i.e., body odor, inferior physical characteristics, association with peculiar blood, diseases, etc.) with negative moral and intellectual characteristics and saw both the former and the latter as inheritable characteristics through transmission of "Jewish blood." See *White Lies*, 12.

Assimilation and Accommodation (Acts 15:1–21)

I contend that interethnic relations in Acts are analogous to the politics of modern bicultural and intercultural relations across deep intercultural divides. Though this dynamic appears in many passages in Luke-Acts, Acts 15 is at the epicenter of attempts to navigate this terrain across chasms of difference. This chapter is where Luke tries to come to grips with the stress of adding newcomers to a more homogeneous population. Despite the affirmation of culture that we saw in Acts 8–11 and the creation of safe spaces for minorities in Acts 6 as discussed in the introduction, Luke pragmatically sets out a framework for biculturalism that attempts to affirm ethnic identification in both cultures. We shall see that Luke promotes a degree of assimilation to the majority culture but does so within limits designed to protect the minority culture, using a framework of practices that are "essential" and "not-burdensome." Nevertheless, well-meaning attempts to bridge implacable divides often result in liminality that leaves no one satisfied. The relative strength and appropriateness of the framework in Acts 15 will also be in the eye of the beholder, and that is the rub.

Literarily, Acts 15 is the centerpiece of Acts and authorizes the Torah-light mission to the Gentiles that Luke describes in the remainder of the work.[89] The story advances with a literary pattern often used in Acts which proceeds in predictable steps. First, a problem fractures the existing harmony (15:1–5). Next, the Christian community finds a solution (15:6–29), which restores harmony (15:30–35) and in turn drives the expansion of the gospel (Acts 16–20). Yet from a theological perspective, most interpreters agree that the passage narrates resolution about the question of table fellowship between Jews and Gentiles; that is, the question of commensality.[90] Here the early church grapples with the fact that table fellowship over foods associated with pagan cultic rituals was deeply offensive to Jews.[91] Functioning as the literary hinge for the

89. Barrett, *Acts of the Apostles*, 2:xxxvi, though Barrett is among many who speak of the spread of a law-free gospel (similarly Weiser, *Apostelgeschichte*, 1:364 and passim). I think it is important to note, as discussed herein, that the final resolution of the conflict in this chapter ends with the Gentile adoption of a small measure of commands from the law.

90. For more discussion about the problems that the Apostolic Decree in 15:19–21 was intended to resolve, and whether these were ethical/theological, social, or cultic/ritualistic problems, see Savelle, "Prohibitions in Acts 15."

91. Though Savelle thinks that the issues in Acts 15 are cultic (see "Prohibitions in Acts 15"), I think that the social issues arising from cultic practices are the more significant ones. Luke is above all interested in describing how harmony drives the growth of the

grand narrative of Acts and the theological linchpin for a Torah-light promulgation of the gospel, this episode defines Luke's vision of how the multiethnic people of God become a blended family in which biculturalism and interculturalism are normative.

Politics and Law

Acts 15 opens as Paul and Barnabas return to their home church after their initial missionary work and bear witness to what God is doing among the Gentiles when some Judean Pharisees challenge their work (15:1–5).[92] These Christian Pharisees seem to believe that embracing the new things in Christ does not necessitate a wholesale rejection of millennia of Israelite tradition. They maintain that Gentiles must be circumcised to be saved. Intriguingly, Torah is described as "the custom of Moses" in 15:1 (cf. 15:5). While some think that this characterization is broadly in accord with Jewish thought for the period,[93] others think that Luke doesn't understand the significance of the Torah in Jewish culture by characterizing it as mere custom.[94] Commenting on this question in a discussion of Acts 6:14, C. K. Barrett says that "it is impossible to turn [the ordinances] into mere customs with no legal authority since what Moses handed down was law."[95] I think that Barrett's opinion may reflect rabbinic opinion in some areas, but 15:1 may represent Luke's view as a Jew from the diaspora where cultic laws would have less salience removed as they were from proximity to the temple. More importantly, I am intrigued with how Luke's thought on this point is closer to how culture functions in an ethnically diverse and pluralistic society.

In verse 2, Paul and Barnabas "argued strongly against" the Pharisees' position, and the language used often appears in contexts describing contentious

---

church. In other words, it is not clear that he thinks of cultic/cultural issues as separate from theological issues, and I certainly don't either. A social problem *is* a theological problem whether it emerges from ritual practice or interpersonal dynamics.

92. It is beyond the scope of this chapter to thoroughly explore the many interesting historical questions that emerge from trying to reconcile Luke's reconstructed account of these important deliberations in Acts 15 with Paul's first-hand account of the conflict and its context found in Gal. 2. Something close to my own thoughts about these questions is captured in Paul Achtemeier's essay on the subject ("Elusive Unity," especially pp. 19–22). For a different reconstruction of these events that is even more skeptical about the historicity of Acts, see Beare, "Sequence of Events in Acts 9–15."

93. E.g., Weiser, *Apostelgeschichte*, 1:377; also Keener, *Acts*, 2:1318–21, citing numerous Greco-Roman parallels.

94. Barrett, *Acts of the Apostles*, 1:329.

95. Barrett, *Acts of the Apostles*, 1:328.

political debate and even outright armed revolt.[96] In this context, I think it is helpful to refrain from dismissing the argument as "just" a religious debate. Instead, I view it in political terms, by which I mean we should think in terms of a debate about values and the power relationships that manifest them. Here "politics" refers to more than electoral processes, pointing to dynamics about how we express allegiances. Especially today, but also in antiquity, one's politics says as much about what they embrace as it says about what they resist. In this light, 15:3–4 paints a picture of how Paul and Barnabas mount a campaign in response to a political problem that pits conservative family members on one side and progressive relatives on the other. Verse 5 crystallizes the primary issue: Notwithstanding the conditions under which Gentiles have *entered* the Christian community, under what conditions should the resulting mixed communities interact? Should Gentiles adhere to the same laws that define Jewish culture? Or should Jews lower the barriers to participation for the newcomers?

A debate about circumcision in the context of Jewish culture is a debate about the center of that culture, since the rite of circumcision is synecdochic for observance of the entire Torah, at least in the view of one famous Pharisee (Gal. 5:3). Indeed, in one argument in Romans, Paul uses the terms *circumcision, justification by works of the law*, and *physical descent from Abraham* in synonymous ways (Rom. 3:27–4:22).[97] For many like Paul, circumcision came to represent the Torah-compliant life and a sign of the covenant between God and Abraham's descendants. This sentiment became especially prominent after the Maccabean revolt, which was the first religious persecution forbidding Jews from circumcising their sons on pain of death.[98] In keeping with this theme, one scholar sees a hendiadys between circumcision and keeping the law of Moses in 15:5.[99] If Gentile believers were to accept the circumcision claim pressed by these believing Pharisees, they would be agreeing to obey the whole Torah.

---

96. "Great dissension/rebellion": στάσις (15:2). Also see Luke 23:19, 25; Acts 19:40; 23:7, 10; 24:5; see also Prov. 17:14 [LXX]; Isa. 22:19 [LXX]; 1 Clem. 1:1; 2:6; 54:2; 1 Macc. 7:12–18; 3 Macc. 1:23; Mark 15:7; Josephus, *Ant.* 1.164; 4.12, 140, 225, 294; 15.135; 17.61; 19.74, 115, 158.

97. Hays, "Have We Found Abraham," 90.

98. Referring to both the Maccabean period and the repression under Hadrian, Friedrich Wilhelm Horn points out that attempts to repress circumcision only strengthened its theological significance. See Horn, "Verzicht auf die Beschneidung," 483; see also Schiffman, *Who Was a Jew?*, 24–25; K.-W. Niebuhr, *Heidenapostel aus Israel*, 105; Hodge, *If Sons, Then Heirs*, 60–61; and Cohen, *Beginning of Jewishness*, 39–40.

99. Seifrid, "Jesus and the Law," 46 and 55n21.

Peter's speech in 15:6–11 reminds the gathering that God has already decided the equal access and standing of Gentile Christians through the Gentile Pentecost episode by making an explicit connection between this passage and Acts 10–11, representing the third and final time that the author rehearses the conversion of the first Gentile. In 15:10, Luke may again express an opinion from the Jewish diaspora at odds with other Judaisms of the day, mainly that the Torah is burdensome and impossible to fulfill. At a minimum, here Luke depicts Peter as "speaking for the race" by making a sweeping statement about the role of the law in Jewish culture that may claim far too much.[100] For instance, Paul believes that he lived a life in full compliance with the law in Philippians 3:6 (cf. Rom. 7:12). An early rabbinic text, m. Aboth 3.5, describes the law as a blessing that lifts burdens: "He that takes upon himself the yoke of the Law, from him shall be taken away the yoke of the kingdom." Jesus's sentiment in Matthew 11:29–30 may be even more explicit on this same point: "Take my yoke upon you and learn from me; for I am gentle and humble in heart, and you will find rest for your souls. For my yoke is easy, and my burden is light."[101] Though reflecting an earlier period, the Maccabean revolt attests to the seriousness of circumcision and obedience to Torah when the Jews faced certain torture and death rather than violate the Torah. The moving testament of the story of Eleazar's torture and death in 2 Maccabees 6:18–20[102] memorializes and propagates these sentiments for a later generation, and Peter's own behavior in Acts 10–11 attests to the ongoing high regard for Torah in an ordinary son of a fisherman.[103] Hence when some Christian Pharisees demand circumcision and obedience to the law in this text, they are making a reasonable demand given that several strands of early Judaism regarded the law as that which orders Jewish life and identifies and preserves the Jewish people.

---

100. "Speaking for the race" is the particular burden of persons from minoritized communities who are often asked, unfairly, to represent "*the* perspective" of their people for majority culture audiences. The views of a diverse and populous people group cannot be adequately represented by one person conditioned by a finite set of experiences. With this in mind, C. K. Barrett's question when commenting on this verse is a good one: "with what right can Peter describe the Law as an intolerable burden which neither he nor his Jewish ancestors have been able to bear?" See *Acts of the Apostles*, 2:xxxvii.

101. Barrett, *Acts of the Apostles*, 2:718.

102. 2 Macc. 6:18–20: "Eleazaros, one of the scribes in high position, a man now advanced in age and of noble presence, was being forced to open his mouth to eat swine's flesh. But he, welcoming death with honor rather than life with pollution, went up to the rack of his own accord, spitting out the flesh, as all ought to do who have the courage to refuse things that it is not right to taste, even for the natural love of life" (NETS).

103. Tiede, "Acts 11:1–18," 1176.

On the other hand, for those in the non-rabbinic Jewish diaspora who received a subset of the law in the absence of a temple cult or those in the early Christian movement raised without the law from infancy, it may well seem that the law is impossible to fulfill. This is possibly the situation that Matthew 23:2–4 has in mind: "The scribes and the Pharisees sit on Moses' seat; therefore, do whatever they teach you and follow it; but do not do as they do, for they do not practice what they teach. They tie up heavy burdens, hard to bear, and lay them on the shoulders of others; but they themselves are unwilling to lift a finger to move them."[104] It may be that the people of the land, the group known in Hebrew as the *'am ha-aretz*, might also have found the demands of the law onerous. One also wonders if Paul's protest in Galatians 5:3 that "every man who lets himself be circumcised . . . is obliged to obey the entire law" may be understood as a warning against bait-and-switch versions of the gospel that *didn't* demand obedience to the whole law, only a part of it.

Joseph B. Tyson notes that the word "yoke" in 15:10[105] is usually used in a positive sense to express the call to obedience to the law, though it does not have that meaning here.[106] This verse and other evidence suggest to Tyson that Acts' implied reader is a Gentile who has limited knowledge about the early Christian community and Jewish religion. Even though such a reader is attracted to Jewish religious life, s/he is not (yet) a Jewish proselyte, like the Godfearers in Acts. Seen through the prism of 15:10, Tyson thinks that the characters in Acts see Torah as a "theologically ineffective burden that includes commands that have not been and cannot be obeyed." For these commands, the Apostolic Decree in 15:19–21 represents a welcome substitute for Gentile believers who would be "encouraged by the removal of a major stumbling block and the reduction of Torah observance to four demands that are characterized as non-burdensome."[107]

The Apostolic Decree

James's speech in 15:15–18 provides the theological foundation for the Apostolic Decree by describing the scriptural connection between the Gentile

---

104. Weiser, *Apostelgeschichte*, 1:381; cf. the negative use of the word "yoke" in 1 Tim. 6:1: "Let all who are under the yoke of slavery regard their masters as worthy of all honor, so that the name of God and the teaching may not be blasphemed." Also see Conzelmann, *Theology of St. Luke*, 83.

105. "Yoke" (15:10): ζυγός.

106. Tyson, "Jews and Judaism in Luke-Acts," 32n29.

107. Tyson, "Jews and Judaism in Luke-Acts," 25, 33.

mission and the long-awaited restoration of Israel through a reworking of Amos 9:11–12. According to the text, the mission to the Gentiles is both a consequence and antecedent of the restoration of Israel.[108] The restoration of Israel "provides the avenue for the Gentile mission . . . through the anti-idolatry preaching of Moses in synagogues" (cf. 15:21).[109] The rebuilding of the "booth" or dwelling of David in 15:16 (cf. Amos 9:11) refers to the regathering of Israel already described in my reading of Acts 1–9.[110] Further, the ordering of the events in these chapters as *before* the conversion of the first Gentile in Acts 10–11 suggests that Luke doesn't think that "the Gospel reaches the Gentiles because Israel or its leaders reject it, but because it corresponds to God's universal salvific will and the promise of the risen Lord."[111] In other words, the Amos text represents the *temporal* ordering of the Gentile mission and not a causal ordering, a view in keeping with the allusion to Isaiah 49:6 in Acts 1:8.

Turning our attention now to the Apostolic Decree itself, the dictum represents a resolution of the question of Jewish and Gentile Christian commensality. But what is sometimes lost, as we will see, is that the Decree also implicitly affirms the validity of the Torah for the people of God. In other words, the Apostolic Decree balances the new work of God in the universalistic mission to the Gentiles with respect for centuries of Jewish tradition. The Decree itself includes several prohibitions, though the number and meaning of them differ among interpreters: abstention from food sacrificed to or contaminated by idols; abstention from blood (or food tainted by blood); abstention from eating strangled animals;[112] and abstention from sexual immorality. The prohibitions are in James's speech in 15:20 and again in the letter from the Jerusalem apostles to the churches in Antioch and elsewhere in the diaspora in 15:29. It also shows up once more in 21:25. The letter emphasizes that while the demand regarding circumcision came from Jerusalem, the leaders in Jerusalem did not authorize the practice. In both 15:20 and 29, the surrounding context frames the three prohibitions in terms of consideration for the recipients of the Decree: Gentiles are not to be troubled (v. 19), and they should receive no further burden beyond the three "essentials" (v. 28).

---

108. Dickinson, "Theology of the Jerusalem Conference," 77.
109. Gaventa, *Acts*, 223–24; Dickinson, "Theology of the Jerusalem Conference," 81.
110. Similarly see Weiser, *Apostelgeschichte*, 1:382.
111. Weiser, *Apostelgeschichte*, 1:271.
112. Refraining from food that was strangled (that is, not properly slaughtered with all the blood drained from the animal) essentially collapses this prohibition on slaughter techniques with the previous one regarding blood.

Even though the Pauline Epistles never mention the Apostolic Decree explicitly, there is some evidence that the Decree was widely known in the early church. For example, Clayton Jefford suggests that the Didache, an early Christian treatise from the late first or early second century AD, corroborates Acts 15:23–29:[113]

> [1] See that no one should lead you astray from this way of the Teaching, since apart from God it teaches you. [2] For if you are able to bear the whole yoke of the Lord, you will be perfect; but if you are not able, do what you are able to do. [3] And concerning food, bear what you are able; but against that which is sacrificed to idols be exceedingly on thy guard; for it is the service of dead gods. (Did. 6:1–3, AT)

According to Jefford, the Didache reflects a community that did not need to make the yoke of the law seem easy, as in Matthew 11:29–30 or 1 John 2:4–6 and 3:11. He suggests that the Didache may come from an earlier form of the yoke teaching in Christian circles.[114] Specifically, three elements in Acts 15:23–29 also appear in Didache 6:1–3, which suggests that some earlier form of the Apostolic Decree may have been the basis for Didache 6 (see table 1).[115] Besides the group of texts in Acts and Didache 6:1–3, Revelation 2:20 is another early Christian text that seems to bear witness to the ideas in the Apostolic Decree:

> But I have this against you: you tolerate that woman Jezebel, who calls herself a prophet and teaches and leads my servants astray to practice fornication, that is, to eat food sacrificed to idols. (Rev. 2:20 AT; cf. 2:14–15)

113. Jefford, "Tradition and Witness in Antioch," 409–19. The Didache was a rather popular early Christian text that even appears on some early canon lists. Part of Jefford's argument concerns a raging debate about whether Paul knew of the Decree since he never makes explicit reference to it in the epistles but deals extensively on the topic of food laws especially in Galatians and 1 Corinthians. Over the course of his essay, he points out that Didache 6 engages topics Paul takes up, even though it does not echo the Pauline Epistles. Further, the Didache was long associated with an Antiochene provenance, and he notes the coincidence that Antioch is known as a center for the Pauline mission (p. 418). Paul Achtemeier also engages this question and points to the odd phrasing in Acts 21:25 as an explanation for the silence about the Decree in the epistles: "If Acts 21:25 is accurate, and Paul learned of it only at the end of his career, one would expect no mention of it in his letters." See Achtemeier, "Elusive Unity," 20n66.

114. Jefford, "Tradition and Witness in Antioch," 415–16.

115. Jefford, "Tradition and Witness in Antioch," 417.

Table 1. Correspondences between Acts 15, Didache 6, and Revelation 2

(1) Threat of false teaching:

Acts 15:24   "... certain persons who have gone out from us ... have said things to disturb you ..."

Didache 6:1   "See that no one should lead you astray ..."

Rev. 2:20   "Jezebel ... is teaching and leading my servants astray ..."

(2) Desire for freedom from an unnecessary yoke/ burden:

Acts 15:28   "... [we] impose on you no further burden than these essentials" (cf. 15:10)

Didache 6:2   "if you can bear the yoke of the Lord"

(3) Prohibition about sacrificed foods:

Acts 15:29a   "abstain from what has been sacrificed to idols ..."

Didache 6:3   "keep strictly away from what is offered to idols"

Rev. 2:20   "leading my servants astray ... to eat food sacrificed to idols"

(4) Prohibition of sexual immorality (πορνεύω):

Acts 15:20   "abstain ... from fornication" (cf. 15:29)

Rev. 2:30   "leading my servants astray to practice fornication"

In Revelation 2, Jezebel likely refers to the leader of a group of less rigorously observant Christians whose practices are critiqued by the author. Some scholars doubt that Jezebel of Thyatira had approved the out-of-bounds practice of eating food sacrificed to idols (cf. 1 Cor. 8–10). Instead, Paul B. Duff argues that Jezebel represents a faction in the church that took a more liberal stance toward the larger pagan society than did John and his followers. Duff thinks that it is more likely that as a teacher, she tolerates eating food sacrificed to idols rather than actively encourages it (perhaps for purposes of social acceptability) and suggests that she may even be following something like Paul's teaching in 1 Corinthians.[116] Indeed, it is "quite possible that 'Jezebel' was merely allowing Christians to eat sacrificial meats in certain circumstances (much as Paul had done several decades earlier)."[117] In other words, the conflict about "Jezebel" may represent a similar debate as that depicted in Acts 15,

116. Duff, *Who Rides the Beast?*, 58.
117. Duff, *Who Rides the Beast?*, 16, 54.

with Jezebel and Paul on one side and John and the Jerusalem-backed Apostolic Decree on the other. Hence, Revelation 2:20 triangulates with Acts 15:23–29 and Didache 6:1–3, which suggests the possibility that some earlier form of the tradition is the basis for the sentiments reflected in all three texts. John was confined to Patmos when he wrote Revelation, but he alludes to a version of the tradition in a circular letter destined for seven cities in the Roman province of Asia. The addition of Revelation 2:20 to the group of texts associated with the Apostolic Decree suggests that churches knew about the tradition behind the Decree far beyond the Syrian Antiochene setting associated with the other two passages.

There is some debate about the underlying sources for the tradition. A survey of this debate uncovered at least four proposals for the origin of the Apostolic Decree. One possibility is that that tradition came out of the typological use of Deuteronomy 12, where Moses commands the people to obey two broad injunctions: refrain from idolatry (12:1–14) and refrain from the consumption of blood (12:15–16).[118] Thus, Houlden suggests that Luke figuratively applied these verses to this conflict between Jewish and Gentile Christians in the two broad parts of the Decree: idolatry (e.g., fornication) and blood (e.g., "things strangled"). We see another potential source for the Decree in early rabbinic literature, which contains similar commands: for example, b. Sanhedrin 74a says that a Jew may compromise to avoid persecution in any area except idolatry, the shedding of blood, and incest.[119] A third possible source of the Decree is the so-called Noachide laws, which were given to Noah and his descendants and hence applied to all humans in Genesis 9:4–6. These Noachide commands may have developed into a more elaborate list of prohibitions in later Jewish literature (Jub. 7:20) and rabbinic teaching (t. ʿAbod. Zar. 8.4; Gen. Rab. 34; b. Sanh. 56b).[120] By far, the majority opinion sees the commands to "the house of Israel and the stranger (גֵּר: *ger*) in your gates" (e.g., 17:8, 10, 12–13; 18:26) in chapters 17–18 of the Holiness Code in Leviticus as the source of the Decree.[121]

118. Houlden, "Response to James D. G. Dunn."

119. Savelle, "Prohibitions in Acts 15," 457–62, 468.

120. This seems to be the choice for Keener, *Acts*, 3:2268–69; Savelle, "Prohibitions in Acts 15," 458–59.

121. Proponents who see Leviticus 17–18 as a background for the Apostolic Decree include Bauckham, "James, Peter and the Gentiles," 172–78; Callan, "Background of the Apostolic Decree," 285; Conzelmann, *Acts*, 118–19; Haenchen, *Acts*, 449nn4–5, 468–72; Jervell, *Luke and the People of God*, 144; Waitz, "Problem des sogenannten"; and Wilson, *Gentile Mission in Luke-Acts*, 188. Terrance Callan's investigation into this possibility is particularly

Callan concludes that it is likely that Luke thinks that the Apostolic Decree is congruent with the minimal requirements for resident aliens who were Gentile adherents of the synagogue.[122] In other words, if Luke believed that the God-fearing converts like Cornelius were already keeping the laws from which the Decree originated (15:21; cf. 10:35), then it makes sense that he thought that the Decree wouldn't be burdensome to them (15:19). I think that Leviticus 17:8–14 and 18:6–29 are most likely to be the source of the Decree, but what is most important for our purposes is the recognition that all of these potential sources are either from the Torah or based on Torah. In other words, even if the Apostolic Decree represents a compromise solution to the problem of table fellowship between Gentile believers and Jewish Christians, the terms of the compromise come from Jewish culture. Indeed, this is the underlying logic expressed in 15:21. These requirements will not be a burden for the Gentiles because, as Godfearers, they are already used to reading Moses every Sabbath, and therefore inviting them to obey a subset of the food laws is not an arduous task.[123] If modern biculturalism is analogous to the intergroup dynamics in Acts 15, then it is Jewish culture that corresponds to the majority culture in this analogy. The Jerusalem compromise does not come from abstract, supracultural concepts from a disinterested third space; it is deeply married to a Jewish social contract. Given that this Torah-light compromise regarding Gentile Christians eventually gave way to a Torah-free ethos among such believers, early Christian history becomes a fascinating example of how this underlying social contract was ultimately reworked and overthrown.

The Politics of Piety

In Acts 10–11, Luke affirms Gentile culture and Gentile identity, especially in the narrative about the conversion of Cornelius. The story shows how God

---

helpful. He begins listing the laws in the OT that apply to both the גֵּר (ger) and the Israelite. He then culls the list by omitting any laws that extend blessings (which are categorically omitted in the prohibitions in the Decree); those lacking the אִישׁ אִישׁ formula (Hebrew: "any person," which emphasizes its universality); and any lacking the "violator will be cut off" formula (which presumes that the ger has been incorporated into Israel in some way). The remaining verses are Lev. 17:8–9; 20:2–3; cf. Ezek. 14:7–8 (together corresponding to idolatry); Lev. 17:13–14 (corresponding to strangulation); Lev. 17:10–12 (corresponding to blood); and Lev. 18:6–29 (corresponding to fornication). Callan's analysis shows how all these might well be summarized by referring to Lev. 17:8–14 and Lev. 18:6–29, as is common in many of these aforementioned studies.

122. Callan, "Background of the Apostolic Decree," 296–97; Weiser, *Apostelgeschichte*, 2:384.

123. Wahlen, "Peter's Vision," 509; also see C. Miller, "Peter's Vision in Acts 10."

persuaded Peter to allow Gentiles to enter the community without becoming Jewish proselytes. Acts 15 seals the case by resisting early Christian traditionalists who were pressing for circumcision. Yet, this episode does not represent an unadulterated victory for the innovators since Jewish culture is affirmed as well, first in negotiating a settlement on the terrain of the Torah, and second in developing a Torah-light approach containing a subset of the law for Gentile adherence. In other words, there are two crucial cultural results in Acts 15: first, the affirmation of Gentile identity in the early Christian movement; and second, the ascendency of Jewish culture. Thus, the compromises negotiated in Acts are analogous to those involved in developing bicultural and intercultural competencies.

Yet, beyond the point at which contemporary life rhymes with the dynamics in Acts, it is essential to explore the shape of that analogy as well as its limits. I've already affirmed how the compromises of Acts 15 broadly align with the contours of biculturalism. Acts 15 manifests the literary sequence depicted in other conflict narratives in this work: problem, fractured harmony, solution, restored harmony, missional growth. As a result of the harmony narrative in Acts 15, Luke adds a dictum with liberative elements. In seasons of cultural conflict and tension, it is essential to reach for a harmony that seeks to blend the old with the new. Acts 15 presents biculturalism as a political act and posture that seeks to preserve ethnic identification even while it also balances the hopes of the faithful traditionalist. It teaches respect for both the tradition and for the new things happening in the present. It urges a cultural sensitivity regarding the long-standing practices of others while also balancing the need to protect vulnerable newcomers. Concern for the newcomer is one of the major liberative elements in this text. The narrative recognizes the potential for harm in forcing new community members to bear the burden of adopting a complex regime of cultural practices that take a lifetime to perfect. This passage shows that assimilation was known to be burdensome even in antiquity. Reducing this burden becomes central to the rationale for a compromise. The council ends up limiting the amount of harm incurred by the minority in this assimilation process. Hence, the request for male Gentile circumcision is analogous to a demand that a minority group wholly assimilate to the majority culture. Without recognition of the costs of assimilation, any requirement for cultural adaptation will be deeply problematic.

We also need to recognize that every culture is particular and that newcomers can't master a new culture without time and a lot of help. Bible readers know just enough about ancient Jewish culture to know that assimilating would be extraordinarily difficult. We need to keep this level of difficulty in mind when thinking about the burdens we impose on the newcomers in our context and the culture shock they experience for months and even years after their arrival. Some decry the fact that immigrants are either slow to master American culture or unwilling to do so. A demand that immigrants instantly master a new language or customs as a precondition for acceptance into the majority culture is unreasonable. It is akin to having to master instantly all the intricacies of the ancient Jewish culture upon which Christian culture is built—a task as impossible today as it was in Luke's day.

The stories also speak to those who think that newcomers should not ask that the broader culture adapts to *them*—that they must adapt to *us*. This reasoning may be "fair" in some social construction that normalizes hierarchies and lopsided power dynamics about who gets to play host in a game about hospitality. These stories reveal that such demands are not consistent with the moral force in these stories. A requirement for assimilation is inconsistent with the gospel that lavishes the gift of the Spirit on all newcomers. It is also at odds with the principle of limiting burdensome harms for those with less power.

This text is also helpful since it endorses the protection of Jewish ethnic boundaries through its legitimization of Jewish culture. While some might argue that the text affirms the unequal power arrangement of Jews and Gentiles in the early Christian period through its legitimization of the Torah as the foundation for the new communities, this ethical stance fails to recognize the broader cultural-historical situation in which this narrative takes place. The Jews were a recently defeated and oppressed *minority group* in the Roman Empire when these events took place, and Christians were a tiny subgroup movement within that minority. In other words, the Jewish-Christian demand for Gentile Christian assimilation should be seen as a demand that cultural outsiders respect the contours of Jewish minority culture. Majority culture outsiders should not have the right to bend a minority culture to their desires, and these stories help protect the integrity of minority culture.[124]

Gentiles have the burden of adapting to the hundreds of commands in the Torah eased, but they also incur the obligation of responding to a subset. Sim-

---

124. Luke's vision to protect Jewish culture is both similar to but also different from the stance taken in Matthew. Whereas Luke prioritizes Jewish culture but reduces the burden on newcomers, the Gospel of Matthew is quite adamant that newcomers should adhere to the particularities of the movement. This concern appears in climactic form in the Great Commission in Matt. 28:16–20: "Go therefore and make disciples of all the nations . . . teaching them to observe *all* that I commanded you"—which of course would include the teaching in Matt. 5:17—"Do not think that I came to abolish the Law or the Prophets; I did not come to abolish but to fulfill." Cf. Luke 16:17: "But it is easier for heaven and earth to pass away than for one stroke of a letter of the Law to fail."

ilarly, the Christian Pharisees of 15:5 obtained concessions regarding commensality from the Apostolic Decree, even if they lost the battle for circumcision. We should not, however, underestimate the magnitude of this concession. Dunn notes that "Obedience to the law on unclean foods had been one of the make-or-break issues in the Maccabean rebellion. Many in Israel stood firm and were resolved in their hearts not to eat unclean food. They chose to die rather than to be defiled by food or to profane the holy covenant; and they did die."[125] In other words, the compromise attempted to minimize the burden on the minority while also asking the newcomer to show respect for the elders' traditions. With so much at stake on either side, even the fact of consensus is remarkable. This text tells us that something holy and powerful happens in building consensus around compromise.[126]

It is essential, of course, to probe the limitations in this analogy and interrogate the spaces where the text leaves us with inadequate resources for navigating intercultural conflict in our contemporary moment. Perhaps because Luke wrote these stories to persuade rather than inform, we find that most of their limitations for ethical reflection concern their missing elements. First, we should note that there really is no deliberation by the Jerusalem Council in Acts. The voices of opposition are missing, and the only people who speak do so in favor of the solution presented. In contrast to the prevailing modes of rhetorical debate, Luke advances his theological agenda by portraying the gospel as irrefutable, persuasive, and appealing.[127] However much that might have worked in the marketplace in Athens, it is completely ill-suited for the plethora of voices and opinions in the modern internet-enabled marketplace of ideas.

Next, we should note the crucial absence of Gentile believers at a conference intended to resolve issues concerning the nature of their participation in the community—perhaps the most serious difficulty in analyzing these dynamics from contemporary horizons. We *have* to do cultural negotiations with equal partners in debates that mediate between what is essential versus what is burdensome. How on earth is it possible to determine what is or is not arduous or unjust for a group of people when it comes to acclimating to a new culture without intimately including them in the discussion? Today we

125. Dunn, "Incident at Antioch," 12. See 1 Macc. 1:62–63.

126. So John N. Suggit: "The actions of human beings and of the Spirit are inextricably intertwined, so that when the members of the community of the Holy Spirit are met together their decisions are those of the Spirit" ("Holy Spirit," 44–45).

127. Joshua Garroway: "In fact, in all three places where he tackles the dispute in the early church about the admission of gentiles—the crucial deliberative issue in Acts—Luke manages to avoid presenting the opposing perspective." See "'Apostolic Irresistibility,'" 751.

see similar kinds of moral blind spots in churches that come together to decide "what to do about the gay folk." It is long past time to make sure that the seats at the table are actualized and not metaphorical when deliberations are taking place that concern a minoritized group. It is quite simply not enough to have advocates and allies speak on behalf of the marginalized because what is "essential" or "not-burdensome" must account for the lived experience of the minoritized group.

This brings us to another gap regarding this contemporary rhyme. Suppose we align majority culture values with the Jewish values in the early Acts church. In that case, we can't assume *a priori* that majority cultural values are the ones that should prevail in a similar debate. If my conjecture about the authorship of the work is correct, Luke made his own values normative and consistent with his Jewish non-rabbinic Afroasiatic diaspora setting. In contemporary society, we would be remiss if we assumed that majority culture values, White values, are the "proper" values to norm in an *a priori* manner in cultural negotiations. In the present cultural moment, we have the much more difficult task of adjudicating between different cultural values emerging from an assortment of US subcultures. We need to negotiate what is essential and burdensome among various *citizen* subcultures, not to mention immigrant cultures, which is an exponentially more complicated task. As we contemplate the extraordinary complexity of such a task, Christians would do well to center the value from this narrative that seeks to prevent harm to the weakest member or group involved in the negotiation.

Acts 15 also assumes that all the Gentile converts involved were Godfearers who had been "reading Moses every Sabbath" (15:21b). In other words, all the Gentiles imagined in this text are "good ones"; they are persons who were already in proximity to the synagogue at the time of conversion. Fleshing out the poetic shape of the rhyme with ethnic negotiations today, we could say that the Godfearers in Acts are analogous to today's biculturals from marginalized communities. The Godfearers of Luke's day were becoming immersed in Jewish culture but still maintained their Gentile identity without taking on circumcision, the most distinctive feature of Jewish identity. Today's biculturals likewise preserve their culture-of-origin identities with their ability to navigate White culture and their home communities dually. Luke treats this group with sensitivity and approval, though their modern analogs have a more complicated situation. While some move easily in the majority culture and accrue benefits like better education, jobs, and social mobility, others accept as the price of biculturalism a level of distrust from some in their communities of origin that spills over in hurtful epithets of banana, apple, oreo, and coconut.

Another gap that is critical to note is the lack of diversity among those who are newcomers. Cultural negotiations must also center the needs of those in marginalized communities with the greatest distance from White culture or risk results that are hollow and unresponsive to material conditions on the ground. It is important to note that Acts 15 completely ignores women and centers the debate on a rite of belonging only accessible to men. It is essential to recognize that this manner of understanding full-fledged membership in the people of God is inherently patriarchal, as feminine membership derives from relationships with circumcised males. Did Luke intentionally depict the newcomers as "good Gentile men" to try to minimize objections to the compromises he narrates? If so, that makes the portrait in Acts akin to the respectability politics seen among contemporary oppressed groups who violently police their own behavior in an attempt to live down virulently unflattering stereotypes. This is not the route to liberation.

Finally, in the world of the narrative, the disciples discern the hand of God through supernatural events, as God, the principal character, steps in and intervenes in the natural order to make the will of God evident. Especially in Acts 10–11 but also in chapter 15, the narrative advances with the aid of supernatural events that superintend an extraordinary cultural shift. I count myself among those who say that it is possible to discern the hand of God moving in contemporary history. Yet, those so inclined would have to admit that it is far harder to achieve agreement about God's providential intervention in recent events. Communal consensus about divine providence does happen, of course, in due season. Consider, for instance, the contemporary western Christian disdain for the institution of slavery. There is little in the Bible that justifies this perspective, so the consensus about slavery itself stands as a testament to the work of the Spirit in helping us discern new essentials and new limits on burdens. Yet considering all the lingering manifestations of oppression in US society, we also must concede that the work of the Spirit is frequently contested. Indeed, the apostle Paul himself stands as an example of how difficult it can be to discern the movement of God in a given moment, given the startling about-face that he experienced in ministry as he moved from persecutor to proselytizer in the blink of an eye. The apostle Paul and nineteenth-century Christian defenders of slavery are cautionary tales about how moral stances can be dead wrong when defending the tradition, causing us to completely miss out when the Spirit moves in a new direction. These stories in Acts summon us to examine our politics, allegiances, and considerations about who our people are. We must continually test ourselves for blind spots, proving our values in the crucibles of diverse viewpoints and a clear-eyed consideration of contemporary suffering when it comes to interrogating burdens that need lifting.

These stories also suggest that designing cultural compromises happens on incredibly fraught terrain where nobody ends up happy in the short term, and agreements are continually renegotiated. The various forms of the Apostolic Decree bear witness to the fact that the compromise itself was repeatedly used and perhaps reworked in multiple locales over time. The Christian Pharisees wanted full law observance for the new Gentile converts, and they got only part of what they wanted. When stacked up against centuries of tradition, it's fair to say that the Apostolic Decree represents a colossal concession for this group. While Gentiles may have wanted a Torah-free Christian practice, the subset of the laws sanctioned by the decree also represents a significant compromise for people new to life with the Torah. For this group, the compromise proved unsustainable over the long run since the Gentile church today, by and large, does not observe the nuances of the Apostolic Decree. In the test of time, the compromises documented in Acts didn't survive. Present realities demand constant negotiation and renegotiation of intercultural adaptation and concessions on the road to Beloved Community. We need the humility of recognizing that our efforts may only represent partial successes. The racism, xenophobia, tribalism, resurgent anti-Semitism, and nationalism in our midst suggest that we need indefatigable partners for the many more cultural negotiations ahead.

6

PRIVILEGE, IDENTITY, AND STATUS
IN 2 CORINTHIANS

For each of us as women,
there is a dark place within,
where hidden and growing
our true spirit rises,
"beautiful and tough as chestnut
stanchions against
(y)our nightmare of weakness."

—Audre Lorde, *"Poetry Is Not Luxury"*[1]

The Broke-Down Pastor

Years ago, I learned about the seductive appeal of the "prosperity gospel" from friends and acquaintances in a Black church in a small town in the rural South. These new friends were generous and loving and threw open the doors of their hearts and homes to me with scarcely a thought for their own scarcity. They were as openhanded in their giving to the church as they were to me, a virtual stranger. Yet, when discussing the prosperity gospel and predatory gimmicks designed to increase contributions from people of color who are sometimes also poor and oppressed, we soon found ourselves at an impasse. Though I denigrated the greed that powers this movement, my friends stunned me with their passionate defense of church leaders in fine suits, fancy cars, and

---

1. In this quotation from the essay "Poetry Is Not a Luxury," Audre Lorde alludes to her poem "Black Mother Woman." See *Sister Outsider*, 36. The essay goes on to unpack the dark place wherein the true spirit of women rises as the ancient and hidden place where emotion and feeling grow. According to Lorde, this dark place is a place suppressed in favor of the world of ideas promoted by the "white fathers"; it is a place where "living is a situation to be experienced" and where "true knowledge . . . and lasting action comes."

209

elaborate homes: "Who wants to follow a broke-down pastor?!" In their view, legitimate pastors must have access to the accoutrements of wealth and power; a "broke-down" pastor is simply not a compelling witness to the power of the gospel. This vignette gives insight into the complicated tangle of faith, wealth, race, and the aspirational desire for status and privilege. Though rooted in the not-too-distant past, this thinking is similar to some of Paul's problems in Roman Corinth, issues that surface mainly in the correspondence now preserved in 2 Corinthians.[2]

This chapter explores the nature of Paul's vision of Christian leadership and ministry and the association between physical identity and privilege. Some interpreters speculate about the arguments advanced by Paul's opponents in Corinth, which gave rise to his responses in 2 Corinthians. However, many suspect that much of the tension emerged from Paul's failure to embody then-contemporary aspirations about a leader's demeanor. Paul assumes the glory of his ministry accomplishments, heritage, and ethnic identity. However, he emphasizes his brokenness, humiliation, and suffering as an "earthen vessel," interpreting these qualities as the preferred expressions of participation in Christ. This chapter considers the implications of this rhetorical strategy for a modern society in which White bodies signify privilege and power, but which regards black and brown bodies as humble, cheap, and disposable. Though Paul's teachings have been the site of controversy in the Black church since before Howard Thurman's grandmother took issue with the deutero-Pauline pro-slavery commands in Ephesians, there are nevertheless liberative moments in his writings too, especially when he wrestles with identity.[3] In this reading of 2 Corinthians, we shall see that Paul's identity illustrates how privilege is relative and dependent on context since he was at the same time both privileged and weak. Though he occupied a privileged

2. Similarly Nave, "2 Corinthians," 310: "Paul's belief that Christian ministry is associated with sacrifice and suffering on behalf of others not only challenged the prosperity-teaching of his opponents, but also challenges much of the teachings of the contemporary prosperity gospel movement. One of the central tenets of the prosperity gospel is the belief that God wills the financial and material prosperity of every Christian. Individual prosperity, rather than affliction and sacrifice on behalf of others, is presented as evidence of God's approval of one's discipleship and ministry. Suffering and affliction are often presented as a sign of living outside of God's intended will. . . . Paul . . . placed his hope and confidence in God, who raised Jesus from the dead. . . . It was also this hope that enabled . . . Sojourner Truth, Harriet Tubman, Martin Luther King Jr. and countless other celebrated and uncelebrated men, women, and children to sacrifice and endure afflictions for the liberation and well-being of poor and oppressed people."

3. See the brief discussion of Howard Thurman's grandmother, Nancy Ambrose, on p. 15 above.

position in his own culture as a widely traveled, professional class Pharisee, he was minoritized as a Jew in those travels across the Roman Empire. Further, out of religious conviction, he writes of enslaving himself to recipients of his ministry, aligning himself with the lowest rungs of the society. We begin with a consideration of privilege and identity before examining how these concepts interact with the situation in 2 Corinthians 3:7–5:21.

The Embodied Nature of Social Identity

Constructs of identity are embodied; they fundamentally involve the nexus of heritage, personality, physical appearance, and social connections. Educators, theologians, and critical theorists alike explore how we understand identity, the human person, and society.[4] In racial and ethnic studies, the embodied nature of identity organically emerges from the fact that these concepts involve value judgments about skin colors, hair textures, facial features, and body types beyond the simple point of physical difference. Recent work in the social sciences no longer focuses on the essentialist enumeration of physical characteristics that belong to particular races or ethnic groups. Instead, scholars in racial and ethnic studies explore how society inscribes social meaning and privileges onto particular bodies. We can narrate the United States' racial history in terms of how interactions in public spaces in the United States manifest embedded value judgments about bodies, ordering them by gender, ethnoracial identity, and apparent sexuality and socioeconomic position.[5] In this society, White bodies signify privilege and power, while black and brown bodies are either expendable, threatening, or both.

The notion of "privilege" is one common theoretical concept that attempts to model how persons inhabit social spaces.[6] Privilege mediates position in a hierarchical ordering of ethnoracial groups by characterizing access to social resources. These resources may be material ones like wealth, credit, property, and access to safe neighborhoods and schools. Alternately, assets may be immaterial and less easy to quantify, such as assumed social status, access to beneficial social networks, employment opportunity, and the presumption of innocence in the legal justice system.[7] Privilege is relative, varying by the

---

4. J. B. Green, *Body, Soul and Human Life*; Westfield, "Called Out"; Tatum, *Why Are All the Black Kids Sitting Together*.

5. See the definition of the term *ethnoracial* on p. 38 above.

6. Feagin, *Systemic Racism*, 33–48. Also see the description of the term *privilege* on p. 41 above.

7. See McIntosh, "White Privilege," 32–35.

complexities of multiple identity attachments, and context-sensitive, varying by social location or setting. That privilege is relative may be seen in the fact that a Black female college professor will enjoy the privileges of educational attainment, but that such privileges will be generally less visible than those accorded to her male colleagues from other ethnic groups.[8] In other words, context matters—if a Black female professor has privilege from educational achievement in certain settings, a White male professor's privilege may be diminished in other contexts if, for instance, he publicly identifies as queer. Though recipients of privilege are often unconscious of its influence, it confers advantages for both the pursuit of happiness and the cultivation of deportment. It smooths the way for its beneficiaries and confers a poise and self-possession that can function as intangible but genuine social resources that confer competitive advantages on the bearers of privilege.

Complicating the concept of privilege is religious social location. Within the larger category of "Christian" in the US scene, there is considerable ethnoracial diversity despite the frequent disembodied, universalistic theorizing of Christian identity. Disembodied constructions of Christian identity appear in modern discourse about Christian theology and are typically wedded in the idea that Christian identity and origins transcend ethnicity and race.[9] Enlightenment and modernist assumptions about the ideal objective observer and the influence of body-soul dualism in the Western philosophical tradition reinforce such disembodied constructs of Christian identity that depict it as a non-ethnic, universal group unmarked by particularity.[10] These constructions are not uncommon in New Testament studies, even those that self-consciously interrogate the intersection of identity theory and biblical studies.[11]

---

8. Westfield, "Called Out."

9. For more on this subject see Hodge, *If Sons, Then Heirs*; Buell, *Why This New Race?*; Sechrest, *Former Jew*; cf. Boyarin and Boyarin, "Diaspora." For a discussion of how whiteness functions in Christian theology see J. K. Carter, *Race*; Douglas, *What's Faith Got to Do with It?*; Jennings, *Christian Imagination*.

10. Douglas, *What's Faith Got to Do with It?*, 3–103. For more on body-soul dualism in Christian theology, see J. B. Green, *Body, Soul and Human Life*, 1–71. The negative effects of a disembodied dualism in Christian thought is aptly captured in Green's comment on this philosophical tradition: "Angst among Christians in recent decades over how to prioritize ministries of 'evangelism' and 'social witness' is simply wrong-headed . . . since the gospel . . . cannot but concern itself with *human need in all of its aspects.* Only an erroneous body-soul dualism could allow—indeed require—'ministry' to become segregated by its relative concern for 'spiritual' vs. 'material' matters" (J. B. Green, *Body, Soul and Human Life*, 70).

11. See for example Cosgrove, "Did Paul Value Ethnicity?"; Duling, "2 Corinthians 11:22." For examples of studies that deliberately challenge this common construction of Christianity

But womanist thought, grounded in the rich soil of Black women's embodied experience at the intersection of interlocking oppressions, trains its critical acumen on the problem of suffering in Christian theology. As Emilie Townes put it, "Womanist ethical reflection rejects suffering as God's will and understands suffering as outrage."[12] Womanist scholars offer penetrating and critical theological insights for understanding suffering in the Christian experience of African American women. They wrestle with the haunting notion that misappropriation of the cross/crucifixion complex can exacerbate an ideological tyranny of minoritized Christians that, effectively, sanctions suffering and violence. As Delores Williams puts it: "The reality is that, at some level, the cross is a constant reminder of innocent suffering and violence, regardless of the messages it is supposed to communicate about salvation. Too often, Christians are thereby taught to believe that something good can result from violence."[13] The pervasive violence in US culture may be rooted in our racist past. Racial stereotypes of even the *prospect* of African American violence can act as a pretext for preemptive subjugation. Via overpolicing and Stand Your Ground laws in twenty-seven states,[14] Whites can kill Blacks with impunity whenever they feel "endangered" in encounters with African American women, men, and children. The 2019–2022 global pandemic also revealed a macabre callousness to suffering in US society to go along with our predilection for violence. I'm sure I'm not the only African American who believes that the astonishing tolerance for the mammoth death toll in the COVID-19 pandemic in the United States at least partly derives from the well-known unequal distribution of black and brown pandemic-related sickness and death. Once there was an association between COVID and Black people, I knew we would see a tragic death toll. The pervasive violence and callous disregard for Black oppression in US society led to an indifference to human suffering.[15] Layering Christian exhortations to endure suffering on top of harmful stereotypes, internalized

---

see Hockey and Horrell, *Ethnicity, Race, Religion*; Hodge, *If Sons, Then Heirs*; Kelley, *Racializing Jesus*; Sechrest, *Former Jew*.

12. Townes, "Living in the New Jerusalem," 78.

13. D. S. Williams, *Sisters in the Wilderness*, 26.

14. The Southern Poverty Law Center maintains that NRA-backed "Stand Your Ground" laws "deepen disparities in the legal system and disproportionately justify the use of violence by people who are white and male against people who are not." See Huang, "Stand Your Ground"; also see the report by the Giffords Law Center, "'Stand Your Ground' Kills."

15. Similarly, D. S. Williams in *Sisters in the Wilderness* points out that common use of the cross and crucifixion arose much later in the church, as late as the eleventh or twelfth century, but doesn't reckon with cross imagery in the earliest NT writings in the Pauline Epistles (e.g., Rom. 8:36; 1 Cor. 1:17–18; Gal. 2:20; 6:14; cf. Matt. 10:38; Mark 8:34; Luke 14:27).

oppression, and the racialized violence in the DNA of American culture produces a piety that sanctimoniously encourages African American women and
other marginalized people to embrace injustice and suffering as a sign of divine
favor and participation in the divine will. A "theology of the cross" that invites
Christians to imitate Christ's passion as found in Paul and the Gospel of Mark
especially is mentioned as the locus of a problematic discourse about oppression that becomes racially loaded in the current context.[16]

Raquel St. Clair's study of Mark 8:31–38, *Call and Consequences*, offers a
book-length study that draws on womanist theological, ethical, and exegetical reflection to examine the relationship between suffering and ministry,
issues that we will see in the forefront in Paul's discourse in 2 Corinthians.
The conception of Jesus as the divine co-sufferer is a central element in the
religious experience of African American women, but womanist scholars
maintain that this ideology casts Black women into a perpetual role of suffering. St. Clair and other womanists suggest that African American women
would benefit by identifying with Jesus's *ministry* versus an exclusive focus
on Jesus's suffering. While womanist scholars outright reject the idea that
suffering is God's will, their theological constructs vary in the degree to
which their views integrate reflection on the cross. For instance, Karen
Baker-Fletcher suggests the reflection on the cross yields an opportunity
to choose between an ethic of risk versus an ethic of sacrifice: "Persecution
and violence suffered by those who resist evil and injustice is the result of an
ethic of risk. The assassination of a Martin King and the crucifixion of Jesus
Christ is part of the risk involved in actively struggling for social justice."[17]
M. Shawn Copeland suggests that enslaved African Americans treasured
the cross because "it enthroned the One who had endured what was their
daily portion . . . who went all the way with them and for them."[18] Rejecting
spiritualized evil or suffering, Copeland constructs a womanist theology of
suffering rooted in resistance. Through remembering and retelling our stories
of oppression and enduring oppression and pain from acts of resistance,
Copeland exhorts womanists to seek to work in partnership with God for
redemption as they risk everything for their own freedom and their children's
lives. These commitments honor the cross and redeem its significance from
misuse as a weapon of oppression.[19]

16. Patterson, *Rituals of Blood*, 229–32.
17. Baker-Fletcher, *Immanuel*, 79–80.
18. Copeland, "Wading through Many Sorrows," 120.
19. Copeland, "Wading through Many Sorrows," 123–24.

By contrast, Delores Williams insists that the cross and crucifixion are symbols of violence and innocent suffering and that we should never assign a positive value to them. Nevertheless, she also suggests that the symbols have an important place in Christian thought as powerful reminders of another sort:

> I do believe there are compelling reasons for remembering the cross and crucifixion. Both are symbols of realism. They are reminders of what can happen to reformers who successfully challenge the status quo and try to bring about a new dispensation of love and power for the poor. For those who really try to live out the two sole commandments Jesus left us—to love God with all our heart, soul, and mind, and to love our neighbor as ourselves—the cross and crucifixion remind us of the struggle that lies ahead.[20]

Kelly Brown Douglas discusses the debate about the crucifixion and how some contest the idea of redemptive suffering as damaging for oppressed peoples whereas others argue that traditional atonement categories have succored and nourished Black Christians amid historical oppression. Douglas herself steers a middle way. She understands the incarnation and resurrection as a single indivisible construct. When viewed this way, the incarnation and resurrection affirm the importance of human bodies and simultaneously participate in God's self-revelation to humanity.[21] According to Douglas, the incarnation/resurrection complex establishes (1) God's identification with human suffering in the context of oppression and unjust uses of power; (2) the incarnation as a declaration of the intrinsic dignity of human flesh as a witness to and medium of God's self-revelation; and (3) God's effective rejection of the ideal of redemptive suffering by the resurrection, since it restores Jesus to embodied life.

However, contrary to Douglas and others who maintain an essential complicity between Pauline theology and hyper-Platonic thought, I suggest Paul espouses similar values in 2 Corinthians, especially concerning the intrinsic dignity of human flesh as a conduit of God's power. Paul's thought differs from Douglas's ideas on how suffering can be redemptive. His thought is more in line with Copeland, who emphasizes partnership with Christ in liberating the oppressed from sin and suffering. Yet, 2 Corinthians does contain Paul's conviction that the promise of the resurrection stimulates active and fearless engagement in the world, a value embraced by several womanist theologians. I suggest that Paul's thought is liberative on this point and can inspire a coura-

---

20. D. S. Williams, *Sisters in the Wilderness*, 27.
21. Douglas, *What's Faith Got to Do with It?*, 89–103.

geous willingness to tolerate suffering if it is the price of retrieving people from broken systems that imprison bodies, souls, and minds. Paul's bold Christian witness is grounded in privileges that emerge from reflection on his rich ethnoracial heritage on the one hand and his identification with the embodied suffering and resurrection of Jesus on the other. Far from denigrating the body, Paul's countercultural ministry affirms the prophetic and embodied nature of Christian life and witness in all its messiness.

Identity and Privilege (2 Corinthians 3:7–4:6)

Paul's extended reflection on Christian ministry in 2 Corinthians 2:14–6:10 is an argument that proceeds in four moves that together address the contrast at the center of the conflict in this epistle: How can authentic ministers fail to exhibit a comparable glory to the glory of God in Christ? In the first move, Paul introduces the topic of sufficiency, maintaining that God is the basis for adequacy as a pastoral leader when one's ministry message symbolizes life and death for its recipients (2:14–3:6). Drawing on Roman triumphal procession imagery, Paul depicts himself as God's captive who tangibly manifests knowledge of God to others. Those accepting the gospel perceive the message and its messengers as a pleasing aroma, while knowledge of God is the odor of death and decay for those who reject it. In the second movement of the argument, Paul contrasts his ministry with Moses's ministry, the most revered leader in Israel's past (3:7–4:6). In the third section, he develops a pottery metaphor wherewith he contrasts God's glorious power with the fragile and common human messenger who is a conduit of that power (4:7–5:10). He characterizes his work as the ministry of reconciliation in the fourth and final move in 5:11–6:10, ending it with a *peristasis*, or catalog of suffering offered as proof of his authenticity. Although we are here concerned with the second and third sections of this discourse, the central issue throughout 2:14–6:10 concerns a tension that rhymes with problems in race relations, and that is the clash between embodied identities on the one hand and social status and privilege on the other.

In 3:7–4:6, Paul does a rereading of Exodus 34:29–35. He introduces the new covenant ministry by contrasting the life-giving Spirit with the "killing" letter, ultimately describing this as a contrast between Moses's ministry and his own via a series of antithetical terms.[22] Post-Shoah interpreters, sensitive

---

22. Though 2:14–6:10 is ostensibly a defense of apostolic ministry in general and Paul's ministry in particular as corroborated by his more direct comments in 2 Cor. 10–13, there are several indications that the comments on ministry in this discourse apply to Christian

to the anti-Semitic roots of the Holocaust, are understandably uncomfortable with this initial comparison and the series of negative images used for Moses's work throughout this paragraph, including "ministry of death," "ministry of condemnation," as well as the possible references to the abolition of the old covenant (e.g., 3:11, 14).[23] A closer reading suggests that these images for the Mosaic ministry were likely chosen less as a realistic or informative description of that ministry for outsiders, but instead to communicate to insiders the extent to which Paul's ministry surpasses Moses's.[24] Paul intends his description of Moses for the consumption of insiders. We should note that Paul simply assumes that his audience will agree that Moses's ministry was glorious. Second, he thinks it is valid to compare the righteousness and life in his own ministry with the condemnation and death in Moses's.[25] By contrast, when discussing the nature of the Mosaic law with outsiders in Romans 7, it is clear that he is addressing people whom he's never met. His description of the law is much lengthier and more nuanced in that passage since he has to argue for his understanding rather than assume it. In the end, it is difficult to imagine a more striking disparity than that between the description of the law as holy, just, and good in Romans 7:12 and Moses's killing ministry of death and condemnation in 2 Corinthians 3:6–9. We can reconcile these different depictions by realizing that the former careful characterization represents Paul's core beliefs, while the latter represents an ad hoc strawman, never intended as a stand-alone exposition, for use only with colleagues in the context of a comparison.

In other words, the Mosaic ministry ministers death only through a vivid contrast with the resurrection life mediated through the new covenant (cf. 2 Cor. 4:14).[26] Paul's esteem for the old covenant is evident in the way that

---

life broadly. J. Lambrecht points out that 2 Cor. 1:3–11 uses much of the same language as 4:7–15: Paul suffers; shares in Christ's suffering; suffers for the sake of Corinthians; and acknowledges God's deliverance of him from death ("Nekrōsis of Jesus," 331–32). Further, 2 Cor. 1:6–7 explicitly maintains that the Corinthians endure the same kind of suffering as Paul does (i.e., the sufferings of Christ; 1:5). Further, the opposition of "we" and "you" in 4:7–15 disappears in the next section, indicating a broadening of the concern to all Christians. The "we all" in 5:10 is explicit and probably applies back to 4:16–18.

23. While interpreters frequently debate whether 3:11 refers to the fading or the abolition of the old covenant, Georgi's exegesis helpfully points out that the contrast here is a contrast between two ministries rather than two covenants. See *Opponents of Paul in Second Corinthians*, 229–56.

24. This is possible evidence for Paul's "solution to plight" pattern of thinking, a phrase popularized by E. P. Sanders in *Paul, the Law, and the Jewish People*; cf. Thielman, *Plight to Solution*.

25. Thrall, *Second Epistle to the Corinthians*, 1:240.

26. E. P. Sanders, *Paul, the Law, and the Jewish People*, 138.

Paul chooses to contrast "glory" with "more glory" rather than using a more negative term as a contrast to glory, such as "dishonor"[27] or "humiliation."[28] When Paul describes the end of veiled readings of the old covenant in Christ in 3:14–17, his reasoning seems focused on the proper *interpretation* of the old covenant through the Spirit versus a focus on its destruction. Indeed, when Paul does develop a foil to contrast with the glory of the new covenant ministry, he will not look to the old covenant, but he will use his own person as an illustration. The glory of the new covenant contrasts with the humble earthen vessel, lacking in all honor, privilege, or inherent power (4:7). Thus, using a *qal vahomer* (i.e., from lesser to greater) argument, Paul establishes the gloriousness of the new covenant ministry by comparing it to something that was for him both self-evident and beyond argument, that is, the intrinsic glory of the Mosaic ministry and covenant (cf. Rom. 7:12).[29] Paul's purposes here are not to denigrate the Mosaic ministry's regime but to establish the glory of the new covenant ministry. Despite Paul's apparent lack of this quality (cf. 10:10), he shows that his ministry is more glorious than the most revered ministry in the central mythomoteur of the people of Israel. In Corinth, Paul's opponents would raise serious doubts about the authenticity of his leadership (10:1–5, 8–9; 11:20–23; 12:11–12) and person (5:12; 10:10), accusing him of poor oratory (10:10; 11:6), inconsistency (10:11; cf. 1:17), and financial fraud (11:7–9; 12:13–18; cf. 2:17; 4:2; 9:20). While we cannot know whether his opponents had already leveled the charges in 2 Corinthians 10–12, it seems probable that this section either responds to something similar or anticipates that such charges would soon be forthcoming.[30]

---

27. "Dishonor": ἀτιμία; see 1 Cor. 11:14–15; 15:43; 2 Cor. 6:8.

28. "Humiliation": ταπείνωσις; see Phil. 3:21. Note also how Paul uses a participle (καταργουμένην) when referring to the passing glory of Moses's face (3:7, 13; cf. 1 Cor. 1:26) and the fading glory of the old covenant (3:14), but that he uses the finite verb (καταργέω) when referring to the removal of the veil over the old covenant (3:14; cf. 1 Cor. 6:13; 13:8, 10; 15:24, 26). The NASB translators capture the distinction between the participial and finite forms of καταργέω well by translating the participle with the less negative "fade" in 3:7, 11, 13 but the verb with "removed" in 3:14, a distinction they preserve in the only other appearance of καταργέω in a participial form in Paul, where the milder translation "fade" also suits the context (cf. 1 Cor. 2:6; 2 Cor. 3:7, 11, 13).

29. On Paul's *qal vahomer* argument, see Thrall, *Second Epistle to the Corinthians*, 1:239–40; Harris, *Second Epistle to the Corinthians*, 279, 290. Cf. Ben Witherington who notes how this argument of the lesser to the greater also appears in Greco-Roman discourse (*Conflict and Community in Corinth*, 380).

30. The temporal relationship between 2 Cor. 1–9 and 10–13 is connected to an interpreter's assessment about the literary integrity of 2 Corinthians. For more on this issue see

One of the key messages in this section appears in the conclusion that Paul draws from his exegesis of Exodus 34:29–35 in 2 Corinthians 3:12. Here Paul infers that the upshot of the new covenant ministry's unveiled and more glorious nature is a ministry characterized by greater boldness.[31] Indeed, it seems likely that the courage and boldness in ministry that issue from Paul's conviction about the gloriousness of the new covenant ministry are closely akin to Paul's confidence[32] in 3:4, which in context refers to the fact that God empowers ministry.[33] Further, Paul's confidence in God's empowerment and the boldness that accompanies his convictions about the surpassing glory of the new covenant ministry also issues in "freedom."[34] The word *freedom* in Paul is usually associated with his thinking about the role of the law for Christians (e.g., Rom. 7:1–6; Gal. 4:4–5). However, the immediate context makes it more likely that he is using all of these words—*freedom*, *confidence*, and *boldness*—as a way of showing that his new covenant ministry is both more glorious and more powerful in overcoming obstacles. Moreover, the phrase "we do not lose heart"[35] (2 Cor. 4:1, 16) simply expresses the same sentiment negatively, that the ministry of the new covenant in Christ will not be diminished by misunderstanding (4:1–4) or danger (4:16; 5:1).[36] Thus, the main idea is that the gloriousness of the ministry of the Spirit outshines the most extraordinary ministry in all of Israel's history, the ministry of the Lawgiver himself, and this conviction produces great confidence and boldness in Paul for the task before him.[37] The willingness to speak urgently, boldly, and with confidence in front of kings, peers, and comrades is where Paul's

---

the discussions in the following: Furnish, *II Corinthians*, 30–48; Barrett, *Second Epistle to the Corinthians*, 11–21; Georgi, *Opponents of Paul in Second Corinthians*, 9–18; and Thrall, *Second Epistle to the Corinthians*, 1:3–61. For more discussion about the identity of Paul's opponents, see the good overview in Bieringer, "Gegner des Paulus," as well as the two frequently cited monographs, Dieter Georgi's *Opponents of Paul in Second Corinthians* and Jerry Sumney's *Identifying Paul's Opponents*.

31. "Boldness" (2 Cor. 3:12): παρρησία.

32. "Confidence" (2 Cor. 3:4): πεποίθησις.

33. Bultmann, *Second Letter to the Corinthians*, 75–76.

34. "Freedom" (3:17): ἐλευθερία. For more on this observation see Bultmann, *Second Letter to the Corinthians*, 75–76; Furnish, *II Corinthians*, 237–38; contra Barrett, *Second Epistle to the Corinthians*, 122–23, who relates freedom in this verse to the law.

35. "We do not lose heart" (2 Cor. 4:1, 6): οὐκ ἐγκακοῦμεν.

36. "Be of good courage" (5:6, 8): θαρροῦντες. This word functions as a synonym for confidence, freedom, and boldness.

37. Also see Matera, *II Corinthians*, 66.

thought is most empowering for those who are hungry to see God's justice manifest among us.

In light of this discussion of the main issues in 2 Corinthians 3:7–4:6, it is necessary to pause to reflect on our earlier discussion about the notion of "privilege." It would not be too much of a stretch for us to see in Paul's confidence, courage, and boldness a network of sentiments analogous to the fearlessness and assuredness that undergirds the modern notion of privilege in critical race theory. Here we see Paul bolstered by the idea that God has empowered his new covenant ministry so that it transcends even the most glorious ministry in his proud ethnic heritage. Though opponents point to Paul's failure to personify then-current standards of conduct for leaders in Corinth, Paul measures himself against Moses, invoking a traditional standard of leadership that was still unassailable within the local community.[38] Paul's argument about the glory of his new ministry in Christ works as a source of empowerment primarily because he has confidence that he and his audience share assumptions about the glory of his ethnoracial heritage.

Read another way, however, one could argue that far from seeking strength from his ethnic heritage, Paul has rejected it since many think that he proclaims the annulment of the old covenant in this passage.[39] This interpretation would not only be countercultural in his ancient context but also conflicts with many goals of contemporary identity theorists who advocate nurturing ethnic sentiment as a way of resisting an oppressive assimilationist ideal, as we discussed in chapter 5. However, this kind of objection reduces ethnoracial identity to ancestry when identification is much more often complicated by multiple associations in which aspects of identity may be emphasized in one setting and subordinated in others. For many Jews of the period, ethnoracial identity included religious sentiment as a critical element alongside ancestry.[40] If Paul's religious sentiments have changed now that he worships the God of Abraham through the new covenant, his focus on Moses affirms that he has nonetheless retained pride in his ancestry as a descendant of Abraham (cf. 2 Cor. 11:22). Paul does not reject his birth identity in this passage any more than he does

38. See Savage, *Power through Weakness*, 54–99, for a discussion of personal characteristics valued in status conscious first-century Corinth.

39. "Cease, annul, destroy" (3:7, 11, 13, 14): καταργέω. So also held by many interpreters: Thrall, *Second Epistle to the Corinthians*, 1:248; Witherington, *Conflict and Community in Corinth*, 279–380; Furnish, *II Corinthians*, 203; Barrett, *Second Epistle to the Corinthians*, 116; cf. Harris, *Second Epistle to the Corinthians*, 290–91. But see note 28 above for a different interpretation of this usage.

40. See chapter 3, "Race and Ethnicity in Antiquity," in Sechrest, *Former Jew*.

in Philippians 3:3–6, a similar passage. Paul's lesser-to-greater/*qal vahomer* reasoning depends on an exalted opinion of that heritage in both contexts. Even more noteworthy is the fact that Paul's pride in his venerable heritage is probably unconscious since it is assumed rather than argued, as mentioned above. His focus is much more on the way that God has empowered the new ministry of the spirit. He takes the gloriousness of his heritage for granted, and the argument's effectiveness rests on this shared and implicit assumption. On the other hand, Paul's attitudes contrast with modern notions of privilege from critical race theory. They are divorced from specifically visible markers like skin color, even though privilege is associated with cultures in both contexts. Indeed, the next section will show that Paul explicitly rules out some visible external markers of status and privilege against then-current expectations.

Embodiment and Identity (2 Corinthians 4:7–5:10)

The Corinthian correspondence does more to establish the embodied nature of Christian identity than any other section of the Pauline corpus. Much of the scholarship on this section concerns the relationship between 2 Corinthians 5:1–10 and 1 Corinthians 15:35–58 and explores the question of whether Paul's views about resurrection in 2 Corinthians 5:1–10 had shifted after he wrote the earlier document.[41] But notwithstanding the question of Paul's eschatology, this segment has important analogical correspondences with contemporary race relations. This section will explore the evidence about Paul's conception of embodiment in 2 Corinthians 4–5, synthesizing it with evidence about how the conflict in Corinth reflected in 2 Corinthians 10–13 concerned rival perceptions about the physical manifestation of leadership qualities. In important ways, the opposition to Paul underlying this epistle is deeply concerned about Paul's public persona[42] and thus analogous to some modern identity dynamics.

---

41. Second Corinthians 5:1–10 has elicited more commentary than just about any other passage in this epistle. One set of questions focuses on the extent to which Paul adopts or rejects Platonic dualism or other Greco-Roman philosophical categories: see Heckel, "Body and Soul in Saint Paul"; Heckel, *Innere Mensch*; Aune, "Anthropological Duality"; J. B. Green, *Body, Soul and Human Life*, 170–78; Betz, "Concept of the Inner Human Being"; Glasson, "2 Corinthians 5:1–10 versus Platonism." For articles on the relationship of this passage to Paul's discussion of resurrection in 1 Cor. 15:35–58 see: Benoit, "Resurrection," 107; Gillman, "Thematic Comparison"; Harris, "Paul's View of Death"; Hettlinger, "2 Corinthians 5:1–10"; Ellis, "2 Corinthians 5:1–10 in Pauline Eschatology"; Perriman, "Paul and the Parousia."

42. Georgi, *Opponents of Paul in Second Corinthians*, 33.

The focal image of this section appears in the opening verse of 4:7–5:21 in the poignant description of the human body as an earthen vessel. Aune reports that this image was a common metaphor for the fragility of the human body in Greco-Roman antiquity, but the Old Testament background for this metaphor adds additional nuances. The human body is not only weak (Dan. 2:42) but also disposable (Lev. 6:28; 11:32; 15:12; cf. Isa. 30:14; Jer. 19:11), cheap (Lam. 4:2), and perhaps forgettable to boot (Ps. 31:12).[43] Yet Paul does not evoke this image to demean human existence, but, as shown in the purpose clause in 4:7, to make the point that the human person is the conduit for the extraordinary power of God. As Paul will make even more apparent in 12:1–9, the fragility and weakness of the human body is a prerequisite for the demonstration of divine power through it.[44] The catalog of suffering in 4:8–9 shows that God's power is evident even amid ostensible defeat: the minister experiences all kinds of affliction but is not crushed; she is neither perplexed nor forsaken; when struck down, she is not ultimately destroyed. Thus, Pauline theology dignifies the fragility and weakness of the human body as an agent for the demonstration of divine power through ministry. *In other words, God prefers to work with stigmatized and, in this context, racialized bodies.* This theological perspective would apply to all kinds of racialized bodies, whether racialized about sexuality, brute strength, promiscuousness, physical passivity, docility, or the like. God uses the weak to shame the strong because all flesh has dignity, and failure to accord it the dignity it deserves is an affront to the Creator. The go-it-alone spirit of individuality valorized by US society and embodied by White male self-sufficiency is an idolatrous independence that belies the everyday work of partnership with God through human agency.[45]

Not only does Paul link the frailty of the human body to divine power, but he goes on to link suffering in the context of Christian life and ministry with the suffering of Jesus in 4:7–15. In this section, Paul several times refers to "Jesus" without adding "Christ" in a departure from his customary practice (4:5, 10, 11, and twice in v. 14; cf. 11:4).[46] However, this usage does not suggest that Paul "separates" the

43. Aune, "Anthropological Duality," 221; Thrall, *Second Epistle to the Corinthians*, 1:322–25. Furnish also mentions the connection of the earthen vessel imagery to the OT metaphor of God as the divine potter and creator of humanity (*II Corinthians*, 253); cf. Harris, *Second Epistle to the Corinthians*, 340; Matera, *II Corinthians*, 108.

44. Savage, *Power through Weakness*, 166–67.

45. See Jennings, *After Whiteness*, for a compelling exploration of the theme of White male self-sufficiency as the misbegotten goal embedded in theological education and western education generally.

46. The evidence is widespread and diverse for both the omission of κύριον ("lord") and

Jesus of history from the Christ of faith or any similar bifurcation.[47] Indeed, Paul refers to the "Lord Jesus" in v. 14 in this particular discourse, an appellation that affirms Jesus's exalted status and nature (cf. 4:5).[48] By and large, however, interpreters do not make constructive proposals about the heavy concentration of this unusual usage in 4:5–15 beyond their insistence on what Paul does not mean.[49] Elsewhere, Paul occasionally references "Jesus" without the much more common addition of "Christ" in texts where he is more interested in his person rather than status (Rom. 3:26; 8:11; Gal. 6:17; Phil. 2:10; 1 Thess. 1:10; 4:14).

Paul also emphasizes Jesus's person over his status in 4:10, where the phrase "the death of Jesus"[50] emphasizes the entire network of events that led to Jesus's earthly death.[51] When Paul speaks of bearing this death process to manifest Jesus's life, he speaks of living a life that continues Jesus's earthly ministry, one which is *oriented to achieve life-giving results for the benefit of others* (4:11–12, 15–16; cf. 1:6). In other words, Paul's ministry participates in the life and death of Jesus inasmuch as a life spent for others is the way of Jesus:[52] "Jesus chose to live his life on behalf of poor and oppressed people, and in so doing endured affliction and suffering."[53] Paul here intertwines the life, death, and ministry of Jesus as a single, undifferentiated whole similar to the emphasis on Jesus's life-giving ministry as advanced by the womanist scholars mentioned above. Paul's suffering in ministry (*not* in oppression!) is for the benefit of those who are being oppressed or defrauded by leaders who are more interested in their own privilege and power than in the example of humble regard of the Other

---

its inclusion in 4:14, though with Metzger, I favor the longer reading "the Lord Jesus" (*Greek New Testament*, 510–11). While the committee maintains that the shorter reading assimilates to Rom. 8:11, I would point to the fact that the inclusion of κύριον is the *lectio difficilior* in 4:7–15 where every other occurrence of Ἰησοῦ ("Jesus") occurs without a title.

47. For a good summary of the scholarly literature on the question see Fraser, "Paul's Knowledge of Jesus."

48. Lambrecht, "Nekrōsis of Jesus," 313–14.

49. See for example Fraser who, after noting the heavy incidence of this usage in 2 Corinthians, merely correlates the usage with Paul's references to Χριστὸς (as opposed to ὁ Χριστὸς), insisting that both usages refer holistically to Jesus's earthly ministry, passion, resurrection, and post-resurrection work ("Paul's Knowledge of Jesus," 299). The exception among scholars might be Georgi, who reads the usage in light of his hypothesis about allegorizing Hellenistic Jewish missionaries (*Opponents of Paul in Second Corinthians*, 271–77); but see Jerry L. Sumney's critique of Georgi's methodology on this point in *Identifying Paul's Opponents*, 49–55.

50. "The death of Jesus" (4:10): τὴν νέκρωσιν τοῦ Ἰησοῦ.

51. See 2 Cor. 4:10; BDAG (s.v. νέκρωσις).

52. Matera, *II Corinthians*, 110–12; Georgi, *Opponents of Paul in Second Corinthians*, 296.

53. Nave, "2 Corinthians," 309.

left by Jesus (5:12–16; cf. 2:17; 4:2; 10:12, 18; 11:5). The overall message in this section is that Paul's ministry embodies Jesus's ministry. His body, like Jesus's, is a concrete conduit for the expression of God's power on behalf of the poor, oppressed, and marginalized in human society.[54]

Second Corinthians 4:16–5:10 is also a premier vehicle for Paul's dialectical eschatology, showcasing his convictions about how a future hope impinges on present existence. The main idea in this passage is that Paul's eschatological hope of renewal assures that he can minister in confidence, notwithstanding the suffering that threatens the integrity of his physical body, his outer person (4:16). As mentioned above, discussion about this passage focuses on whether his views about resurrection have shifted since the writing of 1 Corinthians 15. The debate seems to spin on two axes, the first concerning whether 5:3 refers to a disembodied intermediate state, and the second surrounding the use of metaphorical language throughout the section, which may or may not refer to bodies.

Paul's eschatology in his earlier discourse in 1 Corinthians 15 is clear: the Christian hope is oriented toward the resurrection of the body in an embodied existence on earth and not, as some think, the hope of a disembodied future in heaven (15:12–34). Second, while different, there is nonetheless continuity between the earthly body and the resurrected body (15:35–50, 53–54), and third, that the transformation from earthly to heavenly takes place at the parousia (15:51–52). Though some scholars think that Paul's views have changed somewhat between the time he wrote 1 Corinthians 15:35–57 and 2 Corinthians 5:1–5, there are many similarities between these passages.[55] Paul contrasts the earthly and the heavenly in both texts (1 Cor. 15:49 vs. 2 Cor. 5:1–2). Similarly, he contrasts the perishable and the imperishable on the one hand (1 Cor. 15:42, 50, 52–53) and the eternal and the temporal on the other (2 Cor. 4:16–5:1). Mortality puts on immortality in 1 Corinthians 15:53–54, and mortality is swallowed by life in 2 Corinthians 5:4.[56] He also uses clothing metaphors similarly in these texts, referring to "putting on" imperishability and immortality in 1 Corinthians 15:53, and using a similar metaphor, "clothed"[57] with the heavenly in 2 Corinthians 5:2 and 4. In 1 Corinthians 15:54, death is "swallowed up" by victory, and in 2 Corinthians 5:4, mortality is "swallowed up"[58] by life. On the one hand, Paul

---

54. According to Georgi, in 4:7–16 Paul says that the significance of the preacher is tied to the earthly Jesus inasmuch as the minister bears Jesus's body in theirs and manifests a continuation of his suffering and death (*Opponents of Paul in Second Corinthians*, 274).

55. See Craig Keener's list of these similarities in *1–2 Corinthians*, 179.

56. "Mortality" (2 Cor. 5:4; cf. 1 Cor. 15:53): τὸ θνητὸν.

57. "Putting on" (1 Cor. 15:53): ἐνδύσασθαι; "clothed" (2 Cor. 5:2, 4): ἐπενδύσασθαι; cf. ἐνδύσασθαι in 1 Cor. 15:53.

58. "Swallowed up" (2 Cor. 5:4; 1 Cor. 15:54): κατεπόθη.

says that the Spirit characterizes resurrection life (1 Cor. 15:44–46), and on the other, he depicts the Spirit as a down payment for being swallowed up by life (2 Cor. 5:5). Indeed, one scholar plausibly suggests that the much-debated "we know" formula in 2 Corinthians 5:1 represents a deliberate allusion to the earlier discourse in 1 Corinthians 15.[59] It seems unlikely that Paul would have significantly changed his views in 2 Corinthians 5:1–5 without a more explicit signal of the change, especially given the prominence of the discourse in 1 Corinthians 15 and the significant similarities between it and 2 Corinthians 5:1–5, which were sent to the same audience.[60]

But what of the differences between the texts: do these imply that Paul changed his views? The most significant differences are those mentioned earlier regarding the metaphorical language in 2 Corinthians 5:1–5 and the specific interpretation of 5:3. While Paul uses the word "body"[61] (σῶμα) eight times in 1 Corinthians 15, he does not use the word at all in 2 Corinthians 5:1–5. Most agree, however, that the earthly tent (2 Cor. 5:1; cf. 5:4) is a metaphor for the human body that reflects the same focus on fragility as the earthen vessel metaphor of 4:7.[62] However, despite this consensus, opinion is divided about whether the building from God (5:1b) or the heavenly dwelling (5:4) likewise refers to individual believers' bodies or refers instead to a corporate residence or metaphor, perhaps during an intermediate state.[63] Yet these interpreters miss the import of the thrice-reiterated comparison between the temporary and the permanent that forms the backdrop for this imagery in 4:16–5:5: momentary versus eternal (4:17); temporary versus eternal (4:18); an earthly tent versus an eternal heavenly dwelling (5:1b–2).[64]

---

59. J. B. Green, *Body, Soul and Human Life*, 177.

60. Matera, *II Corinthians*, 170.

61. "Body" (1 Cor. 15:35, 37–38, 40, 44): σῶμα.

62. Matera (*II Corinthians*, 120) mentions the "broad agreement" on this point; see also Thrall, *Second Epistle to the Corinthians*, 362, 367–71; Harris, *Second Epistle to the Corinthians*, 370; Aune, "Anthropological Duality," 224.

63. See Thrall for a comprehensive discussion of the interpretive options in this section, beginning with the possible interpretations of the "dwelling from God": the resurrection body; an intermediate state; a present "spiritual garment"; the resurrected body of Christ; a heavenly temple (*Second Epistle to the Corinthians*, 363–68). Thrall herself, in agreement with "older scholarship," opts to understand the reference to the believer's resurrection body, which is available at the moment of death (pp. 367–68); cf. Furnish, who sees a reference to existence in a future eschatological age (*II Corinthians*, 294–95), and Harris, who interprets the section with reference to Paul's desire to avoid a disembodied intermediate state ("Paul's View of Death").

64. Note that the difference between the permanent and temporary is also an important issue in Paul's interpretation of how the new covenant differs from the old (3:7–18).

That the tent and eternal dwelling, alongside all of the clothing metaphors in this passage, symbolize bodies is reinforced in the parallel structures in 2 Corinthians 5:2–4, which vividly recall the earlier discourse in
1 Corinthians 15:53–54:[65]

(2a)	in this [tent] we *groan longing*		(A)
	(2b)	to be <u>clothed over with a dwelling</u>	(B)
	(3a)	If <u>clothed</u>[66]	(C)
	(3b)	then we won't be naked	(D)
(4a)	in this tent we *groan burdened*		(A')
	(4b)	because we do <u>not</u> want to be <u>unclothed</u>	(B')
	(4c)	but <u>clothed over</u>	(C')
	(4d)	that mortality might be swallowed by life	(D')

Given Paul's earlier use of clothing metaphors and virtually identical sentiments in 1 Corinthians 15:54d and 2 Corinthians 5:4d, it is plausible that "nakedness" is not a reference to a corporate existence or possible intermediate
state as maintained by some.[67] Instead, we can see nakedness as a synonym
for a death in which the believer's mortality has not yet been swallowed by life
(see D-D'). We can read this passage as another way of saying that the believer
never has to worry about a (shameful) disembodied state, even if the present
home in the body is destroyed by death.[68] Far from longing for a Platonic liberation of the mind from the prison of the body, I read Paul as describing an
abhorrence for a disembodied existence. He groans not to take off one body for
another, but to be further embodied, a sentiment that he elsewhere describes
as a groaning for the redemption of our bodies (Rom. 8:23).

Thus in 4:7–5:10, Paul emphasizes the embodied nature of Christian life
and ministry in three ways. First, he dignifies human somatic fragility as the
preferred agency of divine power through the focal image of the earthen vessel.

65. Adapted from Matera, *II Corinthians*, 121.

66. There is much stronger manuscript support for ἐνδυσάμενοι (P[46], a, B, C, D[2], Y, etc.;
see NASB) than for ἐκδυσάμενοι (D*) in 5:3 (see NRSV).

67. E.g., Aune, "Anthropological Duality"; cf. Furnish, *II Corinthians*, 292–99, who interprets the heavenly dwelling of 5:1 as a corporate reference to the eschatological age versus
a reference to individualistic concerns about embodiment.

68. Harris, "Paul's View of Death"; Harris, *Second Epistle to the Corinthians*, 384–89. For an
exploration of the association of "shame" with nakedness in Jewish literature see J. B. Green,
Body, Soul and Human Life, 170–71, as well as Harris, *Second Epistle to the Corinthians*, 385–86.

Second, he connects human suffering for the sake of others with the earthly suffering of Jesus as a way of manifesting Jesus's continuing ministry to the oppressed. And finally, he insists on the embodied nature of human life in this age and the next. Indeed, these three elements are foundational for his argument that a weak or ignoble body can manifest the glory of God and participation in Christ. The promise of a resurrection body liberates the minister from concern with the fragility of human existence, enabling her to use a new boldness in ministry that goes beyond the great heroes of the past.

Thus, the modern penchant for a Christian life that prioritizes the soul at the expense or neglect of the body is anti-Pauline, as are the associated implications for contemporary Christian ministry. It is more than wrongheaded to allow an erroneous body-soul dualism to require ministry to become segregated into relative concerns for "spiritual" evangelism versus "material" social justice as some would have it.[69] Moreover, a desire for "colorblindness," that is, a goodly and pseudo-godly attempt to disregard racial difference as immaterial and perhaps even unseemly—a view rampant in Christian circles—is equally misguided. The imprudent think that a colorblind approach to encountering racial difference is godly in that this approach assumes that racial difference is a flaw that generous people should overlook. Interestingly, this approach is not only politically untenable in that it implicitly normalizes one kind of racial difference while marginalizing all others, but this approach is theologically untenable as well. What some Christians deem a handicap, Paul emphasizes as a means of participating in the work of Jesus since racial stigmas metaphorically and literally weaken racialized bodies through social forces. In other words, colorblindness inhibits God's way of working in the world. This approach disregards how bodies are connected with identities and, according to the texts we have considered, sunders the connection with Christian ministry in its embodiment of Christ's suffering and glorification. From Paul's perspective, attempts to transcend the nature of earthen vessels like that found in the American myth of the self-sufficient White male run counter to the way of Jesus. We can see the myth of self-sufficiency as an attempt to subvert the power of God at work in the world since God uses the weak to shame the wise and, in our context, to upend privileges manifest in racial hierarchies.

As mentioned above, Douglas and other womanists rightly raise the concern that an emphasis on participation in the suffering of Jesus as we see here in Paul can be dangerous theology for those already occupying a demeaned position. We should hear a message emphasizing suffering for those experi-

---

69. J. B. Green, *Body, Soul and Human Life*, 70.

encing oppression as a demand to endure the evils inflicted by an unjust society, which can have the additional negative effect of reinscribing internalized racism.[70] As Guy Nave puts it in his comments on 2 Corinthians 4:16–5:10:

> It is important to realize that living with confidence in the midst of suffering is not the same thing as passively accepting suffering and waiting for one's "pie in the sky when I die." Slave masters often encouraged slaves to passively accept their oppressive plight of slavery on the basis that they would be rewarded in heaven. The belief that one's present reality was not the final reality, however, not only empowered slaves not to lose heart and to confidently endure, but also enabled them to reject their current reality. Confident belief that a better reality was their future and God's will was based on their understanding of God's vindication of Jesus, who lived and died resisting oppression and setting captives free. Faith in God and belief that freedom is God's will empowered them to work and fight for that will, praying as Jesus had taught them, "Your will be done, *on earth* as it is in heaven."[71]

Indeed, it is critical to note that Paul does not endorse all suffering, nor does he advocate that Christians seek out suffering. Instead, Paul speaks of suffering endured because it is concomitant with service on behalf of others.[72] The grief and pressure that he speaks of here come from the Christian's engagement with the forces of evil. Paul's ethic is on full display in the freedom fighters' ethic of nonviolent direct engagement in the Jim Crow South. It is not idealizing some ascetic ideal that pressures broken peoples to mute their resistance to oppression. Paul emphasizes suffering that is endured—not embraced—as part of the cost of following the way of Jesus in ministering life and liberation to others in this life (4:11–12, 15–16; cf. 1:6).

Racial Identity and Status in Corinth (2 Corinthians 5:16–17 and 11:1–12:10)

Though there is considerable debate about the identity of Paul's opposition in Corinth that gave rise to 2 Corinthians, it is clear that these critics challenged Paul's authentic Jewish identity (3:6–18; 11:22), leadership as an apostle (11:5, 12–13; 12:11), and status as a servant of Christ (3:6; 6:4; 11:23). In reviewing the specifics of the dispute, we will find that their charges rhyme with discourse

---

70. For a definition of internalized racism see J. M. Jones, *Prejudice and Racism*, 56, 290.
71. Nave, "2 Corinthians," 316.
72. Lambrecht, "Nekrōsis of Jesus," 328.

about race and privilege in modern society. The opponents' accusations about Paul's leadership deficiencies are analogous to modern racist rhetoric that inhibits the full participation of minoritized groups in US society.

The extended reflection on ministry in 2 Corinthians 2:14–6:10 seems to be an oblique answer to questions about the character of Paul's ministry and person, questions that emerge more forcefully and directly in 2 Corinthians 10:1–13:10. Paul describes the life and death consequences of ministry using the olfactory metaphors of aroma and fragrance. He asks, "Who is sufficient?" for a ministry with life and death consequences (2:16), making it clear that questions about qualifications are at the heart of the conflict. Indeed, comments about letters of recommendation in 3:1–3 interrupt his response to the question of adequacy in 2:16. This telling parenthesis suggests that one of the criteria for leadership in the opponents' eyes was evidence of support from recognized authorities (cf. 4:5; 10:12–18; 11:4). In other words, Paul faced challenges about his legitimacy concerning a perceived lack of endorsement from crucial contacts. We will see that at Corinth, the interrogation of legitimacy went well beyond the mere question of contacts and encompassed the sufficiency of the leader's total public persona, including their appearance, pedigree, finances, and public actions and demeanor. While Paul's opponents invalidate his ministry because they believe it embodies weakness, Paul maintains that his ministry embodies Christ's resurrection life and boldly participates in the new creation as an aroma of Christ that achieves the divine will in any circumstance.[73]

Paul may hint at some of the opposition against him again in 5:12, where he talks about people who boast, in a phrase usually translated "boast in appearance."[74] Because 10:10 does indicate that his opponents maligned his appearance, many interpret 5:12 similarly, an interpretation that seems strengthened by Paul's tacit admission about his own unassuming appearance in 4:7. Yet, the immediate context of 5:12 suggests another possibility. Verse 13 most likely introduces the kind of response that Paul wants to offer those who boast in appearances. Paul says that the Corinthians could boast that he continues the mission of Christ through self-sacrificial actions for the benefit of others (vv. 14–15), rather than reveling in ecstatic behavior or tongues (v. 13; cf. 1 Cor. 14:18–19).[75] Paul affirms that the love of Christ constrains him from offering ecstatic displays as evidence of his legitimacy when these displays do not benefit

---

73. Aernie, "Life of the Believer," 449.

74. Literally "boast in the face" (τοὺς ἐν προσώπῳ καυχωμένους; 2 Cor. 5:12); see Sumney, *Identifying Paul's Opponents*, 129.

75. According to Clair Mesick, the dominant interpretation of 5:13 is that it denotes "some form of religious or ecstatic phenomenon: heavenly ascent, mystical visions, or glossolalia" ("Driven by Grief," 140). Though Mesick offers an interpretation that in 5:13–15 "Paul

the community. While it may be true that the opponents' boasts concern physical appearances, as some interpret 5:12, the seamless way that Paul elaborates
on the phrase "boasting in appearances" in 5:13–15 suggests that this boasting
may go beyond appearances to include certain kinds of actions as well.

Several interpreters remark on the way that "knowing/recognizing according to the flesh" in 2 Corinthians 5:16 is parallel to "boasting in appearances"
in 5:12 and see in this parallelism support for the idea that these phrases refer
only to appearances.[76] However, the alternation in verbs of knowing in 5:16
goes beyond the connections between 5:12 and 5:13–15 discussed above. The
use of these verbs supports my hypothesis that "appearance" and "according
to the flesh" encompass more than superficial physical appearances.[77] When
Paul uses "recognize" in 5:16a (οἴδαμεν) and forms of "know" in the rest of
verse 16 (γινώσκω), he appears to be using these two lexemes as synonyms for
the idea of "knowing about."[78] However, the alternation in these lexemes may
well go beyond simple stylistic variation in that the tense forms of the words for
"know" in these verses communicate verbal aspect.[79] In the New Testament,

intends to address and reinterpret his emotionally charged self-defense," the approach taken
here sees an allusion in 5:13 to displays of charismatic gifts.

76. O'Neill, "Absence of the 'In Christ' Theology," 104; Georgi, *Opponents of Paul in
Second Corinthians*, 252–53. Aernie also sees the "appearance" theme in 5:7 in the translation
"For we walk by faith and not by appearance (εἴδους)" ("Life of the Believer," 443–45).
Also note that there may be a similar parallelism between "according to the flesh" (κατὰ
σάρκα) in 10:3 and "according to appearance" (κατὰ πρόσωπον) in 10:7 as is suggested here
between "boasting in appearances" (5:12: τοὺς ἐν προσώπῳ καυχωμένους) and "knowing/
recognizing according to the flesh" (5:16: οἴδαμεν/ἐγνώκαμεν κατὰ σάρκα).

77. The Greek reads ἐν προσώπῳ (2 Cor. 5:12; "appearance") and κατὰ σάρκα (2 Cor.
5:16; "according to the flesh"). With others, I think that the evidence slightly favors an adverbial construal of κατὰ σάρκα in 5:16 (e.g., Thrall, "Second Epistle to the Corinthians,"
418; Fraser, "Paul's Knowledge of Jesus," 298), though it is not inconceivable that Paul is
intentionally ambiguous here. If Paul normally places κατὰ σάρκα after a noun when using
it adjectivally (e.g., Δαυὶδ κατὰ σάρκα; Rom. 1:3) and before the verb when using it adver-
bially (e.g., κατὰ σάρκα βουλεύομαι; 2 Cor. 1:17), he could not have been more ambiguous
than he was in 2 Cor. 5:16 where it appears *before* the noun and *after* the verb (ἐγνώκαμεν
κατὰ σάρκα Χριστόν; cf. 2 Cor. 10:18). Thus, it is possible that both senses are alluded to
here and we will not be able to rule out the idea that the phrase "according to the flesh"
(κατὰ σάρκα) includes the notion of physical descent, which is normally associated with an
adjectival understanding of the phrase, alongside an adverbial interpretation of "knowing
κατὰ σάρκα." See the discussion on κατὰ σάρκα in 2 Cor. 11:22 below.

78. See Fraser, "Paul's Knowledge of Jesus," 293–313, for a full discussion of the history of
scholarship on the question of "knowing" in 2 Cor. 5:16 and whether Paul had encountered
the historical Jesus.

79. For more on verbal aspect see Porter, *Verbal Aspect*.

the Greek word for "recognize" (οἶδα; usually translated "know") was well on the way to being a frozen form and was thus not helpful in communicating the author's perspective on the action.[80] When Paul uses a different word to speak of "knowing Christ according to the flesh" using the perfect tense (ἐγνώκαμεν), he emphasizes the complexity of the "knowing" and the stative aspect. When he says, "now we know (γινώσκομεν) him no longer in that way" with the present tense, he denies that this kind of knowledge constitutes a meaningful way of *continuing* participation in Christ by using the imperfective aspect. If all this is true, then 5:16b does not at all refer to Paul's earlier encounter with the historical Jesus as some maintain, but, as we will see, to a complex state of "knowing" that goes beyond a superficial engagement with the flesh or its physical appearance.[81] It is as if Paul acknowledges that a narrative about Christ that focuses on outward impressions would produce a thoroughly unattractive judgment. It is easy to imagine someone assessing Christ's life and status using some set of "fleshly" criteria that evaluate Christ's earthen vessel, humble ministry, and ignoble death as contemptible. Yet, Paul maintains that Christ's resurrection nullifies these standards and inaugurates a wholly fresh way of engaging others in the new age.[82] Christians must eschew judging by fleshly superficialities in

---

80. The author's perspective on the action communicates "verbal aspect." Paul uses the perfect tense form for the Greek word οἶδα ("I know") fifty-eight times and the pluperfect tense of this word only once, usage that suggests that this word is aspectually vague since authors could not choose from among multiple viable tense forms for this lexeme. Usage in the rest of the New Testament supports this idea since the word appears in only two tenses: two hundred and twenty-eight times in the perfect and thirty-one times in the pluperfect. That Paul uses two forms of "know" γινώσκω in 5:16b, one of which is in a tense form that was not available for the word translated "recognize" (οἶδα), may indicate that Paul switches to a different verb for "knowing" to communicate verbal aspect. For more on interpreting the aspect associated with perfect and present tense forms see Porter, *Idioms*, 20–42; Porter, *Verbal Aspect*, 75–108, 211–38, 251–59.

81. See Porter, *Verbal Aspect*, 256–59, for more on the way that the perfect tense communicates an author's focus on the complexity of the state of action in a verb used in this form. Here Paul refers to a complex understanding that emerges from judgments made in accordance with a common set of standards (e.g., κατὰ σάρκα) that goes far beyond the simple temporal question of knowing Jesus in the past. Below we explore this set of standards as they are illuminated in 2 Cor. 11:22–12:10 when Paul ironically "boasts" κατὰ σάρκα.

82. Georgi rightly notes that the argument in 5:16–17 is an argument from the greater to the lesser, extending standards used in forming opinions about the most important figure in God's economy to everyone participating in the new order (*Opponents of Paul in Second Corinthians*, 253). O'Neill, on the other hand, thinks that it is nonsensical to think that Paul would advocate disregarding Christ's miracles, earthly ministry, or his humility as a servant ("Absence of the 'In Christ' Theology," 101–2).

the case of Christ's glorious status as Messiah. According to Paul, it is undoubtedly appropriate to reject this criterion in all lesser cases as well.

Paul's other uses of the phrase "according to the flesh"[83] in 2 Corinthians can help us discern the nature of the complexities associated with "knowing according to the flesh." Paul's earliest uses of the phrase may occur in Galatians 4:23 and 29, referring to physical decent and specifically to a biological means of producing converts to the gospel (e.g., making converts through circumcision).[84] In that passage, the phrase stands in contrast to "according to the spirit,"[85] which is Paul's preferred means of incorporating people into the gospel community. Uses of the phrase in other epistles are compatible with this meaning,[86] but there is evidence in 2 Corinthians that Paul responds to his opponents' usage of the phrase.[87] In 2 Corinthians 1:17, Paul seems to be responding to a charge that he is weak-minded, indecisive, or overly obsequious. In 10:1–2, we see that this charge has explicitly originated from opponents:[88]

> When I planned this, did I do it lightly? Or do I make my plans in a worldly manner [lit. "according to the flesh"; κατὰ σάρκα] so that in the same breath I say, "Yes, yes" and "No, no"? (2 Cor. 1:17 NIB)

> By the meekness and gentleness of Christ, I appeal to you—I, Paul, who am "timid" when face to face with you, but "bold" when away! [2]I beg you that when I come I may not have to be as bold as I expect to be towards some people who think that we live by the standards of this world [lit. "that we walk according to the flesh"; κατὰ σάρκα περιπατοῦντας]. (2 Cor. 10:1–2 NIB)

83. "According to the flesh" (2 Cor. 1:17; 5:16; 10:2–3; 11:18): κατὰ σάρκα.

84. Martyn, *Galatians*, 451–54.

85. "According to the spirit" (Gal. 4:29): κατὰ πνεῦμα.

86. See Rom. 1:3; 4:1; 9:3; 1 Cor. 10:18. For more on the use of κατὰ σάρκα in 1 Cor. 10:18, see Schweizer, "σάρξ, σαρκικός, σάρκινος"; Sechrest, *Former Jew*, 132, 142–44.

87. Georgi infers that the opponents accuse Paul of acting "according to the flesh" (κατὰ σάρκα) in 10:2 because he acts contrary to their own "according to the Spirit" (κατὰ πνεῦμα) proclivities (*Opponents of Paul in Second Corinthians*, 236–37 and 289n60). Sumney on the other hand thinks that the phrase κατὰ σάρκα originates with the opponents, though he does not reckon with the different use of the phrase in Galatians and 1 Corinthians, epistles that precede 2 Corinthians chronologically (1 Cor. 10:18; possibly 1 Cor. 1:26; Gal. 4:23, 29), or in usages like those that appear in Rom. 1:3; 4:1; 9:3, 5; cf. 8:4–5, 12–13 (*Identifying Paul's Opponents*, 156).

88. For more on allegations from Paul's opponents that he was a "flatterer" see P. Marshall, *Enmity in Corinth*.

Though the phrase "according to the flesh" is still ambiguous in 10:2, it seems that the phrase refers to public behavior that lacks strength of purpose and cravenly caters to public opinion. That is, though Paul aligned his demeanor with Christ's in 10:2 in rebuttal, the preceding sentence reveals that he has been accused of weakness and inconsistent behavior in a way that is somewhat reminiscent of 1:17.

Paul's use of the phrase in 2 Corinthians 11:18 is more illuminating for our study of what is involved in "knowing according to the flesh," especially since the use of the phrase in this verse is most similar syntactically to the usage in 5:16. In 11:18, the phrase occurs at the end of the prologue to the so-called Fool's Boast in 11:1–21. This discourse begins in 11:22 and runs through 12:10, where Paul depicts himself as being forced to engage in the same foolish boasting and self-commendation that his opponents undertake (11:1, 16, 21). Yet even though Paul responds to the boasting of his opponents, many suggest that he refuses to boast in kind, deftly using irony so that he boasts in a way that is consistent with his theological convictions about ministry. On the other hand, Ryan Schellenberg thinks Paul doesn't use irony so much as he boasts of characteristics and accomplishments implicated in his compromised status at Corinth. According to Schellenberg, Paul seeks to reclaim lost standing in Corinth by boasting in an exotic eastern ethnoreligious wisdom, which though fraught with marginality as a rarity in Roman Corinth, was still fascinating to ordinary people (when authentic!) if also disdained by elites.[89] Thus while Paul's rivals, who were Israelites themselves, successfully portrayed social success despite their marginalized position in Corinth, Paul acknowledged his weakness in an attempt to refigure it as a mark of divine strength.[90]

What is revealing for our purposes is the fact that Paul himself names this kind of discourse "boasting according to the flesh." Thus, we can expect that when Paul engages in his own boasts, however ironic or marginalized the *contents* of the boasts, the *topical scope* of the boasts in the discourse will shed light on whether and how "according to the flesh" goes beyond mere physical appearance to include a complex set of behaviors and demeanors as we have surmised above. When Paul boasts according to the flesh as a rebuttal to his

89. Schellenberg, "Constraints of Boasting," 525–26. Here Schellenberg leans on work by Cavan Concannon on the likely dearth of Jews in Roman Corinth (Concannon, *When You Were Gentiles*), on Heidi Wendt's description of "freelance religious experts" of the period (Wendt, *At the Temple Gates*), as well as on Georgi, *Opponents of Paul in Second Corinthians* and on Pauline Ripat's discussion in "Expelling Misconceptions" on the importance of authenticity in such religious portrayals.

90. Schellenberg, "Constraints of Boasting," 527, 535.

opponents, he uses categories that suggest that there are at least three standards of evaluation involved in assessing the legitimacy of his apostleship.

First, boasting according to the flesh includes boasting in a well-regarded ethnic heritage (11:22; cf. Phil. 3:3–9).[91] By way of showing his equivalence with the "super apostles," Paul boasts that he, too, shares the same language, ancestry, and nationality with them.[92] While we can only speculate about whether the opponents emphasize their service to and identity in Christ over their ethnic heritage, there can be no doubt of Paul's emphasis both here and in 3:7–18. Nevertheless, Paul's mention of these ethnic terms suggests that boasting in this ethnic heritage had social valence with the letter's audience, as Schellenberg suggests.

Second, boasting according to the flesh includes boasting about status—here the status of being a servant of Christ. The evidence suggests that the opponents relied on their own self-representations as well as outside recommendations to substantiate their status as servants of Christ (3:1; 10:12, 18; cf. 4:2; 5:12; 6:4). For his part, Paul focuses attention on the breadth, depth, and intensity of his service to Christ to speak for the legitimacy of his leadership (11:23–27). His halfhearted boast about charismatic visions in 12:1–9 (cf. 5:13) hints that the opponents have additionally relied on charismatic displays to substantiate their claims to leadership status.[93] Taken together, Paul's boasts about suffering and weaknesses in 11:23–12:9 may be intended as ironic contrasts to the opponents' boasts about activities that substantiate claims about being a servant of Christ.

Third, boasting or walking according to the flesh involves bearing a forceful public demeanor that contrasts with Paul's physical demeanor (11:30–33; cf. 10:1–2, 10; 11:20–21; 13:2–3). The comparatively numerous references to Paul's weak public persona expose this as one of the major areas of contention between Paul and the opponents. In addition, it is likely that mention of Paul's unprepossessing physical appearance and lack of eloquence also contribute to this motif (4:7–9; 5:12; 10:10; 11:6). Where his rivals boast in their superiority to believers in Corinth, Paul deliberately draws attention to his own weakness, among other things recounting his furtive escape from the King of Damascus (11:30–33; 12:1–9; cf. 4:7). Indeed, some in Corinth may have interpreted

91. Cf. Duling, "2 Corinthians 11:22," 831.

92. The word "Hebrew" in other Jewish literature in the Greek-speaking diaspora seems to be the preferred way of talking about Aramaic, the language commonly spoken among Palestinian Jews in the Second Temple period; see for example K.-W. Niebuhr, *Heidenapostel aus Israel*, 105–7.

93. Charismatic displays of spiritual power play important roles in Sumney's identification of the opponents as Pneumatics (*Identifying Paul's Opponents*, 177–79) and Georgi's proposal about the Hellenistic θεῖος ἀνήρ (*Opponents of Paul in Second Corinthians*, 254–83).

Paul's practice of renouncing the Corinthians' patronage as an admission of illegitimacy, as if by rejecting this financial support, Paul was admitting that he had no right to support as an apostle (2:17; 11:7–11; cf. 1 Cor. 9:3–14).[94]

Thus, the use of the phrase "according to the flesh" in 2 Corinthians indicates that the term includes a broad array of social value judgments, including ethnoracial identity, social status, contacts, and a particular kind of forceful public behavior. When Paul's rivals contested his sufficiency for leadership, they challenged him on his demeanor as a leader, including assessments of his pedigree, social contacts, actions (i.e., miracles, ecstatic utterances, etc.), and his ability to project strength in his speech and presence. In 5:16–17, therefore, we can deduce that knowing according to the flesh likely encompasses a similar complex network of elements. In the context of the leadership crisis at Corinth, it is clear that some group or contingent in Corinth thought that Paul failed to measure up to their image of what leaders or ministers personify. Instead of someone with gravitas, social standing, mighty deeds, and the accoutrements of glory and wealth, they got Paul, a "broke-down" pastor, who publicly gloried in sharing the fate of a crucified Lord.

The opponents' according-to-the-flesh standards are analogous to judgments made in the context of modern race discourse. Contemporary identity politics involves embodied social constructs and the nexus of heritage, personality, physical appearance, and social connections, and we have seen that these same elements were in contention in Paul's defense of his ministerial identity in Corinth. Our consideration of the fleshly standards operating there suggests that Paul's opponents had concepts of identity animated by forces that were not too dissimilar from modern identity dynamics. The opponents boasted in a privileged ethnic heritage and an elevated social status as servants of Christ. Ancient status privilege manifested itself in charismatic deeds, acceptance of financial support, letters of recommendations, and a boastful demeanor, behaviors that Paul described as inconsistent with his ministry of identification and participation in Christ's other-focused ministry. In Corinth, the rivals malign Paul's physical appearance and public demeanor as one that does not meet the then-current expectations associated with high status. Today, minorities often face obstacles in public life because they, too, fail to "look or act the part" due to negative stereotypes about people of color and cultural behavioral norms and statuses that are keyed to whiteness.

Paul's situation also exhibits how privilege is relative: though he shares a privileged heritage with his opponents, by refusing support and practic-

94. Sumney, *Identifying Paul's Opponents*, 164; Schellenberg, "Constraints of Boasting," 529–30.

ing manual labor, he incurs condemnation and inhabits a lower social status (11:7–9; 1 Cor. 4:12; cf. Acts 18:3).[95] The discourse on Moses in 2 Corinthians 3:7–18 also illustrates how privileged persons have the luxury of temporarily forgoing their privilege. In a society that revered antiquity, Paul can point to an ancient and glorious ancestor. Still, he is secure enough in his status when writing this section of 2 Corinthians that he can relativize the esteem accorded to that figure. Yet, when the situation degraded to the point that he felt forced to address the charges against him in another part of this composite epistle, he makes an explicit appeal to his ethnic heritage, even though he has to concede that doing so risks public disdain for foolishness (11:16, 21, 23).[96] Such ambivalence might be praiseworthy if it were the case that Paul recognized the power of his proud heritage but only took it up in service of the greater good, pressing *through* suffering toward embodied life on the other side of resurrection (cf. Phil. 3:4–11).

This conclusion does not imply that when Paul rejects knowing Jesus according to the flesh, he is undermining Jesus's Jewish heritage; Paul is clear on the point that Jesus's Jewishness demonstrates God's faithfulness to Israel (Rom. 9:5; cf. 1:4). Instead, from Paul's perspective, both he and Jesus inhabit privileged identities, but their confidence in God enables them to eschew these social privileges to become effective conduits of divine power. As a coda to a section that began by exploring the paradoxical juxtaposition of weak human vessels with the manifest power of God, Paul grants that even the most privileged identities will reject privilege in the new age. Further, he also makes this humility normative wherever privilege is located, whether in sexual identity, gender, ethnoracial heritage, socioeconomic status, or educational attainment.

Conclusion

The overall arc of Paul's personal narrative is a fascinating study when examined with interest in race relations. We have only to consider the remarkable nature of how Paul moved from stylized attitudes about Greeks, Gentile sinners, barbarians, and others (Rom. 1:18–32; Gal. 2:15; Col. 3:11) to becoming a "slave" of such people through his missionary endeavors. Paul went from being "blameless" concerning the law as a Pharisee who outstripped his colleagues in zeal for the traditions (Gal. 1:14; Phil. 3:4–6) to being a broke-down preacher in Corinth

95. Sumney, *Identifying Paul's Opponents*, 165.
96. Schellenberg, "Constraints of Boasting," 533–34.

who needed to *remind* people that he shared that proud ethnic heritage. In comments in 2 Corinthians 2:14–6:10, Paul tries to preempt the growing opposition to him that emerges directly in 2 Corinthians 10–12. He defends his identity as a leader who can be compared favorably with Moses, as one who is bolder and more confident in his ability to speak as an ambassador for God. Yet even there, this breathtakingly audacious claim is juxtaposed with an acknowledgment of his likeness to a common, humble, disposable, and fragile piece of clay pottery. Later in 2 Corinthians 10–12, when the defense of his ministry is more direct and full-throated, he identifies himself as one of the weak and despised of the age while still maintaining that his authority and standing are equal to any others to whom he is being compared (10:6; 11:5–6; 12–14).

We do not need to pretend that this epistle says only one thing. A womanist reading of 2 Corinthians could see the message divided into one exhortation for the majority race in the United States and another for minoritized groups. On the one hand, we could encourage privileged groups to imitate the way that Paul embraced weakness as a prerequisite for authentic, other-focused ministry, reminding them that the path of Jesus is a lifestyle that endures for the sake of others. Similarly, we could exhort the oppressed to mimic Paul's boldness and confidence in their confrontation of the evils of gendered, racial, and ethnic injustice. Paul's boasts about heritage, service, and weakness in 11:23–12:9 may be ironic contrasts to his opponents' boasts. Alternately, Paul may be trying to reclaim lost standing in Corinth by boasting in an exotic eastern ethno-religious wisdom. Whatever strategy we see in play here, it is clear that the boasting accomplishes the same rhetorical ends. *He is reframing as a strength what his opponents demean as weakness.* Indeed, it is in this trajectory that the Audre Lorde quote that opened this chapter was evocative. The "dark place within" is not a place of suffering and anguish but the nexus of spiritual growth and change that is redemptive, a fertile place of feminine power wherein women muster the courage to seek liberation for themselves and their peoples.

That said, women and other oppressed groups must understand which of these two messages represents the best analogical correspondence, the most resonant rhyme between 2 Corinthians and their own contemporary circumstances, because there is great potential for tragedy in a misalignment. For most of my life, I have resisted interrogating or allowing my pain to be a stimulant or legitimate basis for resistance. I vigorously fight against unjust oppression in my context, but I have stood silent about my own injuries from sexism or racism. These sentiments were rooted in the idea that there is greater legitimacy in activism that is free from self-interest. In doing so, I had misappropriated a message of surrendered privilege that better aligns with conditions in communities with higher social status and privilege than my own. I have recently begun to challenge that reflex on the grounds that Paul's legacy to the underprivileged calls them to manifest divine power through marginalized and stigmatized bodies. For the sake of themselves, their children, and the men and women they love, they must boldly and courageously seek liberation and resurrection life in every season and epoch.

Yet, it is also interesting to note Paul's dialectical theology and expectation of an imminent parousia straddles both of these perspectives. In other words, an eschatological vision that yearns for Beloved Community would insist that both of these behaviors, confidence and humility, strength and weakness, should reside in the same servant of Christ. In 2 Corinthians, Paul describes his countercultural ministry with a combination of subtlety and boldness, alterations that probably reflect changing strategies, circumstances, or shifts in his opposition. It may be that a Beloved Community adaptation of his ethics for race relations in the United States sees privilege and humility as two sides of the same coin, both deployed for the sake of and in the service of liberation for those with less relative privilege and status than our own.

7

LIGAMENTAL LEADERSHIP FOR
THE HOUSEHOLD OF GOD IN EPHESIANS

When we define ourselves,
when I define myself,
the place in which I am like you
and the place in which I am not like you,
I'm not excluding you from the joining—
I am broadening the joining.

—Audre Lorde[1]

The Politics of Division

Presidential politics in the United States since 2007 offers vivid illustrations of the intersection of race, gender, and power. The American people are never more transparent than when we engage in the quadrennial courtship between the people and potential occupants of the White House. Leadership, involving social influence, also consists of an identity function by which leaders serve as models for group behavior, thought, and interactions with other groups.[2] With this in mind, we can see that our national electoral campaign season says something about the leadership culture—indeed the leadership crisis—in early twenty-first-century US politics.[3]

1. This quote from Audre Lorde originally appeared in an interview in the *Feminist Renaissance*, which is reproduced in Bereano, "Introduction."
2. Northouse, *Leadership*, 3; Sanchez-Hucles and Davis, "Women of Color in Leadership," 171; J. L. Chin, "Introduction," 153.
3. Hogg, "From Group Conflict to Social Harmony," 17; Hogg, "Social Identity Theory of Leadership," 191. Another perspective holds that groups seek leaders who are "prototypical, not of themselves, but of their shared ideas about the attributes of good leaders." See Eagly, "Few Women at the Top," 82. We will return to this idea in the latter portion of this essay.

The Democratic primary campaign in 2007–2008 was between Hillary Clinton, a White female two-term US senator from New York, and Barack Obama, a Black male US senator from Illinois in his first term. Clinton was also a former first lady of the United States and first lady of Arkansas and was active in policy initiatives in both roles. In contrast, Obama had served for seven years as a senator in the Illinois State House before his presidential run. The occasionally acrimonious charges of sexism and racism from supporters of both candidates played out on a national stage for a time before both candidates learned to submerge such allegations (to win) and refrain from ruffling the sensibilities of a Democratic electorate that was ill-equipped to engage the topics substantively. Clinton was derided for her dress, hairstyle, and voice, attention to which no previous male candidate had been subjected. For his part, Obama swallowed insults about his participation in a Black mainline Protestant congregation along with innuendo about his citizenship and birth in Hawaii (e.g., "birtherism" that questioned his US citizenship)—more firsts in national politics. Once elected, the questions about Obama's citizenship and legitimacy continued and represented at least a partial rejection of his ability to serve the modeling function for national leadership.[4] But, as bad as the Obama years were for those traumatized by the intense interplay of race in the politics of American leadership at the federal level, what we did not know but should have expected was that things were about to get substantially worse.

The presidential campaign of 2016 involved an even wider public service experience gap than the one from the Clinton-Obama primary contest, when Clinton, now with service as Obama's Secretary of State added to her resume, faced Donald Trump in the general election. This time she was competing against a White male business leader with no service in government and with four business bankruptcies to his credit. The sexism and racism in 2015–2016 cast similar dynamics from the 2007–2008 Democratic primaries into the shade. Vaulting into national politics by his support for birtherism, Trump was initially condemned by politicians from his own party for his uncivil and misogynistic discourse, sexual assault allegations, racism, name calling, and media bullying. A deeply inexperienced candidate, Trump went on to pull off a narrow electoral college win while losing the popular vote to Clinton, who was arguably one of the most qualified (female) candidates in US history, a result that speaks volumes about the powerful undertow of misogyny in American culture. By 2020 Black women, rubbed raw by microaggressions in the media through these turbulent years, were ready to flex their muscles again in Dem-

4. Coates, "My President Was Black"; Hogg, "Social Identity Theory of Leadership."

ocratic party politics. Yet, many alternated between hope and despair at the thought of a Black woman like US Senator Kamala Harris on the presidential ticket, weighing their understanding of the downward pull of American misogynoir[5] against a desperately felt need to block a second term for Trump.

Studies on the influence of race and gender in leadership selection, evaluation, and effectiveness reveal that women and minorities are the subjects of unequal standards when it comes to assessments of their capacities for leadership and leadership performance. Whites are cheerfully willing to support and help Blacks and other minorities when they occupy lower responsibilities in organizations. Yet, Whites resist Black leadership when Blacks exercise real institutional power.[6] Likewise, women are harshly penalized in assessments of their leadership capacity when seeking power, though they are often praised for their work once actually occupying positions of power.[7] These kinds of implicit biases against women and minorities in leadership played out on the national stage in the presidential candidacies of Barack Obama and Hillary Clinton. Further, these well-documented biases are multiplied and not just added in cases of the overlapping identities of minority females, a phenomenon known as intersectionality.[8] The simple fact is that the American people do not like being led by women or out-group minorities—and especially not by out-group women.

Demographic shifts are roiling our already volatile and racialized politics. Though Whites in the United States will remain the largest ethnic group in the country for the foreseeable future, as they become more aware that they are losing their status as the outright majority, they become more threatened by the idea of demographic change.[9] Studies show that Whites exhibit less tolerant attitudes toward minorities when notified about demographic changes

5. See Bailey, Moya, and Trudy, "On Misogynoir," 762: "Misogynoir describes the anti-Black racist misogyny that Black women experience."

6. Knight et al., "Out of Role? Out of Luck."

7. Doyle, "America Loves Women Like Hillary Clinton"; Pittman, "Sexist Hypocrisy." Prior to her presidential run, Hillary Clinton was the most admired female leader on the global scale, leading a Gallup poll on the question twenty-two times between 1993 and 2020 (https://news.gallup.com/poll/1678/most-admired-man-woman.aspx).

8. An idea first coined by legal scholar Kimberlé Crenshaw, intersectionality refers to the overlapping and interconnected nature of social identity rooted in race, gender, class, sexuality, etc. While these identities each result in experiences of oppression or disadvantage, the combination of factors produces intensified and unique experiences of oppression that aren't captured in each of the other categories separately.

9. Metzl, *Dying of Whiteness*; Craig and Richeson, "'Majority-Minority' America"; Craig and Richeson, "More Diverse Yet Less Tolerant?"; Quadagno, *Color of Welfare*.

resulting in the "browning of America." Such research may help explain the incomprehensible election of a bigot who routinely trumpeted a stream of nakedly racist and sexist insults and innuendo. The fearful attitudes documented in this research may also help explain the overwhelming evangelical support for Trump, which was puzzling to some given earlier rhetoric from this movement about the importance of character during Bill Clinton's impeachment. Other studies indicate that evangelicals have more racial anxiety than other parts of the American church,[10] so this group was probably more susceptible to the triggering fears of demographic shifts in the first place. The United States is entering an era in which our capacity to find leaders with gifts for managing diversity will determine our society's ability to persist and thrive. In these tumultuous times, we are better off choosing leaders promoting strategies like "Yes We Can," "Stronger Together," or "Compassionate Conservatism," rather than "Build the Wall."[11] After the Trump presidency, we must ask ourselves whether the United States can remain a multiethnic democracy while also achieving a measure of long overdue power sharing in this representative democratic republic.

Ephesians, an epistle containing striking language about unity, is a well-known New Testament destination for exploring race relations in such turbulent times, especially for those interested in "racial reconciliation."[12] Ephesians was ostensibly written by a Jewish-Christian minoritized leader in the late first or early second century; the implied recipients are Gentile Christians. The terminology "Gentile" is a framing that emerges from within Judaism, and the term lumps all non-Jews into the same category. However, non-Jewish Christians would have come from a variety of ethnic peoples conquered by the Romans. Given widespread anti-Jewish sentiment in the period, it is possible that many of these non-Jewish members of the early Christian movement

10. Shelton and Emerson, *Blacks and Whites in Christian America*.

11. These were the campaign slogans for the Obama 2008, Clinton 2016, and Bush 2000 presidential campaigns respectively. "Build the Wall" was a common chant at Trump 2016 political rallies but may not have been an official campaign slogan.

12. There are numerous problems with the so-called racial reconciliation framework. First and foremost, the perspective usually forefronts affect and emotion while ignoring needed structural and material considerations in improving race relations. Second, "reconciliation" language assumes the existence of an initial harmony between Blacks and Whites, and third, the perspective often fails to account for how other ethnic groups are racialized and thus operates on a Black-White binary. For more on the racial reconciliation movement in evangelicalism see Harvey, *Dear White Christians*; Walker-Barnes, *I Bring the Voices of My People*. Because of these problems, my own preference is to talk about improving race relations rather than use the term *racial reconciliation*.

would come from peoples with higher status in the empire than Jews.[13] Many of them may have been unsure about their welcome or their place in the early Jesus movement as they aligned with this fringe movement on the edge of Jewish society. This situation rhymes with some dynamics in contemporary US society as multiple minority groups wrangle for power and position in a turbulent landscape alongside newly minoritized Whites jostling for position vis-à-vis other more deeply marginalized groups.

Arguably written in a leadership crisis caused by demographic changes in the church, Ephesians speaks to the church's relationship to God's power and hostile powers all around the church. It has a thick discourse about wielding power and the ethics of appropriating and deploying it. The epistle portrays God as one who exerts power and empowers the church, a God who also overpowers the forces of evil en route to gathering up all creation in Christ. With a strong emphasis on ethical paraenesis, the book has a lot to say about how Christians should behave when they exercise power, tightly linking that activity to the model provided by Christ (Eph. 5:18–6:9). Thus, the author of Ephesians writes to instill a sense of confidence among the newly and more deeply minoritized Gentiles in his audience. Despite the fact that they find themselves in a new society, they genuinely belong and can have confidence that God has the power to act on their behalf as they participate in God's creative, convening, conjoining plans to connect the cosmos.

The discourse about the exercise of power in Ephesians thus leads back to considering the interplay between leadership influence and group membership. Leadership and identity are closely linked in turn since identity is formed, at least in part, through interaction with others in informal and formal interactions. Consequently, leaders can shape identity and model ways of negotiating difference through how their actions manifest perceptions of the Other.[14] In other words, a leader's exercise of power is a social process that influences the formation of self-identity, group identity, and the negotiation of gender and ethnic differences. Leaders thus play a pivotal role in identity formation by shaping the self-concepts of fellow group members. Ephesians develops a social theology that participates in these identity-forming leadership processes by connecting imitation of Christ and pursuit of God's goals vis-à-vis the church with the leadership of Christian communities.[15]

---

13. According to Slater, "some non-Jewish Christians would be extremely reluctant to disavow their socially acceptable anti-Jewish bigotry" (*Ephesians*, 25; also see 18–20).

14. Sanchez-Hucles and Davis, "Women of Color in Leadership," 176.

15. Sanchez-Hucles and Davis, "Women of Color in Leadership," 176; Slater, *Ephesians*, 17.

In this chapter, I explore the ethics of intergroup leadership in Ephesians against the backdrop of current literature on leadership and ethnic and gender diversity. First, we will review the leadership literature on gender and race to explore the challenges women of color face as leaders and the challenges of leading a diverse cluster of subgroups. Next, we move to a consideration of the themes and structure of Ephesians. The heart of this chapter interprets Ephesians 4:7–16 vis-à-vis themes in leadership and diversity. I contend that when read as a text for minoritized persons who lead multiracial organizations, Ephesians can help equip Christian leaders to wield power using the androgynous agentic and communal intercultural skills needed in our increasingly pluralistic and diverse society.

Leadership and Difference

Leadership scholars define the discipline as one that studies processes that encourage groups to achieve common goals through the exercise of interpersonal influence, power, and authority.[16] This definition captures the idea that persuasion and power are central in leadership processes and that leading is fundamentally about the relationships between leaders and other group members. Many leadership paradigms have successively taken center stage over the years, from a group process or skills acquisition orientation to a power relationship focus to a more recent concentration on transformational leadership, emphasizing motivational capacities.[17] But just as earlier generations of scholars effectively neglected followers in their attention to leader selection and development, most also virtually ignored the role of gender and ethnoracial difference. This circumstance is no surprise given the overwhelmingly White male demographics of leaders in the United States.[18] This posture resulted in neglect of all kinds of barriers faced by women and minorities in leader emergence and development, including stereotypes and other in-group–out-group

---

16. Northouse, *Leadership*, 3; Sanchez-Hucles and Davis, "Women of Color in Leadership," 171; J. L. Chin, "Introduction," 153.

17. Northouse, *Leadership*, 2–3.

18. Sanchez-Hucles and Davis, "Women of Color in Leadership," 172. In 2004, a sixty-two-country research project attempted to describe a model of leadership that transcended regional contexts. While there was evidence of certain "universal" elements of the model (e.g., charismatic leadership), there was also extensive evidence that the manifestation of these universals was heavily context dependent (House et al., *Culture, Leadership, and Organizations*). Other research suggests that leadership behaviors such as hierarchy, power, and close supervision are a function of culture (e.g., Ayman and Korabik, "Leadership," 160).

dynamics, role expectations, power and status gaps, and differential evaluations, attributions, and rewards for similar performance.[19]

Over the last ten to fifteen years, scholars in leadership studies and social psychology have begun to attend to the influence of ethnoracial and gender diversity regarding leadership selection and the challenges of leading diverse groups. The difficulties that women and people of color face in navigating leadership selection are numerous enough that a standard set of metaphors have emerged to name these challenges. There is the "glass ceiling," which usually refers to the transparent but less tangible obstacles faced by women in advancing to the highest levels of organizational leadership; the "bamboo ceiling," a variation on this theme which attempts to name the stereotypes that impede Asian American advancement; the "sticky floor" or "concrete ceiling," metaphors that capture the bewildering labyrinth of severe obstructions faced by women of color and other doubly-disadvantaged people; and the phenomenon of "glass cliff assignments" that describe high visibility tasks that are likely to end in failure but that are sometimes the only leadership assignments given to women and people of color.[20] Ironically, the nation's first minoritized President took office under glass cliff circumstances during the onset of the globalized Great Recession at the end of 2008.

There are widespread and gendered assumptions about masculine and feminine leadership styles. Men are associated with traits that are said to be *agentic,* including intelligence, ambition, initiative, and dominance, which are commonly associated with leadership.[21] Women's *communal* characteristics include warmth, kindness, gentleness, and the use of collaborative facilitation techniques that combine to create styles found in subservient roles.[22] These stereotypes about masculine and feminine behavior have significant consequences for women aspiring to leadership. Such widespread thinking makes it less likely that women will be mentored and subsequently appointed to leadership. They will be more likely penalized for acting masculine if they do conform to expectations about successful leadership capacity. They may even be punished for not meeting feminine role expectations if they do exhibit

19. Ayman and Korabik, "Leadership," 157.

20. For "glass ceiling," see Sanchez-Hucles and Davis, "Women of Color in Leadership"; for "bamboo ceiling," see Hyun, *Breaking the Bamboo Ceiling*; for "sticky floor/concrete ceiling," see Sanchez-Hucles and Davis, "Women of Color in Leadership"; for "glass cliff," see Ryan and Haslam, "Glass Cliff."

21. Rosette and Tost, "Agentic Women and Communal Leadership," 222.

22. Eagly and Chin, "Diversity and Leadership"; Sanchez-Hucles and Davis, "Women of Color in Leadership," 173; Rosette and Tost, "Agentic Women and Communal Leadership," 222.

agentic behavior. As one group of scholars put it, women must operate in the "narrow range between not too wimpy and not too bitchy."[23] On the other hand, studies in transformational leadership suggest a correlation between a more androgynous style that combines a high-instrumentality task focus and high-expressivity relational traits.[24] At stake in this discussion are models for what the exercise of leadership power looks like and how that imagery impacts the leadership legitimacy of women and people of color.

The potential for prejudice is present when stereotypes condition expectations about a whole social group, whether these derive from gender, ethnicity, race, sexuality, or sexual expression. Barriers from a misalignment of role expectations derived from White male behavioral ideals and stereotypes also impede leadership emergence among people of color. Stereotypes of African Americans depict them as criminal, antagonistic, and lacking competence, and Hispanics as uneducated and unambitious. Asian Americans are seen as quiet and unassertive or, in keeping with the model minority stereotype, dismissed as overqualified.[25] The intersectionality of identity also multiplies barriers for minority women: African American women experience harsher negative stereotypes and lower promotion rates than their male counterparts. They face more significant backlash for gender role violations in which their behaviors are deemed "unfeminine," femininity as keyed to whiteness.[26] Since White male leaders report a greater willingness to accept White women than African American women, we can surmise that Black women are too different from White women who benefit from being White. Likewise, these Black women are rejected for being too different from African American men who benefit from male privilege. Lack of access to support systems and mentoring networks will have similar effects on Latina and Asian women leaders.[27]

If organizations exclude women and people of color as leaders for one reason or another, these minoritized leaders face enormous pressure to perform if ever assigned to these roles. *Stereotype threat* imperils the performance of many women and minorities; it is a term that names the additional stress that can cause impaired performance when doing tasks that trigger negative stereotypes.

23. Sanchez-Hucles and Davis, "Women of Color in Leadership," 173. Also see J. L. Chin et al., "Overview: Women and Leadership," 312.

24. Ayman and Korabik, "Leadership," 161.

25. Carton and Rosette, "Explaining Bias against Black Leaders," 1143; Eagly and Chin, "Diversity and Leadership," 218; Hyun, *Breaking the Bamboo Ceiling*.

26. Livingston, Rosette, and Washington, "Can an Agentic Black Woman Get Ahead?," 354; P. H. Collins, *Black Sexual Politics*.

27. Sanchez-Hucles and Davis, "Women of Color in Leadership," 174–75.

In other words, stereotype threat results in increased self-doubt about whether one's behavior will confirm the negative stereotype and thus activate more performance anxiety.[28] Suppose a woman knows about stereotypical expectations that she doesn't have "the right stuff" for demanding leadership tasks. In that case, her leadership performance may be impaired by stereotype threat if she is reminded about these expectations while attempting to lead. If, despite all this, women and minorities actually do receive leadership assignments and perform well in them, they then frequently experience backlash from people who resent the fact that they are overturning expectations about implicit hierarchies. They receive more negative performance assessments from aversive prejudice, and the intensity of the backlash appears to depend on the degree of misalignment between the applicable stereotypes and the role requirements.[29] This dynamic is a tale of the entire Obama presidency and helps explain the rise of the naked racism of the Trump era. The backlash was triggered by the simple fact that Obama led, and it was amplified by the fact that he led well.

Just as scholars are turning their attention to questions about how women and minorities ascend into leadership and perform as leaders, the United States is entering an era wherein the capacity to lead diverse groups is ever more critical. By 2045 the country will be "majority-minority," and there will be no single ethnoracial group in the United States that will comprise a majority of the population. By the year 2027 this will already be the case among those who are eighteen to twenty-nine years old.[30] Analysis of US Census data suggests that this condition already prevails in five states and the District of Columbia. California and New Mexico are states where Latinx peoples are already the largest single ethnic category; Hawaii is the only state that has never had a White majority; and Arizona and Texas are states where Whites are the largest single minority group.[31] Trends indicate that Nevada, Georgia, and Maryland

28. Eagly and Chin, "Diversity and Leadership," 219.

29. Aversive racism is a subtle form of prejudice that emerges when people can use other factors as a proxy for race to express negative feelings towards Blacks; see Knight et al., "Out of Role? Out of Luck"; Eagly and Chin, "Diversity and Leadership," 219. For more information about role incongruity see Eagly and Karau, "Role Congruity Theory" and Eagly and Diekman, "What Is the Problem?"

30. https://www.brookings.edu/blog/the-avenue/2018/03/14/the-us-will-become-minority-white-in-2045-census-projects/.

31. US Census data available at: https://www.census.gov/popest/?intcmp=serp; Kaiser Family Foundation data available at: http://kff.org/other/state-indicator/distribution-by-raceethnicity/?currentTimeframe=0&sortModel=%7B%22colId%22:%22Location%22,%22sort%22:%22asc%22%7D.

are likely next to join this list of majority-minority states.[32] Some Americans, especially White Americans, perceive the growing ethnoracial diversity of the nation as a threat, increasing the possibility of misunderstandings, divisiveness, and hostile intergroup relations.[33]

Yet contrary to a narrative that suggests that the diversity of the United States is a problem to be overcome, the nation's ethnoracial diversity *could be* one of its greatest assets for innovation and progress, since exposure to multiple cultures in and of itself can enhance creativity.[34] Multicultural experiences and intercultural collaboration may enhance creativity in at least six ways.[35] First, these experiences can provide direct access to novel ideas and concepts from other cultures. Second, intercultural expertise can create the ability to see multiple underlying functions behind the same cultural form. For example, exposure to multiple cultures can help reveal how a norm like leaving food on a plate as an expression of appreciation as in China or Jordan can, in other cultures like Indonesia, be construed as an insult. Third, exposure to different cultures destabilizes routinized knowledge structures that interrupt culturally expected answers, leading to innovation rather than reproducing the status quo. Fourth, immersion in multicultural spaces creates a psychological readiness to recruit ideas from unfamiliar sources and places. Fifth, multicultural experience stimulates associative reasoning that synthesizes new concepts from seemingly incompatible ideas from diverse cultures. Finally, some studies show that heterogeneous opinions spur group creativity. In sum, while simple tasks are probably best accomplished by homogeneous groups who can rely on shared communication regimes, more complex tasks requiring innovation approaches are best tackled by groups characterized by diversity.[36]

Thus, we need leadership paradigms that help us to avoid divisiveness on

32. US Census data available at: https://www.census.gov/popest/?intcmp=serp; Kaiser Family Foundation data available at: http://kff.org/other/state-indicator/distribution-by-raceethnicity/?currentTimeframe=0&sortModel=%7B%22colId%22:%22Location%22,%22sort%22:%22asc%22%7D.

33. For more on this topic see C. Anderson, *White Rage*.

34. Leung et al., "Multicultural Experience Enhances Creativity," 172. Chi-yue Chiu and Ying-yi Hong define culture as a set of loosely organized ideas and practices produced and reproduced by a network of interconnected individuals; see Chiu and Hong, "Cultural Processes: Basic Principles."

35. The first five benefits for creativity from multicultural experience are from Leung et al., "Multicultural Experience Enhances Creativity." The sixth benefit is from Nemeth and Wachtler, "Creative Problem Solving," and Simonton, "Scientific Creativity."

36. Phillips, "How Diversity Makes Us Smarter"; Eagly and Chin, "Diversity and Leadership," 220.

the one hand while reaping the rewards of the creative tension from social heterogeneity on the other. As discussed in chapters 3 and 5, it is reasonable to expect that leaders from ethnoracial minoritized groups can bring sensibilities to the leadership task well suited for this moment in American history. Such bicultural or multicultural people bring intercultural competence, flexibility, and openness to creative change based on their ability to shift between the majority culture and their own subcultural contexts; a heightened concern for subgroup equality and justice; a more collectivist orientation that can forefront group concerns over those of their own subgroup; and experience of a greater range of male and female emotional expression than is typically found among Americans of European descent.[37] Yet, how do we ensure that society can value these leaders for the perspectives they bring?[38] How should leaders negotiate power and motivate group members toward a shared mission when difference is the group's principal characteristic?

Until recently, there was broad agreement that in-group identity emerges at least partially from opposition to the Other,[39] but research suggests that strong in-group affiliations do not necessarily lead to negative attitudes toward out-groups. One promising leadership paradigm, intergroup leadership, is appearing in the context of these considerations.[40] Improving relations between different social identity groups requires two kinds of action: that which decreases prejudice; and a set of separate and independent interventions that enhance "allophilia," that is, positive intergroup relationships based on cross-group liking.[41] Intergroup leadership involves influence across group bound-

37. Eagly and Chin, "Diversity and Leadership," 219–20. The study by Durik et al. has very interesting findings on differences in male and female emotional expression across minority and White American subgroups, which may in part emerge from greater emphasis on group social norms among minorities versus White individualism; see Durik et al., "Ethnicity and Gender Stereotypes of Emotion."

38. Floor Rink and Naomi Ellemers maintain that clear expectations about diversity lead to positive perceptions of decision-making processes. This clarity also results in a situation where diversity is valued by group members because they recognize that mutual differences contribute to the common goals and tasks of the group. See Rink and Ellemers, "Managing Diversity in Work Groups."

39. Anthony Smith is among the researchers who posit that ethnic identity is partially constructed in response to conflict with other people groups. See *Ethnic Origins of Nations*, 22–32.

40. For descriptions of intergroup leadership, see the following resources: Pittinsky, "Two-Dimensional Model of Intergroup Leadership"; Pittinsky, "Intergroup Leadership." The brief discussion of allophilia and intergroup leadership that follows draws on all these resources.

41. Allophilia is etymologically derived from two Greek words meaning liking or love

aries to bring groups together without trying to eliminate their differences.[42] Those advocating this approach stress cultivating a superordinate identity that represents a "third neutral identity space" to help decrease prejudice. This neutral identity can be a resource to foster interdependent work toward common goals.[43]

In the context of racialized headwinds in the United States, minoritized individuals with strong ethnic identification can be healthier than those with weak ties to their cultures of origin, as described in chapter 5. So those looking for effective intergroup leadership strategies will recognize that elimination of subgroup identities is not at all desirable. Neither the enduring legacies of slavery nor ongoing and hardened institutional racism laid bare in national tragedies like Hurricane Katrina or the COVID-19 pandemic permit amnesia about threats to the most marginalized. On the other hand, given the findings regarding the benefits of diversity on group creativity, we would be foolish to abandon the compelling advantage inherent in the rich diversity of the US population in favor of the sameness of a neutral identity. Therefore, any cultivated neutral third space must be additive instead of supersessionist. In my judgment, the way forward lies with a greater emphasis on the second dimension of intergroup leadership, which focuses on creating and modeling positive intergroup relations through allophilia toward all out-groups. Ephesians is well known for its emphasis on a third identity space (Eph. 2:15). Still, we must interrogate whether its third identity space is additive instead of supersessionist and promotes positive intergroup relations.

Power, Peace, and Mission (Ephesians 1–3)

While the Pauline Epistles are notorious for being embedded in a particular historical situation, it is much more challenging to locate the historical circumstances that prompted the composition of Ephesians.[44] This situation may

---

(φίλος) for the other (ἄλλος), a term that refers to the positive feelings of kinship, affection, and enthusiasm for members of groups different from one's own. See Pittinsky, "Intergroup Leadership," xviii.

42. Pittinsky, "Intergroup Leadership," xii–xvi.

43. Robin DiAngelo describes common tensions between Whites and minority leadership in the context of anti-racist action; see "White Fragility." Also see chapter 2 for a theological consideration of allyship across group boundaries, a form of intergroup functioning.

44. Ephesians was called "an epistle in search of a life setting" by one biblical scholar in an article by the same name (Martin, "Epistle in Search of a Life Setting"). Though the epistle was well-established in the New Testament canon and likely written late in the first

frustrate our ability to find its underlying narrative trajectory and complicate identification of the analogs required for associative hermeneutics. For example, there are good reasons to doubt that the epistle was intended for the congregation(s) at Ephesus. Very early Greek manuscripts of Ephesians lack the phrase "in Ephesus" in 1:1. The epistle gives only general advice and does not offer details regarding any events in its recipients' lives or specific conditions in the church as witnessed in the Epistles to the Galatians, Philippians, Philemon, the Corinthians, and Thessalonians.[45] In penning Romans, Paul wrote

---

century, the authorship of Ephesians is disputed. The majority of critical scholars argue that the author of this work is the same person who composed such letters as Romans, the Corinthian correspondence, Galatians, Philippians, Philemon, and 1 Thessalonians. Some propose a Pauline "school" composed of close associates who may have developed Paul's thought after his death wrote 2 Thessalonians, the Pastoral Epistles, and perhaps Luke-Acts (e.g., Best, *Ephesians*, 36–40). This matter generally involves weighing evidence regarding the epistle's literary style (i.e., unusual vocabulary appearing infrequently elsewhere in the New Testament; words more common to second-century Christianity; prepositions and genitives typical of an elevated liturgical style; complex syntax that differs from the undisputed Pauline Epistles), distinct theological emphases (i.e., Christ as head of the body; the church universal versus local only; prophets as guides not the foundation of the church; vertical versus horizontal reconciliation; no law; all Gentile churches; see Best, *Ephesians*, 35 and passim), literary dependence on Colossians (see e.g., Col. 3:16–4:1 and Eph. 5:19–6:9; Col. 1:25–26 and Eph. 3:2–3; and the mention of Tychicus in Col. 4:7 and Eph. 6:21; for more on this topic see especially Van Kooten, *Cosmic Christology,* and also Lincoln, *Ephesians*; contra Best, *Ephesians*), and the historical reconstruction of the apostle's life and ministry (e.g., Lincoln and Wedderburn, *Theology of Later Pauline Epistles*). Based on all this I think it is more likely that the Paul of the undisputed Pauline Epistles is *not* the author of Ephesians, but I interact with many scholars in this chapter who do not hold this view. For convenience I will refer to the implied author as "the author of Ephesians," though I recognize the author's desire to adapt the historical Paul's theological legacy for a different ecclesial moment. For a thorough and nuanced discussion of Pauline authorship see Best, *Ephesians*, 6–36; also Schnackenburg, *Ephesians*; cf. E. P. Sanders, "Literary Dependence in Colossians." For a defense of Pauline authorship for Ephesians, see Barth, *Ephesians*.

45. One might contrast two approaches to interpreting Ephesians by comparing the commentary of Allen Verhey and Joseph Harvard versus that of Pheme Perkins. The former assumes that the epistle was written in the close aftermath of the Jewish War of AD 66–73 due to what they see as the Jew-Gentile enmity alluded to in Eph. 2:1–22. However, it is worth noting, first, that the "enmity" of Ephesians is much more muted than that in Galatians and other texts mentioned above, and second, that the Jewish War of AD 135 might equally serve as a suitable context for the enmity observed and there is little in the text of Ephesians that could help choose decisively between these two periods. For her part, Perkins is interested in drawing parallels between the language of the epistle's author and the sectarian Jews in the Qumran community without adducing direct dependencies one way or the other. Her approach attempts to situate the teaching of Ephesians vis-à-vis

to a congregation that he had never visited. Yet, its last chapter nevertheless exhibits many personal connections between the apostle and the church and implies that he might have gained detailed knowledge about issues in Rome from those sources. Many scholars suggest that a close reading of Ephesians 1:15, 2:20 (cf. 1 Cor. 3:10), and 3:2a implies that the author was unknown to the audience of this epistle. This state wouldn't have prevailed if the author was indeed Paul and the epistle was intended for a Pauline congregation at Ephesus. Paul himself was well known in that city and spent about three years with the ethnically diverse Jewish and Gentile churches there (Acts 19:17; 20:21).[46] Another scholar suggests that a leadership crisis in the wake of the passing of first-generation Christian leaders might have created a void into which this author speaks. He writes to apply Pauline concepts to a new moment to form new leaders in multiple locations (Eph. 2:20; 4:11), a reading that makes sense of much of the data from the epistle.[47]

Though there is still ambiguity, we can say that the author is likely a Jewish Christian who takes on the persona of Paul, the apostle to the Gentiles. He writes to the Gentiles as a minority group in the early Christian movement, a small offshoot of early Judaism. Adapting Pauline theology for a new moment requiring new ethical appeals, the author urges these Christian converts to live out a faith that anticipates the gathering up of all things in Christ (1:10, 22; 3:10). He reminds these communities that the union of Jews and Gentiles in Christ anticipates[48] God's reordering the cosmos, even or especially in the face of hostile Powers in

---

another sectarian Jewish movement in the period also anchored in the scriptures of Israel. My own preference is best expressed by Schnackenburg, who posits an origin for the epistle around AD 90 (*Ephesians*, 33).

46. While there is a significant emphasis on unity in the church in Ephesians, there is no mention of the concrete issues that divided such congregations, such as adherence to Jewish food laws (Rom. 14:15–21; 1 Cor. 10:19–21) and festivals (Gal. 4:10; Col. 2:16), participation in sexual immorality (1 Thess. 4:6 NLT; 1 Cor. 6:18), or controversial theological constructs like circumcision (Rom. 2:25–29; Gal. 5:2–3, 6–12), the Spirit (1 Cor. 12:1–3; 2 Cor. 3:15–18), or the resurrection (1 Cor. 15).

47. Schnackenburg, *Ephesians*, 33.

48. See Van Kooten's very interesting work in understanding the literary and theological relationship between Ephesians and Colossians (*Cosmic Christology*). Van Kooten reads Ephesians as a correction to the cosmic Christology of the earlier Colossians. He maintains that the author of Ephesians reworks much of the material from Colossians and adds new material (Eph. 2:11–22; 4:1–16; 6:10–17) that depicts the church as the opening stage in the gathering up of the cosmos in Christ, something already depicted as accomplished in the body of Christ in Colossians. See also Schnackenburg, *Ephesians*, 30–32.

their context that seem overwhelming.[49] The author discusses a new blended humanity, the church's power over the Powers through the sufficiency of gifts given from God, and its connection to a loving God who sent Christ to be the head over all things, including the Powers. As we shall see, we will be able to read the ethics of Ephesians as a discourse about power that looks to empower out-group (Gentile) leaders and members of the body of Christ to exercise power in the Lord and Christian communities. The idea that God's power is available to and deployed on behalf of the powerless is likely consonant with the frequent use of Ephesians in African American and other minoritized churches since it affirms that "a greater power is at work in us than the one at work in the world."[50]

For our purposes, we will note two intertwined themes that connect the theological message of the epistle with our interest in leaders who embody and guide minoritized communities. The first theme we will explore concerns the discourse in Ephesians about God's power and evil Powers and how this focus on power rhymes with the theme of institutional racism. Second, we'll describe how Ephesians conceptualizes the relationship between leaders and church members as together they bear witness to the spiritual Powers of evil.

Divine Power against the Principalities and Powers (Ephesians 1)

The depiction of God's power and glory in Ephesians emerges most clearly in 1:18–22, where the author piles up words and images in a portrait of the sheer overwhelming magnitude of God's power as a force that exercises complete and sweeping authority to order the cosmos and every force ranged against God's will:

> [18] . . . so that you may know what is the hope of his calling, what is the riches of the glory of God's inheritance among the saints, [19] and what is the surpassing greatness of God's power for us who believe, by the active force of the strength of God's might. [20] God's power was working in Christ when God raised him from the dead and seated him at the right side in the heavenly realm [21] above every Principality and Authority and Power and Dominion and every Name that is named, not only in this age but also in the age to come. [22] And God subjected all things under Christ's feet and appointed him

49. I capitalize references to "Powers" whenever I am alluding to the idea that the author of Ephesians conceives of these entities as personal spiritual forces capable of independent action that can influence human beings.

50. M. J. Smith, *Insights*, 352.

as head over all things for the church, [23]which is his body, the fullness of which is the One who fills all things in all ways. (Eph. 1:18–22 AT)

Then, in the verses immediately following this section, the author describes how these supernatural Powers leave alienated humans in an utterly helpless state of perpetual sin:

[1]And you were dead in your trespasses and your sins, [2]living like this world age, following the Ruler of the Authority of the Air, the Spirit of the present age who works among the children of disobedience. [3]Among them, we all also formerly lived in the lusts of the flesh, enacting the desires of the flesh and the senses, and we were children of wrath by disposition just like the rest were. (Eph. 2:1–3 AT)

The author describes God's power as emanating in a glorious inheritance for the saints, which on examination appears to be nothing less than the saints' access to God's power ("for us who believe"; cf. 3:16). There are no less than five synonyms and images that refer to God's power in 1:19: it is a power[51] that is surpassing in its greatness; that works with an active force;[52] that exhibits the strength[53] of God's might;[54] all of these shown in the mighty power at work in the resurrection (1:20). Christ's resurrection is not simply a power that overcomes death; it is also a power that raised Christ far above a series of animate and hostile spiritual Powers in the realm of heaven. There can be no more potent example of the magnitude of God's power than the fact that it can overcome death itself. Such power would be a source of immeasurable comfort for Gentiles, who in Christ would be expected to renounce dependence on magic or idols to alleviate oppression by evil, hostile powers.[55] In Galatians, Paul speaks of Gentiles as those who are in slavery to idols thought to be gods, though Christ reveals that these idols are "weak and beggarly," and similar rhetoric is at work here.[56] When Paul remarks that the worship of idols is the worship of demons (1 Cor. 10:20) and that the Gentiles are vulnerable to deception by these powerless idols (1 Cor. 8:4–5; 12:2), he is describing the worldview of many in his context. But in Ephesians, we find

51. "Power": δυνάμεως.
52. "Active force": ἐνέργειαν.
53. "Strength": κράτους.
54. "Might": ἰσχύος.
55. See Eph. 2:2; 3:10, 16–20; 6:10, 12; cf. Acts 19; Col. 1:16; 2:10; 1 Thess. 1:9.
56. Gal. 4:8–9; cf. Gal. 4:3; Heb. 7:18.

the idea that Christians have access to the power of God and are not helpless before these malevolent forces.[57] A key phrase in Ephesians 1:19 communicates the directional focus of God's power: it is "for us who believe." This phrase communicates that God's power in Christ is *for* the church's use (1:22). God's power conveys strength to the church for glorifying God through a mission to exhibit God's wisdom in gathering together an ethnically diverse church (3:21).

Ephesians contains more language about power than almost any other section of the New Testament, which may be due to the author's attempt to address widespread fears about hostile supernatural forces. Whereas some resist these powers through magic rituals and artifacts (cf. Acts 19:17–19), Ephesians comforts believers by depicting the exalted power of God in Christ. The epistle maintains that God has already achieved a decisive win against these entities through Christ's elevation over these powers (1:20). Likewise, Christ supplies strength to Gentile believers to renounce their old practices and trust in God's power to protect them from evil.[58] In the cosmology of Ephesians, the Powers are spiritual beings, here named as rulers, authorities, powers, and dominions, but the epistle also includes other terminology that refers to personal named supernatural agents of evil in opposition to God's will: "the Prince of the power of the air" (Eph. 2:2) and the Devil (4:26–27; 6:11). It is less likely but still possible that 2:2 may be an early reference to a named power known as "Aion,"[59] which became a technical term in later Gnostic thought for forces opposed to God.[60] More likely, we should interpret this reference through the lenses of Hellenistic Judaism and ancient Israelite religion, which attest to notions of how angelic powers both cooperate with and resist the God of Israel.[61] In Ephesians, the text says that these forces reside in the heavenly

---

57. Lincoln and Wedderburn, *Theology of Later Pauline Epistles*, 83.

58. Clinton Arnold's work *Power and Magic* posits the discourse in Ephesians against the background of heavy activity around Ephesus in Asia Minor concerning magic, exploring magical papyri and artifacts, and the cult of Artemis in Ephesus. Though his arguments are less persuasive as a reason to situate this epistle in Ephesus given the textual uncertainty of the relevant phrase in 1:1, he nonetheless helpfully illuminates the fear of "power and magic" as something to which the author of Ephesians responds, beliefs that were widespread in the areas in which early Christianity flourished.

59. "Aion" or τὸν αἰῶνα in 2:2.

60. See Lincoln, *Ephesians*, 94, for more on this possibility, in a way that connects the cult of Aion with second-century BC Egypt rather than Gnosticism (cf. 1 Cor. 2:6, 8; 2 Cor. 4:4), though he ultimately opts against this reading. Also see Arnold, *Power and Magic*, 59–60.

61. See J. J. Collins, "Powers in Heaven." This essay not only provides information about how our author might have understood the powers by exploring another contemporary

realm, and it is clear that the author thinks they influence human life. Note that the influence of the powers is *in cooperation with* human "desires of the flesh" (2:1–3), though counteracted by supernaturally empowered human resistance (6:10–12).[62]

Amid ever-present fears about powerful gods and demi-gods, many people in the period grasped at magic, incantations, and amulets as a means of controlling these supernatural powers. There is debate about how to correlate or build a rhyme that associates the Powers discussed in this epistle with current belief systems in the West that eschew reliance on magic. Do the Powers discussed in Ephesians represent human political rulers or dynamics, or should we imagine them as ongoing forces operating within the context of peoples and nations (e.g., as the spirit of the times)? If Judaism and Christianity referred to such powers as political opponents and supernatural beings attached to nations, clans, or tribes (cf. Dan. 7, 10; Rev. 2–3), surely modern readers do not have to adopt this cosmology wholesale. Walter Wink suggests that a "demythologized" cosmology is already at work in Paul, which the author of Ephesians extends via an amalgamation of spiritual and human forces of evil.[63] According to Wink, Ephesians 2:1–2 represents:

> a heaping up of terms to describe the ineffable, invisible world-enveloping reach of . . . not only demons and kings but the world atmosphere and power invested in institutions, laws, traditions and rituals as well. . . . So formidable a phalanx of hostility demands spiritual weaponry, for it is clear that we contend not against human beings as such ("blood and flesh") but against the legitimations, seats of authority, hierarchical systems, ideological justifications, and punitive sanctions which their human incumbents exercise and which transcend these incumbents in both time and power. It is the suprahuman dimension of power in institutions and the cosmos which must be fought, not the mere human agent. For the institution will guarantee the replacement of this person with another virtually the

---

sectarian Jewish community, but also is helpful for understanding how Ephesians conceptualized the saints as "seated in the heavenly realm" while still also living an angelic life on earth (13, 23–24). Also see Wink, *Naming the Powers*, 13–35; Barth, *Ephesians*, 170–75.

62. Best, *Ephesians*, 220.

63. Wink (*Naming the Powers*, 60–64) speaks of demythologizing as a process that substitutes a naming of forces that influence human life, such as angels and demons and the like, for the "actual physical, psychic, and social forces at work in us, in society, and in the universe" (62). For a persuasive critique of the idea that Paul has a demythologized cosmology see Arnold, *Power and Magic*, 129–34.

same, who despite personal preferences will replicate decisions made by a whole string of predecessors because that is what the institution requires for its survival.[64]

Indeed, the ancients did not draw hard and fast lines between the supernatural and the natural as we do today, and they perceived the religious, the magical, and the political to be intimately bound up with each other in ways that are impossible to disentangle. Jews and early Christians saw themselves as under the power of both supernatural powers and human authorities like kings and other rulers, for good and for ill. Wink's critics point out that Ephesians depicts these as powers in the air or the heavens, and Wink's exegesis of Ephesians persistently overlooks these details by fusing the idea that Jews and Christians sometimes depicted authorities as earthly and other times as supernatural into supposing that both concepts are in mind in the epistle.

On the other hand, Ernst Best's modernistic thinking that reduces human life to only that which we can measure and observe seems more flawed, denuding us of the opportunity to let the ancient text open up space for reflection about our present condition:

> It is not part of the purpose of this commentary to explain the powers in twentieth-century terms either as political, social, and economic forces, or as the power of tradition, ethical custom, race, or as psychological psychoses or forces like sex . . . which we cannot control. . . . For [the readers of Ephesians] the powers are supernatural and cannot be reduced to, and explained in natural terms. . . . [I]n other words the same kinds of tragedies happen to us as happened in the ancient world, but we attribute them to natural and not supernatural causes; we seek rational, not magical, explanations for them and, in so far as it is possible, scientific means for their cure. . . . While [the author] and his readers might in some way accept the concept that supernatural beings are already subject to Christ their conqueror, we cannot understand, to take an example, the car accident in which some innocent person dies as an event subject to Christ. . . . It is probably therefore wrong to attempt to transform the powers into anything which we can observe and measure, though many of the things we can observe and measure affect us in unexpected ways.[65]

64. Wink, *Naming the Powers*, 85–86.
65. Best, *Ephesians*, 179–80.

When thinking about the modern world, Best assumes that naturalistic explanations eliminate the need to talk about spiritual phenomena. For Best, material causes can supply exhaustive discourse about the nature of reality. This position leaves out a whole host of phenomena that cannot be reduced to materialistic terms. Religious experience, emotion, social forces, and personality are all things that might have been named "spiritual" in an earlier age, as, indeed are many of the things discussed in Wink's work. Persuaded by science, today we reject reliance on magical incantations, amulets, and potions to manipulate unseen forces. But there remains a realm of reality containing forces like racism, misogyny, impoverished despair, greed, and fear of the Other, that, while intangible, is still outside of what can be observed and measured. This realm and these forces may still resist control except through wise, concerted, cooperative—and hopefully inspired!—collective human effort.[66] Therefore, we can identify some natural forces as *analogous* to those named by the ancients that control and influence the cosmos. Some of these natural forces, like gravity, light, and biological instincts, are embedded in the material world. Others, like psychosocial functioning, markets, racism, sexism, xenophobia, homophobia, and ageism, are invisible, immaterial, and pressing, but no less *real*.

In naming the powers described in the New Testament in ways that frame these phenomena in accessible ways for modern readers, Wink has engaged in analogical reasoning as discussed in this work. Indeed, Wink's formulation regarding hostile institutional powers that guarantee that replacing this person with another will replicate decisions made by a whole string of predecessors because of a prevailing spirit or ethos comes close to being a textbook definition of institutional racism. Institutional racism, or racism without racists as one scholar puts it, describes the suprapersonal cultural forces that influence the material lives of minorities in ways that are observable and measurable, or that are unreal and invisible, depending on your point of view.[67] Systems

66. Contrast Aune's ideas in "Magic in Early Christianity" with H. S. Versnel's in "Some Reflections on the Relationship." Though they each struggle with the way that normative pressures sometimes create a tension between understanding the difference between magic and religion (i.e., one person's magic is another person's miracle), they adduce similar concepts in the final analysis. In Aune's words: "Goals . . . are magical when attained in such a way that results are virtually guaranteed" (1515–16). Also see Aune's later work on this topic ("'Magic' in Early Christianity"), in which he advocates dispensing with the entire category as an analytical tool, perhaps in favor of using a new term, *sorcery*, that has no overlap with "religion" as a category.

67. Bonilla-Silva, *Racism without Racists*.

built on rules that serve one population while disadvantaging another—like police departments, courts, schools, financial systems, industries, markets, and voting systems—are sometimes so powerfully entrenched that they take on a life of their own. A cloud of preferential assumptions about who has the freedom to have, challenge, or resist authority hovers like a spiritual smog over most of our social, religious, and political arrangements. These strangling forces have pernicious, sometimes murderous effects that weigh down those living in the grip of them.[68]

Today, with our growing understanding of God's world, we can identify the principles by which gravity, psychology, and biology affect human life. With new vocabularies available to us, we can eschew some of the language that the ancients used when naming the forces that governed their lives. In this vein, Wink's argument and its penchant for collapsing ancient and modern phenomena has not been convincing in some quarters. I suggest that his approach is better described as a contextualized reading rather than as a first-line historical description.[69] Yet, for those who are still the subject of unwieldy evil forces influencing human life like racism, sexism, or poverty, Wink's way of naming the powers is compelling. His framework allows contemporary readers to read themselves into the story told in Ephesians and to hope in the power of the God who raised Jesus from the dead. By participating in this story, they also participate in God's work of defeating the powers of racism and sexism and homophobia and every other oppressive power that darkens the human spirit and corrupts human thriving.

Missional Ethics (Ephesians 2–3)

The God of Ephesians is a grand architect, executing a plan for redemption that already exists before creation and any human sin or good deed. But the God of Ephesians is not an impersonal digital God who boots up the cosmos and retreats into impenetrable darkness. The God of Ephesians is a God of love who plans to gather up the cosmos into a harmonious whole that leaves nothing isolated and abandoned (1:4–6, 10; 2:4; 3:7; 5:1–2). The opening verses of the epistle begin to set out God's mysterious plan and the church's role in it:

68. Tatum, *Why Are All the Black Kids Sitting Together*.
69. Wink, *Naming the Powers*; Wink, *Unmasking the Powers*; Wink, *Engaging the Powers*. Indeed, Wink's trilogy was deeply motivated by his work among the poor and marginalized. That his own sensibilities were engaged in contextualizing the biblical message for work alongside communities that suffer oppression and injustice is best showcased in his smaller work *When the Powers Fall*.

[8]With all wisdom and insight [9]God made known to us the mystery of God's own will, under the kind intention which was planned in Christ [10]for structuring the cosmos in the fullness of time, that God would gather all things up together in Christ, both things in heaven and the things on the earth. In Christ [11]we received an inheritance, having been destined according to God's purpose which accomplishes all things according to this plan, [12]so that we who have already hoped in Christ might bring honor to God. (Eph. 1:8b–12 AT)

In Ephesians 1:9, the "mystery" is the gathering up together of all things in Christ, which shows that God's gift to humanity is the privilege of participating in the opening chords of this grand opera. The unification of Jews and Gentiles in the church bears witness to God's great plan for structuring the cosmos around Christ.[70] From this perspective, the existence of the inclusive church is the means of accruing additional glory to God. Consequently, the church's failure to manifest the accomplishment of this work represents its failure to live up to its calling.

Just as God reveals this plan "with all wisdom and insight," so too will the church participate in demonstrating the wisdom of this plan to the Principalities and Powers who resist the unfolding plan (3:4, 10). In Ephesians, gifts of knowledge and insight reveal God's ultimate purpose of gathering up all things in Christ, as well as the church's role in that plan (1:8–9, 17–18). The next section of the epistle gives teaching about what Christ's work accomplishes in the church. As we saw above, the section starts in 2:1–3 and develops that story by describing how the saints straddle the turn of the ages and how their own lives bear witness to being released from the power of evil and personal sin to embrace a new identity and mission in Christ. In 2:1–10, we see only a tantalizing hint about the mission of the church that will unfold more explicitly in 3:1–10. The mission has to do with living out good works that God has foreordained, language that recalls the assertion that believers were predestined by election and anticipates the discourse in chapter 4 about living out their call.

In the long paraenesis of Ephesians 4:1–6:9, there are multiple exhortations about Christians being able to live out their calling as the first fruits of God's plan for cosmic reconciliation. Believers must walk in a manner worthy of God's calling (4:1): they must eschew walking in darkness like the Gentiles do (4:17–18) and walk in love, being able to give out love even as they have been loved (5:1–2), and walk as children of light (5:8). The logical connections

70. Van Kooten, *Cosmic Christology*, 147–203.

between chapters 2–4 imply that the foreordained good works that God supplies for the church of reconciled ethnic groups (2:10–22) represent nothing less than a life of unity in keeping with the calling of God (4:1–3). Indeed, the ethnoracially reconciled church active in the God-given work of creating and protecting unity is the church that manifests and proclaims God's wisdom in reconciling the cosmos to God's self (3:10).

In chapter 2, Ephesians attempts to construct a new superordinate identity that helps unify the converts from different ethnic groups. Interestingly, these groups are not labeled Jewish or Gentile as we might expect a Jewish-Christian author like this one to use (cf. Rom. 9:24; 1 Cor. 10:32; Gal. 2:15). The author refers to one group with two names: "the Uncircumcision" and "Gentiles in the flesh." On the other hand, he names a second group "the so-called Circumcision" (2:11, 12). Altogether, he uses terminology that distances him from both groups, fostering a third superordinate identity.[71] In 2:14–15, we learn that Christ "is our peace," phrasing that echoes Israel's traditions in Isaiah 52:7 and 57:19 that are reused later in Ephesians. These traditions evoke the conceptualization of shalom from the Hebrew scriptures and communicate the *nature* of the harmony between Jews and Gentiles envisaged for the church (2:17; 4:3; 6:15). "Peace" certainly refers to the absence of war[72] but also includes a positive concern for safety and security,[73] healing, comfort, good health,[74] positive good,[75] abundance, and fruitfulness.[76] It involves vertical righteousness and harmony between humanity and God[77] and horizontal justice and harmony among peoples doing good to one another.[78] More importantly, because the epistle describes Christ as our peace and refers to the bond of peace later in 4:3, it becomes apparent that the word "peace" functions to sum up God's entire work of convening and gathering up the cosmos in Christ.

In other words, Christ is the glue that holds this new entity together and in whom God creates a third group, a human group with a superordinate identity inhabiting the space of a new third race in a Jewish-Christian socio-relational map.[79] Thus, these verses with 3:3–6 represent a partial fulfillment of God's

---

71. Lincoln, *Ephesians*, 135–36.
72. Judg. 6:23; Jer. 14:13; Mic. 3:5; 1 Macc. 7:28.
73. Isa. 32:17; 52:7; Ezek. 38:11; 39:26.
74. 1 Sam. 25:5–6; Isa. 57:19; Jer. 8:15; 14:13.
75. Ps. 33:15; Jer. 8:15; 14:13.
76. Ps. 121:6–8; Isa. 27:5–6; 32:17; Zech. 8:12.
77. Isa. 48:18; 52:7; 54:10; Ezek. 37:26.
78. Pss. 27:3; 121:6–8; Isa. 54:13; Jer. 36:7; Ezek. 13:10; 34:29; 39:26; 3 Macc. 6:27.
79. For more on third race dynamics in Pauline theology, see Sechrest, *Former Jew*. For

plan to unify the cosmos, as witnessed in Ephesians 1:9 and following.[80] The question we need to ask regarding this superordinate identity is whether it *replaces* the previous ethnic identities—a question that is analogous to the theological question about supersessionism—or whether the author is saying that this new identity is simply added to already existing ones. The scandal of supersessionism, that a superordinate Christian identity and group *replaces* Jews as the people of God, rhymes with the scandalous suggestion that racialized minorities should somehow shed their particular identities in favor of a common "superior" American identity. When we realize that some Whites claim American identity as uniquely belonging to them, we find ourselves deeper in the scandal.

The comments about the status of the law for these Gentiles in Ephesians 2:14–15 may help us reflect on these questions:

A   [14]abolishing the dividing wall,
  B   that is, the hostility between us by his flesh
A   [15]destroying the law of commandments in decrees

The parallelism between "abolishing" and "destroying" suggests a similar correspondence between "dividing wall" and "commandments in decrees." It could be that what is being destroyed is not the whole law but the part of the law that represents hostility between Jews and others. In other words, the destruction of decrees and commandments from within the law is parallel to the abrogation of the antagonism that makes fellowship between Jews and Gentiles difficult. We could read the text as indicating that Christ destroys the causes of hostility in the law. Still, based on the positive references to scripture elsewhere in Ephesians, some of the law's identity-forming elements that preserve distinctiveness remain.[81] Thus, we have something similar to the two-pronged intergroup leadership ideation described above, which both helps cultivate participation in a superordinate identity while also participating, preserving, and emphasizing the distinctive cultural identities of subgroups. Ephesians affirms a new superordinate identity that can be a starting point for

---

an interesting contrasting opinion that Ephesians conceives of the church of Jews and Gentiles in a way that is more Lukan in outlook, see Dahl, "Gentiles, Christians, and Israelites in Ephesians."

80. Best, *Ephesians*, 313; Van Kooten, *Cosmic Christology*, 147–203.

81. Examples of allusions to the OT in Ephesians include: the mention of Israel (2:12); allusions to Isa. 52:7 and 57:19 (2:17); a quotation of Ps. 68 (4:8); references to OT prophecy (3:3–4) and theology (4:6); and a reference to the Divine warrior imagery of Isa. 11:5 (6:14).

more positive intergroup relations, an idea prominent in much evangelical reflection on the text. The author affirms the bonds of community in the super-ordinate new humanity peace in Christ. Likewise, the author goes out of the way to avoid inflammatory, alien, and imposed ethnic labels in 2:11. Yet even with this logic, we must face the fact squarely that while the author affirms Jewish perspectives and the importance of Jewish texts, nowhere does the text acknowledge Gentile identity as we saw earlier in Acts. Indeed, Gentile identity is explicitly disavowed:

> [17] So I'm telling you this, and I insist on it in the Lord: you shouldn't live your life like the Gentiles anymore. They base their lives on pointless thinking, [18] and they are in the dark in their reasoning. They are disconnected from God's life because of their ignorance and their closed hearts. [19] They are peo-ple who lack all sense of right and wrong and who have turned themselves over to doing whatever feels good and to practicing every sort of corruption along with greed. (Eph. 4:17–19 AT)

Nevertheless, with the emphasis on a perfected union in the church across ethnoracial lines depicted in Ephesians 2–3, it is no wonder that this epistle has been a preeminent site of Christian thought on race relations. Reflection on the ancient union of Jews and Gentiles in Christ and present-day ethnic ten-sions in the American experiment can and has been done in a single, tragically oversimplified step, absent of consideration of where the analogs between our times and Ephesians breaks down. Historically, the American experiment in the United States seeks to form a single multi-nation state out of the union of many diverse peoples. When we recognize that nations are much more often the product of a single people occupying a well-defined territory, the sheer hubris of the American experiment becomes clear.[82] Sadly, the initial land grab and rejection of the indigenous peoples in North America in the thirteen original colonies was more in line with the single-people model than the multi-nation state project in which we are now engaged. Remarkably, our union also seeks a government "by the people" in the world's first and oldest con-stitutional democracy. But we must ask, "Who gets to count as 'the people'"? Our history on this front is one in which the ideology of White supremacy has collided dismally, tragically, and often violently in the oppression of people group after people group across the centuries. For all of its beauteous aspira-tions, our history indicates that the United States is not a hospitable nation.

---

82. A. Smith, *Ethnic Origins of Nations.*

It is easy to associate Gentiles who were "estranged from citizenship in Israel" in Ephesians with over four hundred years of oppression of African Americans by slavery and segregation. This phrase also evokes the Trail of Tears and the wholesale genocide of Indigenous peoples stripped of their land and civilization and abandoned on barren reservations. Further, we can associate estrangement in Ephesians with the Chinese Exclusion Act of 1882, followed by the Scott Act of 1888 that made reentry impossible for Chinese immigrants after visiting China. There's also alienation in the renewed Chinese exclusion legislation of 1892 and the new legislation in 1902, which broadened exclusion to cover people from Hawaii and the Philippines. None of these were repealed until 1943. We must also not forget the internment of Japanese Americans during World War II and the forcible deportation in 1954 of hundreds of thousands of Mexicans brought in to fill American labor shortages alongside many Mexican American citizens caught up in the dragnet of Operation Wetback. All of this only sets the stage for present-day raging hostility toward undocumented short and long-term Mexican immigrants and their Mexican American children in families displaced by the economic fallout from the North American Free Trade Act. How can we read about "strangers to the covenants of promise" and fail to think about these broken treaties and broken promises, along with the exclusion of such peoples from the New Deal legislation enacting the Social Security program? These peoples were excluded from unions, from the benefits of FHA secured loans, and from the GI Bill benefits that together helped create the American *White* middle class.

Even with these assonances, we must avoid a facile collapse that moves too quickly between the biblical text and the contemporary situation, regarding either our thinking about US society or our ideal for churches or congregations. There are far too many differences between the United States and the recipients of Ephesians to gloss over, including the uncomfortable fact that Ephesians doesn't address the complexities of life in diverse communities in antiquity any more than it addresses multiethnic/multicultural churches in the United States.[83] A well-meaning desire to "follow the Bible" can be harmful without a thoughtful and disciplined method for reconciling these two narratives. In my judgment, these gaps are evident in many of the forward-looking and well-meaning attempts at integration that I have seen in some evangelical multiethnic megachurches amid the radical population diversity in southern

83. DeYoung et al., *United by Faith*, 74; Emerson and Smith, *Divided by Faith*; Shelton and Emerson, *Blacks and Whites in Christian America*.

California.[84] These churches would boast significant populations of minority subgroups in the congregation with one or two minority leaders on the pastoral staff. But as these staff members would privately admit, the power in those churches was inevitably held by White leaders and a dominant White ethos and culture prevailed overall. In other words, these churches were multiethnic in representational terms regarding the bodies gathered, but not multi- or intercultural in terms of the dominance of White cultural norms. Indeed, this last point is one way this situation does rhyme with the power dynamics in Ephesians in that the epistle affirms Jewish perspectives and Jewish texts, but it deliberately disaffirms Gentile/minority culture.

And this is terrain that I understand firsthand as I take a moment to describe my own well-meaning commitment to this phantom ideal manifest in years of trying to integrate White spaces and naively, take on White supremacist normativity on my back. I have stories about attending White churches with my husband and two daughters for months and becoming a "member" only to be greeted time after time as visitors. I am intimately acquainted with the tokenism that never had my comfort in mind, but which allowed the White members around me to congratulate themselves on their open-mindedness. I remember the day I spent in a White United Methodist congregation when the congregation celebrated the bluegrass music that made my flight-or-fight survival instincts swamp my front cortex. I remember my jaundiced eye the last time I ventured into these spaces with even a modicum of interest in participating in this endeavor. I remember watching with revulsion the tender, gentle, *weak* attempts of Black leaders in a multiethnic evangelical megachurch to explain African American anguish in the aftermath of the police lynching of Michael Brown. I remember my sense of betrayal when I saw those efforts ultimately abandoned in the wake of the unspoken but ever-present pressure to maintain the White comfort that made this particular multiethnic congregation possible.

After over a decade of working alongside students trying to do analogical reasoning about the Ephesian ideal of the diverse church congregation, I've concluded that it is misguided and oppressive for Blacks and other marginalized peoples to try to live out this ideal in twenty-first-century American churches where White majorities prevail.[85] No other topic generated as much

---

84. Smietana, "Efrim Smith"; Garces-Foley, "Multiethnic Congregations"; Goodrich, "Multiracial Congregations."

85. For more on the value of segregation for the health and well-being of the Black church tradition see Riggs, "Socio-Religious Ethical Tradition," 130.

heat in class discussions as when well-meaning Whites and other earnest evangelicals of color insisted on a biblical mandate for integrated churches from Ephesians. For their part, some immigrants and different Blacks launched vivid and compelling descriptions about the life-sustaining role of segregated, non-White ethnic churches, of how they help constituents survive in a patently and perennially hostile and sometimes murderous American society. These debates highlighted the difficulties that the multicultural church faces: lopsided racial power dynamics; White fragility; clash of worship styles and music choices; passive and aversive racism; cultural assumptions about parenting; and more.[86] It is oppressive to try to guilt Christians into participation in multiethnic churches when these churches put the burden of integration on the victims of the racist divide in the American church instead of on the White majority where it properly belongs. I still believe in and long for the Beloved Community ideal, but as we shall see below, this is an ideal that is considerably more complicated in the flesh.

Leaders as Ligaments (Ephesians 4:1–16)

[1]Therefore I beg you as a prisoner in the Lord, to live in a manner that is worthy of God's call. [2]With all humility, gentleness, and patience—that is, lovingly being patient with each other— [3]earnestly keep the unity of the Spirit in the Peace that is the unifying bond. . . .

[7]Grace is given to each one of us according to the measure of the gift of Christ. [8]Therefore, scripture says, "When he ascended to the heights, he captured prisoners; he gave gifts to humanity." [9]What does the phrase "he ascended" mean but that he had also descended to the lower parts, that is, the earth? [10]Christ, the one who descended, is also the one who ascended far above all the heavens so that he could fill all things.

[11]It is Christ who gives the gifts of apostles, prophets, evangelists, and pastoral teachers to the church. [12]They are given for repair work among the saints so that saints may do the work of serving and building up the body of Christ. [13]These leaders work until we all arrive at the unity of faith and knowledge of the son of God, to mature adulthood, to be fully grown into the full stature of Christ. [14]He gives these gifts, these leaders, that we might no longer be infants who are tossed about here and there, being carried away by every doctrine in the wind, by human capriciousness, or by scheming and deceitful craftiness. [15]But speaking the truth in love, let us grow in every way

86. DeYoung et al., *United by Faith.*

into him who is the head of the church, that is into Christ. [16]From him, the whole body produces the growth of the body toward its edification in love. The body is fitted and held together by what each provided ligament supplies, according to each part's functioning capacity. (Eph. 4:1–3, 7–16 AT)

Most think of Ephesians as composed of two halves, the first section focused on theological reflection and the second on ethical paraenesis, with a hinge connecting the two parts in 4:1–6. Though it is difficult to discern the occasion and purpose of this epistle, the two halves of Ephesians 1–3 and 4–6 are nonetheless intimately and obviously connected.[87] How the church relates to Christ and how its members relate to each other are the themes that unify the work. A long ethical section begins after the bridge in 4:1–6, and in 4:7–16, the author discusses the origin and function of church leaders. After that follows a series of general exhortations about conduct directed toward all believers stretching from 4:17–5:17. These appeals are loosely connected as a discourse, but interspersed throughout is a literary pattern that pairs positive and negative commands together: "Be angry but do not sin" (4:26); "Put away . . . all bitterness and wrath . . . and be kind to one another" (4:31–32); "Do not get drunk with wine, for that is debauchery; but be filled with the Spirit" (5:18).

A more unified paraenetic section called the Household Code (abbreviated HT, i.e., *Haustafeln*) starts at 5:18 and ends at 6:9. A literary form common in Greek and Roman philosophy and Hellenistic Judaism, the HT seems to have emerged as an amalgamation of several earlier literary forms like Stoic duty lists, Hellenistic philosophical propaganda, and traditional Jewish instruction, all of which were concerned with ordering society by addressing moral instruction to the family unit as its most fundamental building block.[88] Yet, it is also true that we must place the relationship between the three household pairs addressed in this unit in the broad context of the patronage system, which ordered social life in Greco-Roman society. Since household relationships were viewed as the foundation of the political system, these moral instructions were as political as they were religious-ethical.[89] Ancient authors such as Plato and the Stoics often saw an analogy between the household and the city or the state

---

87. Best, *Ephesians*, 64.

88. Westfall, "This Is a Great Metaphor!," 563.

89. According to Slater, the family was considered the cornerstone of Roman society, where the entire empire was conceived as a family with the emperor as the imperial father (Slater, *Ephesians*, 29–30). The Christian Household Code in Ephesians thus participates in common moral rhetoric, with distinctive emphases on humility and the Christian's responsibilities to those of lower social status.

so that, as DeSilva observes, the household represented a kind of microcosm of society's structures.[90] Since the patron or the benefactor in the relationship, the husband, represents rulers and the mighty who hold power in the relationship, we can say that the HT is thus addressed to household leaders, at least one section of which urges them to imitate Christ (5:25–26, 29).[91] In other words, the ethical section of Ephesians both begins and ends with a focus on leadership in the context of an ethnically mixed social group, even if only an imagined mixed congregation. The final exordium in 6:10–20 on spiritual warfare returns to themes from the beginning of the work and offers summative reflection for leaders on appropriating God's power for the sake of the group.

Ephesians 4:1–16 has two major sections. The beginning in 4:1–6 contains the exhortation to live in a manner worthy of God's purposes for the church in light of the great doctrines of the church. The second section in 4:7–16 explores the source and purpose of leaders, depicted as Christ's gifts to humanity and the church.[92] Together, 4:1–6, with its appeal to live worthy of God's call to unity, and 4:7–16, with its instructions about how leaders and believers work together, set the framework for 4:17–6:9, which discusses how members should interact in God's household.

Though we will focus more particularly on 4:7–16, a word or two is in order about the tone set in 4:1–6 that also permeates the entire latter half of Ephesians. Ephesians 4:2–3 especially sets the tone for the long section on Christian ethics, emphasizing humility, gentleness, and love. As a result of having been rooted and grounded in Christ's love (3:17–19), the emphasis in chapter 4 now shifts to focus on the love that believers must show each other.

---

90. DeSilva, *Honor, Patronage, Kinship and Purity*, 21, 180; Westfall, "This Is a Great Metaphor!," 565–66; Balch, "Household Codes," 61–62.

91. Westfall, "This Is a Great Metaphor!," 567.

92. John M. G. Barclay's magisterial exploration of the notion of "gift" in biblical and Second Temple literature (*Paul and the Gift*) provides a useful framework for evaluating the language of "gift" in Ephesians, which would include both the word "grace" (χάρις) and the word "gift" (δωρεά), both used in 4:7. The discourse in Ephesians explores many of the "perfections" of grace mentioned in Barclay's framework, but not all of them. In Ephesians grace has the following properties: superabundance (1:3, 6–8; 2:7); singularity/ benevolence (2:4–7); incongruity regarding the indiscriminate nature of the gift (2:5); and efficacy (3:7–8). In addition, there are also hints about the temporal priority of Christ's gift, inasmuch as 4:7–10 links the giving of gifts with the resurrection. On the other hand, the author does not stress the non-circularity (i.e., the lack of an expectation of reciprocity) of these gifts, for even though they have been lavished on sinners, the author clearly expects good works to be offered to God as a fitting response to God's gift (2:8–10; 4:12).

With an emphasis on speaking truth to one another in love within the church (4:15, 25), members are to bear with one another in love (4:2) and build up one another in love (4:16). Members are to be kind, tenderhearted, selfless, and forgiving to one another in imitation of Christ (4:32). The emphasis on humility is both countercultural in the New Testament period and today's stereotypes of leaders as heroic saviors who sweep in and restore order.[93] In the New Testament writings, humility is linked with powerlessness[94] and communal values[95] and is the antithesis of the agentic behavior we described early in this chapter.[96] "Humble" has both servile and nonassertive connotations and may be the quality that best prevents the destruction of the community from unchecked privilege. It is not *necessarily* associated with self-abasement or low self-esteem, but it does promote a consideration for others that places their interests before one's own.[97]

On the other hand, words associated with humility are derogatory in Greek culture since elites despised the habit of servility. As such, this emphasis may have been surprising for the Gentile readers of Ephesians.[98] The Community Rule at Qumran also stresses these communal virtues using similar themes as found in Ephesians. The mention of money and Gentile proselytes in column five of the Community Rule may imply that these sectarians knew well that this emphasis was countercultural and counterintuitive for Gentile converts:

> This is the rule for the men of the Yaḥad who volunteer to repent from all evil and to hold fast to all that He, by His goodwill, has commanded. . . . They are to come together as one with respect to Law and wealth. . . . They are to practice truth together with humility, charity, justice, lovingkindness, and modesty in all their ways. Accordingly, none will continue in a willful heart and thus be seduced, not by his heart, neither by his eyes nor yet by his lower nature. Together they shall circumcise the foreskin of this nature, this stiff

---

93. Again, from the 2016 presidential campaign we could juxtapose Hillary Clinton's campaign motto "Stronger Together" with an iconic line from Donald Trump's speech at the Republican National Convention: "I alone can fix it."

94. Luke 1:52; Acts 20:19.

95. Phil. 2:3; James 1:9; cf. 1QS II, 24–25.

96. For more on the theme of humility in womanist interpretation of the Gospel of Matthew, see Sechrest, "Humbled among the Nations," 299.

97. 1 Cor. 10:24; Phil. 2:4; cf. 1 Cor. 13:4–5.

98. Best, *Ephesians*, 362; Slater, *Ephesians*, 29–30. Note the words with the ταπει* Greek root in Col. 2:18, 23; 3:12; cf. Prov. 18:12 [LXX] and Epictetus, *Discourses* 3.24.56.

neck, and so establish a foundation of truth for Israel—that is to say, for the Yaḥad of the Eternal Covenant. They are to atone for all those in Aaron who volunteer for holiness, and for those in Israel who belong to truth, and for Gentile proselytes who join them in community. (1QS V, 1–6)[99]

Thus, the ethics in Ephesians is profoundly relational and at home in a Jewish milieu. Indeed, to the extent that the hortatory section begins (4:7–16) and ends (5:21–6:9) with a focus on leadership, we might say that the leadership ethics in Ephesians reflects a relational and communal emphasis that rhymes with today's so-called feminine leadership styles. As contemporary leadership theory shifts to focus on leading teams, there is far more emphasis on relational capacities and collaboration as effective leadership strategies for both men and women, even amid stereotyped folk expectations that women are warmer and more collaborative than men who are more task-oriented and individualistic.[100] It is interesting that in Ephesians, Christian leaders are gifts to the whole human race in 4:8 ("he gave gifts to humanity")[101] notwithstanding a focus on the church in 4:11–16, an idea that coheres with the conception that the genre of the HT carries political implications for society as well as the direct appeal to the family. Thus the ecclesiology of this epistle is as sweeping in its vision for the cosmos as is its Christology.

Turning our attention now to 4:7–16, we can see that several issues can be illuminated by attending to the intertextuality in Ephesians 4:8 with Psalm 68:18 [67:19 LXX] and the citation's role in this part of Ephesians.[102] Many ancient

---

99. Wise et al., *The Dead Sea Scrolls*, 122.

100. Rice, "Collaboration and Leadership," 128.

101. The translation of τοῖς ἀνθρώποις in Eph. 4:8 is fairly evenly divided between the English phrases "to his people" (NRSV, NIV, NLT) and the more categorical idea of "to people/humanity/men" (CEB, RSV, NET, NASB). While the former seems to fit the focus on the church in the immediately preceding and succeeding paragraphs, the latter makes this christological statement in this verse match with the cosmic reach of the Christology that pervades the entire epistle.

102. The relationship between Ps. 68:18 and Eph. 4:8 is more apparent in the Greek than in English translations:

Ps. 68:18 [67:19 LXX]
You ascended on high; you led captivity captive; you received gifts by a man
ἀνέβης εἰς ὕψος ᾐχμαλώτευσας αἰχμαλωσίαν ἔλαβες δόματα ἐν ἀνθρώπῳ
Eph. 4:8
When he ascended to the heights, he captured prisoners; he gave gifts to humanity
ἀναβὰς εἰς ὕψος ᾐχμαλώτευσεν αἰχμαλωσίαν, ἔδωκεν δόματα τοῖς ἀνθρώποις.

Jewish and Christian authors, including those who wrote the New Testament writings, did not operate with modern sensibilities about verbatim quotation and slavish attention to the original context of the Old Testament texts. Likewise, our author freely interacts with the Septuagint—the Greek version of the Hebrew Bible—to undergird his argument while also adapting the psalm for this new setting, in effect finding the rhyme between Scripture and the theological needs of his day.[103] Psalm 68 depicts God taking booty from the rebellious nations who have illegally camped on Mt. Zion as God ascends, in effect clearing the holy mountain of the rebellious squatter nations so that God may resume dwelling among the faithful in the holy city. But this message has been reworked in Ephesians 4:8–10 to tell a new story about Jesus's interaction with the church. First, there is a change in the *dramatis personae*: in Ephesians, the focus is on Christ instead of the psalmist's focus on God. Second, in Ephesians, the prisoners are the Powers instead of the rebellious nations in the psalm.[104] Third, there is a change of venue: instead of God's ascent up Mt. Zion in Psalm 68, in Ephesians Christ ascends into the heavenly realm after the resurrection, as 4:9–10 makes clear. Fourth, instead of taking tribute *from* the peoples (i.e., the nations) as in Psalm 68, here Christ is giving gifts *to* humanity. Fifth, the author of Ephesians removes the part of the original verse that shows God dwelling on Mt. Zion in the aftermath of victory over the nations. In Ephesians, a new metaphor emerges that depicts Christ filling up the entire cosmos, from earth to heaven in 4:9–10, and especially manifest in the church through the blending of anatomical and architectural imagery in 4:16.

The surrounding verses give more information about the nature and recipients of the gifts that Christ dispenses. Ephesians 4:7 tells us that Christ gives gifts to all believers ("each one of us") and uses an expression ("according to the measure")[105] that elsewhere suggests that gifts are bequeathed in differing amounts or levels of intensity. In other words, each person must exercise the gift in a way that corresponds to the extent of the donation. In 4:9–10, we see an explanatory gloss that insists that the person who descends is the same person who ascended and thus provides a scriptural referent for the idea that God begins to fill up the cosmos in Christ.[106] But in 4:11, the focus shifts from attention to the gifts that "each one" receives to a focus on the church that

---

103. For more on how authors of the New Testament interact with Scripture see Hays, *Echoes of Scripture in the Letters of Paul*; Hays, *Echoes of Scripture in the Gospels*.

104. Lincoln, *Ephesians*, 243.

105. Cf. Matt. 25:15; Rom. 12:3, 6. On gifts given in varying amounts "according to the measure" in 4:7, see Slater, *Ephesians*, 109–10.

106. Van Kooten, *Cosmic Christology*, 185–86.

obtains the leaders—the apostles, prophets, evangelists, and pastoral teachers—whom Christ gives as gifts. Many understand the naming of these gifts as the naming the various leadership offices in the church in a particularly agentic understanding of leadership.

Yet this agentic prism is complicated in the following lines. Verse 12 describes the function of these leaders in relation to the rest of the body in three prepositional clauses. The first clause, "for repair work among the saints,"[107] gives the divine purpose served by the gift of the leaders. The two subsequent parallel clauses in 4:12 illuminate the work of a unified body of saints, including leaders and saints: together they are to serve through doing [good] work (cf. 2:10: "created in Christ Jesus for good works"). Christ gives the leaders to collaborate in the function of building up the body in love (cf. 4:16: "the *whole body* produces the growth of the body towards its edification in love"). The word I translate "repair work"[108] in 4:12 appears as "equip" in the NRSV and is rare in the New Testament though cognate words appear here and there in biblical literature.[109] The term may refer to training or discipline, though here I suggest, it has the idea of "restoration" as in setting a bone, an idea that applies an anatomical twist to the architectural metaphor.[110] Thus Christ-appointed leaders function to repair the breaks in the body of Christ, that is, to repair any fissures occurring in the group and collaborate in the work of serving and building the social body in love.

Following the three clauses in verse 12 are a new set of three clauses in verse 13 that specify the goals for the ministry of church leaders. They are to work:

1. until the church attains the unity of faith and the knowledge of Christ (εἰς τὴν ἑνότητα τῆς πίστεως καὶ τῆς ἐπιγνώσεως τοῦ υἱοῦ τοῦ θεοῦ)
2. until the church attains to full-grown maturity (lit. "attains to the perfect man") (εἰς ἄνδρα τέλειον)
3. until the church reaches the full stature of Christ (εἰς μέτρον ἡλικίας τοῦ πληρώματος τοῦ Χριστοῦ).

Because the first and last of these three clauses explicitly mentions Christ, it is likely that the clause in the middle also has Christ in mind when it talks

---

107. "For repair work among the saints" is my translation of πρὸς τὸν καταρτισμὸν τῶν ἁγίων in 4:12.

108. "Repair work": καταρτισμός.

109. Ezra 4:13, 16; 5:3, 9 [LXX]; Matt. 4:21 (par. Mark 1:19); 2 Cor. 13:9, 11; Gal. 6:1.

110. See Liddell-Scott (s.v. καταρτισμός).

about reaching the measure of the "perfect man."[111] In addition, it may be that the use of a word that refers to males,[112] especially in this middle clause, subtly anticipates the discourse in 5:21–6:9. The culturally loaded HT section in 5:21–6:9 offers a Christian adaptation of a literary form generally associated with instructing wealthy men to manage the home and fulfill their duties as citizens.[113] In keeping with the associative reasoning in chapter 1, analogical appropriation of the biblical imagery for leaders means extending leadership roles across gender, sexual orientation, or sexual expression, despite the masculine language here.[114] Nevertheless, the use of "male" (ἀνήρ) in 4:12c in this ancient cultural context of patriarchal leadership is a textual detail that reinforces the idea that leadership is broadly in view in both 4:11–16 as it is later in the HT sections. In true womanist fashion, verses 12–13 say that leaders should inspire us to "act grown," that is, to renounce childishness and double-mindedness. Leaders should encourage us to know for ourselves what is true and good and remind each of us of the irreplaceable and indomitable grace bestowed on each of us by God.[115] Black leaders should also renounce a Du Boisian double-consciousness and help their communities see themselves through God's eyes, and not through the deceptions propagated by any who would demean their human dignity.[116]

Verses 15–16 return us to a wide-angle perspective that shows how leaders and individual saints cooperate in the health and vitality of the church as the body of Christ. With a dual emphasis on the responsibilities of the members as well as leaders, Ephesians 4:16 says that the overall body is fitted and held together by ligaments that do the particular function of binding the parts of the

---

111. "Perfect man": ἄνδρα τέλειον.

112. "Males": ἄνδρα.

113. See 4:12c: "to the mature man [ἄνδρα]." Cf. the phrase "act like men" (ἀνδρίζεσθε) in 1 Cor. 16:13 (NASB). See also Best, *Ephesians*, 401–2. For more on the HT, see Muddiman, *Ephesians*, 203; cf. Schnackenburg, *Ephesians*, 184, who thinks that the maturity in view here is not gendered.

114. See the analysis of 1 Timothy 2 in chapter 1 for another discussion about analogical correlations involving ancient, gendered discourse, an analysis that would be especially important for associations involving the Household Code in Ephesians.

115. So says womanist interpreter Layli Maparyan: "In other words, we should know—of our own knowledge, and not just by received knowledge—what is true and good, and we should stick to it, as the true and good is what will transform us into saints. Does this not sound like Alice Walker's (1984) womanist—'Responsible. In charge. Serious. . . . Always wanting to know more and in greater depth than is considered "good" for one'?" See Maparyan, "Miracles and Gifts," 336.

116. Du Bois, *Black Folk*, 45. Also see note 25 on p. 172 above.

body together.[117] The symbolic interpretation of the ligaments in 4:16 as the leaders Christ gives to the church makes sense of the imagery in the surrounding verses. The author interweaves discussion of the many individual saints in the body (e.g., "each one of us" in 4:7; "we" and "we all" in 4:13–14) with logical connections to 4:11–14, which describe leaders as equipping, serving, and building up the church. These leaders work for the church for as long as it takes to see the church reach full maturity, preventing perpetual immaturity and thus stabilizing the whole edifice (cf. οἰκοδομή in 4:12, 16).

Imagery drawn from Colossians 2:19b (lit. "through the joints and ligaments *being supplied*") is more ambiguous in Ephesians 4:16 (lit. "ligament *of supply*").[118] The ambiguity raises questions about whether we should understand Ephesians as stating that Christ is supplying these leaders as special binding body parts, as is evident in Colossians, or whether somehow the leader-ligaments provide assistance of some kind. Two major interpretations of the phrase "ligament of supply" emerge in the standard English versions of the Bible. Some versions choose the phrase "the supporting ligament"[119] in translating the Greek, while another version uses the phrase "the ligament being supplied."[120] In other words, some interpretations stress the work that the ligament does, while another, echoing Colossians, underscores the fact that the ligament is given as a gift.

On the one hand, the preference for the idea "supporting ligament" makes good sense of the context. The danger of instability depicted in 4:14 comports with the somatic metaphor developed here in 4:16. In this reading, the ligaments help provide stability for the body and prevent individual bones or members from spinning off, presumably because of stormy conditions or trickery (4:14). On the other hand, the idea that the ligaments are gifts is also in the context of this passage, especially clear in 4:8, 11.[121] Verses 4:11–13 show that a

117. Some versions of 4:16 identify these body parts literally as "joints" (NASB, NJB, KJV) though other versions use the word "ligaments" (NRSV, CEB, NET, TNIV) because this word better captures contemporary understanding about the body parts that function to connect bones and provide stability for the human skeleton.

118. Col. 2:19b: "through the joints and ligaments being supplied" (διὰ τῶν ἁφῶν καὶ συνδέσμων ἐπιχορηγούμενον) versus Eph. 4:16: "ligament of supply" (ἁφῆς τῆς ἐπιχορηγίας).

119. Major English versions that choose the objective genitive interpretation, "the supporting ligament" or "that which the ligament supplies" are the CEB, NASB, NET, NIV, NJB, and NKJV.

120. The only major English version choosing the interpretation "ligament being supplied" is the NRSV.

121. The lack of ambiguity in Colossians derives mostly from the different syntax there ("through the ligaments being supplied"; διὰ τῶν ἁφῶν . . . ἐπιχορηγούμενον) but could

Col. 2:19	Eph. 4:16
Line 1	*Line 1*
From whom the whole body,	From whom the whole body,
Line 2	*Line 2*
being supplied and held together by the joints and ligaments,	being fitted and being held together by what every provided ligament supplies.
Line 3	*Line 3*
grows with a growth which is from God.	According to the working at capacity of each one of the parts, the whole body produces the growth of the body for the edification of itself in love.
In Colossians God gives ligaments to provide structure; God provides the growth	In Ephesians Christ gives ligaments to provide structure and supply assistance; the body produces growth

Figure 7.1. Comparison of Colossians 2:19 and Ephesians 4:16

major thrust in the section is that Christ gives the gift of leaders to the church to promote stability, repel deceit and trickery, and foster unity. Hence this may be the rare occasion in which both interpretive trajectories are affirmed by the context and warranted by the underlying grammar (see figure 7.1).[122] The ligaments are given first as gifts and second as assistance and support to the body. Yet, lest we lose sight of the cooperative thrust of this verse, 4:16 insists that while *stability and support* come from the ministry of leaders given as gifts, *growth* is a function of the whole church where each member operates according to their own giftedness (cf. 4:7). Further, even as this vision calls for Christ-given leaders who work for the church, it also insists that leaders do

still be supported by the grammar in Eph. 4:16. On the other hand, Ephesians uses a genitive noun phrase (ἀφῆς τῆς ἐπιχορηγίας; 4:16) rather than a passive voice construction using a verbal cognate as in Colossians (διὰ τῶν ἀφῶν καὶ συνδέσμων ἐπιχορηγούμενον; 2:19). The "ligament being supplied" interpretation is still possible here in Eph. 4:16 via the subjective genitive interpretation (see notes 119 and 120 above).

122. For more on this "plenary genitive" interpretation, that is, where both subjective and objective genitive interpretations are warranted, see Wallace, *Greek Grammar*, 119–20.

good for the whole cosmos and all humanity even beyond their direct duties to the church (4:8; cf. 1:23; 3:10, 15).

Thus 4:1–16 flows out of a description of the church as the first act in God's work of creating order in the cosmos by unifying all things under Christ (1:10, 23). Further, the church is to bear witness to that unity (2:13–16; 3:10). The passage also reveals something about how God empowers the church in Christ to maintain unity. While God gives grace to each Christian in the body's pursuit of full maturity in Christ, we also saw in Ephesians 1 that God gives power to the church. In this passage, we learn that such power, at least in part, takes the form of leaders who exercise influence to maintain the unity of the body, an action that, in turn, empowers the growth and work of the body.

A vision latent in this text highlights plural leadership by concentrating on the metaphor of leaders as ligaments that bind and connect the members of the body to each other. This vision is inspiring given today's need for leaders who can operate as binding agents in a hopelessly fractured and tangled polis. There are between 260 and 270 different skeletal parts in the human body, each bound together with ligaments in combinations that allow a myriad of physiological functions to operate freely. Just as hundreds of ligaments in the body bind and connect the parts together, so too do leaders need to come in bundles. In contrast to ideas about leadership that commonly construct the leader as a heroic figure who "alone can fix it," at its best, sophisticated leadership theory invites leaders into nurturing group accomplishments in pursuing shared goals. We can insist that the theological version of leadership that is normed in Ephesians conceives of leadership as an inherently plural and variegated activity, one that can't be envisioned apart from deep, intimate, and organic relationships to all the parts of the body through a variety of kinds of leaders. The more the body needs either movement or stability, the more multiple and variegated ligaments need to facilitate motion or steadiness. Leadership in Ephesians is fundamentally about holding the body together and supplying whatever is required to maintain connections between different parts of the body—it is not a leadership vision wherein leaders seek to maximize their own ends. With the sheer number of connections between subgroups and individuals that modern leaders need to sustain in contemporary society, this analogy becomes a powerful metaphor for how God calls Christian leaders to hold the body's shape. When groups of leaders function this way, the church can manifest the pluriform manifold wisdom of God among all the families and ethnicities on earth, thereby achieving the mission of demonstrating the power and glory of God to all the spiritual powers of White supremacy (cf. 3:8–15 CEB).

With our more precise understanding of the human body and the different ways that ligaments function, the ancient metaphor packs an even more potent punch. For instance, if we were to adapt knee ligaments as a leadership metaphor, then we might say that leaders function as the connective tissue of the body of Christ, providing flexibility and agility. This imagery is reminiscent of Rosabeth Moss Kanter's advice that "leaders must not let differences harden" among those they lead.[123] While ligaments are essential for maintaining the stability of the joint while it is in motion, they also specifically prevent unwanted and potentially damaging movement. This agentic imagery recalls the teaching in Ephesians that leader-ligaments provide the kind of strength that resists the winds of false teaching and heresy and keeps the body from being buffeted and tossed about by waves of trickery, craftiness, and error. The metaphor of leaders as ligaments allows free movement of the body while also holding the shape of the skeleton, preventing bones from falling away from each other permanently. The leader-ligaments of Ephesians have the strength to call out racism, sexism, and all other phobias that weaken the connections between peoples. But, critically, the leader-ligaments are only effective to the extent that each member contributes their giftedness toward the growth of the whole. We are only as strong together as is the strength of our weakest link.

Yet, the body imagery above, while helpful, is not without its problems. The ideal society in antiquity wasn't one in which the evils of discrimination, inequality, and structural racism were nonexistent. For the ancients, the ideal society was one in which the powerful were free to pursue their interests unhindered by everyday concerns.[124] This section implicitly recognizes that the community is comprised of both the powerful and the powerless, and that Christ gives gifts to both kinds of people in the church, though in varying amounts. Yet here we see that Christ gives these separate and different gifts for the same set of aims. Contrary to much modern discourse about unity, this epistle does not envisage equality or sameness as a byproduct of unity. Instead, the discourse is about how those who are more and less powerful should act together in a way that preserves unity.

On the other hand, the ideal society in antiquity was rigidly deterministic, and metaphors that liken society to the body envision a structure in which the poor and marginalized in society forever remain so, placed just so in the body to sustain embedded and enduring hierarchies. In other words, the somatic imagery works both ways in this text, both promoting the harmony of the

123. Kanter, "Creating Common Ground."
124. Neutel, *Cosmopolitan Ideal.*

variegated whole and preserving the determinism embedded in the organic ordering of the body. So rather than focusing on deterministic and unequal apportionments and a lopsided concentration of power that surely saturated the society envisioned by this author, I choose to shift from body imagery to network imagery. Rather than imagining a body where each part is fixed in its relation to others, the metaphor of a network still envisions connection without the implications for rigid and permanently placed nodes. Instead, a network involves connections that can be made and remade as needed.

In addition, the "unity of knowledge" to which leaders aspire, as suggested by the text, will be far more challenging than what our ancient author could have imagined. The original passage may well have envisioned leaders as guarding against damage to the Christian community from external frameworks rather than from diverse perspectives *about* Christianity from within plural forms of Christianity as is the case today. The level of diversity within the Christian confession alone eclipses that envisioned by this author, even accounting for the already diverse group of early Judaisms in that context, not to mention the complex religious pluralism in contemporary US society. The perspective of dividing the world into Jews and Gentiles was always more complicated on the ground than it was philosophically. Even then, "Gentile" was an identity construction that collapsed a myriad of non-Jewish identities, analogous, you might say, to ethnic categories like "Asian" or "Hispanic." As one Korean Canadian friend put it, "Asia" cannot be found on the ground in the Far East—residents of China or South Korea or Japan would typically self-identify in those terms. Indeed, ethnic categories that erase particularity among different national and regional identities also apply for Hispanics and Blacks, including Afro-Caribbeans, a plethora of first- and second-generation African or South American immigrants, and the native-born descendants of the African slavery in North America. Today it might be better to say that a lack of diverse perspectives is more of a mark of *immaturity* in Christian circles than its opposite.

Networked Ligamental Leadership for the Inclusive Church

At stake in this chapter is the question about what the exercise of leadership power looks like in our society, especially among Christians who follow a crucified Savior. Our times require a vision of leadership that can reckon with the winds of demographic change that are buffeting our society. No longer can we put off the centuries-long overdue reckoning regarding our racialized history. Today, leaders need androgynous leadership capacities that include a facility with intergroup politics and group social dynamics as never before. Leaders need to model favorable relations with out-groups and promote enough of a shared group identity to focus group energies positively. One of the biggest obstacles for leadership concerns fears about loss of status that enflame Whites contemplating the idea that they will transition from being the majority group to being the largest minority group. Adding to the volatile mix are the long-standing and repeatedly validated fears of minority groups that their interests are illegitimate when stacked against Whites' interests. The best leaders today must navigate this terrain while promoting missional objectives. Rather than "heroic" leaders who go it alone or "power through" problems with domination or manipulation, leaders inside and outside of the Christian movement need to focus on the health and well-being of the group rather than on what benefits the individual leader.

I read Ephesians as offering reflection on similar problems during demographic shifts in the early Christian movement. The author writes to instill among the Gentiles in his audience a sense of confidence in belonging. Even though they find themselves newly minoritized within the fledgling Christian movement, they receive assurance of belonging and gain confidence that God's power will be deployed on their behalf. No longer do they need to worry about dangerous and fearsome spiritual forces buffeting them on all sides. Though magnified and magnificent, God's power in Ephesians does not emerge as a dominating, crushing power. Instead, it is a creative, convening, gathering energy that brings peoples together in Christ, bringing out the new while also conjoining everything in the cosmos. With a strong emphasis on ethical paraenesis, Ephesians has a lot to say about how Christians should behave when they exercise power, tightly linking that activity to the convening, serving, peace-making model provided by Christ. According to our author, leaders are binding agents just like Christ. Through Christ comes a peace that embodies the creation of a new, unified, and superordinate identity on the one hand, along with the shalom that results in healing, harmony, comfort and good health, abundance, and fruitfulness on the other hand. It involves vertical righteousness and harmony between humanity and God and horizontal justice and harmony among peoples, doing good to one another. Exhorting them to remember who they are, the author urges these Christian converts to live out a faith that anticipates the gathering up of all things in Christ and proclaims the glory of God to the universe (1:10, 22; 3:10). The author reminds these communities that the union of Jews and Gentiles in Christ anticipates God's reordering of the cosmos, even or especially in the face of Powers that, in their context, seem to be overwhelming.

We found a rhyme between the frightening spiritual forces of evil in the cosmology of ancient Gentiles and contemporary institutional racism as a set of cultural forces that oppress people of color by disadvantaging them in a myriad of ways: through inhibiting their access to the vote and fairness in the justice system, and through lack of good housing, good jobs, good education, and health care. The ancients sought amulets and magical incantations to gain good material conditions. Today minoritized peoples seek the same security in the face of overwhelming institutional systems crafted to bring and keep bodies of color under social control and quartered in low-paying jobs and low-performing schools. Some Whites, instinctively reckoning that it is better to be in the majority, are recoiling at the prospect of entering these same dismal conditions that are, rhetorically at least, the province of minorities. They, too, fear the swirling forces of unchecked institutions that favor the elite, worried that their crushing weight may be colorblind after all as they fear their own consignment to the margins of low-paying jobs and low-performing schools in a newly emerging but still dominating White minority.

Though addressed to all-male leaders in its historical context, today's leadership ethics in Ephesians 4–6 address leaders of any gender, sex, or orientation. It promotes androgynous strategies encompassing both agentic and relational traits, the so-called masculine and feminine styles. Leaders provide stability and relational networked connectivity that holds the body together in cooperative action as it seeks the missional unity that testifies to the Powers. Leaders have the responsibility to hold societies and groups together and protect them from error and deception, which in turn frees the group to focus its energies on achieving the full maturity of life in Christ. In the final analysis, it is not the agentic leader-ligament that directs the growth and health of the body. Instead, each node in the networked group receives resources and responsibility for their part in pursuing the church's mission. "The whole body produces the growth of the body" (Eph. 4:16 AT) as leader-ligaments tend to the structural integrity of the groups they lead, giving it the best chance to achieve mature growth. The ligaments are both given as gifts and provide assistance and support. In the leadership vision of Ephesians, leaders help hold the shape of the group to maintain its inherent diversity; they help keep the church's energies directed toward its God-given task of bearing witness to evil, oppressive Powers of the glorious, convening, gathering, conjoining power of God. They tell the truth in their God-given responsibilities to help protect the body from deception and error.

There is much in our society that undermines social unity. On the political right is a devotion to colorblindness that undermines the particularity of ethnic group cultures and thus endangers them. On the political left lives a so-called cancel culture that rhetorically penalizes every failure to perfectly embody values in the coalition for justice among the myriad of its members. To conclude our consideration of how the leadership vision in Ephesians rhymes with leadership needs and models today, we focus on truth-telling and exposing deception (4:14–15, 25) as crucial leadership functions. In any era, they help the body avoid "being carried away by every doctrine in the wind, by human capriciousness, or by scheming and deceitful craftiness" (4:14). Here we focus on one of the most pernicious pieces of trickery concerning the deployment of the rhetoric of racial justice in ways that redound against its aspirations and victims.

Now sixty years past the Civil Rights movement, one can frequently find such tactics employed in right-wing political commentary. Most commonly, this strategy involves labeling as racist anyone who is exposing or pointing out racial disparities wherever these disparities manifest. Recalling our conversation about racial projects from chapter 1, we can refute this by pointing out that projects are *racist* whenever they promote racial hierarchy or discrimination and are *anti-racist* whenever they undermine such. Identification of racial inequities does not promote or establish racial hierarchies; it merely calls attention to existing discriminatory outcomes.

On the other hand, a version of this tactic on the political left is less easy to identify, even though it is becoming more common. It happens when activists deploy the rhetoric of civil rights and the language of justice against allies and other marginalized peoples who are pursuing justice. This happens, for instance, when Obama is accused of failing to address racism. However, such critics fail to note that his signature achievement, Obamacare, disproportionately increased healthcare access for people of color, thus addressing some of the most egregious racial disparities in our society. I am not saying that Blacks, females, or other leaders from minoritized communities are exempt from holding prejudices against other people groups. Nor does this observation preclude the possibility that some of these people may promote racist hierarchies, far from it. Supreme Court Justice Clarence Thomas's vote to gut the preclearance protections in the Voting Rights Act that opened up a wave of tactics to suppress Black voters across the country not seen in decades is a clear example of a Black man with power who is promoting and perpetuating racist inequity.[125] However, I am trying to question whether Obama's lapses and Thomas's antics deserve to be characterized with similar rhetoric.

125. Newkirk, "Shelby County v. Holder."

Tensions that fragment coalitions for justice where Blacks and others work together to dismantle White supremacy deserve more attention. My own trajectory as a Black woman emerging from the whiteness of the evangelical movement toward leadership in a liberal mainline seminary illustrates some of these complexities. My early formation in theological education was in an evangelical institution with a faculty and executive leadership team that was 85 percent White and nearly all male. I received many early opportunities to develop my leadership gifts as Whites were indeed cheerfully willing to help me grow as a junior faculty member. Still, I was eventually stymied by a concrete ceiling beyond which my gifts could not take me. By contrast, when I finally received an opportunity to lead, it was at a liberal mainline institution where the faculty is about 55 percent White, the top two executives are females, and half of the vice presidents minoritized. When I first got there, I thought I was in heaven—here was Beloved Community for sure!

But I've since learned that leadership in the Beloved Community is a tricky proposition. It turns out that the White male normativity in my evangelical roots rhymed with some of the gender and racial dynamics in my new progressive mainline Christian setting. Though nearly everyone in my new community had firm commitments to equity and inclusiveness, the optics of justice still varied in the eye of the beholder. Collectively we tended to assume that the shape of justice in a given situation was a fixed and tangible good that would have precise contours that all could affirm. But there were times when the community could not mediate simultaneously among the varying needs for justice from multiple diverse and overlapping marginalized groups. A focus on making sure that we distributed power equitably sometimes resulted in marginalizing people at the intersection of interlocking oppressions. In one episode, ironically, I was excluded from participation in a group of anti-racist activists against my will, not because I had demonstrated any egregious behavior, action, or lack of commitment, but because as a leader I had "too much power to be in the group." Instead of celebrating the power that I could have deployed on behalf of the group's aims, at least rhetorically, the group's message to me was that my presence as a Black female leader made some group members feel unsafe, a reprise of the Angry Black Woman stereotype discussed in chapter 4. At a different moment, international students, often the most marginalized groups in higher education in the United States and especially so in the Trump era, were in frightening and precarious situations on campus. But I found that there were times when the rush to find justice for this group sometimes trampled over Black concerns, falling into the well-worn ruts in American history of trends that privilege newcomers of every hue over native-born Blacks. Yet there was joy in this community too. It was a fragile, holy sign of Beloved Community when the persons who helped our community out of a painful impasse were Black international students who exhibited inspiring intergroup leadership, standing in the breach and holding multiple groups together in dialogue to benefit the whole.

I am not at all suggesting that my diverse leadership team or wonderfully diverse collegium led or lived in tune with the same racist values on display in the Trump presidency or in misogynistic spaces in the church or industry that I'd inhabited before. Nor was the angry White "blacklash" that propelled Donald Trump to the presidency anything like the innovative, praiseworthy, and sustained but imperfect stumbling toward justice in my new community. The truth is I'd rather be in this community that is closer to Beloved Community than just about anywhere else. But I am suggesting that rhetoric about justice can sometimes result in situations where Black voices get subordinated to norms about justice that overlook Black concerns and especially Black female concerns. Outspoken, truth-telling Black female leadership in a diverse community is a complicated affair and is subject to the dangers named earlier in this chapter. This woman will be overscrutinized and subject to the same stereotypes heaped on Black women in other roles. She will be accused of being incompetent if she carefully charts a lower profile as a leader with a more communal leadership style. But she will be demonized as an angry colonizer or accused of being a sellout to Whites if she exercises the agentic behavior that usually brings praise to White men. Worst yet, if she is successful, she may unwittingly, unintentionally, unknowingly be the pivot around which a tragic backlash takes hold, as it did in the wake of our first Black President.

Musings about womanist leadership and the values of truth-telling and networked communities collided with the world outside my office door on May 25, 2020. Who can forget how African American Minneapolis resident George Floyd died while White police officer Derek Chauvin pinned him with a chokehold by kneeling on Floyd's neck for nine minutes, nearly the whole encounter captured on video released in real time. Chauvin was not arrested or charged until four days later. Four days of peaceful protests became violent by night, coinciding with a press conference where prosecutors declined to announce charges against the officers, alluding to mysterious evidence that might exonerate the officers of criminal wrongdoing. Unlike the all-too-frequent and now scripted cycle of police brutality, Black death, and the lack of consequences, this episode happened in the middle of a pandemic disproportionately affecting Blacks and with attendant depression-era levels of unemployment affecting Blacks. The nation was a dry tinderbox, and protestors were not in a mood for patience. Tensions exposed in this incident were compounded by other recent cases of police brutality and White vigilante terrorism.[126] The protestors' chants of "No justice, No peace!" seemed to say it all.[127]

I was intrigued by how civic and government leaders responded to the violence enacted on the margins of the protests, curious about how they would hold the shape of the polis under these extraordinarily stressful circumstances. What does "speaking the truth in love" look like in this context? White, Black, and Brown leaders thrust into the national limelight in those days felt the pressure to decry the looting and rioting, even though the massive protests were 99 percent peaceful. Democratic White male Minnesota governor Tim Walz was plainly sympathetic to the protestors and vilified on the right for it, but insisted that peace had to prevail because "protecting private property is the first priority." After the first night of violent protests, he openly acknowledged the irony of deploying police to respond to rioting about police brutality. Complicating easy answers, he and others noted that "all the protestors arrested so far for violence were from out of state," implying that the violence was being done *to Minneapolis*, not *by Minneapolis*. There were also allegations that White supremacist organizations and foreign actors were taking the opportunity to amplify racial tensions, especially to help portray Black protest as criminal, thuggish, etc. Though he acknowledged the legitimate anger of the protestors and defended their constitutional right to protest, by the third day of rioting, Gov. Walz insisted that continued rioting was "no longer about George Floyd but attacking our society." As I sat glued to news coverage about the protests and the fringe riots, I only once heard someone, in this case Black feminist scholar Brittney Cooper, challenge the growing fixation on property damage versus the need to stay focused on state-sanctioned violence against Blacks.

The massive peaceful multiracial protest went on for weeks and emerged in thirty cities across the United States and in multiple international cities as well. African American mayor and Democrat Keisha Lance Bottoms was leading Atlanta, and her impassioned words as protests targeted property in the area were widely lauded. Having moved swiftly to discipline police committing acts of brutality caught on tape during the protests, she was outraged at the

126. Christian Cooper and the Central Park birdwatching incident: Nir, "Two Lives Collided"; Breonna Taylor and the mistaken no-knock warrant: Oppel et al., "Breonna Taylor's Death"; vigilante lynching of Ahmaud Arbery: Taylor and Vinson, "Ahmaud Arbery."

127. The rallying cry "No justice, No peace!" was first articulated in the protests over the acquittal of four White police officers accused of police brutality in the beating of Rodney King, brutality that had been captured live on video and broadcast nationally. See Baker-Fletcher and Baker-Fletcher, *My Sister, My Brother*, 8.

attacks against property in the Atlanta area. Bottoms's rebuke to the violent protestors went viral as she insisted that Atlanta had a legacy of Black mayors, Black police chiefs, and a thriving base of Black-owned businesses so that any damage was against "our community." Bottoms wanted the violent protestors to go home rather than dishonor the legacy of the Civil Rights movement in Atlanta.[128] Violent attacks against the CNN building and other spaces "honors neither George Floyd nor Martin Luther King, Jr. . . . If you want change in America, go out and register to vote. Show up to the polls on November 10th [*sic*]." I can imagine myself saying similar things if I was in a similar role and probably not as well as she did. Still, while it was a masterful demonstration of what "holding the shape of the body" might look like, I wasn't sure that it was also the kind of truth-telling that would unmask the forces of racism at work in the moment.

For me, the decentralized, networked leadership model of the Black Lives Matter movement was the most generative in the swirling days of the massive protest movement that erupted in summer 2020. More so than ever before seen in my lifetime, young Black leaders best embodied the morally centered, plural, and ligamental leadership envisioned in Ephesians. Author and activist Kimberly Latrice Jones's viral video at the moment eloquently and powerfully unmasked the evils of racism and economic hardship that led to the explosion of protest and violence. She invoked a metaphor of Blacks playing an impossible-to-win 450-year-long Monopoly™ game as enslaved, segregated, abused, and then economically crippled. Her unwillingness to discard either the looters or the protestors was a stunning act of empathy and model of "holding the shape of the body" as she described the historical and economic pressures that bear on the act of looting:

> So, I have obviously seen a lot of things, people making commentary. Interestingly enough, the ones I've noticed who've been making the commentary are wealthy Black people making the commentary: "You should not be rioting. We should not be looting. We should not be tearing up our own communities." And then there's been an argument on the other side: "We should be hitting them in the pocket. We should be focusing on the blackout days where we don't spend money."
>
> But, you know, I feel like we should do both, and I feel like I support both. And I'll tell you why I support both. I support both because when you have a civil unrest like this, there are three types of people in the streets.

128. For video of Bottom's remarks see https://youtu.be/VO7z6m2os2g.

There are the protesters; there are the rioters, and there are the looters. The protesters are there because they actually care about what is happening in the community. They want to raise their voices, and they're there strictly to protest. You have the rioters who are angry, who are anarchists, who really just want to just fuck shit up, and that's what they're going to do regardless. And then you have the looters, and the looters are almost exclusively—are just there to do that—to loot. . . .

Let's ask ourselves why in this country, in 2020, where the financial gap between poor blacks and the rest of the world is at such a distance that people feel like their only hope and only opportunity to get some of the things that we flaunt and flash in front of them all the time, is to walk through a broken glass window and get it. But they are so hopeless that getting that necklace, getting that TV, getting that change, getting that bed, getting that phone—whatever it is they're going to—is that in that moment when the riots happened and if they present an opportunity for looting, that's their only opportunity to get it. We need to be questioning "Why?" Why are people that poor? Why are people that broke? Why are people that food insecure, that clothing insecure that they feel like their only shot . . . [is] by walking through a broken glass window to get what they need?

Let me explain to you something about economics in America. . . . Now, if I . . . decided that I wanted to play Monopoly with you, and for 400 rounds of playing Monopoly, I didn't allow you to have any money. I didn't allow you to have anything on the board. I didn't allow for you to have anything. And then we played another 50 rounds of Monopoly, and everything that you have and you earned while you were playing that round of Monopoly was taken from you. That was Tulsa, that was Rosewood: Those are places where we built Black economic wealth, where we were self-sufficient, where we owned our stores, where we owned our property, and they burned them to the ground! . . .

So, when they say, "Why do you burn down the community? Why do you burn down your own neighborhood?" It's not ours! We don't own anything! . . . There's a social contract that we all have, that if you steal or if I steal, then the person who is the authority comes in and they fix the situation. But the person who fixes the situation is killing us! So, the social contract is broken. . . . *You* broke the contract when you killed us in the streets and didn't give a fuck. You broke the contract when for 400 years, we played your game and built your wealth. You broke the contract when we built *our* wealth again on our own, by our bootstraps in Tulsa, and you dropped bombs on us. When we built it in Rosewood, and you came in, and you slaughtered us. You broke the contract! . . . And they are *lucky* that what Black people are looking for is equality and not revenge.[129]

It is a truism of the Civil Rights movement that Martin Luther King Jr. was demonized as an "outside agitator," just as the well-meaning liberal governor of Minnesota marginalized the protestors and looters in his state and Keisha Lance Bottoms did the same in her city. Calls for peace that are nothing more than calls for a return to the same status quo ante that allows these senseless killings to happen over and over again are not calls for the peace of the Crucified One. But Jones's truth-telling demonstrated love for the least of these as she held the shape of the most marginalized bodies in the Black community. This Black woman had a masterful grasp of Black political history in the United States. She brilliantly unpacked a powerful metaphor for institutional racism with truth-telling suitable for these awful days of televised, state-sponsored Black lynchings. We need more leaders like her who can hold the shape of a networked polis by refusing to cast off the least desirable in the urgency of the mission to unmask the Powers of racism.

129. To view Jones's video, see https://youtu.be/1MA9oQrBpww. Also see her website at https://www.kimjoneswrites.com/.

WAKING UP ON THE WRONG SIDE OF EMPIRE
IN ROMANS AND REVELATION

Now, look here! John saw the city, didn't he?
Yes, John saw the city. Well, what did he see?
He saw twelve gates; three of those gates was on the North,
three of them was on the East, and three of them was on the West.
But there was three of them on the South too;
and I reckon if they kill me down there,
I'll get into one of them gates, don't you?

—*Harriet Tubman*[1]

Prophets and Police

It has never been more important for Christians to do moral reflection on the proper relationship between the church, the state, and the values of Empire.[2] It is an understatement to say that the 2016 election season was among the most acrimonious and divisive in recent US history, laying bare divisions in race, gender, religion, and education. Further, if millions longed for a reversion to "normal" afterward, the 2020 election left us in no doubt when a riotous mob bent on insurrection stormed a session of Congress to prevent the peaceful transfer of presidential power: We are a long way away from normal. Though journalists frequently note the strong evangelical vote in support of

---

1. From Bradford, *Scenes in the Life of Harriet Tubman*, 36, with amendments. I have eliminated the dialect that Bradford used to capture Tubman's words, preferring to reflect the speech act rendered by Tubman by changing such words as "de, dem, dose" to "the, them, those." Other wording tracks what appears in Bradford.

2. Throughout this chapter I capitalize *Empire* when referring to it as a collection of values or ideologies. The word appears in lowercase type when referring to historical political entities like the Babylonian or Roman empires.

the Republican candidate in these elections, deep divides in the vote between White evangelicals and evangelicals of color received less attention when the latter voted for the Democratic candidate by roughly the same numbers as the White group voted for Trump.[3] If both groups were voting their conscience following biblical principles, how do we explain two such radically different outcomes? Recent research concludes that one's ethnoracial identity and political party are more powerful predictors of voting than evangelical religious convictions alone.[4]

Evangelical conversations about the Christian's relationship toward governing authorities often begin with the apostle Paul's framing of the issue in Romans 13. Paul writes that God has instituted governing authorities for the welfare of the people and that Christians should submit to them because of that. Yet, to the dismay of Christians who wake up and get out of bed on the wrong side of Empire, there is no explicit "out" when these readers live under the thumb of oppressive regimes. On the other hand, John's Apocalypse ostensibly portrays an utterly different posture toward the Roman government. Rather than suggesting that imperial authorities are worthy of all deference, the latter half of the book of Revelation unveils the demonic influences that seek to deceive the faithful into being complicit with Empire and its values, values that idolize wealth, global trade, and economic security. According to John, Christians must prophetically and publicly resist Empire in every way possible, even at the cost of their lives. Thus these texts have apparently divergent instructions about relating to the government even though it is the same entity—the Roman Empire—that is the subject of these teachings.

We can see the message of Romans manifest in a newer register in public rhetoric associated with the Trump administration. In a section of the Trump era Whitehouse.gov website devoted to law enforcement, we read:

> The Trump Administration will be a law and order administration. President Trump will honor our men and women in uniform and will support their mission of protecting the public. . . . Our job is not to make life more comfortable for the rioter, the looter, or the violent disrupter. . . . *It is the*

---

3. LifeWay Research polls used a definition of an "evangelical" drawn from the National Association of Evangelicals and found that, when disaggregated by race, White evangelicals supported Trump at 65 percent while evangelicals of color supported Clinton at 62 percent (Smietana, "Election Exposes Evangelical Divides"). The same group found similar racial splits among evangelicals by race at roughly a similar point in 2020 (Earls, "Most Evangelicals Choose Trump over Biden").

4. Earls, "Most Evangelicals Choose Trump over Biden."

first duty of government to keep the innocent safe, and President Donald Trump will fight for the safety of every American.[5] (emphasis added)

Thus this rhetoric associates the avenging sword of government in Romans 13:4 with the contemporary police officer. If this is true, what might be an analogous symbol of the church's posture toward Empire preserved in Revelation? New Testament scholar Brian Blount suggests that the 1960s era Civil Rights movement captures the prophetic message in Revelation.[6] The person of Marissa Johnson, a Black Lives Matter (BLM) protestor from Seattle, may represent a twenty-first-century update on Blount's instinct. Though BLM protestors are either dismissed as undisciplined "thugs" or hailed as freedom fighters depending on your point of view, Marissa Johnson's story captured my attention. Johnson and a companion disrupted a Bernie Sanders rally during the Democratic primary in 2016 with all of the disruptive and edgy energy that seems typical of the movement. Intriguingly, Johnson is the mixed-race offspring of a Black father and White mother who, as evangelicals, were both active in the Tea Party movement that is diametrically opposed to Marissa's politics.[7] For her part, Johnson says that her BLM activism emerges specifically from her deep convictions as an evangelical Christian. She says that her activism doesn't come from "right-wing" religious convictions but that her religion "says you lay down your life for other people and the most marginalized."[8] She calls herself a Christian extremist,[9] and like it or not, that has got to be just about the best way to describe the great prophets of Israel that I've ever heard. Jeremiah had his crazy acted parables, Elijah his edgy and in-your-face boldness, and Moses chose "to share ill-treatment with the people of God rather than enjoy . . . the pleasures of sin" (Heb. 11:25), extremists one and all.

To say that contemporary American politics is polarized is a massive understatement. Further, our polarization always has been but is now even more

---

5. Retrieved March 14, 2017, from https://www.whitehouse.gov/law-enforcement -community. As of June 19, 2021, this website is no longer accessible. A similar statement on law enforcement under the Biden administration contains these words: "My Administration is committed to advancing the rule of law within the United States so that everyone is ensured equal justice under the law, an equal place in our democracy, and the opportunity to fulfill their potential free from abuses of power." See The Whitehouse Briefing Room statement "A Proclamation on Law Day."

6. Blount, *Can I Get a Witness?*

7. E. Sanders, "In Her Own Words."

8. E. Sanders, "In Her Own Words."

9. E. Sanders, "In Her Own Words."

deeply racialized. Even the two representative iconic images for these two texts, the police officer and the BLM protestor, are drawn from different racialized narratives. In contemporary politics in the West, racism is inextricably linked to Empire; thus, the center of the Christian response to Empire must also involve prophetic resistance to racism. This chapter explores the Christian postures toward governing authorities emerging from Romans 13 and key passages in Revelation in chapters 2–3 and 11. In addition, I examine the nature of witting and unwitting alignment with Empire values that idolize wealth and exploitative relationships in both biblical books and contemporary life. These readings offer tools for discerning our complicity with Empire and our role in resisting the racist evil at the heart of it. I pursue this agenda in four segments. First, I'll look briefly at the nexus of prejudice and racism and discuss how these concepts are embedded in social structures and identities. Second, I explore a rhyme between Romans 13 and the social welfare state in the United States. This section looks at how racism aligns with Empire values via Monya Stubbs's womanist ideological reading of Romans 13. Third, we'll look at the situation underlying the prophetic message in three chapters in Revelation. We'll see that in chapters 2–3 and 11, John unveils the demonic lure of economic security that leads to compromise with Empire and the structures and values that support it. I conclude with moral reflection on how texts in Romans and Revelation can help the church wake up and resist the racism at the heart of Empire.

Prejudice, Racism, and Group Identity

One scholar points out that modern society has finally found a racial epithet that enrages Whites in a way that approaches the deep hurt and anger engendered among minority communities at words like "Nigger," "Wetback," "Raghead," "Red-skin," "Christ-killer," or "Chink."[10] Whites feel deeply dehumanized and insulted when dubbed "Racists," even though the word lacks the dangerous history of the epithets applied to people of color. Most Whites think that if they are not slave owners or violent bigots, racism can't possibly apply to them; today, some even make exceptions about violence.

On this point, I've found that one of the most helpful constructs in teaching about race is to differentiate the concept of prejudice from the idea of racism.[11] Prejudice involves holding positive or negative attitudes or beliefs

10. Emerson, "Persistent Problem."

11. For more on these topics see Tatum, *Why Are All the Black Kids Sitting Together*; Walker-Barnes, *I Bring the Voices of My People*; J. M. Jones, *Prejudice and Racism*.

about a group, generalized from limited information about the group.[12] It is essential to recognize that ever-present images, words, pictures, and media subtly influence our thinking and feeling about other groups. Thus, prejudice is almost an automatic response to living in a racialized society, a condition that Beverly Daniel Tatum compellingly likens to smog. According to Tatum, racism is "in the air" and affects each of us whether we are aware of it or not.[13] We inadvertently and implicitly respond to people based on that person's group membership through the operation of prejudicial biases, which turns every individual encounter into an intergroup encounter.[14] Prejudice can be manipulated to ebb or flow in response to contextual factors. This variability makes prejudice a more manageable sin than racism because when the issues driving prejudice are removed, group relations can sometimes be restored. For example, prejudice is likely to rise if two nations are warring over control of land. Still, we can imagine that those nations could normalize relations over time after they resolved the land dispute. This situation broadly characterizes territorial conflict between the United States and Mexico. Yet, one wonders if the same can happen during other hostilities, such as the current one regarding the Israeli-occupied territories in Palestine.

Racism, on the other hand, is the ideology undergirding a system of advantage based on racial typologies. It assumes the ranking of races and the ideas, customs, and practices associated with them. Unlike prejudice, which is pervasive across peoples and times, racism is a property of societies involving hierarchically ordered ethnoracial groups, arranged from the best to the worst. Psychologist Beverly Daniel Tatum describes how people sometimes collapse or confuse the concepts of prejudice and racism in answering questions about whether people of color can be "racist." If one equates racism with prejudice, then, yes, people of color are racist since people groups across various eras

12. J. M. Jones, *Prejudice and Racism*, 8–9; Tatum, *Why Are All the Black Kids Sitting Together*, 85.
13. Tatum, *Why Are All the Black Kids Sitting Together*, 86.
14. Implicit biases are stereotypes, prejudices, attitudes, and beliefs about minoritized communities or women that people are either unable or unwilling to report. There are a number of instruments that attempt to measure these biases: the most widely known are the Implicit Attitudes test, the Evaluative Priming Task, and the Affect Misattribution Procedure. These tests are not intended as tools to label people or predict behavior; rather, they highlight implicit bias in order to help people resist active discrimination. See Hahn and Gawronski, "Facing One's Implicit Biases"; FitzGerald et al., "Interventions Designed to Reduce Implicit Prejudices." For more on this topic see Devine et al., "Long-Term Reduction in Implicit Race Bias"; Charlesworth and Banaji, "Patterns of Implicit and Explicit Attitudes."

have held positive and negative attitudes about communities around them. But when we define racism as a system of advantage based on race as in the United States, then in a system that advantages Whites, it is not true that minoritized groups are racists in this race-based society.[15]

Tatum develops another helpful metaphor, this time for the difference between racism and anti-racism:

> I sometimes visualize the ongoing cycle of racism as a moving walkway at the airport. Active racist behavior is equivalent to walking fast on the conveyor belt. The person engaged in active racist behavior has identified with the ideology of White supremacy and is moving with it. Passive racist behavior is equivalent to standing still on the walkway. No overt effort is being made, but the conveyor belt moves the bystanders along to the same destination as those who are actively walking. . . . But unless they are walking actively in the opposite direction at a speed faster than the conveyor belt—unless they are actively antiracist—they will find themselves carried along with the others.[16]

With this in mind, we can identify positions or policies as racist when they create or perpetuate racial hierarchies. So, in contrast to the earlier example about how prejudices may operate in the context of a land dispute, race-based slavery is wholly different. For instance, it would have been less horrible if Whites enslaved Blacks strictly based on differences in weapon technologies; it is infinitely worse that slavery included ideologies that portrayed Blacks as subhuman. In this case, racist assumptions about the inferiority of Blacks persist even after the institution of slavery has ended.

In connection with our focus on the Christian's relationship with Empire, it will also be helpful to explore the concept of institutional racism. Institutional racism is one of the many modes of racism that embeds hierarchical relationships between ethnoracial groups into the laws and institutions in society. Institutional racism restricts the choices, rights, and social mobility of different ethnoracial groups by limiting the access of some racial groups to needed social and material resources. This systemic form of racism embeds unequal access to material goods, biased habits, laws, and practices in social institutions. For instance, US tax policies currently favor the accumulation and preservation of intergenerational wealth for corporate elites. Our political

15. Tatum, *Why Are All the Black Kids Sitting Together*, 90.
16. Tatum, *Why Are All the Black Kids Sitting Together*, 91.

system could resume earlier tax policies on corporations and the ultra-wealthy that funded social benefits for Whites in the days of legalized racial discrimination. Renewed attention to such programs without discrimination against Blacks would help ameliorate the historical, state-sponsored, and race-based theft of wages and wealth from Black people during slavery and Jim Crow. By favoring corporations who disproportionately benefit from the institutions in this country relative to what they pay into them, we will continue to perpetuate structural socioeconomic deficits for historically disadvantaged ethnoracial groups and reinforce the status quo. The concept of institutional racism is crucial for the study of Revelation because of how that work questions how structural evil is embedded in everyday life through ideologies, commerce, and politics warped by greed.[17]

A widely read book by Christian Smith and Michael O. Emerson suggests that many White evangelical Christians are stymied in their understanding of racism on just this very point.[18] Smith and Emerson's study describes White evangelicals as even more likely than other Whites to use individualistic language and frameworks when engaging the topic of race. According to these scholars, evangelicals have three commitments in their "tool kit" that impede their ability to understand the effects of institutional racism. First, these evangelicals have a deeply rooted commitment to accountable freewill individualism in which people are individually and personally responsible for their sins. Second, they prioritize the view that social life consists of individuals interacting with other individuals so that change comes one heart at a time. Third, there is an explicit rejection among them of the idea that social structures influence our beliefs and practices.[19] In other words, White evangelicals are especially prone to confuse prejudice, which is about personal attitudes, with racism, which involves institutions and widespread practices. From the perspective of American individualism, it becomes all too easy to blame the poor for their poverty and fault disadvantaged minorities for circumstances and structures beyond their control.

Hence, White evangelicals tend to talk about changing hearts and minds when thinking about race and racism with little or no focus on attending to material conditions. Christians of color, however, tend to think about the group and speak about justice and changing structures. A study by Jason Shelton

---

17. Kraybill, *Apocalypse and Allegiance*, 153.

18. Smith and Emerson, *Divided by Faith*.

19. See Smith and Emerson, *Divided by Faith*; Glaude, Review of *Divided by Faith*; Emerson, "Persistent Problem."

and Michael Emerson examines differences between Black Protestants and White evangelicals and found that Black Protestants emphasize the community's well-being and openly express a greater sense of dependence on God through prayer. Anecdotally I've found that these differences are broadly true in comparable groups in other immigrant and domestic communities of color. Shelton and Emerson also report that White evangelicals place great importance on orthodoxy. For Whites, denominational affiliation played a more decisive role in shaping their religious identity than Black Protestants.

On the other hand, Black Protestants prize orthopraxy over orthodoxy, preferring to ensure that practices and ethics align with doctrine and values.[20] This study found that attitudes on nineteen topics concerning racial identity, equality, political ideologies, and voter preferences differ across race and denominational affiliations. The gap is the widest between Black Protestants and White evangelicals, who differed on ten of the nineteen elements. Big differences were also extant between Black Protestants and White mainline Protestants, who differed on seven of these measures. Intriguingly, Black and White non-Protestants differed on only four elements, which suggests to me that racial problems are deeper among Christians.[21] The authors conclude that: (1) racial group membership has more influence than denominational affiliation for Black attitudes about race, identity, and politics; (2) religious affiliations strongly influence White attitudes on these topics, particularly those within Protestantism; and (3) non-Protestant attitudes among Blacks and Whites were strongly correlated with political affiliation.[22] In other words, the results of this 2012 study essentially predict the racialized vote inside and outside of evangelicalism in the 2016 and 2020 elections, pointing to enduring chasms of difference.

Empire and Racism (Romans 13)

Having briefly engaged key concepts regarding racism, prejudice, and group dynamics, we are in a good position to examine the nature of Empire in this section. Richard Horsley helpfully describes some components of imperial civilizations in biblical periods that will illuminate the portrait of Empire underlying many of the New Testament writings. Because of the relatively infrequent contact between populations and the slow rate of social change in antiquity, the economic conditions prevailing in Iron Age empires were not

20. Shelton and Emerson, *Blacks and Whites in Christian America*, 67–78.
21. Shelton and Emerson, *Blacks and Whites in Christian America*, 177–81.
22. Shelton and Emerson, *Blacks and Whites in Christian America*, 180–81.

too dissimilar from the economics of the Roman Empire centuries later.[23] Horsley schematizes biblical empires using the classic economic pyramid. A population of individual peasant families forms the units of production on the bottom of the pyramid, supporting a tiny class of priests and religiopolitical elites at the top. Imperial elites extracted taxes, tithes, and offerings from the families on the bottom. In rural areas with agrarian economies, kings needed farmers' output to feed workers and participate in building projects, such as the pyramids in Egypt or the Solomonic and Herodian temples in Israel. And as the prophet warns in 1 Samuel 8, kings, and presumably emperors too, were prone to procure luxury items for themselves on the backs of the peasantry by taxing the production of family farmers. In fact, in the Roman era, trade was the primary means by which the aristocracy acquired luxury goods by extracting the resources of families that were farther afield. Loss of such luxuries would prompt deep mourning, as the angel proclaims regarding the prospect of the fall of the Roman Empire in the book of Revelation:

> [2]"Fallen, fallen is Babylon the great! . . . [3]All the nations have drunk of the wine of the wrath of her adultery, and the kings of the earth have committed adultery with her, and the merchants of the earth have grown rich from the power of her luxury." . . .
>
> [11]And the merchants of the earth weep and mourn for her, since no one buys their cargo anymore, [12]cargo of gold, silver, jewels and pearls, fine linen, purple, silk and scarlet, all kinds of scented wood, all articles of ivory, all articles of costly wood, bronze, iron, and marble, [13]cinnamon, spice, incense, myrrh, frankincense, wine, olive oil, choice flour and wheat, cattle and sheep, horses and chariots, slaves—even human souls. (Rev. 18:2a, 3, 11–13 AT)

Early agrarian empires could only grow their economies through the conquest of foreign temple cities and the villages and farming families that supported them,[24] creating something analogous to sharecropper relationships with these farmers. When families couldn't produce enough to meet their own subsistence needs because of famine or because of the burden of taxes and tribute, they had to go into increasing amounts of debt to the ruling elites to survive, eventually losing their ancestral lands to those local rulers.[25] Thus, the antics of antebellum Southern leaders to restrict the flow of social benefits

---

23. Horsley, *Covenant Economics*, 3–16.
24. Horsley, *Covenant Economics*, 5–8.
25. Horsley, *Covenant Economics*, 12–13.

to poor Blacks to increase the sharecroppers' indebtedness are rooted in the ancient practices of Empire (cf. Gen. 47:19–26).

The economic realities of the Roman Empire followed this same basic pattern, though with several complicating factors.[26] Roman armies tended to terrorize the countryside in their initial annexation of lands as a way of inculcating submission, imagery that seems to come alive in the four horsemen of the Apocalypse, where the first horseman, Conquest, is followed by Slaughter, Famine, and Plague (Rev. 6:2–8). During this period, Rome levied heavy tribute upon the Jews, on top of tithes and offerings supporting the priesthood and temple complex. Rome's client kings and local authorities were also free to enhance their wealth by extracting a third layer of taxes from the farming families. Like Herod the Great, the client king of Judea, these rulers often engaged in elaborate building projects to honor Rome, which helped them demonstrate their devotion to the empire, fueling the same cycle of taxes and tribute compounded by high-interest loans and slavish control through debt.[27] This description of the many layers of taxes and debt during the empire may provide background for Romans 13:6–7, as we shall see.

Womanist scholar Monya Stubbs takes an ideological approach when looking at how Paul engages Empire in Romans 13, which can help us forge con-

26. Horsley, *Covenant Economics*, 88–91.

27. Many assert rightly that politics and religion in the ancient world are qualitatively different from their substantiations in the modern United States. What these theorists usually have in mind is that the complete interpenetration of religion with politics and economics in antiquity is fundamentally different from the secularization of modern politics and economics. Yet if one considers the relationship of religious identity to ethnoracial identity in general, the differences between antiquity and modernity become differences of degree more so than differences in kind. Ancient societies can be viewed as constructed around ethnic difference when one considers that worship of gods generally varied by kinship networks, and in the largely sedentary agrarian societies of antiquity religion was less of a voluntary association than a status ascribed at birth. Thus, while ethnoracial identity was mediated in terms of religious belief in ancient Israelite thought, contemporary societies vary in terms of the ethnoracial identifiers that serve as primary indicators of belonging, sometimes keyed to religion or language and at other times mediated by skin color, country of origin, or tribe, etc. This suggests that we can make a case that the ancient worldview involved the enmeshment of politics, economics, and ethnoracial identity whereby the dominant mode of ethnoracial identity among ancient Jews and Christians was mediated via religious beliefs. For more on this subject see Sechrest, *Former Jew*. In the next section I am going to argue that contemporary US politics and economics are likewise deeply influenced by ethnoracial considerations, though the primary indicators of identity in modern society are mediated via physical characteristics versus religion. Hence in both cases, ethnoracial identity networks provide a framework for public social relations.

nections between Empire, racism, and anti-racism. In her book *Indebted Love*, Stubbs describes Empire as an ideology by appropriating Paul's language referring to "governing authorities" (Rom. 13:1, 5). For Stubbs, the *Pax Romana* is a culturally hegemonic, dominating force that competes with the power of the gospel for control of human interaction, involving willing, unwilling, or unconscious submission.[28] Governing ideologies represent a mindset that is a form of bondage that negates the human capacity to engage or even imagine mutually edifying relationships.[29] Empire values of militaristic conflict, reverence for the imperial cult, and a patron-client system promote domination in social relationships, which in the Roman Empire were thought to protect peace and prosperity through willing submission to Caesar. Patronage in the empire involved a delicate dance of domination and subjugation, as each party in the relationship rendered services of benefaction or honor mediating permanent relations of inequality.

Methodologically, Stubbs uses a strategy similar to associative reasoning to connect Harriet Tubman's lived experience under subjection to slavery with Paul's discourse about subjection to Rome. She finds an epistemological subjection-reflection-transformation pattern of empowerment in Tubman's thought similar to Paul's. The first step in the model involves naming the powers of subjugation in an environment as a way of recognizing the world as it is. Next, one reflects on the nature of reality revealed in that naming and the desire for a new reality by imagining how the world could be. Finally, this reflection calls for transformation so that people can bridge the gap between what is and what ought to be through their speech and actions. Stubbs sees this pattern in Tubman's brutal honesty about how slavery operated as a cruel and oppressive governing authority denying Black humanity, and her reflection on how slavery contrasts with liberty as an ideal in US society led her to transformation and a determination that she would seize her own freedom and help others to do the same.[30]

---

28. Stubbs also describes a second important governing authority in Romans that she identifies as Sin's Encounter with the Law, though I do not focus on her development of that theme here. This second governing authority is vividly apparent in Rom. 2:17–29 according to Stubbs, and she maintains that Paul uses a subjection-reflection-transformation model in this passage to identify and transform ideologies of ethnic elitism that can emerge from relationships influenced by this governing power. Stubbs sees 2:17–20 as the section that names the dominant ideology, 2:21–27 as the reflection section, and 2:28–29 as the transformation section. See *Indebted Love*, 18–23.

29. Stubbs, *Indebted Love*, 12, 25.

30. Stubbs, *Indebted Love*, 7.

Stubbs's analysis of a widely noted Tubman quotation shows a compressed form of the subjection-reflection-transformation pattern, and, even more importantly, focuses attention on the role that ideology plays in Stubbs's reading:

> When asked how she felt about the success she experienced in leading so many enslaved men, women, and children to the free North . . . [a] source quotes Tubman saying, "I freed a thousand slaves. If I could have convinced more slaves that they were slaves, I could have freed thousands more." . . . The greatest challenge Tubman encountered . . . was not the enslaved men and women's fear of capture or death . . . the greatest challenge she faced was one of ideology. The enslaved men and women whom she could not convince understood the institution of slavery as natural and absolute. . . . Therefore, when Tubman states she could not convince the enslaved men and women that they were slaves, the implication is that she could not convince them . . . [that] their enslavement was not the result of the natural course of history or the ordained will of God.[31]

Stubbs's analysis of Romans 1:18–32 can help connect the ideology of Empire with the problem of racism as a governing authority in the context of American imperialistic values. She sees Romans 1:18–32 as Paul's description of the subjugation of humanity in epistemic bondage to a mindset that refuses to acknowledge God's will expressed through the gospel. According to Paul, sinners refuse to admit that created things reveal critical information about God's nature and God's will. By worshipping created things instead of the Creator, they engage in exploitative behavior and disordered human relationships. Using this insight, we can see that a retelling of Romans 1:18–32 that addresses racism might similarly describe contemporary people in the grip of racist ideologies as those who suppress the clear evidence that humans across race, ethnicity, and sexual expression possess worth and dignity. A womanist retelling of this passage would insist that all humans, no matter how differently constructed or variously abled, are endowed with gifts of creativity and ingenuity for the world. The distortion and devaluing of those created in the image of God result in a disordered, de facto worship of a segment of human creation and the emergence of ideologies that privilege that group's needs and perspectives. They exploit the bodies and minds of peoples and groups at the bottom of a racialized hierarchy, all as a result of a deranged mindset that cannot imagine human relationships that *aren't* based on hoarded wealth,

---

31. Stubbs, *Indebted Love*, 29–30.

elitism, and exploitation, but which seem natural and inevitable to all dominated by the ideology. Those exploited by the ideology are as much in thrall to it as those benefiting, just like the slaves Tubman referenced who could not imagine a world in which they were free.

Stubbs's reading of Romans features the concept of indebted love as well as the triad of subjugation-reflection-transformation. I think her vision of reciprocity in indebted love is helpful as a theological paradigm for anti-racism. Reflecting on Romans 12:1, she talks about indebtedness as a capacity "to walk in the world as a living sacrifice . . . to offer oneself to God and thus to others as a gift—to give freely of oneself . . . with the expectation that you will get something in return: the ability to discern and demonstrate the will of God in the world and the privilege of living in a mutually indebted relationship to others."[32]

Critically, Stubbs does not see indebted love as a concept that requires the abnegation of the self for the sake of the other. Instead, it entails a "radical reciprocity," an interdependence that takes stock of the gifts that each brings, deploying them for the needs of one another.[33] Stubbs later connects the idea of reciprocity and mutual indebtedness to the interdependence of salvation in the olive tree metaphor in Romans 11, where Jews and Gentiles as people groups are each deployed by God in the plan of salvation for the other.[34]

Combining the three governing ideologies in Romans with the idea of indebtedness to the other, Stubbs takes on Paul's meaning in Romans 13:1–7 in light of the *Pax Romana*. She sees an analogy between how Tubman imagined countercultural values about living a life of obedience to God while contending against the governing authorities of chattel slavery and how Paul also contended with governing authorities in tension with the righteousness of God. Ultimately Stubbs interprets Romans 13:1–7 as a *description* of the prevailing ethos in the Roman Empire rather than as prescriptive commands about a Christian posture toward government.[35] She explores the ambiguity in the middle-passive voice inflection of the verb "be subject" in 13:1, 5. Reviewing the middle voice interpretation ("Let every person subject her or himself to governing authorities") and the passive voice interpretation ("Let every person be subjected by governing authorities"), she concludes that the broader context of Romans 13 involves both willing volition (12:1–2) and imposed subjugation (13:1, 5). She notes how paraenesis can be subversive in calling for a new social

---

32. Stubbs, *Indebted Love*, 9.
33. Stubbs, *Indebted Love*, 13.
34. Stubbs, *Indebted Love*, 49–51.
35. Stubbs, *Indebted Love*, 99.

order in the context of liminality. Using this paradigm, she suggests that the paraenesis in Romans 13:1–7 represents "Paul's partial conformity to the normative values" of the Roman Empire, "to secure both the safety of the Christian community at Rome and the continued expansion of his missionary activity."[36] For a Christian community in the liminality of the already-and-not-yet, 13:1–7 awakens the community to a *conscious* knowledge regarding the influence of Rome's dominant ideology as rhetorical shock therapy.[37] Verses 8–10, then, serve as the reflection on the dominant ideology. This section illuminates the call to indebted love that exists alongside the dominant ideology for Christians at Rome. At the same time, 13:11–14 represents the transformative moment that makes the wake-up call for new action explicit: "Do all this knowing *that the time is now* for you to wake from sleep" (Rom. 13:11).

Stubbs finds in Tubman's memoirs an evocative, transformative sequence that narrates a former slave's awakening from the hegemony of chattel slavery. Stubbs relates the story from Tubman's biography about Joe's awakening, analyzing a whipping Joe received as a transformative event that helped him see beyond distorted realities, likening Joe's transformation to that which Paul sees as possible through the power of the gospel.

Joe was a noble specimen of a negro, and was hired out by his master to a man for whom he worked faithfully for six years, saving him the expense of an overseer and taking all trouble off his hands. At length this man found him so absolutely necessary to him that he determined to buy him at any cost. His master held him proportionally high. However, by paying a thousand dollars down for him and promising to pay another thousand in a certain time, Joe passed into the hands of his new master.

As may be imagined, Joe was somewhat surprised when the first order issued from his master's lips was, "Now, Joe, strip and take a whipping!" . . . [Joe,] naturally enough, demurred, and at first thought of resisting. But . . . he had witnessed [a whipping] . . . the particulars of which are . . . horrible . . . and he thought it best to submit. . . .

"Master," said Joe, "haven't I always been faithful to you? Haven't I worked through sun and rain, early in the morning and late at night; haven't I saved you an overseer by doing his work; have you had anything to complain of against me?" The master replied, "No Joe, I've no complaint to make of you; you're a good nigger, and you've always worked well; but the

36. Stubbs, *Indebted Love*, 111.
37. Stubbs, *Indebted Love*, 121.

first lesson my niggers have to learn is that I am master and that they are not to resist or refuse to obey anything I tell them to do. So the first thing they've got to do is to be whipped; if they resist, they get it all the harder; and so I'll go on, till I kill them, but they've got to give up at last, and learn that I am master."[38]

Stubbs goes on to point out that although Joe initially submitted to the whipping and participated in the hegemonic contours of slavery by giving in to the destructive authority wielded by his new master, his submission was not total:

At the completion of his whipping, Joe draws his "clothes up over his torn and bleeding back" and states, "This is the last!" That night he . . . went . . . to Harriet's father, and said, "Next time Moses comes, let me know." The whipping he endured, and equally, the "master's" reasoning as to why the whipping was necessary, awakened Joe and allowed him to envision and pursue freedom. . . . Joe assumed that a level of inherent dignity existed within the institution of chattel slavery. Instead, his consciousness is raised; and Joe acted on the awareness that rather than mutual edification, mutual loyalty, or mutual indebtedness, the ideological reality of slavery advances the systemic dehumanization of those subjected by its rule, whether enslaved or slave owners.[39]

In Revelation, this transformational moment comes at the climax of the text in Revelation 17–18 in the vision of the Harlot of Babylon, as John unveils the rot at the core of Rome's alliances with political rulers and the Satanic synergies of Empire. The violent fall of the Harlot/Babylon/Rome symbol causes the merchants and kings to mourn her loss. Though we are never told about whether they repent and turn to the Lion-Lamb, the fact they mourn Rome's downfall is perhaps its own answer. Interestingly, both Joe's transformation and the transformational opportunity in Revelation occur in the aftermath of violence. There has been a similar transformational opportunity for awakening in the aftermath of the violence in American life as the nation watched the nine minutes of George Floyd's televised murder in horror. There was indeed something apocalyptic about the summer of 2020 as American society unraveled

---

38. Stubbs, *Indebted Love*, 97–98, citing Bradford, *Scenes in the Life of Harriet Tubman*, 27–30.

39. Stubbs, *Indebted Love*, 98.

that spring and summer. While the novel coronavirus swept across the country almost entirely unchecked, especially in Black and Indigenous communities, multiple highly publicized cases of police brutality against Black women and men occurred alongside growing numbers of hate crimes against Asian Americans. The cavalier racism evident in George Floyd's death at the hands of an indifferent cop mingled with the institutional racism of inequalities in health care and essential worker conditions that left Black, Indigenous, and other people of color disproportionately exposed, infected, and struck down.

The unique convergence of events of that period prompted a national reckoning about race and the role of government in public life, though it is not yet clear whether real transformation will emerge from this cauldron. From my perspective, 2021 yielded only continuing racial tension as states across the union enacted a wave of voter suppression laws not seen since the Jim Crow era. By contrast, modern political philosophy suggests that the most basic function of government is the protection of the citizenry. This view is the one undergirding many readings of Romans 13. Whether Paul is simply describing the role of the empire or whether, as Stubbs suggests, he is trying to subvert its dominion, he maintains that God institutes the governing authority to protect and preserve "law and order" (Rom. 13:3–4). The specific mention of taxes in Romans 13:6–7 reminds us that Paul was writing with local issues in mind, as is the case with all of the epistles. It is possible that here he warns against participation in incipient or imminent tax revolts that periodically roiled the city's populace.[40]

40. There were numerous tax revolts and revolts with underlying issues around taxation in imperial Rome, some with respect to land taxes and others emerging from the onerous and hated practice of exacting tribute from conquered peoples. David F. Burg ("Tax Rebellions") lists no fewer than sixteen rebellions and resistance movements in the latter republic and imperial period protesting Roman socio-economic control, from opposition to John Hyrcanus's desire to use taxes to fund a Hellenistic monarchy complete with a standing army of mercenaries in 67 BC to the increased taxes on Jews after the war with Rome in AD 71. Nero's tax reforms in AD 58 likely arose because of great protests against taxes levied partially to fund the emperor's excesses and partially to rebuild the city in the wake of the great fires (see Tacitus, *Annals* 13.50–51; 15.38–44; Suetonius, *Life of Nero* 38). Though other ancient sources are less certain about it, Suetonius indicates that Nero did indeed set the fire: "For under cover of displeasure at the ugliness of the old buildings and the narrow, crooked streets, he set fire to the city. . . . For six days and seven nights destruction raged, while the people were driven for shelter to monuments and tombs. . . . Viewing the conflagration from the tower of Maecenas and exulting, as he said, in 'the beauty of the flames,' he sang . . . in his regular stage costume. Furthermore, to gain . . . from the contributions which he not only received, but even demanded, he nearly bankrupted the provinces and exhausted the resources of individuals" (Suetonius, *Life of Nero* 38 [Rolfe]). It is impossible at this distance to be sure that the Neronian tax increases form the historical background for Paul's

Indeed, a focus on local events regarding security and taxes requires us to note that one's experience of Empire is radically affected by whether or not one is a citizen of that empire. While many US citizens do not think of the United States as an empire, those who read Revelation in the two-thirds world regularly identify it as the modern-day analog for the Roman Empire.[41] Further, one's status as an imperial insider may be contested. It is not an overstatement to say that today there are millions of native-born US residents whose experience of the United States is sometimes more analogous to the experience of foreigners than that of protected citizens. Thus, if it is possible to interpret Romans 13 as an insider's perspective on Empire as a protected citizen, Revelation's perspective of Empire is best described as the view from the underside of Empire. John focuses on Empire as a consumer of goods, gold, kingdoms, people, and worship and sees himself as belonging to a community that Empire is trampling. Thus, by analogy, both Revelation and Romans 13:1–7 comment on the Christian's relationship with the structures of the state.

Romans 13 describes Christians in submissive and subjugated thrall to imperialistic governing authorities, though Stubbs offers a reading that suggests that Paul hopes for far more from a Christian community awakened from slumber. In her reading, he hopes that there would be indebted love and mutual reciprocity of diverse gifts among people empowered by the gospel in willing, loving, mutual submission (Rom. 12; 13:8–14). Christians submitting themselves to the power of the gospel undertake care for one another that extends far beyond what some governmental authority deigns to share. But even Paul's description of a normative ideology in 13:1–7 lays out a political theology that views the state's protection of those under its span of care as divine favor. As God's servant, the government should seek security and benefits for each individual: "The governing authority is God's servant for your well-being" (13:4a).[42] Romans 13:1–7 ends by urging Christians to pay their

---

commands in Rom. 13. Yet even if Nero's tax program came after Paul's epistle, it is possible that the apostle's commands were given in a context in which dissatisfaction with taxes had been rising across the empire, even if it would take the aftermath of the fires and Nero's possible part in that disaster for the dissatisfaction to spill over into outright revolt and riots.

41. Maier, "Coming out of Babylon."

42. Here are some translation notes for Rom. 13:4a, which I render, "The governing authority is God's servant for your well-being" (AT; cf. 13:1). Literally the phrase reads, "It/He is a servant of God for your [singular] good"), but there is ambiguity about the antecedent of "it." I am interpreting "it" as a general reference to the governing authority as an entity involving many persons, similar to several English versions (NRSV, NIV, NLT), as opposed to a reference to a single person exercising authority (NIB, RSV; cf. "rulers" in 13:3). Second, the emphasis in this discussion that I place on the well-being for *each individual* derives from

taxes as a material element in submission to government, taxes that facilitate the purpose of government to protect and serve. I suggest that the benefits described in 13:4 and the taxes discussed in 13:6–7 are analogous to the modern social welfare state. Stubbs's reading can help us imagine a Christian vision of a robust welfare state that cares for the sick, lifts the poor from poverty, protects the human dignity of all, and equips all citizens to flourish as they offer their gifts back to society in mutual interdependence.

Hence, the Bible says nothing that exempts minorities from the benefits and protections of the state. Yet despite this biblical injunction in a nation purportedly founded on Judeo-Christian values, our history forces us to conclude that racism is a major factor poisoning the social welfare state in this country that has failed to protect and serve its minority citizens. In *The Color of Welfare* Jill Quadagno argues that race is the critical factor that has inhibited the creation of "social rights" in the United States even as racialized gaps in political rights and civil rights have narrowed somewhat over time. Other western democracies with only a fraction of the ethnoracial diversity of the United States have been able to grant social rights to citizens by enacting national welfare programs like universal public health insurance, childcare, parental leave, and education through the university level.[43]

Some suggest that Americans prefer a weak welfare state because of their commitment to individual rights, private property, and small government. However, Quadagno points out that Americans tolerated major exceptions to that anti-government ethos when they welcomed public spending after the Civil War and the Great Depression, as well as in Great Society legisla-

---

the singular inflection of the second-person pronoun "your." Finally, I interpret the Greek phrase τὸ ἀγαθόν (lit. "the good") in a broad sense. Paul uses this phrase thirteen times in the undisputed corpus, and in nine of these instances it has the sense of "moral good" as in Rom. 13:3: "Then do *what is good*, and you will receive the authority's approval" (similarly 12:2; 14:6). Here the sense doesn't seem associated with an individual's moral action, but with an abstract conception of good things conferred by the governing authority on an individual who is governed by that authority, captured by the phrase "well-being."

43. According to Quadagno, social rights emerged in the late nineteenth century as industrialized nations began to construct social welfare states. Social rights, as opposed to political or civil rights, provide three kinds of protections for citizens. Some social rights protect the poor from the exigencies of capitalism as well as employees from unemployment, old age, or losses for injuries on the job. A second class of social rights help stabilize consumer markets and help provide income security for the working class. Third, social rights stabilize the labor supply, and include job training, employment-referral systems, day-care provisions, paid parental leave, and full-employment policies (*Color of Welfare*, 18).

tion.[44] Moreover, she argues that values-oriented explanations fail to account adequately for race as a major structural dynamic in American society. Her book shows how "efforts to use government intervention to extend *positive liberties* to African Americans clashed with the *negative liberties* of whites to dominate local politics, to control membership in their unions, and to choose their neighbors."[45] Such conflicts undergird a racial fault line in public policy that accounts for the lack of widespread public support for robust social welfare rights.[46]

Indeed, the creation of White middle class wealth in the United States is largely a product of the post–World War II economic policies that intentionally excluded Blacks, women, and other people of color. Franklin Delano Roosevelt needed support from southerners in Congress to get his post-Depression New Deal programs passed. In exchange for these votes, he agreed to exclude African Americans and most working women from the core programs of the Social Security Act by excluding the occupations containing the vast majority of Blacks and women. New Deal legislation initiated the social right to a floor of protection for the industrial working class but did this in ways that reinforced racial segregation. Legislative bargains with southern members of Congress denied benefits to Blacks wherever possible. This legislation achieved this mainly by creating an infrastructure that ensured that monetary benefits would never be given directly to African Americans, using the mechanism of "local control" of benefits dollars in ways that protected White social and financial control of Blacks through debt. Tragically, this political backroom bargaining would become a template for other programs designed to create "universal" access to social welfare benefits, like Medicaid in the mid-1960s and the Affordable Care Act in the early 2010s. We should also discern that this is nothing more than a modern analog for ancient imperial economics of control reprised through post-Reconstruction sharecropping, Jim Crow arrangements, and New Deal compromises all the way up to our most recent legislative expansions of the social safety net.

Homeownership has been the ticket to better public services, education, and wealth for most American families. Nothing did more than post–World War II housing policy to create the White middle class, and these changes initiated a massive intergenerational accumulation of wealth. African Americans and other citizens of color were excluded from the easy terms for acquiring

44. Quadagno, *Color of Welfare*, 5.
45. Emphasis added.
46. Quadagno, *Color of Welfare*, 6.

a first home in the post–World War II boom by redlining and other forms of federally imposed discrimination. These exclusions drastically constrained Black opportunities to build and access family capital to help lift their families out of poverty.[47] In summary, we can say that social rights for citizens are consistent with many readings of Romans 13 and the taxes and mandate for well-being found there. The expansion of social rights in the American context, a goal in keeping with these readings of Romans 13, effectively ended just as it became illegal to discriminate against Blacks and other minorities. In other words, from the founding of this country until now, the idea of "America first" has, with few exceptions, only ever been about improving the lives of White Americans.[48] We shall see that the domination, greed, and racism that fueled this trajectory align with the trends that John addresses in Revelation. In this work, he is especially keen to expose the demonic lure of economic security that leads to compromise with Empire and the structures and values that support it. In the next section, I explore four of the letters to the churches in Revelation 2–3 before a brief mention of the church's role in Revelation 11.

Resisting Imperial Values (Revelation 2–3 and 11)

The letters to the seven churches of Asia are the most easily decoded sections of Revelation. In them, Christ sends tailored messages to each congregation that John also intends for the group as a whole.[49] The letters to Smyrna and Philadelphia are the only ones among the seven that lack any criticism from Christ. The letters to these two churches also contain striking references to the "synagogue of Satan" (2:9; 3:9).[50] This fraught ethnic rhetoric *could* refer to tension between the Jewish and Christian communities in these cities, signaling that Jews and Jesus's followers are in open conflict. In effect, the suggestion is that members of the Jesus movement, who would be "true Jews" to John, are being "outed" to the authorities by Jews who are opposed to the Jesus movement

---

47. Asante-Muhammed et al., "Ever Growing Gap"; Shapiro, *Hidden Cost*, 2–3.

48. See Rothman, "Long History," for the isolationist, anti-Semite history of "America First" foreign policy prior to its adoption as a campaign slogan during the Trump 2016 presidential campaign.

49. The letters to each of the seven churches addressed in Revelation end with: "If you can hear, listen to what the Spirit is saying to the churches" (2:7, 11, 17, 29; 3:6, 13, 22).

50. Blount observes that we should not regard the "synagogue of Satan" as racist anti-Jewish rhetoric, because it is discourse that reflects an inter-ethnic Jewish debate (*Revelation*, 54). The idea is that John writes as a Jew to others whom he considers to be members of Israel.

(i.e., "blasphemy, or slander"; 2:9).[51] Another interpretation is that the rhetoric represents *intra*-ethnic tension within the church, similar to the internal conflict evident in Matthew as discussed in chapter 2. In this latter case, among a group of Jesus movement people, whether Jewish or Gentile, John labels some of them as "fake," probably because some are not as observant of essentials as John expects. Throughout the Apocalypse, it is apparent that John thinks that he and faithful followers of the Messiah *are* the "true" Jews, and here John says that his opponents do not deserve to identify themselves this way.[52]

The latter suggestion is more attractive than the former. The background behind the first idea is that these "false Jews" are not eligible for the protections that Roman law guaranteed Jews of the period. But there is little or no evidence of Jewish cooperation of this kind with Roman authorities in the period.[53] Nevertheless, the threat of imprisonment in 2:10 suggests that the practices at issue ostensibly bring them into conflict with Rome, as indicated by the demonizing language used here: "synagogue of Satan" in 2:9 and "devil" in 2:10. Elsewhere in the Apocalypse, this kind of imagery is associated with opponents of the Jesus movement (cf. 12:9, 12–13). And as the devil imagery morphs seamlessly into the dragon imagery in chapters 12 and 13, it is easy to see that the serpent/devil/dragon motif symbolizes the demonic spiritual forces behind the beast-like Roman Empire (12:17–13:3). In other words, the symbolical assertions in these later images are already at work in this early epistolary section. Just as John shows that the satanic devil-dragon stands behind Rome, so too does the

---

51. Blount, *Revelation*, 54–55; Charles, *Revelation of St. John*, 1:56, 58. John appropriates all the iconic symbolism of Israel when describing members in the Jesus movement (i.e., the church with twelve gates, twelve tribes, twelve fruit in the holy city, the Israel/Jacob imagery associated with the woman in Rev. 12:1–2; cf. Gen. 37:3–11). Further, he insists on cultic purity with reference to food and prohibitions on idolatry from Torah throughout. When John speaks of "those who say they are Jews but are not" in Rev. 2:9 and 3:9, it is clear that these false Jews are the antithesis of an unnamed but logically required group of faithful true Jews who are being addressed in these letters. Together with all the Israel symbolism and the emphasis on purity, it is hard to escape the idea that John thinks that "true Jews" are those who are faithful to both Jesus and the Torah. Apparently the "false Jews" in view in 2:9 and 3:9 are those who are faithful to only one of these non-negotiable commitment structures.

52. Frankfurter, "Jews or Not?" Frankfurter suggests that the people whom John regards as fake Christians are historically Pauline Gentile Jesus believers who are law observant though insufficiently concerned with purity to fit John's sectarian notions. The identification of Pauline Christians as the opponents is helpful and is in keeping with the observation that Jezebel of Thyatira's apparent willingness to countenance participation in idolatry has long been associated with a certain reading of Pauline Christianity. See Duff, *Who Rides the Beast?*

53. Frankfurter, "Jews or Not?," 404–6.

use of similar language in Revelation 2 suggest that John believes that Rome is aligned with one of these Christian factions in this internal dispute.

Alleging that his opponents in Smyrna are aligned somehow with Rome, John thinks they are unworthy of sharing the group identity reserved for the faithful. When we recall that the "true" Smyrna group is commended for suffering poverty due to their posture, we might imagine that the opponents of the poor Smyrna group from the Jesus movement are not experiencing that same hardship. While the alignment with Rome could have been manifest in either political, economic, or social terms, the particular issues at Smyrna likely focused on economic policy or practices, given the emphasis on poverty in this letter. Was the threat of imprisonment derived from refusing to worship the emperor? Were the so-called "false" Smyrna believers advocating participation in the imperial cult and local trade guilds while John's "true" believers were renouncing the idolatry involved in these activities, eschewing involvement in the city's economic life?[54]

According to David Frankfurter, John's great concern was with the purity of the halakhic observance of people inside the nascent Jesus movement. For Frankfurter, the author's principal opponents among the churches of Asia were Jezebel, the Nicolaitans, neo-Balaamites, and opponents at Smyrna and Philadelphia, all of which were likely (neo-)Pauline Christians. As fellow members of the Jesus movement, they are the subject of vitriolic rhetoric for their lack of halakhic purity.[55] They are "so-called Jews" because they were

54. Osborne, *Revelation*, 127, 130. Citing Osborne, see Sechrest, "Antitypes, Stereotypes and Antetypes," 123: "Eating is a moral choice in the apocalypse, something that is especially highlighted in the letters to the seven churches. In Pergamum, some members of the church are rebuked for eating food sacrificed to idols, and Christ promises that those in this city who resist eating food sacrificed to idols will eat manna instead, God's special food (2:17). The letter also attributes the teaching that promotes eating food sacrificed to idols to the Nicolaitans (2:14–15), which implies that the eating of idol food had been a problem in the church of Ephesus as well since the Nicolaitans are also mentioned in that letter (2:6). Indeed, the letter to Ephesus likewise offers an opportunity to eat God's food instead of idol food, when Christ gives overcomers permission to eat from the tree of life (2:7). Food sacrificed to idols may be the central issue in Thyatira, especially if the fornication mentioned in 2:20 is simply a way of symbolizing the unfaithfulness of eating food sacrificed to idols mentioned in that same verse (πορνεῦσαι καὶ φαγεῖν εἰδωλόθυτα: to fornicate, that is, to eat food sacrificed to idols). In addition, one might also surmise that the relative poverty of Smyrna and wealth of Laodicea is connected to the degree to which the Christians in these communities were integrated into the socioeconomic fabric of the cities, an integration which might well involve participation in the imperial cult or local trade guilds and thus activities that would likewise involve moral choices about eating."

55. Frankfurter, "Jews or Not?," 413–19, 422.

not following Jewish practice. Frankfurter speculates that some may have been devout Gentiles who are "Jews on the inside" with circumcision of the heart, whom Paul contrasts with people who are Jews by appearance (only) in Romans 2:28–29.[56] Paul's more liberal attitude toward eating meat from the marketplace that had been sacrificed in pagan rituals as in 1 Corinthians 10:25–30 would have been scandalous to a purist like John. The rhetoric and imagery noted above suggest that he saw this as nothing short of collusion with Rome, possibly through participation in the imperial cult in Smyrna, which was known for its devotion and loyalty to the empire.[57] John contends that devilish Roman authorities are throwing "pure" Smyrna Jesus followers into prison and poverty due to their actions. From John's perspective, it's a small leap to reckon that the opponents of the poverty-stricken faithful are possibly reaping direct or indirect financial advantage through cooperation with Roman practices. Perhaps they were reaping the social benefits of "regular" participation in the politico-religious life of the community. Since the messages in these seven letters are meant to be read by all seven congregations, the pure, poor Smyrna Messiah people may be a deliberate contrast with the church full of wealthy Laodiceans that we will discuss below.

If the situation in Smyrna results in the poverty and affliction of that church, the situation in Philadelphia concerns a church that is experiencing sociopolitical exclusion and powerlessness. The Philadelphian church seems to be internally divided into "true" and "false" Jesus followers as in Smyrna since John is using the same "synagogue of Satan" rhetoric. But instead of a focus on poverty, in this letter, the accent is on the power to control social inclusion or exclusion, something that would comfort a marginalized church. In verses 7–8, Christ is the one (1) who opens locks; (2) who controls the opening and closing of doors; (3) who has given the Philadelphians an open door; and (4) offers in verse 12 the promise of a permanent place in the temple of God. As at Smyrna, Christ accuses the opponents at Philadelphia of lying and slander. It may be

56. Frankfurter, "Jews or Not?," 419. Compare translations of 2:29: "The real Jew is the one who is inwardly a Jew, and real circumcision is in the heart" (NJB; similarly NLT, NIV) versus "It is the person who is a Jew inside, who is circumcised in spirit" (CEB; similarly NRSV). According to Frankfurter, "Paul and John of Patmos illustrate the diversity of Gentile self-definition within the Jesus movement: Gentiles labelling themselves Jews because of adherence to some degree of halakhic practices; Gentiles considering themselves 'inward' Jews according to Paul's dicta; and Gentiles in various stages of conversion to Judaism. Such Gentile 'Judaizers' seem to have been a significant force in the Jesus movement throughout the second century" ("Jews or Not?," 420).

57. Gorman, *Reading Revelation Responsibly*, 92–93.

that these falsehoods have resulted in some level of social exclusion or exile for the "true" group in that city. Just as at Smyrna, though John calls them "Jews," it is clear that he is talking about people in the early Jesus movement. This conclusion receives support from Christ's praise for the Philadelphians, who publicly align with him despite the lies and slander from those in the synagogue of Satan (3:8–9). In John's view, this "false" group of believers in the synagogue have made a bargain with the devil in exchange for political power and social acceptability from the empire. Again, the concluding appeal that all churches heed the messages to each church suggests that John wants everyone to know that political compromise with Empire is only a devil's bargain.

The poverty, powerlessness, and social marginalization of the churches at Smyrna and Philadelphia are the signs of churches that are at odds with Empire. These are the churches that are being excluded from government protections in social, political, and economic terms. In the modern scene, marginalized people are excluded because of their ethnicity or race and not necessarily because they have resisted Empire as is the case in Revelation 2–3, but it is nevertheless true that their experience of being excluded and thereby marginal, poor, and powerless is what helps them cultivate a greater willingness to resist Empire. There is something about being on the wrong side of Empire that allows you to be more clear-eyed about its excesses. Just as stereotypes slander the humanity of Black, Indigenous, Asian, and Latinx people and depict them as alien and prone to crime, the imperial resisters from Smyrna and Philadelphia are the subjects of lying and slanderous rhetoric, which results in situations where their freedoms are threatened or removed. Contemporary people are analogous to those in Smyrna who are on the wrong side of Empire when they lack access to poverty-alleviating social rights. Modern minorities are also analogous to the group in Philadelphia who are on the wrong side of Empire when their opponents dominate local politics, control membership to schools, clubs, and unions, and have the power to include or exclude them from neighborhoods and jobs. In both New Testament letters, we should note that it was the compromised group, the members in name only, who were enabling the marginalization of siblings in Christ through the silent and tacit tolerance of imperialistic values and indifference to practices that exploit and exclude marginalized citizens. This, too, seems analogous to the wide opinion gaps between Black and White Protestants on race and politics that we surveyed in a previous section.

While the churches in Smyrna and Philadelphia were experiencing severe poverty, prison, or exile, probably due to their principled withdrawal from religious or social complicity with the empire, the Christians in Laodicea were in a completely different situation. Founded at the intersection of major trade routes, this city was wealthy as a result of its lively commerce and banking industry. When other cities in the region needed Rome's help in rebuilding in the aftermath of a major earthquake in recent memory, Laodicea was able to go it alone in rugged individualism: "I am rich, I have prospered, and I need nothing" (3:17).[58] They are so profoundly attached to their economic prosperity that in 3:15–16, the Lord of the church is absolutely sickened by them to the point of vomiting. Though the imagery in these verses is sometimes misunderstood, the symbolism draws on the architecture of Laodicea's water supply, which they piped in from other cities. By the time it reached the city, the water was brackish and tepid from a long journey in mineral-encrusted, sunbaked pipes. Through these symbols, Christ indicts the church's internalization of Empire values by likening the church to tepid water that is indistinguishable from its surrounding environment. They think that they are prosperous and self-sufficient when verses 17–18 say that they are spiritually poor, blind, and completely unclothed. This last description is a profoundly devastating critique when one realizes that in Revelation white clothing symbolizes the righteous deeds of faithful witnesses engaged in imitation of Christ (see 19:7–8).[59] Though the city was renowned for its eye institutes, textiles, and banking (3:17–18), Christ lambastes the church for failing to see that it has lost its witness.[60] In contrast to the image of Christ wandering among lampstand churches (1:19), in this letter, Christ stands outside of the church beseeching the occupants for entry. This church is so compromised that it has failed to recognize that it is no longer actually a church.

The deceived and insensible state of Laodicea represents the ultimate end of a journey that begins with compromise. An earlier waystation on the way to being overtaken by Empire values emerges in the portrait of the church in Thyatira, the longest letter in Revelation 2–3. This letter describes an error that also seems to prevail in some of the other churches as well, and several features about society in Thyatira help reveal this. First, Thyatira had the distinction of being early in designating the emperor Domitian as the incarnation of Apollo and thus the "Son of Zeus," a move that made it very difficult for people in Thyatira to opt out of religious devotion because of the political implications.[61] Second, it boasted a local trade deity by the same name: Apol-

58. Hemer, *Letters to the Seven Churches*.
59. Sechrest, "Antitypes, Stereotypes and Antetypes," 120.
60. Sechrest, "Antitypes, Stereotypes and Antetypes," 120.
61. Blount, *Revelation*, 62; Beale, *Revelation*, 259.

los Tyrimnaeus.[62] So when Christ is depicted as "Son of God" in 2:18, it had special local significance within the local context of Thyatira. This title was as much a political statement of civil disobedience as it was a statement about economic practice and religion.

Thyatira also had numerous prominent trade guilds for various occupations: guilds for dyers, shoemakers, bronzesmiths, clothiers, bakers, potters, slave traders, etc. These trade guilds facilitated access to participation in various crafts and thus the economic livelihood of the craftsmen. Ancient trade guilds seem to be roughly analogous to contemporary labor unions, which also mediate involvement in the craft. Each craftsman would belong to a guild, which occupied a square in the city and functioned as the center of that part of the community's civic, social, and economic life. Since each guild had a patron god or goddess, gatherings of these guilds were frequently religious in character, and abstaining from these feasts meant being excluded from the economic and civic life of the trade community. Thus, attendance at guild meetings inevitably meant participation in idolatry.[63]

As noted in our discussion of Smyrna, the problem regarding the teaching in Thyatira may have concerned Paul's teaching about Christian liberty or possibly even a popular corruption of it.[64] Instead of Paul's nuanced teaching about eating food sacrificed to idols in 1 Corinthians 8–10, Jezebel of Thyatira may have sanctioned outright participation in trade guild idolatry for the sake of economic security and integration into the life of the city (2:20).[65] When John says that she "calls herself a prophet," he uses language that labels her an outsider and a false prophet in not-so-subtle terms. John believes that all Jesus followers must hold to the "testimony of Jesus." When he later defines the testimony of Jesus as "the spirit of prophecy" (19:10), John effectively calls Jezebel and her followers false Christians.[66] Indeed, John doesn't call her "false" outright, but the deliberately drawn similarities between Jezebel and the Harlot

---

62. Aune, *Revelation*, 2:201; Beale, *Revelation*, 259; Osborne, *Revelation*, 151.

63. Osborne, *Revelation*, 151–52.

64. Frankfurter, "Jews or Not?," 416–22.

65. Frankfurter, "Jews or Not?," 416–22 and those cited there. Compare Frankfurter's interpretation with the nuanced reading of Paul's teaching in 1 Cor. 8–10 in Thiselton, *First Epistle to the Corinthians*.

66. One scholar points out that John crafts intentional similarities between Jezebel imagery and the description of the Harlot "Babylon" in chapters 17–18: both are queens, both associated with sexual immorality, both spill the blood of the people of God, and both have their flesh devoured by scavengers in their respective stories. See Duff, *Who Rides the Beast?*, 90.

of Babylon are telling: they are both economically secure foreign queens accused of sexual immorality.[67] His use of the word "deceive"[68] in 2:20 is likewise illuminating. Though some English translations soften this word to "beguile" or "mislead" in this context, it is the same word that is translated "deceive" in references to Satan and the second beast later on (12:9; 13:14; 19:20; 20:10). Thus the critical issue in the message to Thyatira is a warning against heterodox teaching that sanctions compromise for the sake of participation in the social, political, and economic life of the empire. "Deception" becomes a prominent motif in Revelation associated with the satanic influences that pervade Empire, and, significantly, the first use of the word occurs here in connection with the teaching of a leader in the church. This placement suggests that a big part of John's communication intent concerns the urgent need to discern the truth about the identity and nature of what is being worshipped. In a word, John is urging the church to renounce Empire and the satanic values that power it. He wants to unveil the nature of Empire to prevent unwitting complicity with it.

If some Jesus people at Smyrna and Philadelphia are analogous to those who wake up on the wrong side of Empire, those at Laodicea and Thyatira live on the imperial upside. They have slipped into a dangerous relationship with Empire through individualism and compromise with the surrounding political, social, and economic structures of Empire. Such compromise can so thoroughly damage witness that these Christians may not even realize that they have ceased to be identifiable as members of the company of the Lamb. Worse, this group is so utterly deceived about its own status that they do not realize the extent to which they are actually *promoting* the interests of Empire. The believers in Laodicea and Thyatira are analogous to those who began resisting the expansion of the social welfare state in modern life in the United States after the end of state-sanctioned discrimination. These believers, politicians, and citizens have absorbed the self-promoting idolatry of wealth by refusing to fund or expand social rights and benefits for all citizens, whether consciously or unwittingly. Asleep and unaware, they participate in exploiting marginalized people whose vulnerabilities became glaringly apparent during the pandemic as the "essential workers" who staffed grocery stores, pharmacies, schools, hospitals, and care facilities at great personal risk while receiving comparatively fewer protections from the state.

Moving now to Revelation 11, we meet two prophets who represent the church because, in John's world, everyone in the church is a prophet (19:10).

---

67. Duff, *Who Rides the Beast?*, 126.
68. "Deceive": πλανάω.

Appearing in an interlude between the sixth and seventh trumpet judgments, the purpose of the episode is to depict the church's actions during the trumpet judgment cycle. With this in mind, the fact that God gives the prophets the capacity to strike the earth with Exodus-like plagues (11:6) suggests that the church's prophetic ministry somehow participates in bringing divine judgments to the earth in the Exodus-like trumpet judgments of Revelation 8.[69] Not only are these witnesses protected from danger during the time of their testimony, but they also have the gift of fiery speech for fighting their enemies (11:6), a power that is reminiscent of Christ's control over life and death through speech acts (1:16). When their testimony is complete, so too is the period of protection, and their enemies are allowed to prevail. But the witnesses are ultimately vindicated through resurrection so that they imitate their Lord in death just as they did in life.

We can best see the *message* of the prophetic church in the letters to the seven churches: that is, the church must resist compromise with the political and economic power of Empire by worshipping God and resisting Caesar and the lure of social standing or wealth, no matter the cost. But the *posture* of the prophetic church is fully exhibited in Revelation 11. The prophetic church conquers through nonviolent witness, a stance that is not to be mistaken for passivity. The church overcomes evil through a testimony that is edgy, bold, confrontational, forward-leaning, in-your-face, and fearless. It shuns a passive, low profile witness and resists the seductive lures of Empire and assimilation to the temperature of the surrounding environment at all costs, willingly accepting the possibility—even the probability—of ostensible defeat as the cost of bearing witness to Jesus. As one scholar put it, John effectively tells the church: "Go out and pick a fight!"[70] This kind of witness has been rightly likened to the active persevering faith of the historic Black church-led Civil

---

69. See Rev. 8:7 (cf. Exod. 9:23–24); Rev. 8:8 (cf. Exod. 7:17); and Rev. 8:12 (cf. Exod. 10:21). The idea that the church participates in initiating these judgments rests partly on the imagery I note above in Rev. 11:6, but also in the imagery in 8:1–5. In this passage, an angel pours out a bowl of incense onto the earth, resulting in initiation of the trumpet judgments. I suggest that the incense in this scene reprises earlier imagery concerning golden bowls full of incense that John describes as *equivalent* to the prayers of the saints (5:8). In other words, we could render 8:3–4: "Another angel came and stood at the altar with a golden censer. He was given a great quantity of incense so that he could offer the prayers of all the saints on the golden altar that is before the throne. And the smoke of the incense containing the prayers of the saints, rose before God from the hand of the angel." Altogether, the imagery suggests that the angel in Rev. 8:1–9 dumps bowls full of prayers onto the earth, which initiates a set of Exodus-like plagues similar to those the prophets call forth in Rev. 11:6.

70. Blount, *Revelation*, 41.

Rights movement.[71] The Black church's quest for liberation through the horrors of slavery, segregation, and the long fight for civil rights was always theologically moored in an effort to secure the freedom to participate with God in the divine agenda to set the world to rights. But I think it is also fair to say that Black Lives Matter activists like Marissa Johnson also fit the bill in a way that captures the particular emphases of Revelation 11. A BLM-type prophetic ministry is fearless in confronting the structures of Empire wherever they may be. Their take-no-prisoners, leave-it-all-on-the-table commitment to liberation rejects the more socially acceptable trappings of those in liberation movements of the past.[72] They are edgy and unapologetic in their bold desire to challenge everyone's alignment between orthodoxy and orthopraxy, testing to see whether actions are consistent with words. They represent the church that Jesus commends, the church on the margins of social acceptability and economic prosperity. This is the kind of church that confronts and resists the economic exploitation at the racist heart of Empire.

Let the Sleeper Awaken—the Church and Governing Authorities

Romans 13 and Revelation have sparked very different responses among Bible readers. Rightly we should criticize the perspective in Romans 13 for its ostensibly conciliatory posture toward the brutality and violence of the Roman Empire. If Paul thought the church shouldn't concern itself with fighting imperialism in the final days before the triumphal return of the Messiah to set the world to rights, readers two thousand years later must certainly take up these matters. Revelation should also receive critique for its thoroughgoing violence and misogynistic imagery. It sometimes reproduces the hierarchical domination of Rome in offering its own vision of the dominion of God. Yet even with all these caveats, these ancient artifacts of more violent times resonate with postures toward dominating governing authorities that we can still see today. We can see misguided analogical appropriations of Romans 13 among those who will excuse government corruption, exploitation, and state-sanctioned violence against its own citizens. Likewise, the violent trampling of Capitol Hill on January 6, 2021, has an eerily literalistic and misguided correspondence with Revelation 11:2. In this case, the modern actors *initiated* violence to defend deceitfully propogated statements about election integrity with no evi-

71. Blount, *Can I Get a Witness?*
72. Sechrest, "Antitypes, Stereotypes and Antetypes."

dentiary basis, unlike the context of Revelation, where the prophetic church is the *recipient* of state-sanctioned violence.

But whatever else you make of these texts, you cannot deny that their basic postures toward governing authorities are fundamentally at odds. Some would say that different views in these texts toward the same historical imperial governing authority make it difficult, if not impossible, to synthesize a posture toward present governing authorities based on both of these texts. Some of us may struggle to recognize that what we see as a benign and localized governing authority is the very definition of Empire for others. For instance, the present troubling rise of inwardly focused nationalism that castigates immigrants crossing our southern border fails to recognize that, at a macro level, our economically imperialistic practices materially contribute to the conditions for mass population upheavals from the global South. In the western hemisphere specifically, trade agreements and farm subsidies undermine Latin American industries so that it is cheaper for other nations to buy US exports than to invest in their own people and means of production. Thus, it is no wonder that displaced workers will migrate to the nation that has effectively swallowed up their jobs. Closing borders or enacting draconian deportation regimes will only further destabilize the home countries of these displaced workers and foment conditions in the western hemisphere that may only exacerbate the problems that the restrictive immigration measures were intended to solve.

Yet, even this perspective that the interior view of Empire is different than the exterior view is overly simplistic. In this country, some citizens are not accorded the full privileges of citizenship. The Justice Department found rampant and routine violations of constitutional rights by the police in Ferguson, Missouri, where Michael Brown died by cop in an incident that sparked massive protests and gave birth to the Black Lives Matter movement.[73] Arizona's controversial law SB 1070 (dubbed a "Papers Please" law) required that police demand proof of citizenship based on "reasonable" suspicion regarding immigration status. Critics said that the law promoted racial profiling, and the Supreme Court struck down three parts of it before it went into effect. African Americans will never recoup centuries of stolen wages, lost capital, and intergenerational wealth from the days of slavery and the Jim Crow era of segregation. Studies of African American life outcomes point more and more to a position as a permanent underclass in American society after centuries of lost wealth and decades of denied social and civil rights. The situation is even worse regarding Indigenous peoples who experienced genocide, theft

---

73. Shaw, *Ferguson Report.*

of lands, desecration of natural resources and sacred sites, and broken treaty after broken treaty. Mexican Americans whose families have lived on the same land in North America for centuries are often now in the situation where they are regarded as interlopers in the land of their ancestors. When Chicanx activists say that "the border crossed me," they refer to the American acquisition of vast swaths of Mexico in the Treaty of Guadalupe Hidalgo, which ended the US-Mexican War, a war that the United States initiated in the wake of an imperialistic annexation of Texas. Asian Americans are regarded as forever foreign, expected to remain submissive in gratitude for their status as "honorary Whites" while never being admitted into true White privilege. Democratic and Republican presidents in the modern era have all presided over de facto colonial regimes in Puerto Rico, Guam, the Virgin Islands, the Mariana Islands, and American Samoa. American policy denies voting rights to these subjects whose US passports read, "The bearer is a United States national and [but?] not a United States citizen."

Whites feel that some of the privileges that they have enjoyed in the past are slipping away. In turn, this promotes fear of giving minority groups access to benefits previously enjoyed by Whites only. This fear erodes popular support for social welfare programs that would benefit everyone. But the feelings of loss come from the perception that the material advantages that Whites have enjoyed over people of color are slowly narrowing, a perception exacerbated by the symbolic power of a two-term African American president. Some fear the day when Whites lose their status as the numerical majority in the population. If you have ever recognized that it is no fun to be a minority in this country, then it is perfectly rational to bemoan the idea that your group is moving into that status. There is no denying that you may well experience the rise of equality as an impending loss if your community is accustomed to unearned privilege.[74] Thus, Whites' perception of dwindling advantages is understandable, even though we cannot also affirm it. Denying needed resources to others because of their ethnoracial belonging because you want to continue hoarding them for yourself is profoundly un-Christian and the very definition of racist.

Romans 13 and Revelation are texts that invite reflection on the church's relationship with the state and its values. As Stubbs does, one may read Romans 13:1–7 *descriptively*, with the balance of the chapter containing a prescriptive wake-up call from tacit complicity with governing systems that oppress and

---

74. Craig and Richeson, "More Diverse Yet Less Tolerant?"; Craig and Richeson, "'Majority-Minority' America."

preserve hierarchy and exploitation. Other readers, using a somewhat better-known *prescriptive* interpretation of 13:1–7, take Paul's commands to submit to government as enduring moral precepts because God establishes governments to serve and protect the governed (13:3–5). On either of these trajectories, readers take little notice of the text's emphasis on the government's role in providing divinely favored benefits through the very ordinary mechanism of taxes (13:4a, 6–7). I contend that this reading of the purpose of government is analogous to how contemporary federal, state, and local taxes fund social welfare rights. This idea has important implications for a Christian posture in a divided society given how deeply racialized the American pursuit of the nation's "general welfare" has been. By contrast, the powerful rebuke of Empire with its worship of wealth in Revelation forms a striking tension. Possibly written in part to criticize Pauline views about participating in the wider society, Revelation implies that a focus on submission to governing ideologies via Romans 13 opens the door to complicity with evil. From this perspective, nothing could be worse than when an imperialistic ideology of exploitation combines with the worship of wealth to undermine government mandates to secure the welfare of people entrusted to it. In these cases, submission to government potentially and dangerously slides into idolatry and needs to be rebuked with prophetic power.

When it comes time to choose one's preferred "governing authorities," Christians must select among competing visions of the relationship between the state and conscience. In this country, many respond by framing their choice in line with one of these texts. Following the line many see in Romans 13, one can pursue a (de facto) submission to governing authorities that prioritizes preserving the peace and restraining evil. Ironically, some following this trajectory are occasionally the very souls who simultaneously undermine the government's *raison d'être* as articulated in that text through a low tax/small-government or no-government platform. Alternately, people might gravitate to Revelation as a text that advocates resistance to an imperialistic status quo. These people might choose disruptive protest against imperialistic values and seek to redistribute wealth by advocating for higher taxes and robust social rights in an expanded welfare state comparable to other western economies.

In the recent past, people of color tended to see their electoral choices in terms of a Revelation 13[75] moment that required resistance to coded promises about restoring a racist past ("America First"). For them, their vote was an act

---

75. Here I am using the phrase "Revelation 13" as shorthand for the interpretation of

of resistance to an imperialistic movement that was in keeping with a history of stolen wages, stolen land, and capricious disregard for the welfare of the marginalized. On the other hand, Whites in the evangelical church, with inferior tools for dealing with structural inequities as described by Smith and Emerson, tended to lean on Romans 13 in formulating their electoral choice. At best, they were people who were not directly affected by institutional racism and who voted in favor of extending state protections to the unborn. In so doing, they continued a posture informed by Romans 13 that trusts that governing authorities will not pursue nefarious or hurtful policies toward people under its dominion. At worst, however, these evangelicals were frightened by approaching minority status and voted because the "America First" rhetoric of the campaign played to their racial fears. Finally, note that while Republican Party identification accounted for most of the Trump vote, racial animus was the next largest category that predicted support for Trump. It was less clear which of these motivations was uppermost in the group in the election's immediate aftermath. However, continued evangelical support for that administration's Muslim ban, defense of Nazis and Klansmen in Charlottesville, and intentional cruelty at the border tipped the balance toward the latter in the minds of many.

My own sympathies are definitely with the former group for reasons I have described here. Sadly, I am aware that others came to different ethical conclusions either by reading Scripture differently or not reading Scripture at all. What I am trying to do, however, is to point out features of both texts that generally receive little emphasis in Bible-reading circles. For those of us who choose to interact with governing authorities based on Revelation, we need to do so ready to accept the consequences of taking a deeply unpopular message into spaces where it is unlikely to be well received. For the sake of our testimony, we need to risk losing favor with our friends and networks and accept the consequences of that witness when it affects our wealth, our jobs, and our privilege. We need to seek a ministry that testifies to Jesus by unmasking all of the deceptive allure of Empire wherever those values crop up. We need to be bolder and more fearless in witness. However, Revelation readers must also make sure that a righteous fervor to resist injustice does not bleed over into unjust slander of the governing authorities. Thus, a resistance informed by Revelation needs to find its own brand of submission to governing authorities.

On the other hand, if you choose to submit to governing authorities based on Romans 13:1–7, perhaps for the sake of the unborn as many maintain, then I pray that you honor all seven verses in that passage. Consider that local, state,

---

Revelation offered above. A Revelation 13 scheme versus a Romans 13 scheme is an evocative one for articulating the contrasts between these interpretive frameworks.

and federal taxes that mitigate poverty, educate the populace, and care for the infirm are commensurate with that worthy goal. According to some studies, over 60 percent of women choose abortion because they cannot financially support the unborn child.[76] Thus, it is counterproductive to eliminate taxes that can provide birth control to poor women on the one hand while decrying abortion rates on the other. More importantly, readers of Romans 13 also need to reckon with the possibility that their submission to Empire has slipped into complicity with it. They need to make sure that they have not been seduced by the fruit of the racism that lies at the heart of Empire, which privileges one group at the expense of all others. As Stubbs's reading of the contexts of that passage reminds us, we must wake up to the power of the gospel and its call to live in interdependent mutuality that does not repay evil for evil but makes provision for what is good for all people (Rom. 12:17; 13:4a, 8).

Let's end by taking up a little nugget of wisdom in an article by Austen Ivereigh analyzing a 2017 interview with Pope Francis conducted by the Spanish newspaper *El País*:

> "In moments of crisis, discernment doesn't work," [the Pope] told the Span-
> ish newspaper in January, around the time of Mr. Trump's inauguration.
> "Discernment" is an important word for the pope; it is key to his Jesuit
> spirituality. He meant in this case the capacity to detect the "spiritual mo-
> tions"—the presence of good and evil—in events. In times of crisis, that
> capacity disappears, and projection, scapegoating and hysteria take over.[77]

O Lord God Almighty, grant us the capacity to discern evil around us and in us. Please help us find the good in our midst and submit to it, and in troubling times help us to avoid projection, scapegoating, and hysteria. But when there is evil around us and in us, I pray that you would give us the power to prophesy against it. By the power of the gospel, O God, help us to be a church that bears witness to our Lord Jesus and be worthy of him when he returns. Even so, come Lord Jesus!

---

76. See for example Biggs, Gould, and Foster, "Understanding Why Women Seek Abortions in the US."

77. https://www.nytimes.com/2017/03/04/opinion/sunday/is-the-pope-the-anti
-trump.html.

APPENDIX

SAMPLE MORAL ANALOGY ASSIGNMENT

This appendix contains a sample assignment that I use to introduce students to associative hermeneutics. This three- to four-page structured paper helps them cultivate analogical correspondences between a biblical text and a modern dilemma in race relations. Students identify the dilemma in race relations in the first section in conversation with course readings and then provide a concise statement of the rhyme between the biblical text and the racial problem in the second section. The poetics or shape of the analogy is developed using a table as a heuristic device to align elements in the modern world with details from the text, and the final section requires an analysis of the analogy, showing where it fits and where it is less helpful for ethical practice. I received permission from the student who wrote this assignment to disseminate this sample anonymously, though it has been edited for clarity and consistency in this venue.

Text: Acts 4:1–22

Statement of Ethical Dilemma

Black people have a history of being silenced in one form or another. In the days of slavery, White masters silenced Blacks with physical force/violence and the denial of basic human rights. These injustices led to Blacks having their voices devalued. Blacks, seen as chattel and property to be bought and sold, were stripped of their voices and reduced to the services they could perform (i.e., physical labor and sexual reproduction) (Collins, *Black Sexual Politics*, 55–57). After slavery, the dominant culture continues to put false identities upon Black people. For example, Black women struggle to find themselves in a system that tries to categorize them as either a promiscuous "jezebel" or an asexual "mammy" (Collins, *Black Sexual Politics*, 72). Black men engage in the same search for identity in a world that easily labels them as criminals. When Black people refuse the identities put upon them and resist assimilation into

White culture, the dominant culture looks to actively or adversely deny them their voice. This silencing is even found in the realms of theology (Sechrest, class notes). The effects are a loss of voice in the public sphere and one's own community due to the internalized frustration of not being given an outlet to speak (Collins, *Black Sexual Politics*, 74).

Given the difficulties of finding one's voice as a Black person, the ethical dilemma is deciding whether or not to resist the dominant culture's demands for silence. There are pros and cons to choosing one or the other. The benefit of choosing to keep one's Black identity silent is that one can potentially be at "peace" with the dominant culture and perhaps even be welcomed into it. (As Collins explains, Black women, for example, can be deemed "decent.") The drawback of this is that the peace is a *pax Romana*—a mere absence of external conflict—rather than a true *shalom*. Internal disputes about identity and denying who one truly is brings anything but peace. (See the themes that run throughout Tatum's work, *Why Are All the Black Kids Sitting Together*.) The benefit of Black people searching for and claiming their voice is that there is an internal refusal to suppress one's own identity. The drawback is that raising one's voice results in conflict with the dominant culture and suffering the anger of the system.

Rhyme of the Moral Analogy

Acts 4:1–22 presents a situation in which certain authorities pressure Christ-followers to no longer speak about the resurrection of Christ, the event that has come to identify them as a church. This is similar to the current situation in which the Black community is pressured to be silent, thereby suppressing its true identity.

Analysis of the Moral Analogy

In Acts 4:1–11, certain community authorities are disturbed by Peter and John's preaching of Jesus's resurrection from the dead (4:2) and order the two men to stop (4:17–18). We can see a similar situation today in that certain powers in the dominant culture are disturbed by the voice of the Black community—which demands justice for its people—and therefore they try to silence it. In Acts, the apostles refuse to be silent, adhering to God's commands rather than to the fear of the authorities (4:19) and continuing to preach the gospel despite the conflict that may result (4:20). They decide to weather the conflict because the church must be a witness to the resurrection of Christ so that people may find healing and restoration (4:20, 22). Giving in to the demands of the authorities would mean denying people their right to the gospel. The early church's

Table 2. Poetic Shape of the Moral Analogy

Elements of Moral Analogy	Biblical Context	Modern Context
Situation	Certain community authorities are disturbed by Peter and John's preaching of Jesus's resurrection from the dead (4:2). They order the men to stop (4:17–18).	Certain powers in the dominant culture are disturbed by the voices of Black people who demand justice, and therefore they try to silence them.
Possible Response	The church gives in to the pressure from the authorities and stops preaching, thereby denying people access to the gospel and the restoration it gives.	Black people could give in to the pressure from the dominant culture and stop speaking out, thereby denying themselves of access to their true identities and the possibility of ending oppressive systems.
Poetic Detail (1) (Enter as many "poetic details" rows here as needed to high-light key verses.)	Adhere to God's commands rather than to the fear of the authorities (4:19).	Adhere to the needs of the Black community for justice rather than the fear of dominant culture. This is in keeping with the tradition of the biblical law and prophets (e.g., Deut. 24:17–22; Jer. 7:5–7).
Poetic Detail (2)	Continue to preach the gospel despite the conflict it may bring with the authorities (4:20).	Continue to speak out despite the conflict it may bring with the dominant culture.
Reasoning	The church must be a witness to the resurrection of Christ so that people may find healing and restoration (4:20, 22).	The Black church should be a witness to God's justice so that it may claim freedom from oppressive systems.

decision here can aid today's Black community in whether or not they should give in to the pressure of the dominant culture. If the community gives in and stops speaking out, it will deny its people access to their true identities and the possibility of ending oppressive systems. Therefore, I would argue that Acts 4:1–11 can be interpreted as an instruction for the Black community: Adhere to the needs of the Black community rather than the fear of the dominant culture and continue to speak out despite the conflict it may bring because the Black community finds its identity and freedom from oppressive systems.

Strengths and Limitations of the Moral Analogy

The strength of this analogy is that it is applicable not only for the Black community but for many other communities who feel silenced by the dominant culture. The Native American community, for example, could easily adapt this analogy to itself. The weakness of this analogy is that not *all* communities could or should apply it to their situation. The KKK, for example, may feel that the dominant culture condemns their message, but for them to speak out despite society's disapproval would not be analogous to Acts 4:1–22 since their message goes against many of the gospel's themes.

There are many ways in which this analogy (in relationship to the Black community) has its complicating factors. One complication is that Acts 4:1–22 shows relatively new oppression (the oppression of Christ followers) and has yet to become systematic. However, for the Black community today, the oppressive systems that they experience stem from the repeated injustices that are deeply rooted in US history. These injustices resulted in White people gaining privileges that Black people do not have. This complicates the analogy since the dominant culture comes at the modern situation benefiting from the oppression, thereby making their voice in the conversation largely ignorant of the Black perspective. This leads to my next point. For the early church and the Black community, there are different senses of "group." In the early church in Acts, there were yet no clear divisions with the Jewish community between those who followed Christ and those who didn't since both held the same cultural center (the synagogue) and followed very similar cultural practices. Therefore, the conflict in Acts 4:1–22 could be considered "in the family." However, for the Black community and the dominant culture, history has drawn deep divisions between the two, and therefore, the conflict could be considered an "us" versus "them" situation. This conflict complicates the analogy for today since Peter and John could speak the "language" of the authorities. At the same time, the Black community and the dominant culture cannot always find the same vocabulary to address one another. Therefore, much of the conflict between the Black community and the dominant culture is complicated by a breakdown in communication.

BIBLIOGRAPHY

Achtemeier, Paul. "An Elusive Unity: Paul, Acts, and the Early Church." *CBQ* 48 (1986): 1–26.

Aernie, Jeffrey W. "Faith, Judgment, and the Life of the Believer: A Reassessment of 2 Corinthians 5:6–10." *CBQ* 79 (2017): 438–54.

Alcoff, Linda Martín. "Latino/as, Asian Americans, and the Black–White Binary." *The Journal of Ethics* 7 (2003): 5–27.

———. "What Should White People Do?" *Hypatia* 13 (1998): 6–26.

Alese, Whitney. "7 Reasons why Respectability Politics are BS." *Medium*, 6 July 2021. https://thereclaimed.medium.com/7-reasons-why-respectability -politics-are-bs-1c97041ccfe2.

Alexander, Michelle. *The New Jim Crow: Mass Incarceration in the Age of Color-blindness*. New York: The New Press, 2010.

Allard, Sharon Angella. "Rethinking Battered Woman Syndrome: A Black Feminist Perspective." *UCLA Women's Law Journal* 1 (1991): 191–207.

Alston, Richard. *Aspects of Roman History AD 14–117*. London and New York: Routledge, 2002.

Alter, Robert. *The Art of Biblical Narrative*. New York: Basic Books, 1981.

Amber, Jeannine. "In Her Own Words: Marissa Alexander Tells Her Story." *Essence*, 27 October 2020. https://www.essence.com/news/marissa-alexan der-exclusive/.

Anderson, Carol. *White Rage: The Unspoken Truth of Our Racial Divide*. New York: Bloomsbury, 2016.

Anderson, Hugh. "Broadening Horizons: The Rejection at Nazareth Pericope of Luke 4:16–30 in Light of Recent Critical Trends." *Interpretation* 18/3 (1964): 259–75.

Aristotle. *Politics*. Translated by H. Rackham. Loeb Classical Library No. 264. Cambridge: Harvard University Press, 1944.

Arnold, Clinton. *Power and Magic: The Concept of Power in Ephesians*. Eugene, OR: Wipf & Stock, 1989.

Asante-Muhammed, Dedrek, Chuck Collins, Josh Hoxie, and Emanuel Nieves. "The Ever Growing Gap: Without Change, African American and Latino Families Won't Match White Wealth for Centuries." CFED and the Institute for Policy Studies. August 2016. https://ips-dc.org/wp-content/uploads/2016/08/The-Ever-Growing-Gap-CFED_IPS-Final-2.pdf.

Aune, David E. "Anthropological Duality in 2 Cor 4:16–5:10." In *Paul beyond the Judaism/Hellenism Divide*, edited by Troels Engberg-Pederson, 353–80. Louisville: Westminster John Knox, 2007.

———. "Magic in Early Christianity." In *Aufstieg und Niedergang der römischen Welt* 2.23.3, edited by Hildegard Temporini and Wolfgang Haase, 1470–557. Berlin: De Gruyter, 1980.

———. "'Magic' in Early Christianity and Its Ancient Mediterranean Context: A Survey of Some Recent Scholarship." *Annali di storia dell'esegesi* 24/2 (2007): 229–94.

———. *Revelation*. 3 vols. WBC 52. Grand Rapids: Zondervan Academic, 2014–2017.

Ayman, Roya, and Karen Korabik. "Leadership: Why Gender and Culture Matter." *American Psychologist* 65/3 (2010): 157–70.

Bagai, Rani. "Bridges Burnt Behind: The Story of Vaishno Das Bagai." Angel Island Immigration Station Foundation. AIISFIV.Org. (2021). Accessed 27 November 2021. https://www.immigrant-voices.aiisf.org/stories-by-author/876-bridges-burnt-behind-the-story-of-vaishno-das-bagai/.

Bailey, Kenneth E. *Finding the Lost: Cultural Keys to Luke 15*. St. Louis: Concordia, 1992.

Bailey, Moya, and Trudy. "On Misogynoir: Citation, Erasure, and Plagiarism." *Feminist Media Studies* 18/4 (2018): 762–68.

Bajard, Jean. "La structure de la péricope de Nazareth en Lc IV, 16–30." *Ephemerides Theologicae Lovanienses* 45 (1969): 165–71.

Baker, F. M. "The Afro-American Life Cycle: Success, Failure, and Mental Health." *Journal of the National Medical Association* 79/6 (1987): 625–33.

Baker-Fletcher, Karen. "Immanuel: Womanist Reflection on Jesus as Dust and Spirit." In *My Sister, My Brother: Womanist and Xodus God-Talk*, edited by Karen Baker-Fletcher and Garth Kasimu Baker-Fletcher, 73–93. Maryknoll, NY: Orbis, 1997.

Baker-Fletcher, Karen, and Garth Kasimu Baker-Fletcher, eds. *My Sister, My Brother: Womanist and Xodus God Talk*. Maryknoll, NY: Orbis Books, 1997.

Balch, D. L. "Household Codes." In *Greco-Roman Literature and the New Testament: Selected Forms and Genres*, edited by David E. Aune, 25–50. SBLSBS 21. Atlanta: Scholars, 1988.

Barclay, John M. G. *Paul and the Gift*. Grand Rapids: Eerdmans, 2015.

Barreto, Eric D. *Ethnic Negotiations: The Function of Race and Ethnicity in Acts 16*. WUNT 2.942. Tübingen: Mohr Siebeck, 2010.

Barrett, C. K. *Acts of the Apostles: A Shorter Commentary*. London: Bloomsbury, 2002.

———. *A Commentary on the Second Epistle to the Corinthians*. BNTC. New York: Harper & Row, 1973.

Barth, Markus. *Ephesians*. AB 34. New York: Doubleday, 1974.

Bauckham, Richard. "James, Peter and the Gentiles (Acts 15:13–21)." In *The Missions of James, Peter, and Paul: Tensions in Early Christianity*, edited by Bruce D. Chilton and Craig Evans, 91–142. Leiden: Brill, 2005.

Baur, F. C. *Paul, the Apostle of Jesus Christ, His Life and Work, His Epistles and His Doctrine: A Contribution to a Critical History of Primitive Christianity*. Translated by Allan Menzies. 2 vols. London: Williams and Norgate, 1876.

Beale, G. K. *The Book of Revelation*. NIGTC. Grand Rapids: Eerdmans, 1998.

Beare, Francis Wright. "The Sequence of Events in Acts 9–15 and the Career of Peter." *JBL* 62 (1943): 295–306.

Beltran, Mary. "The Hollywood Latina Body as Site of Social Struggle: Media Constructions of Stardom and Jennifer Lopez's Crossover Butt." *Quarterly Review of Film and Video* 19/1 (2002): 71–86.

Benoit, Pierre. "Resurrection: At the End of Time or Immediately after Death?" *Concilium* 10 (1970): 103–14.

Bereano, Nancy K. "Introduction." In *Sister Outsider: Essays and Speeches of Audre Lorde*, 7–12. Berkeley: Crossing Press, 1983.

Bertram, Robert W. "The Complete Centurion." *Concordia Theological Monthly* 39 (1968): 311–27.

Berzon, Todd. "Ethnicity and Early Christianity: New Approaches to Religious Kinship and Community." *Currents in Biblical Research* (2018): 191–227.

Best, Ernst. *A Critical and Exegetical Commentary on Ephesians*. ICC. Edinburgh: T&T Clark, 1998.

Betz, Hans Dieter. "The Concept of the Inner Human Being." *NTS* 46 (2000): 315–41.

Bhabha, Homi. *The Location of Culture*. London and New York: Routledge, 1994.

———. *Nation and Narration*. London and New York: Routledge, 1990.

Bieringer, R. "Die Gegner des Paulus im 2. Korintherbriefes." In *Studies on 2 Corinthians*, edited by R. Bieringer and J. Lambrecht, 181–221. Leuven: Leuven University Press, 1994.

Biggs, M. Antonia, Heather Gould, and Diana Greene Foster. "Understanding Why Women Seek Abortions in the US." *BMC Womens Health* 13/29 (2013): 1–13.

Bird, Michael. "Who Comes from the East and West? Luke 13.28–29/Matt 8.11–12 and the Historical Jesus." *NTS* 52 (2006): 441–57.

Blount, Brian. *Can I Get a Witness? Reading Revelation through African American Culture.* Louisville: Westminster John Knox, 2005.

———. *Revelation: A Commentary.* NTL. Louisville: Westminster John Knox, 2009.

———. *Then the Whisper Put on Flesh: New Testament Ethics in an African American Context.* Nashville: Abingdon, 2001.

Bock, Darrell L. *Luke.* 2 vols. BECNT. Grand Rapids: Baker, 1994.

Bonilla-Silva, Eduardo. *Racism without Racists: Color-Blind Racism and the Persistence of Racial Inequality in the United States.* Lanham, MD: Rowman & Littlefield, 2006.

Boring, M. Eugene. "The Gospel of Matthew." In *The New Interpreter's Bible.* Vol. 8. Nashville: Abingdon, 1994.

Bornkamm, Günther. *Jesus of Nazareth.* Translated by Irene McLuskey, Frase Mc-Luskey and James Robinson. New York: Harper, 1960.

Boyarin, Daniel, and Jonathan Boyarin. "Diaspora: Generation and the Ground of Jewish Identity." *Critical Inquiry* 19/4 (1993): 693–725.

Bradford, Sarah H. *Scenes in the Life of Harriet Tubman.* Auburn, NY: W. J. Moses, 1869.

Brant, Jo-Ann A. "Husband Hunting: Characterization and Narrative Art in the Gospel of John." *Biblical Interpretation* 4/2 (1996): 205–23.

Brock, Eleanor. "The Truth about Women of Color Behind Bars." *Logikcull,* 15 September 2018. https://www.logikcull.com/blog/women-color-behind-bars.

Brodkin, Karen. *How Jews Became White Folks and What That Says about Race in America.* New Brunswick, NJ: Rutgers University Press, 1999.

Broido, Ellen M. "The Development of Social Justice Allies during College: A Phenomenological Investigation." *Journal of College Student Development* 41/1 (2000): 3–18.

Brown, Marilyn M., and Meda Chesney-Lind. "Women's Incarceration in the United States: Continuity and Change." In *Routledge Handbook of Corrections in the United States,* edited by O. Hayden Griffin III and Vanessa H. Woodward, 127–34. New York: Routledge, 2017.

Brown, Michael Joseph. *Blackening of the Bible: The Aims of African American Biblical Scholarship.* Harrisburg, PA: Trinity Press International, 2005.

———. "The Gospel of Matthew." In *True to Our Native Land: An African American New Testament Commentary,* edited by Brian K. Blount, Cain Hope Felder, Clarice J. Martin, and Emerson B. Powery, 85–120. Minneapolis: Fortress Press, 2007.

Brown, Raymond E. *The Gospel according to John I–XII*. AB 29. New York: Doubleday, 1966.

Brown, Schuyler. "The Matthean Community and the Gentile Mission." *NovT* 22 (1980): 193–221.

———. "Mission to Israel in Matthew's Central Section (Matt 9:35–11:1)." *ZNW* 69 (1978): 73–90.

Bruce, F. F. *The Book of Acts*. NICNT. Rev. ed. Grand Rapids: Eerdmans, 1988.

Buell, Denise Kimber. "Rethinking the Relevance of Race for Early Christian Self-Definition." *HTR* 94 (2001): 449–76.

———. *Why This New Race? Ethnic Reasoning in Early Christianity*. New York: Columbia University Press, 2008.

Buell, Denise Kimber, and Caroline Johnson Hodge. "The Politics of Interpretation: The Rhetoric of Race and Ethnicity in Paul." *JBL* 123 (2004): 235–51.

Bultmann, Rudolf. *History of the Synoptic Tradition*. Oxford: Blackwell, 1968.

———. *The Second Letter to the Corinthians*. Edited by Erich Dinkler. Translated by Roy A. Harrisville. Minneapolis: Augsburg, 1985.

Burg, David F. *A World History of Tax Rebellions: An Encyclopedia of Tax Rebels, Revolts, and Riots from Antiquity to the Present*. New York and London: Routledge, 2004.

Burrell, David B. *Analogy and Philosophical Language*. Eugene, OR: Wipf & Stock, 1973.

Burrow, Rufus, Jr. "The Beloved Community: Martin Luther King, Jr. and Josiah Royce." *Encounter* 73/1 (2012): 37–64.

Butler, Anthea. "Shooters of Color Are Called 'Terrorists' and 'Thugs.' Why Are White Shooters Called 'Mentally Ill'?" *Washington Post*. 18 June 2015. https://www.washingtonpost.com/posteverything/wp/2015/06/18/call-the-charleston-church-shooting-what-it-is-terrorism.

Byron, Gay L. *Symbolic Blackness and Ethnic Difference in Early Christian Literature*. London: Routledge, 2003.

Caird, George B. *New Testament Theology*. Edited by L. D. Hurst. Oxford: Clarendon, 1994.

Callan, Terrance. "The Background of the Apostolic Decree (Acts 15:20, 29; 21:25)." *CBQ* 55 (1993): 284–97.

Cannon, Katie Geneva. *Katie's Canon: Womanism and the Soul of the Black Community*. London and New York: Continuum, 1995.

Cannon, Katie Geneva, Emilie M. Townes, and Angela D. Sims, eds. *Womanist Theological Ethics: A Reader*. Louisville: Westminster John Knox, 2011.

Carroll, John T. *Luke: A Commentary*. NTL. Louisville: Westminster John Knox, 2012.

Carson, Donald A. *The Gospel according to John*. PNTC. Grand Rapids: Eerdmans, 1991.

Carter, J. Kameron. *Race: A Theological Account*. Oxford and New York: Oxford University Press, 2008.

Carter, Warren. "Matthew and the Gentiles: Individual Conversion and/or Systemic Transformation." *JSNT* 263 (2004): 259–82.

———. "Resisting and Imitating the Empire: Imperial Paradigms in Two Matthean Parables." *Interpretation* 56 (2002): 260–72.

Carton, Andrew M., and Ashleigh Shelby Rosette. "Explaining Bias against Black Leaders: Integrating Theory on Information Processing and Goal-Based Stereotyping." *Academy of Management Journal* 54/6 (2011): 1141–58.

Case, Kim A. "Discovering the Privilege of Whiteness: White Women's Reflections on Anti-racist Identity and Ally Behavior." *Journal of Social Issues* 68/1 (2012): 78–96.

Chaitin, Gilbert D. "Metonymy/Metaphor." In *The Encyclopedia of Contemporary Literary Theory: Approaches, Scholars, Terms*, edited by Irene Rima Makaryk, 589–90. Toronto: University of Toronto Press, 1993.

Charles, Robert Henry. *A Critical and Exegetical Commentary on the Revelation of St. John: With Introduction, Notes, and Indices, Also the Greek Text and English Translation*. 2 vols. Edinburgh: T&T Clark, 1920.

Charlesworth, Tessa E. S., and Mahzarin R. Banaji. "Patterns of Implicit and Explicit Attitudes: I. Long-Term Change and Stability from 2007 to 2016." *Psychological Science* 30/2 (2019): 174–92.

Chavez-Dueñas, Nayeli Y., Hector Y. Adames, and Kurt C. Organista. "Skin-Color Prejudice and Within-Group Racial Discrimination: Historical and Current Impact on Latino/a Populations." *Hispanic Journal of Behavioral Sciences* 36/1 (2014): 3–26.

Chin, Jean Lau. "Introduction to the Special Issue on Diversity and Leadership." *American Psychologist* 65/3 (2010): 150–56.

Chin, Jean Lau, Bernice Lott, Joy Rice, and Janis Sanchez-Hucles. "Overview: Women and Leadership: Transforming Visions and Diverse Voices." In *Women and leadership: Transforming Visions and Diverse Voices*, edited by Jean Lau Chin, Bernice Lott, Joy Rice, and Janis Sanchez-Hucles, 1–18. Hoboken, NJ: John Wiley & Sons, 2008.

Chiu, C.-y., and Hong, Y.-y. "Cultural Processes: Basic Principles." In *Social Psychology: Handbook of Basic Principles*, edited by E. T. Higgins and A. E. Kruglanski, 785–806. New York: Guilford Press, 2007.

Cho, Sumi K. "Converging Stereotypes in Racialized Sexual Harassment: Where the Model Minority Meets Suzie Wong." *Journal of Gender, Race, & Justice* 1 (1997): 177–211.

Clanton, Dan W., Jr. "(Re)Dating the Story of Susanna: A Proposal." *JSJ* 34/2 (2003): 121–40.

Clayton, Edward T. "The Tragedy of Amos 'n' Andy." *Ebony* 16/12 (October 1961).

Coates, Ta-Nehisi. "My President Was Black." *The Atlantic*, January/February 2017.

Cohen, Shaye. *The Beginning of Jewishness*. Berkeley: University of California Press, 1999.

Cohick, Lynn. *Women in the World of the Earliest Christians: Illuminating Ancient Ways of Life*. Grand Rapids: Baker Academic, 2009.

Collins, John J. "Powers in Heaven: God, Gods, and Angels in the Dead Sea Scrolls." In *Religion in the Dead Sea Scrolls*, edited by J. J. Collins and R. A. Kugler, 9–28. Grand Rapids: Eerdmans, 2000.

Collins, Patricia Hill. *Black Sexual Politics: African American, Gender, and the New Racism*. New York: Routledge, 2004.

Concannon, Cavan W. *When You Were Gentiles: Specters of Ethnicity in Roman Corinth and Paul's Corinthian Correspondence*. New Haven, CT: Yale University Press, 2014.

Conway, Colleen M. *Men and Women in the Fourth Gospel: Gender and Johannine Characterization*. Atlanta: Scholars, 1999.

Conzelmann, Hans. *Acts of the Apostles*. Hermeneia. Philadelphia: Fortress, 1987.

———. *The Theology of St. Luke*. New York: Harper & Row, 1960.

Cope, Lamar. "Matthew XXV:31–46 'The Sheep and the Goats' Reinterpreted." *NovT* 11 (1969): 32–44.

Copeland, M. Shawn. "Wading through Many Sorrows: Toward a Theology of Suffering in Womanist Perspective." In *A Troubling in My Soul: Womanist Perspectives on Evil and Suffering*, edited by Emilie Townes, 109–29. Maryknoll, NY: Orbis, 1993.

Copher, Charles B. "The Black Presence in the Old Testament." In *Stony the Road We Trod: African American Biblical Interpretation*, edited by Cain Hope Felder, 146–64. Minneapolis: Fortress, 1991.

Cosby, Bill, and Alvin F. Poussaint. *Come On People: On the Path from Victims to Victors*. Nashville: Thomas Nelson, 2007.

Cosgrove, Charles. "Did Paul Value Ethnicity?" *CBQ* 68 (2006): 268–90.

Cousland, J. R. C. "The Feeding of the Four Thousand Gentiles in Matthew? Matthew 15:29–39 as a Test Case." *NovT* 41 (1999): 1–23.

Craig, Maureen A., and Jennifer A. Richeson. "More Diverse Yet Less Tolerant? How the Increasingly Diverse Racial Landscape Affects White Americans' Racial Attitudes." *Personality and Social Psychology Bulletin* 40/6 (2014): 750–61.

———. "On the Precipice of a 'Majority-Minority' America: Perceived Status

Threat from the Racial Demographic Shift Affects White Americans' Political Ideology." *Psychological Science* 25/6 (2014): 1189–97.

Crenshaw, Kimberlé, Neil Gotanda, Gary Peller, and Kendall Thomas, eds. *Critical Race Theory: The Key Writings That Formed the Movement*. New York: The New Press, 1995.

Crenshaw, Kimberlé, Priscilla Ocen, and Jyoti Nand. "Black Girls Matter: Pushed Out, Overpoliced, and Underprotected." Center for Intersectionality and Social Policy Studies. New York: African American Policy Forum, 2015.

Crockett, Larrimore C. "Luke 4:25–37 and Jewish-Gentile Relations in Luke-Acts." *JBL* 88 (1969): 177–83.

Crowder, Stephanie Buchanan. 2007. "The Gospel of Luke." In *True to Our Native Land: An African American New Testament Commentary*, edited by Brian K. Blount, Cain Hope Felder, Clarice J. Martin, and Emerson B. Powery, 158–85. Minneapolis: Fortress, 2007.

———. *When Momma Speaks: The Bible and Motherhood from a Womanist Perspective*. Louisville: Westminster John Knox, 2016.

Culbertson, Philip L. "Reclaiming the Matthean Vineyard Parables." *Encounter* 49/4 (1998): 257–58.

Dahl, Nils Alstrup. "Gentiles, Christians, and Israelites in the Epistle to the Ephesians." *HTR* 79 (1986): 31–39.

Dalmage, Heather M. "Discovering Racial Borders." In *Rethinking the Color Line: Readings in Race and Ethnicity*, edited by Charles A. Gallagher, 542–53. New York: McGraw Hill, 2007.

Dance, Darryl Cumber. *From My People: 400 Years of African American Folklore*. New York and London: W. W. Norton, 2002.

Daniels, Jessie. *White Lies: Race, Class, Gender, and Sexuality in White Supremacist Discourse*. New York: Routledge, 1997.

Darden, Lynn St. Clair. "A Womanist-Postcolonial Reading of the Samaritan Woman at the Well and Mary Magdalene at the Tomb." In *I Found God in Me: A Womanist Biblical Hermeneutics Reader*, edited by Mitzi J. Smith, 183–202. Eugene, OR: Cascade, 2015.

Davies, W. D., and Dale C. Allison Jr. *A Critical and Exegetical Commentary on the Gospel according to Saint Matthew*. 3 vols. ICC. Edinburgh: T&T Clark, 1988–1997.

Delgado, Richard, and Jean Stefancic. *Critical White Studies: Looking behind the Mirror*. Philadelphia: Temple University Press, 1997.

Derrett, J. Duncan M. "Law in the New Testament: The Syro-Phoenician Woman and the Centurion of Capernaum." *NovT* 15 (1973): 161–86.

DeSilva, David A. *Honor, Patronage, Kinship and Purity: Unlocking New Testament Culture*. Downers Grove, IL: InterVarsity, 2012.

Devine, Patricia G., Patrick S. Forscher, Anthony J. Austin, and William T. L. Cox. "Long-Term Reduction in Implicit Race Bias: A Prejudice Habitbreaking Intervention." *Journal of Experimental Social Psychology* 48/6 (2012): 1267–78.

DeYoung, Curtiss Paul, Michael O. Emerson, George Yancey, and Karen Chai Kim. *United by Faith: The Multiracial Congregation as an Answer to the Problem of Race.* New York: Oxford University Press, 2003.

DiAngelo, Robin. "White Fragility." *International Journal of Critical Pedagogy* 3/3 (2011): 54–70.

———. *White Fragility: Why It's So Hard for White People to Talk about Racism.* Boston: Beacon, 2018.

Dickerson, Febbie C. "Acts 9:36–43: The Many Faces of Tabitha, a Womanist Reading." In *I Found God in Me: A Womanist Biblical Hermeneutics Reader*, edited by Mitzi J. Smith, 296–312. Eugene, OR: Cascade, 2015.

Dickinson, Royce, Jr. "The Theology of the Jerusalem Conference: Acts 15:1–35." *Restoration Quarterly* 32/2 (1990): 65–83.

Douglas, Kelly Brown. "Marginalized People, Liberating Perspectives: A Womanist Approach to Biblical Interpretation." *Anglican Theological Review* 83/1 (2001): 41–47.

———. *What's Faith Got to Do with It? Black Bodies/Christian Souls.* Maryknoll, NY: Orbis Books, 2005.

———. "When the Subjugated Come to the Center." *Journal of Religious Thought* 52/2–53/1 (1996): 37–43.

Doyle, Sady. "America Loves Women like Hillary Clinton—As Long as They're Not Asking for a Promotion." *Quartz.* 25 February 2016. https://qz.com/624346/america-loves-women-like-hillary-clinton-as-long-as-theyre-not-asking-for-a-promotion/.

Du Bois, W. E. B. *The Souls of Black Folk, with a New Introduction by Randall Kenan.* New York: Signet, 1995.

Dube Shomanah, Musa W. *Postcolonial Feminist Interpretation of the Bible.* St. Louis: Chalice, 2000.

Duff, Paul B. *Who Rides the Beast? Prophetic Rivalry and the Rhetoric of Crisis in the Churches of the Apocalypse.* New York: Oxford University Press, 2001.

Dukes, Kristin N. "An Overlooked Link: Popular Media, Stereotypes, and the Incarceration of Black Girls and Young Women." In *Caged Women: Incarceration, Representation, and Media*, edited by Shirley A. Jackson and Laurie L. Gordy, 52–63. New York: Routledge, 2018.

Duling, Dennis. "2 Corinthians 11:22: Historical Context, Rhetoric, and Ethnicity." *Hervormde Teologiese Studies* 64/2 (2008): 819–43.

Dunn, James D. G. "The Incident at Antioch (Gal. 2:11–18)." *JSNT* 18 (1983): 3–57.

Durik, Amanda M., Janet Shibley Hyde, Amanda C. Marks, Amanda L. Roy, Debra Anaya, and Gretchen Schultz. "Ethnicity and Gender Stereotypes of Emotion." *Sex Roles* 54 (2006): 429–45.

Dyer, Jeff, Hal Gregersen, and Clayton M. Christensen. *The Innovator's DNA: Mastering the Five Skills of Disruptive Innovators*. Boston: Harvard Business Press, 2011.

Eagly, Alice H. "Few Women at the Top: How Role Incongruity Produces Prejudice and the Glass Ceiling." In *Leadership and Power: Identity Processes in Groups and Organizations*, edited by Daan van Knippenberg and Michael A. Hogg, 79–93. London: Sage, 2003.

Eagly, Alice H., and Jean Lau Chin. "Diversity and Leadership in a Changing World." *American Psychologist* 65/3 (2010): 216–24.

Eagly, Alice H., and Amanda B. Diekman. "What Is the Problem? Prejudice as an Attitude-in-Context." In *On the Nature of Prejudice: Fifty Years after Allport*, edited by John F. Dovidio, Peter Glick, and Laurie A. Rudman, 19–35. Malden, MA: Blackwell, 2005.

Eagly, Alice H., and Steven J. Karau. "Role Congruity Theory of Prejudice toward Female Leaders." *Psychological Review* 109/3 (2002): 573–98.

Earls, Aaron. "Most Evangelicals Choose Trump Over Biden, but Clear Divides Exist." *Lifeway Research*. 29 September 2020. https://lifewayresearch .com/2020/09/29/most-evangelicals-choose-trump-over-biden-but-clear -divides-exist/.

Easton, Burton Scott. *The Gospel before the Gospels*. London: Allen & Unwin, 1928.

Eichstedt, Jennifer L. "Problematic White Identities and a Search for Racial Justice." *Sociological Forum* 16 (2001): 445–70.

Elkins, Stanley M. *Slavery: A Problem in American Institutional and Intellectual Life*. Chicago: University of Chicago Press, 1959.

Ellis, E. Earle. "2 Corinthians 5:1–10 in Pauline Eschatology." *NTS* 6 (1960): 211–24.

Emerson, Michael O. "The Persistent Problem." Baylor University Center for Christian Ethics. https://www.baylor.edu/content/services/document .php/110974.pdf.

Emerson, Michael O., and Christian Smith. *Divided by Faith: Evangelical Religion and the Problem of Race in America*. New York: Oxford University Press, 2001.

Eng, David L. *Racial Castration: Managing Masculinity in Asian America*. Durham, NC: Duke University Press, 2001.

Espin, O. M. "Cultural and Historical Influences on Sexuality in Hispanic/Latin Women." In *All American Women: Lines That Divide, Ties That Bind*, edited by Johnnetta B. Cole, 272–84. New York: Free Press, 1986.

Evans, C. F. *Saint Luke*. Philadelphia: Trinity, 1990.

———, assisted by Danny Zacharias, Matt Walsh, and Scott Kohler. *The Pseudepigrapha* (English). Oaktree Software, 2008.

Faber, Judy. "CBS Fires Don Imus Over Racial Slur." *CBS News*. 12 April 2007. http://www.cbsnews.com/news/cbs-fires-don-imus-over-racial-slur/.

Feagin, Joe R. *Systemic Racism: A Theory of Oppression*. New York and London: Routledge, 2006.

Feeley-Harnick, Gillian. *The Lord's Table. Eucharist and Passover in Early Christianity*. Philadelphia: University of Pennsylvania Press, 1981.

Felder, Cain Hope. *Race, Racism, and the Biblical Narratives*. Minneapolis: Fortress, 2002.

Fernandez, John P. "The Impact of Racism on Whites in Corporate America." In *The Impacts of Racism on White Americans*, edited by Benjamin P. Bowser and Raymond G. Hunt, 157–78. Thousand Oaks, CA: Sage, 1996.

FitzGerald, Chloë, Angela Martin, Delphine Berner, and Samia Hurst. "Interventions Designed to Reduce Implicit Prejudices and Implicit Stereotypes in Real World Contexts: A Systematic Review." *BMC Psychology* 7/29 (2019): 1–12.

Fitzmyer, Joseph A. *The Gospel according to Luke*. 2 vols. AB 28–28A. Garden City, NY: Doubleday, 1981–1985.

Flender, Helmut. *St. Luke: Theologian of Redemptive History*. Philadelphia: Fortress, 1967.

Forbes, Greg. "Repentance and Conflict in the Parable of the Lost Son (Luke 15:11–32)." *JETS* 42/4 (1999): 211–30.

Forsyth, Craig J., Raymond W. Biggar, York A. Forsyth, and Holly Howat. "The Punishment Gap: Racial/Ethnic Comparisons in School Infractions by Objective and Subjective Definitions." *Deviant Behavior* 36 (2015): 276–87.

France, R. T. *Matthew: An Introduction and Commentary*. TNTC. Grand Rapids: Eerdmans, 1985.

Frankenberg, Ruth. *White Women, Race Matters: The Social Construction of Whiteness*. Minneapolis: University of Minnesota Press, 1993.

Frankfurter, David. "Jews or Not? Reconstructing the Other in Rev 2.9 and 3.9." *HTR* 94 (2001): 403–25.

Franklin, Eric. *Luke: Interpreter of Paul, Critic of Matthew*. JSNTSup 92. Sheffield: JSOT Press, 1994.

Fraser, John W. "Paul's Knowledge of Jesus: II Corinthians V.16 Once More." *NTS* 17 (1971): 293–97.

Freire, Paolo. *Pedagogy of the Oppressed*. New York: Herder & Herder, 1970.

Furnish, Victor Paul. *II Corinthians*. AB 32A. Garden City, NY: Doubleday, 1984.

Gafney, Wilda C. "A Black Feminist Approach to Biblical Studies." *Encounter* 67/4 (2006): 391–403.

———. *Womanist Midrash: A Reintroduction to the Women of the Torah and the Throne*. Louisville: Westminster John Knox, 2017.

Garces-Foley, Kathleen. "Multiethnic Congregations—Baylor University." Baylor University Center for Christian Ethics. https://www.baylor.edu/content /services/document.php/110977.pdf.

Garcia, Amber L., Heidi R. Riggio, Subha Palavinelu, and Lane Locher Culpepper. "Latinos' Perceptions of Interethnic Couples." *Hispanic Journal of Behavioral Sciences* 34/2 (2012): 349–62.

Garroway, Joshua D. "'Apostolic Irresistibility' and the Interrupted Speeches in Acts." *CBQ* 74 (2012): 738–52.

Gaventa, Beverly Roberts. *Acts*. ANTC. Nashville: Abingdon, 2003.

Geertz, Clifford. *Interpretation of Cultures*. New York: Basic Books, 1973.

Gehman, Henry Snyder. *The New Westminster Dictionary of the Bible*. Philadelphia: Westminster, 1970.

Georgi, Dieter. *The Opponents of Paul in Second Corinthians: A Study of Religious Propaganda in Late Antiquity*. Philadelphia: Fortress, 1986.

Gibson, Campbell, and Kay Jung. "Historical Census Statistics on Population Totals by Race, 1790 to 1990, and by Hispanic Origin, 1970 to 1990, for the United States, Regions, Divisions, and States." U.S. Census Bureau, Working Paper Series No. 56, September 2002. https://web.archive.org/web /20141224151538/http://www.census.gov/population/www/documenta tion/twps0056/twps0056.html.

Giffords Law Center. "'Stand Your Ground' Kills: How These NRA-Backed Laws Promote Racist Violence." Southern Poverty Law Center, 31 July 2020. https://www.splcenter.org/sites/default/files/_stand_your_ground_kills _-_how_these_nra-backed_laws_promote_racist_violence_1.pdf.

Gillman, John. "A Thematic Comparison: 1 Cor 15:50–57 and 2 Cor 5:1–5." *JBL* 107 (1988): 439–54.

Glasson, Thomas Francis. "2 Corinthians 5:1–10 Versus Platonism." *Scottish Journal of Theology* 43/2 (1990): 145–55.

Glaude, Eddie S., Jr. Review of *Divided by Faith: Evangelical Religion and the Problem of Race in America*, by Michael O. Emerson and Christian Smith. *Journal of Religion* 83/3 (2003): 513–14.

Glenn, Evelyn Nakano. *Shades of Difference: Why Skin Color Matters*. Stanford: Stanford University Press, 2009.

Goodacre, Mark S. *The Case Against Q: Studies in Markan Priority and the Synoptic Problem*. Harrisburg, PA: Trinity Press International, 2002.

Goodman, Diane. *Promoting Diversity and Social Justice: Educating People from Privileged Groups.* Thousand Oaks, CA: Sage, 2001.

Goodrich, Terry. "Multiracial Congregations Have Nearly Doubled, but They Still Lag behind the Makeup of Neighborhoods." Baylor University Media and Public Relations, 20 June 2018. https://www.baylor.edu/mediacommuni cations/news.php?action=story&story=199850.

Goodwyn, Wade. "Charleston's Black Leaders Want to See Justice as Much as Forgiveness." *NPR Morning Edition.* 2 July 2015. http://www.npr.org/2015 /07/02/419405863/charlestons-black-leaders-want-justice-as-much-as -forgiveness.

Gorman, Michael J. *Reading Revelation Responsibly: Uncivil Worship and Witness; Following the Lamb into the New Creation.* Eugene, OR: Cascade, 2011.

Goto, Courtney T. "Beyond the Black–White Binary of U.S. Race Relations: A Next Step in Religious Education." *Religious Education* 112/1 (2017): 33–45.

Goulder, Michael D. *Luke: A New Paradigm.* 2 vols. JSNTSup 20. Sheffield: JSOT Press, 1989.

Green, Bridgett A. "'Nobody's Free Until Everybody's Free': Exploring Gender and Class Injustice in a Story about Children (Luke 18:15–17)." In *Womanist Interpretation of the Bible: Expanding the Discourse*, edited by Gay L. Byron and Vanessa Lovelace, 291–310. Atlanta: Society of Biblical Literature, 2016.

Green, Joel B. *The Gospel of Luke.* NICNT. Grand Rapids: Eerdmans, 1997.

———. *Body, Soul and Human Life: The Nature of Humanity in the Bible.* Grand Rapids: Baker Academic, 2008.

Greenberg, Julie. "Beyond Allyship: Multiracial Work to End Racism." *Tikkun* 29/1 (2014): 11–18.

Gross, Kali Nicole. "African American Women, Mass Incarceration, and the Politics of Protection." *Journal of American History* 102/1 (2015): 25–33.

Guardiola-Sáenz, Leticia A. "Borderless Women and Borderless Texts: A Cultural Reading of Matthew 15:21–28." *Semeia* 78 (1997): 69–81.

Guelich, Robert A. *The Sermon on the Mount: A Foundation for Understanding.* Waco, TX: Word Books, 1982.

Guenther, Katja M., Sadie Pendaz, and Fortunata Songora Makene. "The Impact of Intersecting Dimensions of Inequality and Identity on the Racial Status of Eastern African Immigrants." *Sociological Forum* 26/1 (2011): 98–120.

Gwin, Minrose Clayton. *Black and White Women of the Old South: The Peculiar Sisterhood in American Literature.* Knoxville: University of Tennessee Press, 1985.

Haenchen, Ernst. *The Acts of the Apostles: A Commentary.* Louisville: Westminster John Knox, 1971.

Hager, Eli. "A Mass Incarceration Mystery." *Washington Post*. 15 December 2017. https://ils.fd.org/sites/ils.fd.org/files/uploaded_files/cja_resources/train ing/01.A%20Mass%20Incarceration%20Mystery_1.pdf.

Hagner, Donald A. *Matthew*. 2 vols. WBC 33. Dallas: Word Books, 1995.

Hahn, Adam, and Bertram Gawronski. "Facing One's Implicit Biases: From Awareness to Acknowledgment." *Journal of Personality and Social Psychology* 116/5 (2019): 1–43.

Hamer, Fannie Lou. "'Nobody's Free Until Everybody's Free': Speech Delivered at the Founding of the National Women's Political Caucus, Washington, D.C., July 10, 1971." In *The Speeches of Fannie Lou Hamer: To Tell It Like It Is*, edited by Fannie Lou Hamer, Maegan Parker Brooks, and Davis W. Houck, 134–39. Jackson, MS: University Press of Mississippi, 2011.

Hanek, Kathrin J., Fiona Lee, and Mary Yoko Brannen. "Individual Differences among Global/Multicultural Individuals: Cultural Experiences, Identity, and Adaptation." *International Studies of Management & Organization* 44/2 (2014): 75–89.

Hanson, John. "Dreams and Visions in the Graeco-Roman World and Early Christianity." In *Aufstieg und Niedergang der römischen Welt* 2.23.3, edited by Hildegard Temporini and Wolfgang Haase, 1395–1427. Berlin: de Gruyter, 1980.

Harlan, Philip A. "Climbing the Ethnic Ladder: Ethnic Hierarchies and Judean Responses." *JBL* 138 (2019): 665–86.

Harnack, Adolf von. *The Acts of the Apostles*. Translated by J. R. Wilkinson. London: Williams and Norgate, 1909.

———. *Luke the Physician: The Author of the Third Gospel and the Acts of the Apostles*. Translated by J. R. Wilkinson. London: Williams and Norgate, 1908.

Harrington, Daniel. "Polemical Parables in Matthew 24–25." *Union Seminary Quarterly Review* 44/3–4 (1991): 287–98.

Harris, Murray J. "Paul's View of Death in 2 Corinthians 5.1–10." In *New Dimensions in New Testament Study*, edited by R. N. Longenecker and M. C. Tenney, 317–28. Grand Rapids: Eerdmans, 1974.

———. *The Second Epistle to the Corinthians*. NIGTC. Grand Rapids: Eerdmans, 2005.

Harrisville, Roy A. "The Woman of Canaan: A Chapter in the History of Exegesis." *Interpretation* 20 (1996): 247–87.

Harvey, Jennifer. *Dear White Christians: For Those Still Longing for Racial Reconciliation*. Grand Rapids: Eerdmans, 2014.

Hauser, Christine. "Florida Woman Whose 'Stand Your Ground' Defense Was Rejected Is Released." *New York Times*. 7 February 2017. https://www.nytimes .com/2017/02/07/us/marissa-alexander-released-stand-your-ground.html.

Hays, Richard B. *Echoes of Scripture in the Gospels.* Waco, TX: Baylor University Press, 2016.

———. *Echoes of Scripture in the Letters of Paul.* Reprint. New Haven, CT: Yale University Press, 1993.

———. "'Have We Found Abraham to Be Our Forefather according to the Flesh?' A Reconsideration of Rom 4:1." *NovT* 27 (1985): 76–98.

———. *The Moral Vision of the New Testament: A Contemporary Introduction to New Testament Ethics.* New York: HarperCollins, 1996.

Heckel, Theo K. "Body and Soul in Saint Paul." In *Psyche and Soma: Physicians and Metaphysicians on the Mind-Body Problem from Antiquity to Enlightenment,* edited by John P. Wright and Paul Potter, 117–31. Oxford: Clarendon, 2000.

———. *Der innere Mensch: Der paulinische Verarbeitung eines platonischen Motivs.* WUNT 2.53. Tübingen: J. C. B. Mohr, 1993.

Hemer, Colin J. *The Letters to the Seven Churches of Asia in Their Local Setting.* JSNTSup 11. Sheffield: JSOT Press, 1986.

Hertig, Paul. "The Jubilee Mission of Jesus in the Gospel of Luke: Reversals of Fortunes." *Missiology: An International Review* 26/2 (1998): 167–79.

Hettlinger, Richard Frederick. "2 Corinthians 5:1–10." *Scottish Journal of Theology* 10/2 (1957): 174–94.

Hiers, Richard H. "Friends by Unrighteous Mammon: The Eschatological Proletariat (Luke 16:9)." *Journal of the American Academy of Religion* 38/1 (1970): 30–36.

Hill, David. "The Rejection of Jesus at Nazareth (Luke iv 16–30)." *NovT* 13/3 (1971): 161–80.

Hockey, Katherine M., and David G. Horrell. *Ethnicity, Race, Religion: Identities and Ideologies in Early Jewish and Christian Texts, and in Modern Biblical Interpretation.* London: Bloomsbury, 2018.

Hodge, Caroline Johnson. *If Sons, Then Heirs: A Study of Kinship and Ethnicity in the Letters of Paul.* New York: Oxford University Press, 2007.

Hoehner, Harold. *Ephesians: An Exegetical Commentary.* Grand Rapids: Baker Academic, 2002.

Hogg, Michael A. "From Group Conflict to Social Harmony: Leading across Diverse and Conflicting Social Identities." In *Crossing the Divide: Intergroup Leadership in a World of Difference,* edited by T. L. Pittinsky, 17–30. Boston: Harvard Business Press, 2009.

———. "A Social Identity Theory of Leadership. Personality and Social Psychology." *Personality and Social Psychology* 5/3 (2001): 184–200.

Hong, Hae-Jung. "Bicultural Competence and Its Impact on Team Effectiveness." *International Journal of Cross Cultural Management* 10/1 (2010): 93–120.

hooks, bell. *Yearning: Race, Gender, and Cultural Politics.* Boston: South End, 1990.

Horn, Friedrich Wilhelm. "Der Verzicht auf die Beschneidung im frühen Christentum." *NTS* 42/4 (1996): 479–505.

Horrell, David G. "'Race', 'Nation', 'People': Ethnic Identity Construction in 1 Peter 2:9." *NTS* 58/1 (2012): 123–43.

———. *Solidarity and Difference: A Contemporary Reading of Paul's Ethics.* 2nd ed. London: Bloomsbury, 2016.

Horsley, Richard A. *Covenant Economics: A Biblical Vision of Justice for All.* Louisville: Westminster John Knox, 2009.

Horvath, Agnes, Bjørn Thomassen, and Harald Wydra. "Introduction: Liminality and Cultures of Change." *International Political Anthropology* 2/1 (2009): 3–4.

Houlden, J. L. "Response to James D. G. Dunn." *JSNT* 19 (1983): 64–65.

House, Colin. "Defilement by Association: Some Insights from the Usage of KOINOΣ/KOINOΩ in Acts 10–11." *Andrews University Seminary Studies* 21/2 (1988): 143–53.

House, R. J., P. J. Hanges, M. Javidan, P. W. Dorfman, and V. Gupta. *Culture, Leadership, and Organizations: The GLOBE Study of 62 Societies.* Thousand Oaks, CA: Sage, 2004.

Huang, Margaret. "'Stand Your Ground'" Kills: A New Report from Giffords Law Center and SPLC Action." Southern Poverty Law Center, 31 July 2020. https://www.splcenter.org/news/2020/07/31/stand-your-ground-kills-new-report-giffords-law-center-and-splc-action?gclid=CjoKCQjw1 6KFBhCgARIsALB0g8IBN01rHorepHPSFcKprEImKvcvY56YgtVUr-Yhg ZNKRSSkclQHcVAaAvdaEALw_wcB.

Hunter, Margaret L. *Race, Gender, and the Politics of Skin Tone.* London and New York: Routledge, 2013.

Hutchinson, John C. "Women, Gentiles, and the Messianic Mission in Matthew's Genealogy." *Bibliotheca Sacra* 158/630 (2001): 152–64.

Hyun, Jane. *Breaking the Bamboo Ceiling: Career Strategies for Asian Americans.* New York: HarperCollins, 2006.

Instone-Brewer, David. "1 Corinthians 7 in the Light of the Jewish Greek and Aramaic Marriage and Divorce Papyri." *Tyndale Bulletin* 52/2 (2001): 225–44.

Jacobson, Matthew Freye. *Whiteness of a Different Color: European Immigrants and the Alchemy of Race.* Boston: Harvard University Press, 1998.

Jefford, Clayton N. "Tradition and Witness in Antioch: Acts 15 and Didache 6." *Perspectives in Religious Studies* 19/4 (1992): 409–19.

Jennings, Theodore W., Jr., and Tat-Siong Benny Liew. "Mistaken Identities but Model Faith: Rereading the Centurion, the Chap, and the Christ in Matthew 8:5–13." *JBL* 123/3 (2004): 467–94.

Jennings, Willie James. *After Whiteness: An Education in Belonging.* Grand Rapids: Eerdmans, 2020.

———. *The Christian Imagination: Theology and the Origins of Race.* New Haven, CT: Yale University Press, 2010.

Jeremias, Joachim. *Jesus' Promise to the Nations.* Translated by S. H. Hooke. London: SCM Press, 1958.

———. *The Parables of Jesus.* Rev. ed. New York: Charles Scribner's Sons, 1963.

Jervell, Jacob. "The Church of Jews and God-Fearers." In *Luke-Acts and the Jewish People: Eight Critical Perspectives*, edited by Joseph B. Tyson, 11–20. Minneapolis: Augsburg, 1988.

———. *Luke and the People of God: A New Look at Luke-Acts.* Repr. Eugene, OR: Wipf & Stock Publishers, 2002.

———. *The Theology of the Acts of the Apostles.* Cambridge: Cambridge University Press, 1996.

Johnson, Judy A. "The Culture Hero: Anansi." In *Critical Survey of Mythology and Folklore: Heroes and Heroines*, edited by B. Kundanis, 273–81. Pasadena, CA: Salem Press, 2013.

Johnson, Luke Timothy. *The Gospel of Luke.* Sacra Pagina. Collegeville, MN: Liturgical Press, 1991.

Johnson, Matthew V., James A. Noel, and Demetrius K. Williams. *Onesimus Our Brother: Reading Religion, Race, and Culture in Philemon.* Minneapolis: Fortress, 2012.

Jones, Chenelle A., and Renita L. Seabrook. "The New Jane Crow: Mass Incarceration and the Denied Maternity of Black Women." In *Race, Ethnicity and Law*, edited by Mathieu Deflem, 135–54. Bingley, UK: Emerald Group Publishing Limited, 2017.

Jones, James M. *Prejudice and Racism.* 2nd ed. New York: McGraw-Hill, 1997.

Juel, Donald. "The Strange Silence of the Bible." *Interpretation* 51/1 (1997): 5–19.

Junior, Nyasha. *An Introduction to Womanist Biblical Interpretation.* Louisville: Westminster John Knox, 2015.

Kaalund, Jennifer. *Reading Hebrews and 1 Peter with the African American Great Migration: Diaspora, Place and Identity.* LNTS 598. London: Bloomsbury, 2018.

Kanter, Rosabeth Moss. "Creating Common Ground." In *Crossing the Divide: Intergroup Leadership in a World of Difference*, edited by Todd L. Pittinsky, 73–86. Boston: Harvard Business Press, 2009.

Keener, Craig. *Acts: An Exegetical Commentary.* 4 vols. Grand Rapids: Baker Academic, 2012–2015.

———. *A Commentary on the Gospel of Matthew.* Grand Rapids: Eerdmans, 1999.

———. *The Gospel of John: A Commentary.* 2 vols. Peabody, MA: Hendrickson, 2003.

———. "Matthew's Missiology: Making Disciples of the Nations (Matthew 28:19–20)." *Asian Journal of Pentecostal Studies* 12 (2009): 3–20.

———. *1–2 Corinthians.* NCBC. Cambridge: Cambridge University Press, 2005.

Keim, Theodor. *The History of Jesus of Nazara.* 6 vols. Translated by A. Ransom and E. Geldart. London: Williams and Norgate, 1876–1883.

Kelley, Shawn. *Racializing Jesus: Race, Ideology and the Formation of Modern Biblical Scholarship.* London: Routledge, 2002.

Kendi, Ibram X. *How to Be an Antiracist.* New York: One World, 2019.

Kim, Bitna. "Asian Female and Caucasian Male Couples: Exploring the Attraction." *Pastoral Psychology* 60 (2011): 233–44.

Kimball, Charles. "Jesus' Exposition of Scripture in Luke 4:16–30: An Inquiry in Light of Jewish Hermeneutics." *Perspectives in Religious Studies* 21/3 (1994): 179–202.

King, Martin Luther, Jr. *The Papers of Martin Luther King, Jr.*, edited by Clayborne Carson, Peter Holloran, Ralph Luker, and Penny A. Russell. Berkeley: University of California Press, 1992.

Kingsbury, Jack Dean. "Observations of the Miracle Chapters of Matthew 8–9." *CBQ* 40 (1978): 559–73.

Knight, Jennifer L., Michelle R. Hebl, Jessica B. Foster, and Laura M. Mannix. "Out of Role? Out of Luck: The Influence of Race and Leadership Status on Performance Appraisals." *The Journal of Leadership and Organizational Studies* 9/3 (2003): 85–93.

Koet, Bart J. *Five Studies on the Interpretation of Scriptures in Luke-Acts.* Leuven: Peeters Publishers, 1989.

Kolasny, Judette. "An Example of Rhetorical Criticism: Luke 4:16–30." In *New Views on Luke and Acts*, edited by Earl Richard, 67–77. Collegeville, MN: Liturgical Press, 1990.

Kraybill, J. Nelson. *Apocalypse and Allegiance: Worship, Politics, and Devotion in the Book of Revelation.* Grand Rapids: Brazos, 2010.

LaFromboise, Teresa, Hardin L. K. Coleman, and Jennifer Gerton. "Psychological Impact of Biculturalism: Evidence and Theory." *Psychological Bulletin* 114/3 (1993): 395–412.

Lambrecht, J. 1994. "The Nekrōsis of Jesus: Ministry and Suffering in 2 Corinthians 4,7–15." In *Studies on 2 Corinthians*, edited by J. Lambrecht and R. Bieringer, 309–33. BETL 112. Leuven: Leuven University Press, 1994.

LaVerdiere, Eugene A., and William G. Thompson. "New Testament Communities in Transition: A Study of Matthew and Luke." *Theological Studies* 37/4 (1976): 567–97.

Lee, Hak Joon. *The Great World House: Martin Luther King, Jr., and Global Ethics.* Cleveland, OH: Pilgrim Press, 2011.

Lee, Jennifer, and Frank D. Bean. "Reinventing the Color Line: Immigration and America's New Racial/Ethnic Divide." *Social Forces* 86/2 (2007): 561–86.

Leung, Angela Ka-yee, William W. Maddux, Adam D. Galinsky, and Chi-yue Chiu. "Multicultural Experience Enhances Creativity: The When and How." *American Psychologist* 63/3 (2008): 169–81.

Levin, Dan. "As More Mothers Fill Prisons, Children Suffer 'A Primal Wound.'" *New York Times*, 28 December 2019. https://www.nytimes.com/2019/12/28/us /prison-mothers-children.html.

Levine, Amy-Jill. "Hemmed in on Every Side: Jews and Women in the Book of Susanna." In *The Feminist Companion to Esther, Judith and Susanna*, edited by Althalya Brenner, 303–23. Sheffield: Sheffield Academic Press, 1995.

———. "Matthew's Advice to a Divided Readership." In *The Gospel of Matthew in Current Study: Studies in Memory of William G. Thompson, S.J.*, edited by David E. Aune, 22–41. Grand Rapids: Eerdmans, 2001.

———. *The Social and Ethnic Dimensions of Matthean Social History: "Go Nowhere among the Gentiles . . ." (Matt. 10:5b)*. Lewiston, NY: Edwin Mellen, 1988.

Lewis, A. E. "'What Group?': Studying Whites and Whiteness in the Era of 'Colorblindness.'" *Sociological Theory* 22 (2004): 623–46.

Liew, Tat-Siong Benny. "Acts." In *Global Bible Commentary*, edited by Daniel Patte, 419–28. Nashville: Abingdon, 2004.

———. "Margins and (Cutting-)Edges: On the (Il)Legitimacy and Intersections of Race, Ethnicity, and (Post)Colonialism." In *Postcolonial Biblical Criticism: Interdisciplinary Intersections*, edited by Stephen D. Moore and Fernando F. Segovia, 114–65. London: A&C Black, 2005.

Lincoln, Andrew T. *Ephesians*. WBC 42. Dallas: Word Books, 1990.

Lincoln, Andrew T., and Alexander J. M. Wedderburn. *Theology of the Later Pauline Epistles.* Cambridge: Cambridge University Press, 1993.

Lischer, Richard. *The Preacher King: Martin Luther King, Jr. and the Word That Moved America.* London and New York: Oxford University Press, 1997.

Livingston, Gretchen, and Anna Brown. "Intermarriage in the U.S. 50 Years after Loving v. Virginia: 1. Trends and Patterns in Intermarriage." Pew Research Center, 18 May 2017. https://www.pewresearch.org/social-trends/2017 /05/18/1-trends-and-patterns-in-intermarriage/.

Livingston, Robert W., Ashleigh Shelby Rosette, and Ella F. Washington. "Can an Agentic Black Woman Get Ahead? The Impact of Race and Interpersonal

Dominance on Perceptions of Female Leaders." *Psychological Science* 23/4 (2012): 354–58.

Lopez, Johana P. "Perspectives in HRD—Speaking with Them or Speaking for Them: A Conversation about the Effect of Stereotypes in the Latina/Hispanic Women's Experiences in the United States." *New Horizons in Adult Education & Human Resource Development* 25/2 (2013): 99–106.

Lorde, Audre. *The Collected Poems of Audre Lorde*. New York: W. W. Norton & Company, 1997.

———. *Sister Outsider: Essays and Speeches by Audre Lorde*. Berkeley: Crossing, 2007.

Luz, Ulrich. *Matthew 8–20: A Commentary*. Translated by James E. Crouch. Minneapolis: Fortress, 2001.

Lysiak, Matthew. "Charleston Massacre: Mental Illness Common Thread for Mass Shootings." *Newsweek*, 19 June 2015. http://www.newsweek.com/charleston-massacre-mental-illness-common-thread-mass-shootings-344789.

Lyttle, Allyn D., Gina G. Barker, and Terry Lynn Cornwell. "Adept through Adaptation: Third Culture Individuals' Interpersonal Sensitivity." *International Journal of Intercultural Relations* 35 (2011): 686–94.

Maier, Harry O. "Coming out of Babylon: A First World Reading of Revelation among Immigrants." In *From Every People and Nation: The Book of Revelation in Intercultural Perspective*, edited by David Rhoads, 62–81. Minneapolis: Fortress, 2005.

Maloy, Simon. "The 20 Worst Racial Attacks Limbaugh's Advertisers Have Sponsored." *Media Matters*, 7 March 2012. http://mediamatters.org/blog/2012/03/07/the-20-worst-racial-attacks-limbaughs-advertise/184776.

Mance, Ajuan Maria. "Sapphire (Stereotype)." In *Writing African American Women: An Encyclopedia of Literature by and about Women of Color*, edited by Elizabeth Ann Beaulieu, 778–79. Westport, CT: Greenwood Press, 2006.

Maparyan, Layli. "Miracles and Gifts: A Womanist Reading of John 14:12–14 and Ephesians 4:11–16." In *Womanist Interpretation of the Bible: Expanding the Discourse*, edited by Gay L. Byron and Vanessa Lovelace, 331–38. Atlanta: Society of Biblical Literature, 2016.

Marchal, Joseph A. "Mimicry and Colonial Differences: Gender, Ethnicity, and Empire in the Interpretation of Pauline Imitation." In *Prejudice and Christian Beginnings: Investigating Race, Gender, and Ethnicity in Early Christian Studies*, edited by Laura Nasrallah and Elisabeth Schüssler Fiorenza, 101–27. Minneapolis: Fortress, 2009.

Marshall, Emily Zobel. "Liminal Anansi: Symbol of Order and Chaos—An Exploration of Anansi's Roots Amongst the Asante of Ghana." *Caribbean Quarterly: A Journal of Caribbean Culture* 53/3 (2007): 30–40.

Marshall, I. Howard. *The Acts of the Apostles: An Introduction and Commentary.* TNTC. Grand Rapids: Eerdmans, 1980.

———. *The Gospel of Luke.* NIGTC. Grand Rapids: Eerdmans, 1978.

Marshall, Peter. *Enmity in Corinth: Social Conventions in Paul's Relations with the Corinthians.* WUNT 2.23. Tübingen: Mohr Siebeck, 1987.

Martin, Ralph P. "An Epistle in Search of a Life Setting." *Expository Times* 79 (1968): 296–302.

Martinez, Elizabeth. "Seeing More Than Black and White: Latinos, Racism, and the Cultural Divide." In *Race, Ethnicity, and Gender*, edited by Joseph F. Healey and Eileen O'Brien, 285–90. Los Angeles: Pine Forge, 2007.

Martyn, J. Louis. *Galatians.* AB 33A. New York: Doubleday, 1997.

Massie, Victoria M. "White Women Benefit Most from Affirmative Action—and Are among Its Fiercest Opponents." *Vox*, 23 June 2016. Accessed 13 February 2021. https://www.vox.com/2016/5/25/11682950/fisher-supreme-court-white-women-affirmative-action.

Matera, Frank J. *II Corinthians: A Commentary.* NTL. Louisville: Westminster John Knox, 2003.

Mbiti, John S. *African Religions and Philosophy.* London: Heinemann, 1969.

McFague, Sallie. *Metaphorical Theology: Models of God in Religious Language.* Philadelphia: Fortress, 1982.

McGhee, Heather. *The Sum of Us: What Racism Costs Everyone and How We Can Prosper Together.* New York: One World, 2021.

McIntosh, Peggy. "White Privilege: Unpacking the Invisible Knapsack." *Independent School* 49/2 (1990): 30–36.

McNeile, A. H. *The Gospel according to St. Matthew.* London: Macmillan, 1915.

McWhorter, John. "Getting over Identity." In *Reinventing the Melting Pot: The New Immigrants and What It Means to Be American*, edited by Tamar Jacoby. New York: Basic Books, 2004.

———. *Losing the Race: Self-Sabotage in Black America.* New York: Free Press, 2000.

Meeks, Wayne A., and Robert L. Wilken. *Jews and Christians in Antioch in the First Four Centuries of the Common Era.* Missoula, MT: Scholars, 1978.

Meier, John P. *A Marginal Jew: Rethinking the Historical Jesus.* Vol. 3. New York: Doubleday, 1991.

Mesick, Clair E. "Driven by Grief, Inspired by Christ: Paul 'Beside Himself' in 2 Cor 5:13." *NovT* 61 (2019): 137–55.

Metzger, Bruce Manning. *Textual Commentary to the Greek New Testament.* 2nd ed. Stuttgart: Deutsche Bibelgesellschaft; London: United Bible Society, 1994.

Metzl, Jonathan M. *Dying of Whiteness: How the Politics of Racial Resentment Is Killing America's Heartland*. New York: Basic Books, 2019.

Michael, Ali, and Mary C. Conger with Susan Bickerstaff, Katherine Crawford-Garrett, and Ellie Fitts Fulmer. "Becoming an Anti-Racist White Ally: How a White Affinity Group Can Help." *Perspectives on Urban Education* 6/1 (2009): 56–60.

Miller, Chris. "Did Peter's Vision in Acts 10 Pertain to Men or the Menu?" *Bibliotheca Sacra* 159 (2002): 302–17.

Miller, John B. "Exploring the Function of Symbolic Dream-Visions in the Literature of Antiquity, with Another Look at 1QapGen 19 and Acts 10." *Perspectives in Religious Studies* 37/4 (2010): 441–55.

Miller, Patrick D., Jr. "Book Review: An Exposition of Luke 4:16–21." *Interpretation* 29/4 (1975): 417–21.

Mills, Charles W. *The Racial Contract*. Ithaca, NY: Cornell University Press, 1997.

Mio, Jeffrey Scott. "Asians on the Edge: The Reciprocity of Allied Behavior." *Cultural Diversity and Ethnic Minority Psychology* 10/1 (2004): 90–94.

Moore, Andrea M. "Confused or Multicultural: A Phenomenological Analysis of the Self-Perception of Third Culture Kids with Regard to Their Cultural Identity." MA Thesis. Liberty University, 2011.

Morris, Edward W., and Brea L. Perry. "Girls Behaving Badly? Race, Gender, and Subjective Evaluation in the Discipline of African American Girls." *Sociology of Education* 90/2 (2017): 127–48.

Morton, Patricia. *Disfigured Images: The Historical Assault on Afro-American Women*. New York: Greenwood, 1991.

Mounce, Robert H. *Matthew, A Good News Commentary*. San Francisco: Harper & Row, 1985.

Muddiman, John. *The Epistle to the Ephesians*. BNTC. London: Continuum, 2001.

Mukasa-Mugerwa, E. *The Camel (Camelus Dromedarius): A Bibliographical Review*. Addis Ababa, Ethiopia: International Livestock Center for Africa, 1981.

Nadar, Sarojini. "Paradigm Shifts in Mission: From an Ethic of Domination to an Ethic of Justice and Love—The Case of 1 Tim. 2:8–15." *Missionalia* 33/2 (2005): 303–14.

Nagel, Caroline R. "Rethinking Geographies of Assimilation." *The Professional Geographer* 61/3 (2009): 400–407.

National Geographic. "Animals Photo Ark: Arabian Camel." 10 May 2011. Accessed 10 June 2021. https://www.nationalgeographic.com/animals/mammals/facts/arabian-camel.

National Research Council. *Racial and Ethnic Differences in the Health of Older Americans*. Washington, DC: The National Academies Press, 1997.

Navarrete, Veronica, and Sharon Rae Jenkins. "Cultural Homelessness, Multiminority Status, Ethnic Identity Development, and Self Esteem." *International Journal of Intercultural Relations* 35 (2011): 791–804.

Nave, Guy. "2 Corinthians." In *True to Our Native Land: An African American New Testament Commentary*, edited by Brian K. Blount, Cain Hope Felder, Clarice J. Martin, and Emerson B. Powery, 307–32. Minneapolis: Fortress, 2007.

Nemeth, C., and J. Wachtler. "Creative Problem Solving as a Result of Majority vs. Minority Influence." *European Journal of Social Psychology* 13/1 (1983): 45–55.

Neumann, Sandra L. "The 'Why's' and 'How's' of Being a Social Justice Ally." In *Getting Culture: Incorporating Diversity Across the Curriculum*, edited by Regan A. R. Gurung and Loreto R. Prieto, 65–75. Sterling, VA: Stylus, 2009.

Neuner, Gerhard. "Socio-Cultural Interim Worlds in Foreign Language Teaching and Learning." In *Intercultural Competence*, edited by Michael Byram, 15–62. Council of Europe. 2003.

Neutel, Karin. *A Cosmopolitan Ideal: Paul's Declaration "Neither Jew nor Greek, Neither Slave nor Free, Neither Male and Female" in the Context of First-Century Thought*. LNTS 513. London: Bloomsbury, 2015.

Newkirk, Vann R., II. "How Shelby County v. Holder Broke America." *The Atlantic*, 10 July 2018. https://www.theatlantic.com/politics/archive/2018/07/how-shelby-county-broke-america/564707/.

Neyrey, Jerome H. "'I Am the Door' (John 10:7, 9): Jesus the Broker in the Fourth Gospel." *CBQ* 69 (2007): 271–91.

Nguyễn, Ann Thúy, and Maya Pendleton. "Recognizing Race in Language: Why We Capitalize 'Black' and 'White.'" Center for the Study of Social Policy, 23 March 2020. https://cssp.org/2020/03/recognizing-race-in-language-why-we-capitalize-black-and-white/.

Niebuhr, Karl-Wilhelm. *Heidenapostel aus Israel: Die jüdische Identität des Paulus nach ihrer Darstellung in seinen Briefen*. WUNT 62. Tübingen: J. C. B. Mohr, 1992.

Niebuhr, Reinhold. *Moral Man and Immoral Society: A Study in Ethics and Politics*. New York: Scribner, 1960.

Nir, Sarah Maslin. "How 2 Lives Collided in Central Park, Rattling the Nation." *The New York Times*, 14 October 2020. https://www.nytimes.com/2020/06/14/nyregion/central-park-amy-cooper-christian-racism.html.

Nolland, John. *The Gospel of Matthew*. NIGTC. Grand Rapids: Eerdmans, 2005.

Nørgaard, Nina, Beatrix Busse, and Rocío Montoro. *Key Terms in Stylistics*. London: A&C Black, 2010.

Northouse, Peter G. *Leadership: Theory and Practice*. 5th ed. New York: Sage Publications, 2010.

Nuamah, Sally A. "In Columbus, Police Killed a Black Teenage Girl. That Fits a Rarely Discussed Pattern." *Washington Post*. 22 April 2021. https://www.washingtonpost.com/politics/2021/04/22/columbus-police-killed-black-teenage-girl-that-fits-rarely-discussed-pattern/

O'Day, Gail R. "John." In *The Women's Bible Commentary*, edited by Carol A. Newsom and Sharon H. Ringe, 293–304. Louisville: Westminster John Knox, 1992.

Okazaki, Sumie. "Teaching Gender Issues in Asian American Psychology: A Pedagogical Framework." *Psychology of Women Quarterly* 22 (1998): 33–52.

Omi, Michael, and Howard Winant. *Racial Formation Theory in the United States: From the 1960's to the 1990's*. Rev. ed. New York: Routledge, 1994.

———. "The Theoretical Status of the Concept of Race." In *Race, Identity and Representation in Education*, edited by Cameron McCarthy, Warren Crichlow, Greg Dimitriadis, and Nadine Dolby, 3–12. New York and London: Routledge, 2005.

O'Neill, John. "The Absence of the 'In Christ' Theology in 2 Corinthians 5." *Australian Biblical Review* 35 (1987): 99–106.

Oppel, Richard A., Jr., Derrick Bryson Taylor, and Nicole Bogel-Burroughs. "What to Know about Breonna Taylor's Death." *New York Times*, 26 April 2021. https://www.nytimes.com/article/breonna-taylor-police.html.

Osborne, Grant R. *Revelation*. BECNT. Grand Rapids: Baker Academic, 2002.

Park, Wongi. *The Politics of Race and Ethnicity in Matthew's Passion Narrative*. New York: Springer, 2019.

Patel, Viraj S. "Moving toward an Inclusive Model of Allyship for Racial Justice." *Vermont Connection* 32 (2011): 78–88.

Patterson, Orlando. *Rituals of Blood: Consequences of Slavery in Two American Centuries*. Washington, DC: Civitas/CounterPoint, 1998.

Perea, Juan F. "The Black/White Binary Paradigm of Race." In *The Latino/a Condition: A Critical Reader*, edited by Richard Delgado and Jean Stefancic, 359–68. New York: New York University Press, 1998.

———. "The Black/White Binary Paradigm of Race: The Normal Science of American Racial Thought." *California Law Review* 85/5 (1997): 1213–58.

Perkins, Pheme. *Ephesians*. ANTC. Nashville: Abingdon, 1997.

Perriman, Andrew C. "Paul and the Parousia: 1 Corinthians 15:50–57 and 2 Corinthians 5:1–5." *NTS* 35/4 (1989): 512–21.

Petzke, G. *Das Sondergut des Evangeliums nach Lukas*. Zurich: Theologischer Verlag, 1990.

Philips, Amber. "Why Is the Confederate Flag Still a Thing Even Though the South Lost the Civil War?" *Washington Post.* 10 July 2015. http://www.washing tonpost.com/news/the-fix/wp/2015/07/10/why-is-the-confederate-flag -still-a-thing-even-though-the-south-lost-the-civil-war/.

Phillips, Katherine W. "How Diversity Makes Us Smarter: Being around People Who Are Different from Us Makes Us More Creative, More Diligent and Harder-Working." *Scientific American* (2014): 43–47.

Philo. *On the Special Laws, On the Virtues, On Rewards and Punishments.* Translated by F. H. Colson. Loeb Classical Library No. 341. Cambridge: Harvard University Press, 1939.

Pierson, Emma, Camelia Simoiu, Jan Overgoor, Sam Corbett-Davies, Daniel Jenson, Amy Shoemaker, Vignesh Ramachandran, Phoebe Barghouty, Cheryl Philips, Ravi Shroff, and Sharad Goel. "A Large-Scale Analysis of Racial Disparities in Police Stops across the United States." *Nature Human Behaviour* 4 (2010): 736–45.

Pippin, Tina. "Jezebel Re-Vamped." *Semeia* 69–70 (1995): 221–33.

Pittinsky, Todd L. "Intergroup Leadership: What It Is, Why It Matters, and How It Is Done." In *Crossing the Divide: Intergroup Leadership in a World of Difference*, edited by T. L. Pittinsky, xi–xxvii. Boston: Harvard Business Press, 2009.

———. "A Two-Dimensional Model of Intergroup Leadership: The Case of National Diversity." *American Psychologist* 65/3 (2010): 194–200.

Pittman, Ashton. "Elizabeth Warren, Hillary Clinton and the Sexist Hypocrisy of the 'Likability' Media Narrative. Here We Go Again." *Think: Opinion, Analysis, Essays.* 5 January 2019. https://www.nbcnews.com/think/opin ion/elizabeth-warren-hillary-clinton-sexist-hypocrisy-likability-media -narrative-here-ncna955021.

Plummer, Alfred. *An Exegetical Commentary on the Gospel according to St. Matthew.* London and New York: Charles Scribner, 1909.

Plutarch. *Moralia.* 2 vols. Translated by F. C. Babbitt. Loeb Classical Library. Boston: Harvard University Press, 1927.

Porter, Stanley E. 1995. Idioms *of the Greek New Testament.* 2nd ed. Sheffield: JSOT Press, 1995.

———. *Verbal Aspect in the Greek of the New Testament.* New York: Peter Lang, 1989.

Poteat, V. Paul, and Lisa B. Spanierman. "Further Validation of the Psychosocial Costs of Racism to Whites Scale among Employed Adults." *The Counseling Psychologist* 36 (2008): 871–94.

Powery, Emerson B. *Jesus Reads Scripture: The Function of Jesus' Use of Scripture in the Synoptic Gospels*. BibInt 63. Leiden: Brill, 2003.

Price, James L. "Luke 15:11–32." *Interpretation* 31/1 (1977): 64–69.

Quadagno, Jill S. *The Color of Welfare: How Racism Undermined the War on Poverty*. New York: Oxford University Press, 1994.

Reason, R. D., and N. J. Evans. "The Complicated Realities of Whiteness: From Color Blind to Racially Cognizant." *New Directions for Student Services* 120 (2007): 67–76.

Red Horse, John G. "Family Structure and Value Orientation in American Indians." *Social Casework* 61/8 (1980): 462–67.

Rhamie, Gifford Charles Alphaeus. "Whiteness, Conviviality and Agency: The Ethiopian Eunuch (Acts 8:26–40) and Conceptuality in the Imperial Imagination of Biblical Studies." PhD dissertation. Canterbury Christ Church University, 2019.

Rice, Joy K. "Collaboration and Leadership." In *Women and Leadership: Transforming Visions and Diverse Voices*, edited by J. L. Chin, B. Lott, J. K. Rice, and J. Sanches-Hucles, 127–139. Malden, MA: Blackwell, 2007.

Riggs, Marcia Y. *Plenty Good Room: Women vs. Male Power in the Black Church*. Eugene, OR: Wipf & Stock, 2003.

———. "The Socio-Religious Ethical Tradition of Black Women: Implications for the Black Church's Role in Black Liberation." *Union Seminary Quarterly Review* 43/4 (1989): 119–32.

Ringe, Sharon H. "Luke 4:16–44: A Portrait of Jesus as Herald of God's Jubilee." *Proceedings of the Eastern Great Lakes Biblical Society* 1 (1981): 73–84.

Rink, Floor, and Naomi Ellemers. "Managing Diversity in Work Groups: How Identity Processes Affect Diverse Work Groups." In *The Glass Ceiling in the 21st Century: Understanding Barriers to Gender Equality*, edited by M. Barreto, M. K. Ryan, and M. T. Schmitt, 281–303. Washington, DC: American Psychological Association, 2009.

Ripat, Pauline. "Expelling Misconceptions: Astrologers at Rome." *Classical Philology* 106 (2011): 115–54.

Ritchie, Andrea J. "Dajerria Becton Survived a Violent Arrest at a Pool Party and Went Viral." *Teen Vogue*. 19 June 2018. https://www.teenvogue.com/story/dajerria-becton-arrest-pool-party-viral.

Roberts, Alexander, and James Donaldson. *The Apostolic Fathers with Justin Martyr and Irenaeus*. Vol. 1. Christian Literature Publishing, 1885; reprint Peabody, MA: Hendrickson, 1994.

Rosette, Ashleigh Shelby, and Leigh Plunkett Tost. "Agentic Women and Communal Leadership: How Role Prescriptions Confer Advantage to Top Women Leaders." *Journal of Applied Psychology* 95/2 (2010): 221–35.

Rothman, Lily. "The Long History Behind Donald Trump's 'America First' Foreign Policy." *Time*, 28 March 2016. https://time.com/4273812/america-first -donald-trump-history/.

Ryan, Michelle K., and S. Alexander Haslam. "The Glass Cliff: Exploring the Dynamics Surrounding the Appointment of Women to Precarious Leadership Positions." *Academy of Management Review* 32/2 (2007): 549–72.

Saddington, D. B. "The Centurion in Matthew 8:5–13: Consideration of the Proposal of Theodore W. Jennings, Jr., and Tat-Siong Benny Liew." *JBL* 125 (2006): 140–42.

Said, Edward. *Orientalism*. New York: Vintage, 1979.

Salomone, Rosemary. "Transnational Schooling and the New Immigrants: Developing Dual Identities in the United States." *Intercultural Education* 19/5 (2008): 383–93.

Sanchez-Hucles, J. V., and D. D. Davis. "Women and Women of Color in Leadership: Complexity, Identity, and Intersectionality." *American Psychologist* 65/3 (2010): 171–81.

Sanders, E. P. *Jesus and Judaism*. Minneapolis: Fortress, 1985.

———. "Literary Dependence in Colossians." *JBL* 85 (1966): 28–45.

———. *Paul, the Law, and the Jewish People*. Philadelphia: Fortress, 1983.

Sanders, E. P., and Margaret Davies. *Studying the Synoptic Gospels*. London: SCM; Philadelphia: Trinity Press International, 1989.

Sanders, Eli. "In Her Own Words: The Political Beliefs of the Protester Who Interrupted Bernie Sanders." *The Stranger*, 11 August 2015. https://www .thestranger.com/blogs/slog/2015/08/11/22680645/in-her-own-words-the -political-beliefs-of-the-protester-who-interrupted-bernie-sanders.

Sanders, Jack T. "The Jewish People in Luke-Acts." In *Luke-Acts and the Jewish People: Eight Critical Perspectives*, edited by Joseph B. Tyson, 51–75. Minneapolis: Augsburg, 1988.

———. *The Jews in Luke-Acts*. Philadelphia: Fortress, 1987.

Sanders, James A. "From Isaiah 61 to Luke 4." In *Christianity, Judaism, and Other Greco-Roman Cults Studies for Morton Smith at Sixty*, edited by Morton Smith and Jacob Neusner, 75–106. Leiden: Brill, 1975.

Savage, Timothy. *Power through Weakness: Paul's Understanding of the Christian Ministry in 2 Corinthians*. New York: Cambridge University Press, 1996.

Savelle, Charles H. "A Reexamination of the Prohibitions in Acts 15." *Bibliotheca Sacra* 161 (2004): 449–68.

Schellenberg, Ryan S. "Paul, Samson Occom, and the Constraints of Boasting:

A Comparative Rereading of 2 Corinthians 10–13." *HTR* 109/4 (2016): 512–35.

Schiffman, Lawrence. *Who Was a Jew?* Hoboken, NJ: Ktav, 1985.

Schlier, Heinrich. *Der Brief an die Epheser: Ein Kommentar.* Düsseldorf: Patmos, 1957.

Schnackenburg, Rudolf. *Epistle to the Ephesians: A Commentary.* Translated by Helen Heron. BNTC. Edinburgh: T&T Clark, 1991.

Schüssler Fiorenza, Elisabeth. *Revelation: Vision of a Just World.* Minneapolis: Fortress, 1991.

Schwarcz, Lilia Moritz. "Not Black, Not White, Just the Opposite: Culture, Race and National Identity in Brazil." Paper for the Centre for Brazilian Studies, 2003.

Schweizer, Eduard. "σάρξ, σαρκικός, σάρκινος." In *Theological Dictionary of the New Testament,* edited by Geoffrey William Bromiley, 8:125–35. Grand Rapids: Eerdmans, 1964.

Scott, Bernard Brandon. *Hear Then the Parable: A Commentary on the Parables of Jesus.* Minneapolis: Fortress, 1989.

Scrivner, Joseph. "African American Interpretation." In *The Oxford Encyclopedia of Biblical Interpretation,* edited by Steven McKenzie, 1–8. Oxford: Oxford University Press, 2013.

Sechrest, Love L. "Antitypes, Stereotypes and Antetypes: Jezebel and the Sun Woman for Contemporary Black Women." In *Womanist Biblical Interpretation: Expanding the Discourse,* edited by Gay L. Byron and Vanessa Lovelace, 113–37. Atlanta: Society of Biblical Literature, 2016.

———. "A Double Vision, a Revolutionary Religion: Race Relations, Moral Analogies, and African American Biblical Interpretation." In *Ethnicity, Race, and Religion: Identities and Ideologies in Early Jewish and Christian Texts, and in the Traditions of Biblical Interpretation,* edited by Katherine M. Hockey and David G. Horrell, 202–18. London: Bloomsbury, 2018.

———. *A Former Jew: Paul and the Dialectics of Race.* LNTS 410. London: T&T Clark, 2009.

———. "Humbled among the Nations: Matthew 15:21–28 in Antiracist Womanist Missiological Engagement." In *Can "White" People Be Saved? Triangulating Race, Theology, and Mission,* edited by Love L. Sechrest, Johnnie Ramirez-Johnson, and Amos Yong, 276–99. Downers Grove, IL: IVP Academic, 2018.

———. "The Perils of Passing: Code-Switching and Intercultural Competency in Acts." In *Confronting Racial Injustice: Theory and Praxis for the Church,* edited by Gerald Hiestand and Joel Lawrence. Eugene, OR: Cascade, forthcoming.

Sechrest, Love L., and Johnny Ramirez-Johnson. "Race and Missiology in Glocal

Perspective." In *Can "White" People Be Saved? Triangulating Race, Theology, and Mission*, edited by Love L. Sechrest, Johnny Ramirez-Johnson, and Amos Yong, 1–24. Downers Grove, IL: IVP Academic, 2018.

Seifrid, M. A. "Jesus and the Law in Acts." *JSNT* 30 (1987): 39–57.

Senior, Donald. "Between Two Worlds: Gentiles and Jewish Christians in Matthew's Gospel." *CBQ* 61 (1999): 1–23.

Sentencing Project. "Incarcerated Women and Girls." The Sentenga Project, November 2020. https://www.sentencingproject.org/wp-content/uploads/2016/02/Incarcerated-Women-and-Girls.pdf.

———. "Parents in Prison." The Sentencing Project, 27 September 2012. https://www.sentencingproject.org/publications/parents-in-prison/.

———. "Trends in U.S. Corrections." The Sentencing Project, 20 May 2021. https://www.sentencingproject.org/publications/trends-in-u-s-corrections/.

Shapiro, Thomas. *The Hidden Cost of Being African American: How Wealth Perpetuates Inequality*. New York: Oxford University Press, 2004.

Shaw, Theodore M. *The Ferguson Report: Department of Justice Investigation of the Ferguson Police Department*. New York: The New Press, 2015.

Shellnutt, Kate. "A Lament for Charleston: What Makes This Mass Shooting Different." *Christianity Today*, 19 June 2015. http://www.christianitytoday.com/gleanings/2015/june/lament-for-charleston-what-makes-this-shooting-different.html.

Shelton, Jason E., and Michael Oluf Emerson. *Blacks and Whites in Christian America: How Racial Discrimination Shapes Religious Convictions*. New York: New York University Press, 2012.

Sifford, Amy, Kok-Mun Ng, and Chuang Wang. "Further Validation of the Psychosocial Costs of Racism to Whites Scale on a Sample of University Students in the Southeastern United States." *Journal of Counseling Psychology* 56 (2009): 585–89.

Siker, Jeffrey S. "'First to the Gentiles': A Literary Analysis of Luke 4:16–30." *JBL* 111 (1992): 73–90.

Sim, David C. *The Gospel of Matthew and Christian Judaism: The History and Social Setting of the Matthean Community*. Edinburgh: A&C Black, 1998.

———. "The Gospel of Matthew and the Gentiles." *JSNT* 57 (1995): 19–48.

Simmons, Tiffany R. "The Effects of the War on Drugs on Black Women: From Early Legislation to Incarceration." *American University Journal of Gender, Social Policy & the Law* 26 (2017): 719–39.

Simonton, D. K. "Scientific Creativity as Constrained Stochastic Behavior: The Integration of Product, Person, and Process Perspectives." *Psychological Bulletin* 129/4 (2003): 475–94.

Skiba, Russell J., Robert H. Homer, Chung Choong-Geun, M. Karenga Rausch,

Seth L. May, and Tary Tobin. "Race Is Not Neutral: A National Investigation of African American and Latino Disproportionality." *School Psychology Review* 40 (2011): 85–107.

Slater, Thomas B. *Ephesians*. Smyth & Helwys Bible Commentary. Macon, GA: Smyth & Helwys, 2012.

Slevin, Colleen, and Patty Nieberg. "Colorado Officers Won't Be Charged for Detaining Black Girls." *ABC News*, 9 January 2021. https://abcnews.go.com /US/wireStory/colorado-officers-wont-charged-detaining-black-girls -75138278.

Smietana, Bob. "2016 Election Exposes Evangelical Divides." Lifeway Research, 14 October 2016. https://lifewayresearch.com/2016/10/14/2016-election -exposes-evangelical-divide/.

———. "Efrim Smith: White Evangelicals Need to Humble Themselves." *Christianity Today*, 1 June 2020. https://www.christianitytoday.com/news/2020 /june/efrem-smith-george-floyd-minneapolis-evangelicals-response.html.

Smith, Andrea. "Indigeneity, Settler Colonialism, White Supremacy." In *Racial Formation in the Twenty-First Century*, edited by Daniel Martinez, Oneka HoSang, and Laura Pulido LaBennett, 66–90. Berkeley: University of California Press, 2012.

Smith, Anthony. *The Ethnic Origins of Nations*. Oxford: Blackwell, 1989.

———. "The Origins of Nations." *Ethnic and Racial Studies* 12/3 (1989): 340–67.

Smith, Christian, and Michael O. Emerson. *Divided by Faith: Evangelical Religion and the Problem of Race in America*. New York: Oxford University Press, 2000.

Smith, Mitzi J. "Ephesians." In *True to Our Native Land: An African American New Testament Commentary*, edited by Brian Blount, Cain Hope Felder, Clarice J. Martin, and Emerson B. Powery, 348–62. Minneapolis: Fortress, 2007.

———, ed. *I Found God in Me: A Womanist Biblical Hermeneutics Reader*. Eugene, OR: Cascade, 2015.

———. *Insights from African American Interpretation*. Philadelphia: Fortress, 2017.

———. "'Knowing More Than Is Good for One': A Womanist Interrogation of the Matthean Great Commission." In *I Found God in Me: A Womanist Biblical Hermeneutics Reader*, edited by Mitzi J. Smith, 236–65. Eugene, OR: Cascade, 2015.

———. "Paul, Timothy, and the Respectability Politics of Race: A Womanist Inter(con)textual Reading of Acts 16:1–5." *Religions* 10/3 (2019): 135–47.

———. "This Little Light of Mine: The Womanist Biblical Scholar as Prophetess, Iconoclast and Activist." In *I Found God in Me: A Womanist Biblical*

Hermeneutics Reader, edited by Mitzi J. Smith, 109–29. Eugene, OR: Cascade, 2015.

—. *Womanist Sass and Talk Back: Social (In)justice, Intersectionality, and Biblical Interpretation.* Eugene, OR: Cascade.

Smith, Mitzi J., and Jin Young Choi. *Minoritized Women Reading Race and Ethnicity: Intersectional Approaches to Constructed Identity and Early Christian Texts.* London: Lexington Books, 2020.

Smith, Mitzi J., and Yung Suk Kim. 2018. *Toward Decentering the New Testament: A Reintroduction.* Foreword by Michael Willett Newheart. Eugene, OR: Cascade, 2018.

Smith, Mitzi J., and Jayachitra Lalitha. *Teaching All Nations: Interrogating the Matthean Great Commission.* Minneapolis: Fortress, 2014.

Smith, Shively T. J. "One More Time with Assata on My Mind: A Womanist Rereading of the Escape to Egypt (Matt 2:13–23) in Dialogue with an African American Woman Fugitive Narrative." In *Womanist Interpretation of the Bible: Expanding the Discourse*, edited by Gay L. Byron and Vanessa Lovelace, 139–64. Atlanta: Society of Biblical Literature, 2016.

Smither, Robert. "Human Migration and the Acculturation of Minorities." *Human Relations* 35/5 (1982): 57–68.

Smokowski, Paul R., Rose Roderick, and Martica L. Bacallao. "Acculturation and Latino Family Processes: How Cultural Involvement, Biculturalism, and Acculturation Gaps Influence Family Dynamics." *Family Relations* 57 (2008): 295–308.

Snodgrass, Klyne R. *Stories with Intent: A Comprehensive Guide to the Parables of Jesus.* Grand Rapids: Eerdmans, 2008.

Snowden, Frank M. *Before Color Prejudice: The Ancient View of Blacks.* Cambridge, MA: Harvard University Press, 1991.

Spanierman, Lisa B., Nathan R. Todd, and Carolyn J. Anderson. "Psychosocial Costs of Racism to Whites: Understanding Patterns among University Students." *Journal of Counseling Psychology* 56 (2009): 239–52.

Spanierman, Lisa B., V. Paul Poteat, Amanda M. Beer, and Patrick Ian Armstrong. "Psychosocial Costs of Racism to Whites: Exploring Patterns through Cluster Analysis." *Journal of Counseling Psychology* 53 (2006): 434–41.

Sparks, H. F. D. "The Centurion's παῖς." *JTS* 42 (1941): 179–80.

Stanton, Graham. *The Gospels and Jesus.* New York: Oxford University Press, 1989.

St. Clair, Raquel. *Call and Consequences.* Minneapolis: Fortress, 2008.

Steffek, Emmanuelle. "Quand juifs et païens se mettent à table (Ac 10)." *Études Théologiques et Religieuses* 80/1 (2005): 103–11.

Stubbs, Monya A. *Indebted Love: Paul's Subjugation Language in Romans*. Eugene, OR: Pickwick, 2013.

Suggit, John. "'The Holy Spirit and We Resolved . . .' (Acts 15:28)." *Journal of Theology for Southern Africa* 79 (1992): 38–48.

Sumney, Jerry. *Identifying Paul's Opponents: The Question of Method in 2 Corinthians*. Sheffield: Sheffield Academic, 1990.

Szmigiera, M. "Countries with the Most Prisoners as of June 2020." Institute for Crime and Justice Policy Research. June 2021. https://www.statista.com /statistics/262961/countries-with-the-most-prisoners/.

Tannehill, Robert C. "Israel in Luke-Acts: A Tragic Story." *JBL* 104 (1985): 69–85.

———. "The Mission of Jesus according to Luke iv 16–30." In *Jesus in Nazareth*, edited by W. Eltester, 51–75. Berlin: De Gruyter, 1972.

———. *The Narrative Unity of Luke-Acts: A Literary Interpretation*. 2 vols. Philadelphia: Fortress, 1986.

———. "Rejection by Jews and Turning to Gentiles: The Pattern of Paul's Mission in Acts." In *Luke-Acts and the Jewish People: Eight Critical Perspectives*, edited by Joseph B. Tyson, 83–101. Minneapolis: Augsburg, 1988.

Tanu, Danau. "Toward an Interdisciplinary Analysis of the Diversity of 'Third Culture Kids.'" In *Migration, Diversity, and Education: Beyond Third Culture Kids*, edited by Fred Dervin and Saija Benjamin, 13–35. London: Palgrave Macmillan, 2015.

Tatum, Beverly Daniel. *"Why Are All the Black Kids Sitting Together in the Cafeteria?" And Other Conversations about Race*. Rev. ed. New York: Basic Books, 2017.

Taylor, Jennifer Rae, and Kayla Vinson. "Ahmaud Arbery and the Local Legacy of Lynching." The Marshall Project, 21 May 2020. https://www.themarshall project.org/2020/05/21/ahmaud-arbery-and-the-local-legacy-of-lynching.

Taylor, Vincent. *The Gospel according to St. Mark: The Greek Text with Introduction, Notes, and Indexes*. London: Macmillan, 1952.

Theriault, Denis C. "Playing a New Race Card." *Portland Mercury*, 28 June 2012. https://www.portlandmercury.com/portland/playing-a-new-race-card /Content?oid=6331210.

Thielman, Frank. *Plight to Solution: A Jewish Framework for Understanding Paul's View of the Law in Galatians and Romans*. Leiden: Brill, 1989.

Thiselton, Anthony C. *The First Epistle to the Corinthians*. NIGTC. Grand Rapids: Eerdmans, 2000.

Thompson, Marianne Meye. *John: A Commentary*. NTL. Louisville: Westminster John Knox, 2015.

Thrall, Margaret E. *The Second Epistle to the Corinthians*. 2 vols. ICC. Edinburgh: T&T Clark, 1994.

Thurman, Howard. *Jesus and the Disinherited*. Nashville: Abingdon, 1949.

Tiede, David L. "Acts 11:1–18." *Interpretation* 42/2 (1988): 175–80.

———. *Prophecy and History in Luke-Acts*. Philadelphia: Fortress, 1980.

Titone, C. "Educating the White Teacher as Ally." In *White Reign: Deploying Whiteness in America*, edited by J. L. Kincheloe, S. R. Steinberg, N. M. Rodriguez, and R. E. Chennault, 159–76. New York: St. Martin's Griffin, 1998.

Torrey, E. Fuller. "Ronald Reagan's Shameful Legacy: Violence, the Homeless, Mental Illness." *Salon*, 29 September 2013. http://www.salon.com/2013/09/29/ronald_reagans_shameful_legacy_violence_the_homeless_mental_illness/.

Townes, Emilie M. "Living in the New Jerusalem: The Rhetoric and Movement of Liberation in the House of Evil." In *A Troubling in My Soul: Womanist Perspectives on Evil and Suffering*, edited by Emilie M. Townes, 78–91. Maryknoll, NY: Orbis Books, 1993.

Tuan, Mia. *Forever Foreigners or Honorary Whites? The Asian Ethnic Experience Today*. New Brunswick, NJ: Rutgers University Press, 1998.

Tuckett, C. M. "Luke 4,16–30, Isaiah and Q." In *Logia: Les paroles de Jésus—The Sayings of Jesus: Mémorial Joseph Coppens*, edited by J. Delobel, 343–54. Leuven: Leuven University Press, 1982.

Tyson, Joseph B. *Images of Judaism in Luke-Acts*. Columbia: University of South Carolina Press, 1992.

———. "Jews and Judaism in Luke-Acts: Reading as a Godfearer." *NTS* 41 (1995): 19–38.

———, ed. *Luke-Acts and the Jewish People: Eight Critical Perspectives*. Minneapolis: Augsburg, 1988.

———. *Luke, Judaism, and the Scholars: Critical Approaches to Luke-Acts*. Columbia: University of South Carolina Press, 1999.

Upkong, Justin. "Luke." In *Global Bible Commentary*, edited by Daniel Patte, 385–94. Nashville: Abingdon, 2004.

Utt, Jamie. "So You Call Yourself an Ally: 10 Things All 'Allies' Need to Know." *Everyday Feminism*, 8 November 2013. http://everydayfeminism.com/2013/11/things-allies-need-to-know/.

Van Kooten, George H. *Cosmic Christology in Paul and the Pauline School: Colossians and Ephesians in the Context of Graeco-Roman Cosmology, with a New Synopsis of the Greek Texts*. WUNT 2.171. Tübingen: Mohr Siebeck, 2003.

Vecsey, Christopher. "The Exception Who Proves the Rules: Ananse the Akan Trickster." *Journal of Religion in Africa* 12/3 (1981): 161–77.

Verhey, Allen, and Joseph S. Harvard. *Ephesians*. Louisville: Westminster John Knox, 2011.

Versnel, H. S. "Some Reflections on the Relationship: Magic–Religion." *Numen* 38/2 (1991): 177–97.

Wahlen, Clinton. "Peter's Vision and Conflicting Definitions of Purity." *NTS* 51/4 (2005): 505–18.

Waitz, H. "Das Problem des sogenannten: Aposteldekrets und die damit zusammenhängenden literarischen und geschichtlichen Probleme des apostolischen Zeitalters." *ZKG* 55 (1936): 227–63.

Walker, Alice. "Coming Apart." In *You Can't Keep a Good Woman Down: Short Stories*, edited by Alice Walker, 41–53. Boston: Mariner Books, 2003.

———. *In Search of Our Mothers' Gardens: Womanist Prose*. San Diego: Harcourt Brace Jovanovich, 1983.

Walker-Barnes, Chanequa. *I Bring the Voices of My People: A Womanist Vision for Racial Reconciliation*. Grand Rapids: Eerdmans, 2019.

Wall, Robert W. "Peter, 'Son' of Jonah: The Conversion of Cornelius in the Context of Canon." *JSNT* 29 (1987): 79–90.

Wallace, Daniel B. *Greek Grammar beyond the Basics: An Exegetical Syntax of the New Testament*. Grand Rapids: Zondervan, 1996.

Wan, Sze-kar. "The Letter to the Galatians." In *A Postcolonial Commentary on the New Testament Writings*, edited by Fernando F. Segovia and Rasiah S. Sugirtharajah, 246–64. London: A&C Black, 2009.

Washington, J., and N. J. Evans. "Becoming an Ally." In *Beyond Tolerance: Gays, Lesbians, and Bisexuals on Campus*, edited by N. J. Evans and V. A. Wall, 195–204. Washington, DC: American College Personnel Association, 1991.

Weems, Renita J. "Reading Her Way through the Struggle: African American Women and the Bible." In *Stony the Road We Trod: African American Biblical Interpretation*, edited by Cain Hope Felder, 57–80. Minneapolis: Fortress, 1991.

———. "Re-Reading for Liberation: African American Women and the Bible." In *Feminist Interpretation of the Bible and the Hermeneutics of Liberation*, edited by Silvia Schorer and Sophia Bietenhard, 19–32. JSNTSup 374. London: Sheffield Academic, 2003.

———. "Womanist Reflections on Biblical Hermeneutics." In *Black Theology: A Documentary History, Vol. 2, 1980–1992*, edited by James H. Cone and Gayraud S. Wilmore, 216–24. Maryknoll, NY: Orbis Books, 1993.

Weiser, Alfons. *Die Apostelgeschichte*. Ökumenischer Taschenbuchkommentar zum Neuen Testament 5/1–2. Gütersloher: Gerd Mohn, 1981–1985.

Wendland, Ernst R. "Finding Some Lost Aspects of Meaning in Christ's Parables of the Lost—and Found (Luke 15)." *Trinity Journal* 17/1 (1996): 19–65.

Wendt, Heidi. *At the Temple Gates: The Religion of Freelance Experts in the Roman Empire*. New York: Oxford University Press, 2016.

Westfall, Cynthia Long. "'This Is a Great Metaphor!' Reciprocity in the Ephesians Household Code." In *Christian Origins and Greco-Roman Culture*, edited by Andrew W. Pitts and Stanley E. Porter, 561–98. Leiden: Brill, 2013.

Westfield, Lynn. "Called Out My Name, or Had I Known You Were Somebody: The Pain of Fending Off Stereotypes." In *Being Black, Teaching Black*, edited by Nancy Lynn Westfield, 61–78. Nashville: Abingdon, 2008.

White, Deborah Gray. *Ain't I a Woman? Female Slaves in the Plantation South*. New York: W. W. Norton, 1985.

Whitehouse Briefing Room. "A Proclamation on Law Day, U.S.A, 2021." 30 April 2021. https://www.whitehouse.gov/briefing-room/presidential-actions /2021/04/30/a-proclamation-on-law-day-u-s-a-2021/.

Williams, Delores S. "'A Crucifixion Double Cross': The Violence of Our Images May Do More Harm Than Good." *Other Side* 29 (1993): 25–27.

———. *Sisters in the Wilderness: The Challenge of Womanist God-Talk*. Maryknoll, NY: Orbis, 1993.

Williams, Demetrius K. "The Acts of the Apostles." In *True to Our Native Land: An African American New Testament Commentary*, edited by Brian K. Blount, Cain Hope Felder, Clarice J. Martin, and Emerson B. Powery, 213–48. Minneapolis: Fortress, 2007.

Wilson, S. G. *The Gentiles and the Gentile Mission in Luke-Acts*. SNTSMS 23. Cambridge: Cambridge University Press, 1973.

Wink, Walter. *Engaging the Powers: Discernment and Resistance in a World of Domination*. Minneapolis: Fortress, 2017.

———. *Naming the Powers: The Language of Power in the New Testament*. Philadelphia: Fortress, 1984.

———. *Unmasking the Powers: The Invisible Forces That Determine Human Existence*. Minneapolis: Fortress, 1993.

———. *When the Powers Fall: Reconciliation in the Healing of Nations*. Minneapolis: Fortress, 1998.

Wise, Michael O., Martin G. Abegg Jr., and Edward M. Cook. *The Dead Sea Scrolls: A New Translation*. New York: HarperCollins, 1996, 2005.

Witherington, Ben, III. *Conflict and Community in Corinth: A Socio-Rhetorical Commentary on 1 and 2 Corinthians*. Grand Rapids: Eerdmans, 1995.

Wright, N. T. *Jesus and the Victory of God*. Minneapolis: Fortress, 1996.

Wu, Frank. "The Changing Face of America: Intermarriage and the Mixed-Race Movement." In *Rethinking the Color Line: Readings in Race and Ethnicity*, edited by Charles A. Gallagher, 554–72. New York: McGraw Hill, 2007.

Yankah, Ekow N. "When Addiction Has a White Face." *New York Times*, 9 February 2016. https://www.nytimes.com/2016/02/09/opinion/when-addiction-has-a-white-face.html.

Yudell, Michael. *Race Unmasked: Biology and Race in the Twentieth Century*. New York: Columbia University Press, 2014.

INDEX OF MODERN AUTHORS

INDEX OF SUBJECTS

leading womanist biblical scholars and texts, 7–13; methodology of associative hermeneutics, 2–4, 13–37; reflections on theology of the cross and redemptive suffering, 213–16, 227–28, 237–38; Stubbs's reading of Romans 13 and Paul's discourse on Empire, 297–305, 321. *See also* associative hermeneutics

"Womanist Interpretation and Preaching in the Black Church" (Cannon), 7–8
Womanist Midrash (Gafney), 9–10
"womanist midrash," 9
Womanist Theological Ethics: A Reader (Cannon, Townes, and Sims), 7–8
World War II, 264

Zimmerman, George, 147–48

INDEX OF SCRIPTURE REFERENCES AND OTHER ANCIENT SOURCES